Secrets *in* Families *and* Family Therapy

Evan Imber-Black, Ph.D.

W·W·Norton & Company · New York · London

A NORTON PROFESSIONAL BOOK

Printed in the United States of America.

First Edition

Composition by Bytheway Typesetting Services, Inc. Manufacturing by Haddon Craftsmen, Inc.

Library of Congress Cataloging-in-Publication Data

Secrets in families and family therapy / [edited by] Evan Imber-Black.
    p.   cm.
    "A Norton professional book" — P. facing the t.p.
    Includes index.
    ISBN 0-393-70147-6
    1. Family psychotherapy.   2. Confidential communications — Family therapists.   3. Communication in the family.   4. Secrecy — Psychological aspects.   5. Family — Mental health.   6. Shame.
I. Imber-Black, Evan.
    [DNLM: 1. Confidentiality.   2. Ethics, Medical.   3. Family.
4. Family Therapy.   5. Physician-Patient Relations.   WM 430.5.F2
S446]
RC488.5.S415   1992
616.89'156 — dc20
DNLM/DLC
for Library of Congress   92-49170   CIP

W.W. Norton & Company, Inc., 500 Fifth Avenue, New York, N.Y. 10110

W.W. Norton & Company, Ltd., 10 Coptic Street, London WC1A 1PU

1 2 3 4 5 6 7 8 9 0

This book is lovingly dedicated
to my sister, Meryle Sue Mitchel,
and my brother, Ariel Barak Imber,
for all the sweet secrets of childhood.

Contents

Foreword

RICHARD CHASIN, M.D.

EVEN IN THE EARLY, unsophisticated years of family therapy, we realized that family secrets would be a thorny problem. When we worked with individuals, we could grant each client the privilege of confidentiality. But when the family became the client, we wondered what to do when one or more members requested that we keep something confidential from others in the same family. This dilemma about confidentiality obligations was compounded by the obvious power imbalances that could be created if we kept secrets from some family members and not others. In fact, some early family therapists were so intimidated by the force field of family politics that they met the family with a distrustful, defensive, even competitive posture, determined at all costs not to be co-opted or pulled into a coalition. A stance on secrecy seemed necessary armor for surviving what was seen as the sinister machinations of family power tactics.

We have faced this dilemma in the context of two cultural trends: a traditional one that honored individual privacy and a newer one that called for candor. Even though family therapists understood the value of privacy, most subscribed to the cultural vogue that openness—even if feared and disruptive—was essential to family health.

In seeking a solution to the problem of secrets, family therapists were undoubtedly caught in the thrall of Platonic idealism that has gripped the Western mind for the past two thousand years. Simplicity, rhapsodized as "elegant" simplicity, seemed always superior to "messy" complexity. One sought simplicity and felt defeated by or, at best, resigned to complexity.

In fact, virtually all early family therapists strove for a simple stance on secrets, even though it was obvious to most of us that no such policy could be defended in all cases. The result was a handful of narrow choices. Some therapists kept individual confidences, but might pressure a client to divulge them or might indirectly foster disclosure by opening the subject of secrecy with the family. Other therapists refused to keep secrets, warning the family that any communication from one family member would be shared with all the others. Some therapists stated their positions when making the initial contract with the family. Others did not reveal their stance until they were confronted with a secret.

Only a few therapists told the family at the outset that they would listen to secrets and deal with them depending on the needs of the situation. Those who took this "it depends" position often were made to feel naive and wishy-washy by their colleagues. Now, after 30 years, "it depends" may be emerging as the only way to go. What has transpired that has allowed us to move from stances that now seem doctrinaire and simplistic to ones that honor the moral and clinical complexity of secrecy?

For one thing, the field as a whole has begun to embrace rather than shrink from complexity. Many of us now believe that truths and changes are most likely to emerge from a detailed exploration of multiple contexts from multiple perspectives—that families develop new ideas and actions from the explosion of information that is frequently set off when the therapist invites the family to make distinctions and entertain complexity where they originally may have held one or two simple, often opposing, beliefs.

In addition to this distinctively nonreductive turn, the growing awareness of endemic family abuse has caused therapists to anticipate the enormous ethical, legal, and clinical challenge that secrets represent. The next family that walks into the consulting room might be one in which disclosure will prevent catastrophe—or one for which disclosure will be catastrophic. Most likely it will be one in which secrecy emerges in a muddy way, indicating no obviously correct ethical, legal, or clinical course to follow.

Along with our awareness of abuse came our appreciation of shame as an engine that drives secrecy, forcing our stories underground and banishing our traumas to dissociated obscurity. Shame and secrecy may destroy lives in one generation and pass like an invisible cursed heirloom to the next, creating traditions of deception and evasion that no longer have a discernible origin.

Feminist critiques of family therapy have opened our eyes to the impact of oppressive forces so deeply embedded in our culture that they remain hidden until courageous sharing and painstaking analysis surface and define them. Social power, whether recognized or not, can determine the import of privacy and secrecy. The secrets of the powerless may be essential for their protection. The privacy of the powerful can act as a screen that conceals their privileged information and blocks their awareness of injustice.

Thus, many issues that are surrounded by secrecy have been substantially exposed and elucidated only in recent years. The careful analysis by family therapists of secrecy itself is also new. In 1980, Karpel published a particularly clarifying article, defining key concepts and suggesting guidelines for action.* A few other important articles followed. Now, 12 years later, we have this book, the first wide-ranging examination of secrets in the family therapy literature. Evan Imber-Black and the other contributors address the topic from multiple perspectives, covering virtually every clinical situation where secrets are vital and problematic. In these theoretically evocative and clinically rich presentations, we find recurring issues such as injury, protection, power, stigma, injustice, shame, and mystification. We can also see that no two sources, contexts, or instances of secrecy are alike, leaving us with the inescapable conclusion that we must try to comprehend the particular factors that stimulate and sustain secrecy in each individual clinical circumstance we encounter. We must be prepared to use our best imagination, judgment, and ethical sensitivity to fashion a distinctive and apt response. Whether family members maintain a secret for their safety or undo it for their liberation, we must attend to them with great care. The chapters that follow will amply inform our efforts.

This book will serve to shift the way we all think about secrets. It will help bring secrecy itself, like so many other fears, prejudices, crimes, and injustices that have fueled it, out of the shadows and into the light. It will help us to see secrecy clearly for what it is: another complex and important player in the family drama, born of fear and love, offering protection and causing pain, but, at last, available for deep understanding and careful healing.

*Karpel, M. (1980). Family secrets. *Family Process, 19*:295 306.

Contributors

Claudia Bepko, M.S.W.
Brunswick, Maine

Lascelles W. Black, M.S.W.
Montefiore Medical Center
Bronx, New York

Nancy Boyd-Franklin, Ph.D.
The Robert Wood Johnson School
    of Medicine and Dentistry
New Brunswick, New Jersey.

Alan Cooklin, M.B.Ch.B.,
    F.R.C. Psych., D.P.N.
Marlborough Hospital
London, England

Ronny Diamond, C.S.W.
Adoption Resource Center
Spence-Chapin Service to Families
    and Children
New York, New York

Gill Gorell Barnes, M.A., M.Sc.
Tavistock Clinic
London, England

Ann Hartman, D.S.W.
Smith College School for Social
    Work
Northampton, Massachusetts

Evan Imber-Black, Ph.D.
Albert Einstein College of Medicine
Bronx, New York

Gus Kaufman, Jr., Ph.D.
Men Stopping Violence
Atlanta, Georgia

Jo-Ann Krestan, M.A., L.S.A.C.
Brunswick, Maine

Joan Laird, M.S.W.
Smith College School for Social
    Work
Northampton, Massachusetts

Marilyn J. Mason, Ph.D.
Minneapolis, Minnesota

Dusty Miller, Ed.D.
Antioch New England Graduate
    School
Keene, New Hampshire

Jane Nagy, R.N., M.N.
University of Calgary
Calgary, Alberta, Canada

Peggy Papp, A.C.S.W.
The Ackerman Institute for Family
    Therapy
New York, New York

Laura Giat Roberto, Psy.D.
Eastern Virginia Medical School
Norfolk, Virginia

Janine Roberts, Ed.D.
University of Massachusetts
Amherst, Massachusetts

Sallyann Roth, M.S.W.
Family Institute of Cambridge
Watertown, Massachusetts

Gary L. Sanders, M.D.,
    F.R.C.P. (C)
University of Calgary
Calgary, Alberta, Canada

Judith Schaffer, M.A.
The Perinatal Cocaine Project
New York, New York

Kathy Weingarten, Ph.D.
Family Institute of Cambridge
Watertown, Massachusetts

Rosmarie Welter-Enderlin, M.S.W.
Ausbildunginstitut für Systemische
    Therapie und Beratung
Meilen, Switzerland

Lorraine Wright, R.N., Ph.D.
University of Calgary
Calgary, Alberta, Canada

Acknowledgments

THE EXPLORATION OF the ideas that have culminated in the creation of this volume was supported in many contexts and through many relationships. I want to thank my colleagues on the family therapy faculty in the Department of Psychiatry, Albert Einstein College of Medicine, for enabling me to explore the topic of secrets in families and family therapy through many dialogues. I also want to thank the faculty of the Family Institute of Westchester for their valuable feedback on my papers relating to secrets that resulted in the opening chapter of this volume.

I want to express my deep appreciation to Monica McGoldrick who helped me to envision this volume, and to Betty Carter who, as always, encouraged me as I worked with these ideas.

Thanks to Gunthard Weber and to Adela Garcia for their dialogues with me about secrets in the German and Argentinian contexts respectively, which helped to broaden and deepen my own thoughts about the effects of sociopolitical secrets on the lives of families and therapists.

I especially thank all of the contributors to this volume. Their diverse ideas and thoughtful contributions to the human struggle with secrecy and openness have made my experience as editor of this volume one of richness, expansiveness, and deep satisfaction.

I want to thank all of the families I have worked with who made courageous, often painful, journeys from secrecy to openness, and who allowed me to witness their struggles and learn more about secrets and about the powerful personal and relationship changes that are possible.

I want to thank my editor, Susan Barrows Munro for her enthusiastic support of this book.

My deep appreciation goes to Marie Mele who assisted me in all of the details connected to preparing the manuscript, including typing, retyping, duplicating, contacting authors, and generally helping me to stay in good spirits.

Finally, this volume would not have been possible without the loving support of my family. My husband, Lascelles Black, not only encouraged the origination of this volume, but helped to expand my thinking through our many touching conversations about the effects of secrets in our own lives and in the lives of our clients. My children, Jason and Jennifer, made room for this work and cheered me on.

Evan Imber-Black

Preface

ORIGINS OF THE BOOK

Among the many clinical dilemmas confronting family therapists, the most compelling for me has been secrets. In my own practice and in conversations with colleagues, I have struggled to develop a position regarding secrets, only to find that this struggle needs to be entered again and again with each new family and each unique secret or pattern of secret-keeping. I have been dissatisfied with what appeared to be simplistic "rules"—"open the secret," "find a way to go around the secret," "don't keep secrets with members of the family," or "only interview about the process of secret-keeping, not the content of the secret," since each family that I met and worked with where secrets pertained seemed to offer an exception to the rule. I have been struck by our field's seeming reluctance to engage the topic of family secrets, for with the exception of a few journal articles and a few brief discussions in longer volumes, secrets have not been a part of our conversation, our literature, or our research.

Perhaps more than any issues with which we deal, secrets bring multiple levels of systems to life in the therapy room, including sociopolitical, economic, cultural, religious, moral, policy, media, larger health, mental health and educational, multigenerational and immediate family, two person relationship, and individual. Secrets, decisions about secrecy and openness, and the management of information are woven into the fabric of our society. The paradoxes of what is to be kept secret and what is to be shared and with whom are all around us and are embedded in each encounter between family and therapist. As this volume was being prepared, the United States fought the Gulf War, and the exquisite contradictions of openness and secrecy confronted us daily, as, on the one hand, the war itself appeared on our television screens, and on the other hand, daily press briefings with the generals were filled with "I can't tell you that," "I can't respond to that," and "I never want to be less than completely honest with you and so I can't reply."

Such confounding messages regarding secrecy and openness, along with challenges to our definitions of privacy, occur daily on television talk shows, promoting an atmosphere of pseudo-openness that finds its way into families and, potentially, our therapy rooms. The current confusion about what is secret, what is private, what should be shared and with whom was exemplified in a recent moment on an Oprah Winfrey show devoted to the topic of secrets, when a man in the audience stood up and said he had never told his family or anyone else "this secret," and proceeded to divulge extremely sensitive sexual matters on national television, with no idea of the relational or personal implications or consequences and no responsibility assumed by anyone else in the immediate context.

The families we see are struggling to make decisions about secrecy and openness within the same environment of contradictory influences in which we, as therapists, live. This volume arose out of my belief that what was needed was a book about secrets in families and family therapy that would eschew simplistic "rules" and would enable the reader to think through the complicated terrain of secrets and struggle with the ethical dilemmas, while having an opportunity to examine effective clinical approaches when secrecy pertains. All of the authors were invited to explore the topic of secrets from many vantage points, including the historical context that shapes a particular secret and patterns of secret-keeping; the multiple levels of system at which a given secret may be located, including the therapeutic system level; the ways in which communication, relationships, power, hierarchy, reliability, trust, and sense of self are effected when secrecy pertains; the interaction of secrets and symptoms; distinctions between secrecy and privacy; issues of timing for opening secrets; effective clinical interviewing and intervention methods; ways to deal with the relational and individual aftermath when a secret is opened; specific medical and legal issues that may pertain; and their own ethical position.

The result is a volume with differentiated positions that both inform and challenge the reader to shape his or her own position.

ORGANIZATION OF THE BOOK

The volume is organized in seven sections. The first section, *Secrets: Dilemmas for Families and Therapists* introduces the volume with two chapters designed to provide an orientation to the issues involved when secrets pertain. In Chapter 1, "Secrets in Families and Family Therapy: An Overview," I start with a review of where the topic of secrets has been in the family therapy field and proceed to discuss major clinical questions and issues as exemplified first in an early case, which challenged me to rethink my position on secrets, and then in a more recent case.

In Chapter 2, "Shame: Reservoir for Family Secrets," Marilyn Mason discusses the complex relationship between secrecy and privacy and relates these to the affective experience of shame. Through an effective clinical case, she enables the reader to examine the multiple levels of system in which shame is embedded, and how one can work with shame and secrets both personally and professionally.

In Section Two, *Secrecy Across the Family Life Cycle*, several authors discuss secrets as they exist in key family life cycle stages and issues. Chapter 3 by Rosmarie Welter-Enderlin addresses "Secrets of Couples and Couples' Therapy." Welter-Enderlin challenges some of the field's favorite truisms regarding couples and secrets. Informed by feminist thinking, her chapter highlights the ways that some secrets may be necessary differentiating steps and how the therapist can support this effectively.

In Chapter 4, "The Worm in the Bud: Secrets Between Parents and Children," Peggy Papp brings her clinical versatility to bear on intergenerational secrets, exemplifying the creativity that is possible even in the face of difficult secrets. Papp offers a useful method for the therapist to evaluate the effects of secrets and illustrates the many talents of children when they must deal with secrets through metaphorical communication.

Chapters 5 and 6 deal with the many secrets surrounding parentage and parental origins, including the sometimes devastating effects of such secrets on relationships and individual development. In Chapter 5, "Secrecy in Adoption," Ann Hartman orients the reader to the social, historical, and legal requirements that engendered secrecy in adoption and tracks the movement from secrecy to openness that may serve as a template for other kinds of secrets. Utilizing narrative therapeutic methodology, Hartman poignantly portrays the effects of opening the adoption secret and enabling the adult adoptee to create a more complete and coherent life story. Chapter 6, "The Secret of Infertility: Private Pain and Secret Stigma" by Judith A. Schaffer and Ronny Diamond, presents the dilemmas of secrets connected to infertility and the new birth technologies. This chapter exemplifies the complex ways that new secrets arise when expected but unmet life cycle transitions interact with technology operating at a speed that is beyond our current ethical positions. The requirement that therapists think through previously unimaginable birth origins, the impact of medical advice on a couple's decision regarding secrecy and openness, religious and moral principles, and family-of-origin influences are carefully illustrated in case examples.

In Chapter 7, Lorraine M. Wright and Jane Nagy discuss "Death: The Most Troublesome Family Secret of All." Using a model called Systemic Belief Therapy, the authors illustrate how beliefs regarding health, illness, death, and secrecy interact among family members and therapists. Through a moving case example involving a life-shortening illness, the authors challenge the reader to consider the existential and unresolvable secret of the time of death and the ways that this secret affects family relationships.

Section Three addresses *Secrecy and Symptoms*. Chapters 8 and 9 illustrate the ways that symptoms, per se, may be kept secret, as well as the ways that symptoms may be profound metaphors for family secrets. In Chapter 8, "On Lies, Secrets, and Silence: The Multiple Levels of Denial in Addictive Families," Jo-Ann Krestan and Claudia Bepko discuss the multiple ways that denial shapes painful secrets in families with alcohol and drug addiction. The authors illustrate the social, family, and therapeutic system levels that may converge to promote secrecy and denial, the complex interplay of loyalty and betrayal in relationships, and effective clinical methods to work with such secrecy. Chapter 9, "Eating Disorders as Family Secrets" by Laura Giat Roberto, discusses eating disorders as a template for family secrets that function to prevent healthy differentiation, autonomous functioning, and conflict resolution. The ways that eating disorders shape and express internal, interpersonal, and social secrets and effective clinical approaches are highlighted in cases involving both adolescents and adults.

Secrets of Violence and Abuse comprise Section Four. Chapters 10 and 11 address dangerous secrets; secrets that may frighten therapists, yet require a carefully thought out clinical and political position. Both chapters address issues of violence and abuse that remained secret in families and in the culture until recently. In Chapter 10, "Incest: The Heart of Darkness," Dusty Miller invites the reader to struggle with the complex issues connected to prematurely opening the secret of incest. She presents an original multimodal treatment model that carefully integrates intrapsychic and systemic theory and practice in order to effectively address the secret of sexual abuse. Chapter 11, "The Mysterious Disappearance of Battered Women in Family Therapists' Offices: Male Privilege Colluding with Male Violence" by Gus Kaufman, Jr., discusses the secret of wife battering and draws our attention to the ways that family therapists have contributed to maintaining this destructive secret. Dealing with the blurred distinctions between secrecy and privacy, Kaufman presents a feminist-informed model for opening this secret and preventing the silencing of women.

In Section Five, *Learning to Hear the Voice of Silence*, a special form of secrecy is addressed, that of silence and taboo. The authors of this section focus our attention on the many ways that our clients', and our own voices may be silenced, how the requirements of silence shape corrosive secrets, and how we may begin to hear those who have been silent. Gary Sanders opens this section with Chapter 12, "The Love That Dares to Speak Its Name: From Secrecy to Openness — Gay and Lesbian Affiliations." Sanders' work illustrates the historical and current dimensions of homophobia and demonstrates the devastating effects of secrecy and silence on self-definition, authenticity, family relationships, and the culture. His clinical work exemplifies a model that challenges effectively social and political constructions in a therapy designed to address personal and interpersonal secrets.

In Chapter 13, "Women's Secrets—Women's Silences," Joan Laird discusses the many ways that women's voices have been silenced. Using a feminist-informed clinical method based on narrative, storytelling, and the creation of new stories, and challenging the notion that conversation is "neutral," Laird orients the reader to creative and effective means for enabling women to open long-held, painful secrets, to speak and to be heard.

Chapter 14, "Speaking the Unspoken: An Agency Consultation to Reopen Dialogue" by Sallyann Roth, describes silence and secrecy that developed within an innovative mental health agency. She weaves among the constraining levels of secrets and taboos from the culture, religion, gender, sexual orientation, family-of-origin, and the personal, and illustrates a sensitively crafted consultation method for enabling open conversation about difference and commonality in human experience. While specifically addressing a crisis regarding homosexuality, Roth's methodology is a template for the restoration of trust when the unspoken has engendered mistrust.

In Chapter 15, "Taboos and Social Order: New Encounters for Family and Therapy," Alan Cooklin and Gill Gorell Barnes orient the reader to the multiple personal, interpersonal, and clinical effects of taboos and how "rules" regarding what cannot be spoken about give rise to symptoms and distress. Through a rich variety of examples, the authors present effective therapeutic interviewing and intervention methods for addressing and altering taboos.

Section Six deals with *Families, Secrets, and the Wider Social Context*. While the entire volume makes reference to the vital importance of the social context level in shaping, maintaining, and altering secrets, the two chapters which comprise this section especially illustrate ways that stigma, bigotry, and racial and ethnic intolerance function to produce toxic secrets in the very victims of oppression. In Chapter 16, Nancy Boyd-Franklin writes about "Racism, Secret-Keeping, and African-American Families." Carefully combining history and contemporary clinical work, Boyd-Franklin draws the reader's attention to secrets of skin color, parentage, and informal adoption. She presents the ways that adaptive and protective secrets affect any potential therapeutic relationship with African-American families, thereby providing a template for considering secrets and ethnic differences in general. Chapter 17, "AIDS and Secrets" by Lascelles Black, presents the reader with the most current challenge to our thinking about secrecy, privacy, and confidentiality. Black discusses intricate ways that medical, legal, mental health, ethnic, family, and individual levels of system converge in AIDS and HIV, shaping and reshaping secrets that may be life-threatening, and offers clinical examples for working with such secrets.

In Section Seven, *Teaching Trainees About Secrets*, two highly experienced family therapy trainers present two different curricula for working with trainees about secrets. In Chapter 18, "On Lies, Secrets, and Not Telling the Truth: A Training Curriculum," Kathy Weingarten offers an orientation to training that considers secrets as detrimental to intimacy. She presents several useful exercises to enable trainees to grasp the complexities involved when secrets pertain. Chapter 19, "On Trainees and Training: Safety, Secrets, and Revelation" by Janine Roberts, is a fitting end to this volume as it presents a curriculum organized to help trainees examine the various positions regarding working with secrets that exist in the family therapy field in order to arrive finally at their own position.

I wish you good reading, productive struggles with the material, and an evolving position on secrets in families and family therapy.

—Evan Imber-Black

Secrets *in* Families *and* Family Therapy

I

SECRETS: DILEMMAS FOR FAMILIES AND THERAPISTS

1

Secrets in Families and Family Therapy: An Overview

EVAN IMBER-BLACK

INTRODUCTION: WHERE HAVE ALL THE SECRETS GONE?

The daily practice of family therapists is replete with secrets, including such intimate and profound areas of individual and family life as birth, adoption, parentage, infertility, abortion, physical and mental illness, sexual orientation and sexuality, incest, rape, violence, addictions, religion, intermarriage, terrorism and wartime behavior, divorce, migration status, suicide, and death. While secrets are often encountered in therapy, with the exception of a few journal articles (Friedman, 1973–1974; Grolnick, 1983; Karpel, 1980; Wendorf & Wendorf, 1985) and some references in very few books (Anderson & Stewart, 1983; Boscolo, Cecchin, Hoffman, & Penn, 1987; Bowen, 1978; Boyd-Franklin, 1989; Haley, 1976; Imber-Black, 1986, 1988; Imber Coppersmith, 1985; Pittman, 1989; Walker, 1991), they remain an area largely unaddressed in the family therapy literature. In short, until very recently in our field, secrets have remained a secret!

There are several explanations for our field's lack of focus on the topic of secrets. In its infancy, in the late 1950's and early 1960's, the family therapy field was occupied with establishing itself. Part of this establishment phase included defining ourselves as *different* from psychoanalysis. This early differentiation and reactivity oriented the field to a sole focus on pattern and away from any focus on content, which effective inquiry into family secrets often requires.

Unlike many areas in family life and family therapy, secrets squarely confront the practicing therapist with the need to examine closely and explicitly his or her own values regarding secrecy and openness across many topics and to devise methodologies that are both ethical and effective. Secrets pose ethical dilemmas that are not resolved through simple "rules." Opening certain secrets may be profoundly healing for individuals and relationships, while opening other secrets may put people in jeopardy, particularly where issues of physical safety are concerned. And then there are secrets that hold the potential of both reconciliation and division, with no guarantees of which will pertain. The small literature on family secrets has attempted to come to terms with the ethical dimension, but often has done so through closure of the ethical question altogether. Thus, Haley (1976) counseled what he referred to as a "courtesy" approach with the family, urging that the therapist not open family secrets but, rather, find an indirect way to deal with them; Boscolo et al. (1987) proposed indirect circular interviewing when the therapist knows there is a secret, even when this secret might be a dangerous one such as incest. At the other end of the continuum, Friedman (1973–1974) insisted that secrets must be opened, and Pittman (1989) took the position that secrets of marital affairs must be opened for trust to be restored. Because the complex ethical dilemmas embedded in family secrets do not yield to simple formula, these attempts to make them do so precludes the careful and deliberate therapeutic struggle that is necessary, issue by issue and family by family.

Until the last decade, our theoretical lenses were insufficient to engage issues of secrecy. The feminist critique of family therapy, the field's examination of ethnic differences in families, attention to affect, particularly shame, and the simultaneous focus on individual and internal experience, on the one hand, and macro system contributions to family dysfunction, on the other, have converged to allow us to begin to hear painful secrets. New lenses are emerging, allowing us to see that some secrets, previously kept out of the therapy room, have deleterious physical, intrapersonal, and interpersonal effects on individual and family well-being.

"IT'S NEVER TOO LATE": A FAMILY'S
SECRET THAT ALTERED MY THINKING

In 1985, at a time when my own practice was informed by the Milan model's belief that focusing solely on the systemic effects of secret-keeping was sufficient, I met and worked with a family whose half-century-old secret had taken a profound toll on each member's well-being and had left all family relationships tied in painful knots, including patterns of cut-off, hidden alliances and debilitating symptoms. Because this family made the coura-

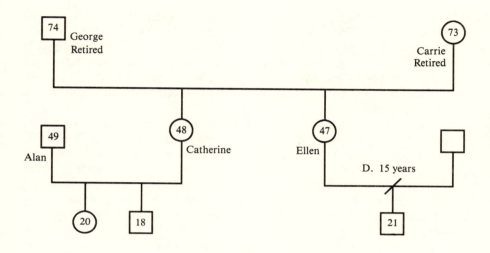

Figure 1.1

geous journey from secrecy to openness after 50 years, and because our work together challenged my own beliefs regarding effective clinical work with secrets, I called this case "It's Never Too Late."

A family was referred to me for consultation by a psychiatric resident. The family included two elderly parents, George, 74, and Carrie, 73, and their two grown daughters, Catherine, 48, and Ellen, 47 (Imber-Black, 1986). Carrie was hospitalized for what was diagnosed as a "phobia" of many years duration. She spoke about a profound fear of germs and refused to touch anyone or be touched. She would not shop for food or clothing, open doors, handle money, or play cards because she feared germs on the surfaces of these objects would contaminate her. She abandoned playing her beloved piano, which she had taught to children. She would not travel, go to her children's homes, or have anyone in her home. Her outings were restricted to medical and psychiatric appointments. She spent hours every day washing her hands. Carrie cried much of every day because she was so unhappy about her situation. When I first met the family during Carrie's second hospitalization for unrelenting anxiety, her fear of germs and her hand-washing had become the *only* allowable topic of family conversation.

Prior to our work together, all manner of interventions had been tried, including behavioral desensitization, cognitive therapy, antidepressant medications, tranquilizers, and couple's therapy. Professionals described Carrie as "resistant," the family as "uncooperative" and the overall prognosis as "hopeless." Carrie was considered a treatment failure and a source of great frustration to the hospital and the family. Serious consideration was being given to psychosurgery and nursing home placement. Both measures were discussed in a punitive tone by the many professionals involved.

When I first met the family, George and Carrie were struggling daily because of her symptoms. He tried to convince her that her fears were foolish, she replied that she could not help herself, and the struggle escalated until she cried and left the room. Both insisted they had absolutely no other problems and there had not been a single difference between them throughout their long marriage! Mirroring the parents' struggle, Catherine and Ellen fought over who would save their parents, and whether mom or dad "had it worse." They alternated supplying new ideas for treatment, such as biofeedback and acupuncture, and they discounted each other's efforts. Ellen was generally solicitous of her parents and angry with professionals, including me, while Catherine was angry with their parents, often cutting off from them for brief periods of time, only to get intensely reinvolved, and acted kindly towards professionals.

Carrie's severely debilitating symptom and George's responses to it had powerful effects on their daughters' lives. Catherine and her husband, Alan, fought frequently over her relationship with her parents, and she felt powerless and ineffective with her adolescent sons. Ellen took a new job during therapy, but stated frequently that she would quit her job and go live with her parents if this would help her mother. Both daughters seemed to be mired in unexplainable guilt and spent most of their free energy bound up with their parents.

There seemed to be a powerful injunction against the acknowledgment of open conflict in any of the relationships. When I inquired about conflict throughout their long marriage, George replied, "I don't remember having any!" In a session with the daughters, each said they believed the parents were hiding their conflicts and pretending all was well, as each parent would complain ferociously about the other in private conversations, then deny this when the spouse was present, and critically attack the daughter for suggesting that there were problems. Thus, a pattern of secrets that everyone knew, but disavowed, permeated the family system.

The family had a "rule" regarding what they called "outsiders," which for Carrie included professional helpers, her husband, her in-laws, and for George included anyone outside immediate family. Outsiders were to be handled with polite and distant diplomacy. Involvement of professional helpers in family issues thus appeared doomed, and yet the family appeared for session after session, inviting me in, while simultaneously keeping me out.

In a session alone with the daughters, Ellen urged me to see her parents separately in order to hear their secret complaints about one another. I turned down this request to become "one of the daughters" and, rather, suggested that the daughters become part of the therapy team, saying to them: "I need your help because, as we all know, I'm an 'outsider' and so your parents are very polite and diplomatic with me. I would like to invite your parents to the next session, and ask that you serve as my consultants, as my team behind the one-way mirror. Call me when you see your parents being very polite or diplomatic with me because I am an outsider, or when there are topics I need to raise. I want to ask you to keep this plan a secret until we meet." The request that they maintain a secret between us until the next session was intended both as a metaphorical comment on secrets and as an attempt to relocate the process of secret-keeping from within the family to between the family and an "outsider."

The session with the daughters as my consultants took place one month later. I began the session by asking the parents' permission to conduct the meeting with their daughters behind the mirror, framing my position as an "outsider" who needed the daughters' assistance. George and Carrie feigned great comfort with this arrangement; as soon as the session was underway, the phone from the observation room immediately began to ring with the first challenges to the family's myths, secrets, and taboos. George and Carrie began to take tiny, frightened steps towards acknowledging painful conflicts for the first time. Both expressed surprise as I gave voice to their children's beliefs and concerns. The phone rang every three or four minutes for nearly an hour with new topics, challenges, and previously unspoken observations about family relationships. As each call came, I put down the phone, named who had called, and relayed the content of the message. This repeated process became the symbolic actions of movement from secrecy to openness.

The tension in the room grew profound, and there were moments, as family rules shattered, when I felt like a villain and questioned my own ethical position as one who was pushing these two people, who were old enough to be my parents, to deal more openly with one another and with me. The power of secrets in the family culminated in an argument behind the mirror, as Catherine felt we were finally getting somewhere and that we needed to push on, and Ellen voiced concern for the parents' health and warned me that they needed to be protected. I reported this natural team split to the parents and asked them to go and consider what we should do next.

I did not hear from George and Carrie for three months. Catherine came to see me and said that an open and powerful argument, the first of its kind in the history of the family, had ensued following the session. The exact nature of the fight seemed less important to her than the fact that people were voicing their differences face-to-face in a manner without precedent in their relationships. Ellen revealed several secrets to the family immediately following the session, secrets that she previously believed would reap disapproval and risk her privileged position with her parents, including that she was living with her boyfriend and that she was struggling with a drinking problem. The family began to have conversations about more complex issues than Carrie's so-called phobia.

After three months, Carrie called and requested a session for George and herself. When they entered, a profoundly different mood prevailed, as they openly began to discuss previously hidden aspects of their lives, revealing a host of formerly denied problems and unspoken conflicts. Many of these conflicts centered on the sexual aspect of their marriage, which they had chosen to handle by totally withdrawing from each other sexually for decades. They slept in separate bedrooms and used Carrie's fear of germs as an excuse not to touch each other. This couple, who had previously insisted that they had a marriage devoid of any conflict except Carrie's symptoms, now painfully acknowledged what Carrie referred to as "many, many more quarrels over sex than we have ever had over washing my hands." Due perhaps to the intimate and authentic nature of our conversation, I was able to joke with them, replacing the grim tone of all of our previous meetings.

As this lighter mood prevailed, Carrie revealed a secret, which had caused her to experience overwhelming shame, confusion, and disabling symptoms. The interactional effects of the secret had established a family whose relationships with each other and with the outside world were marked by fear, defensiveness, criticism, and dissatisfying distance. The power of the unspoken, the unvoiced, and the secret to shape family relationships became apparent as Carrie told me that Catherine was born before she and George were married. In response to my question about whether her daughters knew this, Carrie replied, "I know they know," and went on to describe how for years the family would look at other people's wedding pictures together and the daughters never once asked to see the pictures from George and Carrie's wedding. Painful shame marked Catherine's birth as they had been banished by Carrie's family and as George's mother had excoriated Carrie (but not George) when Catherine was born. The painful secret affected family rituals as they celebrated no anniversaries or birthdays and lived a joyless existence.

As is often true, when painful secrets told to a therapist are met with empathy and receptivity, this is a new experience for the family, and they may begin to change rapidly and in unexpected ways. Carrie began to play the piano again and requested a meeting with what she referred to as a "germ expert" in order to put her fears to rest. George went on a fishing trip, and Carrie stayed at her sister's home for the first time in 40 years. I was at least ten steps behind them when I suggested that we make a video of their story to show their daughters, and George, the previous master of circuitous conversation, said, "No, that's too indirect — let's just bring them in and tell them!" In a session in which I served primarily as a witness to relationship healing, George and Carrie courageously struggled to open all that had been hidden, telling the daughters the secret they already knew and lifting the half-century prohibition on talking about it. At the conclusion, Carrie honored me with the graphic evidence of her own new freedom, taking my two hands in hers and touching another human being for the first time in many years.

This family both taught me a lot and raised many questions that have shaped my subsequent work with secrets.

CLINICAL QUESTIONS AND ISSUES POSED BY SECRETS

How Do Secrets Shape Family and Therapeutic Relationships?

Secrets are systemic phenomena. They are relational, shaping dyads, triangles, hidden alliances, splits, cut-offs, defining boundaries of who is "in" and who is "out," and calibrating closeness and distance in relationships. Certainly the questions "Who knows the secret?" and, by implication, "Who does not know the secret?" orient us to the ways that secrets affect relationship possibilities.

The triangles shaped by secrets can become especially convoluted as the existence of the secret-keeping dyad per se becomes a secret. Rapid triangular shifts may occur in families where secret-keeping has become the relational *modus vivendi*. For example, in one family, a mother agreed to keep a secret with an adult son, promising that she would not reveal his drug abuse to his father. Within hours, she told the father, who, in turn, agreed to keep his knowledge a secret from both the son and from me, their therapist. The father came to the next therapy session alone and began by telling me the secret, while insisting that I not tell his wife that he had done so! A joint family session, focusing on the ways information flowed in the family and on the mutually felt experience of constant betrayal in a family whose spoken aim was to protect one another from harm, finally began to shift this pattern.

Intergenerational family loyalties are often shaped by secrets. Such loyalties may appear as otherwise unexplainable behavior that repeats across the generations. One may see, for instance, affairs, reclusiveness, delinquency, refusal to go to doctors in the face of serious illness, suicide attempts at a particular age, etc., all of which make a new kind of sense when a long-held family secret is opened. In George and Carrie's family, Catherine, too, became pregnant before marriage, as did her own young adult daughter.

Such repetition may be seen and framed as a misguided attempt to finally open the family secret.

The very meaning of family loyalty may narrow in the presence of required secret-keeping, such that a family member comes to believe that only by maintaining a secret can one demonstrate loyalty and that to open a secret is the supreme act of disloyalty. The capacity to be loyal in relationships can also be undermined by secret-keeping (Bok, 1983). When a child is required to keep a secret with a parent that excludes the other parent, or when one spouse keeps a secret that directly affects the well-being of the other spouse, then loyalty is seriously compromised. Effective therapy with secrets often involves enabling participants to develop new and expanded definitions of loyalty both cognitively and experientially.

The presence of a secret or many secrets can also affect the family-therapist relationship. In George and Carrie's family, I was kept at a polite distance until the one-way mirror session allowed me to reposition myself between the two generations as a conduit, rather than as an "outsider." In other therapeutic systems, the therapist may be invited into a secret but rendered ineffective by the requirement of confidentiality, as when one family member tells the therapist a secret but forbids the therapist to open it with others. Triangles in the family that are shaped by secrets are thus replicated at the family-therapist level.

In George and Carrie's story, the secret of Catherine's birth had shaped a family system with a high degree of interpersonal distance in all areas except Carrie's symptoms, which provided the only closeness and intensity allowed. All family members knew the secret, but the prohibition against speaking about it erected a wall between family members and between the whole family and the outside world, metaphorically referred to as "outsiders." However, a focus *only* on the relationship effects of the secret and secret-keeping was insufficient in this case.

What Is the Specific Content of a Secret?

Earlier work regarding secrets suggested that it was unnecessary for the therapist to know the specific content of a given secret (Boscolo et al., 1987; Haley, 1976; Imber Coppersmith, 1985). More recently, as the family therapy field has shifted to an interest in stories, narrative, and the social construction of beliefs and meanings, attention to content has both become possible and recognized as necessary (see Laird, Chapter 13). It is often in the specific content of a secret that one finds the origins of stigma, shame, and fear of revelation and family dissolution that so powerfully drives the process of secret-keeping.

The content of a given secret allows the therapist to create categories for clinical action. Thus, some secrets are *positive*, such as the temporary secrets involved in many rituals or in gift-giving, the secrets that adolescents keep from parents in order to begin differentiation, the "pillow talk" secrets of vulnerability that couples keep, or the secrets that oppressed people keep from their oppressors that provide a source of bonding and strength.

Some secrets are *toxic*, engendering debilitating symptoms and erosion of relationship reliability. Toxic secrets are often long-standing. They require careful work and timing by the therapist to open them and deal with the aftermath. They are frequently about actions that occurred in the past, but whose power to affect relationships and individual well-being remains alive in the present. Thus, George and Carrie's secret was a half-century old. Following the one-way mirror session, in which many family rules were broken and the decision regarding whether to go further was put squarely in the couple's hands, it took three months for George and Carrie to decide to open their painful secret. Opening their secret to me led them to take the more difficult step of opening it with their daughters. Over several months, more and more aspects of relationship healing occurred, as Carrie attended her granddaughter's wedding, which her earlier phobia would have prevented, and Catherine and Ellen worked together to make the first anniversary celebration in their parents' lives.

Some secrets, such as current sexual and physical abuse, are *dangerous*, requiring immediate steps by the therapist to insure safety (see Kaufman, Chapter 11). Certainly it is no longer acceptable in our work (if, indeed, it ever was) to say that the content of secrets such as incest, abuse, and physical or emotional harm are simply "systemic" and that these can and should be explored obliquely.

Working with the Meanings of Secrets

The content of any given secret will have various meanings to different families, family members, and therapists. Such meanings generally flow from social constructions in the culture. This requires that therapists carefully consider the meanings they might attach to particular secrets and that they examine and question where such meanings originate.

A change in what is kept secret often results from a change in meanings. For instance, adoption used to carry a meaning of stigma and shame, due both to the so-called "illegitimacy" of the adopted person and the likely infertility of the adopting couple (see Hartman, Chapter 5). When this set of meanings prevailed, adoption was kept secret, sometimes even from the adopted person. Such meanings supported keeping alcoholism a secret within a family (see Krestan and Bepko, Chapter 8). As new meanings became available, which defined alcoholism as a disease, more people became willing to seek treatment. Likewise, opening a particular secret can enable new meanings to emerge. For instance, as public figures, like Betty Ford, have become open about previously secret addictions, such openness has assumed the meaning of courage.

The meanings attached to secrets are often challenged by broad social movements, often reinforced by the media. Thus, adult adoptees, families of the mentally ill, disability rights advocates, and the recovery movement have all challenged and changed the previously stigmatized meanings attached to particular secrets. One useful way to examine narrow meanings attached to secrets is to imagine the effects of a yet-to-be-formed social movement on a particular kind of secret.

Any given secret may have multiple meanings within a family. Parents may define a particular secret as having a protective meaning, as for instance, when a child is not told that a father is actually a stepfather (see Weingarten, Chapter 18 for an example). This same secret may carry the meaning of deception for the child. Similarly, a secret affair may mean differentiation and autonomy to one partner (see Welter-Enderlin, Chapter 3) and relationship betrayal to the other partner. Effective therapy with secrets requires the capacity to create an environment sufficient to hold and express the multiple and often disparate meanings attached to secrets and secret-keeping.

The therapy room is often a place where the meanings of secrets can be explored, questioned, and ultimately changed. The specific content of George and Carrie's secret was a so-called "illegitimate" birth. The meanings attached to this secret involved strongly held social beliefs regarding premarital sex and the need to punish a woman's sexuality. In therapy, we were able to examine these beliefs and the unnecessary pain they had caused. Placing the strongly held social beliefs of the 1940's within a 1980's context allowed George and Carrie simultaneously to challenge and forgive their own parents' actions that originated the secret-keeping. In a session with their daughters, the meanings of the secret were broadened further to include the mutual, though misguided, attempts by family members to protect one another. As the definitions attached to the secret shifted, healing across the generations became possible.

Occasionally, a therapist encounters a family with a toxic secret — the content of which is known by all affected members — who are adamant about excluding the therapist. In an earlier paper (Imber Coppersmith, 1985), I described a couple who had a secret that they kept from their therapist and that they fought about constantly, saying, "We fight whenever either one of us brings up the past, but we don't want to talk about the past in here. We tried it once in another therapy, and it made things worse!" We determined that the content of the secret resided far in the past, was known by both partners, and was spoken of often and angrily by both.

In this case, the therapeutic task was not to open the content to the therapist, but to enable the couple to change the *meaning* of the content from that which caused conflict to that which joined them in humor and playfulness. A burial ritual was devised that allowed the couple to bury the specific content of the secret, in effect, to bury the past, get it out of their daily lives, and go on. The couple was asked to agree that if they began to fight about the past, they would get in their car and drive to where the past was now buried and finish their fight. The change in the meaning of their secret was evident in the joke they created whenever either one would bring up the past during an argument about present matters: They would look at one another and declare "Take a trip!" which would be followed by laughter and settlement of the current issue.

The Effects of Secrets on Communication

The presence of a central secret in a family or a relationship distorts and mystifies communication processes (Karpel, 1980). Family members may become "deaf," "blind," and "mute" regarding information. For instance, a family came to therapy for elective mutism in a small child. During the first session, the mother whispered several family secrets to the therapist while the child played and effectively pretended not to hear what her mother was saying.

In George and Carrie's situation, all family members knew the central secret but acted as if they did not know. Allowable topics for conversation became narrower and narrower, lest the secret emerge. Finally, only Carrie's pervasive symptoms were safe topics for what became endless perseverating discussion.

Since the presence of a toxic secret can disallow conversation in many areas, a family's ability to solve problems or to confront normal developmental issues may be seriously impaired. In one family, a teenage son had died two years before the birth of a daughter. The parents and oldest sister kept this son's very existence a secret from the youngest child, who grew up in an atmosphere of deep, unexplainable sadness. The mother's yearly depressions, coincidental with the anniversary of the son's death, went "unnoticed" and unattended. The father's hypervigilant attention to every action of the young girl led to seemingly unexplainable and ultimately dangerous rebellious behavior on her part, including breaking and entering homes in the neighborhood, no doubt a metaphorical communication in a family where critical information was blocked. When the family first entered therapy, the only allowable topic of conversation was the girl's grades in school, even though it was obvious from their nonverbal communication that something much more serious was affecting the family's well-being.

When relationships are bound up by a secret, the family's overall communication style may become one marked by secret-keeping in areas totally unrelated to the initial secret. Both deliberate lies and withheld information may erode interpersonal trust and relationship reliability.

Secrets and Symptoms

The relationship of secrets and symptoms can be seen in four ways. First, particular symptoms may be kept a secret, either by the symptomatic person or the family. Examples of symptoms as secrets include alcoholism, drug addiction, eating disorders, and mental illness (see Krestan and Bepko, Chapter 8, and Giat Roberto, Chapter 9). Physical symptoms and diseases such as AIDS are also often kept secret (see Black, Chapter 17). When symptoms are kept secret, most often it is because shame and stigma are attached to the particular symptom. Such shame engenders secrecy, which, in turn, engenders a deepening sense of shame (see Mason, Chapter 2). When symptoms remain a secret, the individual and family remain without access to the resources needed to address the symptom and its personal and relational effects.

Second, certain symptoms may function as metaphors for particular secrets. A young child's refusal to speak outside the family, an adolescent's lying and stealing, or a young woman's bulimia may be ways to comment metaphorically on the unmentionable. A symptom may be a symbolic expression of powerful emotions connected to the secret. Thus, Carrie's seemingly irrational fear of germs and constant hand-washing, which led to her inability to function in the outside world, neatly encapsulated all of the family's fear and overwhelming shame regarding their secret.

Third, symptoms may serve as effective distractions from otherwise unbearable secrets, providing family members with a safe topic of conversation. As in Carrie's case, therapist after therapist may get busy intervening at the wrong level of the system, attempting to address the symptom at the biological, behavioral, or even interpersonal level, while completely missing the core system of secrecy in which the symptom is embedded.

Finally, symptoms of anxiety and guilt may result from secrecy. As Karpel (1980) noted, those who know the secret become anxious as they constantly fear disclosure and constantly have to guard the direction of conversations, and those who are kept out of the secret become anxious as they experience the interpersonal tension that surrounds secrets. Those who "know but aren't allowed to know" a secret often describe feeling burdened by an unexplainable sense of guilt.

The intricate relationship of secrets and symptoms and the dissolution of disabling and even chronic symptoms when a toxic secret is carefully opened can be seen in a case which I call "Finding Our Voices."

The Green family called for therapy in the midst of a severe crisis. The family consisted of the mother and stepfather, John and Sara Green, 45 and 38; a son, James, 22; and a daughter, Ella, 17. Sara Green had been a single parent, raising both children alone from shortly after their births until 1986 when she married. The family is African-American. The mother's extended family lives nearby and relies on her to do most instrumental functioning for the entire family — she is seen by everyone as extraordinarily strong, capable, and having few needs of her own.

The daughter, Ella, has spoken very little since early childhood. She was diagnosed with moderate mental retardation and learning disabilities. She attends special education classes, and her mother has been extremely diligent in getting appropriate services for her.

A crisis of enormous magnitude in Ella's life brought the family into therapy, as it was discovered that she had been repeatedly raped by two janitors at her school. Ella kept this violent abuse a secret for many months, because she was frightened of getting anyone in trouble and was especially concerned that she might upset her mother. Ella and her mother had a warm and loving relationship, but Ella seemed to sense that her mother needed protection, despite her overt strengths. Over the months of secret sexual abuse, Ella showed profound personality changes, becoming intensely hostile, angry, and enraged toward family members, in contrast to her previously sweet and docile nature. Finally, her mother took her to the doctor, where it was discovered that she had become pregnant: In this way, the first secret, the secret of the rapes, became known. It was at this moment that the family entered therapy.

From the outset, this was an unusual family therapy, as the family sought help simultaneously from our team* and from their church. They placed our work with them within the context of their faith, which dictated that our work with them was, in fact, sent by God. They secured permission from their church for Ella to have an abortion, which was ordinarily prohibited by their religion. The parents moved swiftly to protect Ella by sending her to her grandmother's and tried to bring criminal charges against the rapists, but they were told by the District Attorney that, due to Ella's disabilities, she was not a credible witness. Our initial work with the family was, in fact,

*Peggy Papp was my collaborator in this clinical work.

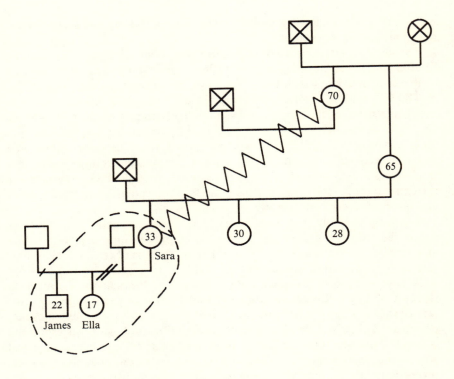

Figure 1.2

crisis intervention, enabling a forum for the expression of their grief and anger, assisting the stepfather and son to reconsider their desire to take the law into their own hands, and helping them to organize a civil suit against the janitorial service, who, in fact, knew of the ongoing sexual abuse and had done nothing to stop it.

The family was handling this terrible crisis in a thoughtful and caring manner in our early sessions, when the mother simply began to deteriorate. She spoke poignantly of her overwhelming guilt, of her feelings that, as the mother, she should have been able to protect Ella, that, if she couldn't protect her daughter, what kind of mother was she. In short, the cultural message that if anything happens to a child, it is the mother's fault was ringing in her ears. Weaving the sociocultural level of beliefs into the family therapy and using our position as two women, Peggy Papp and I challenged the notion that what happened to Ella was in any way the mother's fault and reflected to her all of the impressive ways that she was handling this terrible crisis for Ella and for the family. She received this opinion from us with great surprise, as she had never before heard praise for her mothering. While she relaxed a bit in that session, the family then reported to us that Sara had continued to decline at home, that she wasn't sleeping or eating, and that she was enormously anxious.

In the next session, the mother insisted that her anxieties were focused on her belief that Ella would "be unable to ever recognize danger" and that nothing could remedy this. She was frantic as she talked about her fear, and while we worked with her and Ella on this issue of being able to recognize danger, it was to no avail. The family referred to the mother as Ella's "best teacher," and we attempted to utilize this resource in a homework task designed to enable her to recognize danger. But, the mother returned and told us she simply couldn't do it and that she was, incomprehensibly, doing worse and worse in her daily functioning. At this point, we made a decision to see the mother alone, as we thought there was something she could not speak about in the family that was perhaps contributing to her deterioration.

Early in this individual session, Sara told me that what had happened to Ella reminded her of something that had happened to her that she had not thought of for 27 years, but she said that she could not speak of it and quickly changed the subject. I asked her, then, if I could explore a bit of family history with her, which we had not done; as we constructed her genogram together, several secrets began to emerge. Some were secrets that the whole family knew, but did not discuss, including that her mother had left her father after discovering his secret affair. She tried to keep her family together but was unable to and sent Sara, then 10 years old, to live with her aunt, while keeping her two other children with her. At first, Sara told me that she really had no idea why she was sent away, but gradually she revealed the secret regarding racism within her family, a secret seldom, if ever, discussed with white people. She told me that she believes that she was sent away because she was the darkest and was then horribly physically abused by her aunt, who was prejudiced against her for being so black (see Boyd-Franklin, Chapter 16 for a discussion of skin color secrets in African-American families).

As we explored this painful and secret legacy of black slavery, a legacy in which lighter-skinned blacks were often treated better by their masters than darker-skinned blacks, but in which lighter skin also spoke of generations of rape and sexual abuse of black women by white men, I felt I had permission to revisit the issue about which Sara had said earlier she could not speak. With enormous anxiety Sara began to tell me of being repeatedly sexually abused by her uncle over a period of five years. As her story unfolded, moments of enormous courage and strength emerged, as she spoke of the ingenious ways she had devised to get away from her uncle.

She attempted to tell her aunt about the abuse, but her aunt called the 10-year-old girl a whore and broke her arm. She ultimately ran away to the North. She never spoke of the abuse again, until this session, and had repressed the painful memories until the sexual abuse of her daughter brought it all back, catching her up in a tornado of excruciating images. The immediate effects of her finding her voice with us, in an atmosphere marked by empathy and receptivity, were visible at the end of the session when she told us that all of her guilt had been lifted and that she felt a lightness she had never before experienced.

In the next session, Sara expressed that she now believed Ella would be able to recognize danger. She spoke of feeling calm and strong and attributed the change in herself to being able finally to find her voice in the previous session.

Her newfound faith in Ella's capacities — a mirror, in fact, of her newly birthed belief in herself, in her own goodness, and in her worth as a woman — were met with many unanticipated changes, first in Ella and then in the whole family system. Prior to even hearing her mother's painful secret, Ella somehow recognized that her mother had a new voice. Ella, who previously could barely speak above a whisper, began to develop a voice of her own, challenging the stigmatizing label of mental retardation and telling me that it was simply not right that handicapped people made less money for doing the same job as people who were not handicapped. Further, she described to me how she had told a girlfriend how to protect herself at school and on the streets. Most dramatically, as Ella witnessed her mother's changes, she changed before our eyes from a little handicapped girl to a competent young woman, holding forth in one session to her stepfather on the rights of women!

Over the next several months, through a careful coaching process, Sara opened the secret of her own sexual abuse to many family members, with many important changes resulting. She decided she wanted to talk first to her own mother and discovered in this conversation that her mother had also been sexually abused and had never spoken of it. An enormous gulf between them was bridged and many relationship issues were gradually healed, as the "rule" requiring women to be silent about being abused was broken across the generations. She spoke next to her sister, whose image of her had been that she never had any problems in life and could handle anything the family asked of her. A more equal relationship between them began to emerge, and her sister was able to focus her on the profound developmental changes appearing in Ella, amplifying these for all to notice.

Finally, during a family argument, which her husband and children were insisting she had to solve as she always solved all other matters for them, she revealed the secret of her abuse and was able to change the previous paradoxical pattern of their seeing her as invincible while, at the same time, believing that she needed great amounts of protection. The capacities of all family members to take care of each other were invoked, replacing the previous arrangement where Sara was expected to care for all while her own needs for care remained hidden and were met covertly.

Secrecy and Privacy — Who Decides?

A central dilemma for therapists working in the area of secrets revolves around the definitions of secrecy and privacy. These definitions shift across time, cultures, and sociopolitical circumstances. Various families will have their own definitions of what is secret and what is private, and so will various therapists. Socially constructed definitions of secrecy and privacy change by what a given culture stigmatizes or values. For instance, the sexual relationship of a heterosexual couple is considered private, while the sexual relationship of a homosexual couple must often be kept secret, as it is not protected by law in some places and is certainly subject to prejudices that violate privacy (see Sanders, Chapter 12).

In a discussion of secrecy and privacy, Bok (1983) defines secrecy as "intentional concealment" and privacy as "being protected from unwanted access by others" (p. 10). When we attempt to apply these definitions in family life or in therapy, however, ethical struggles regarding their overlap and who is doing the defining become apparent. A husband may define his affair as "private" while his wife may experience it as "secret." A biological mother who gives her child up for adoption may claim a right to privacy regarding ever being contacted by this child, and the state may even codify such privacy into law, while the adult adoptee regards the information as a secret being kept from him. An adolescent may regard her sexual life as private, while her parents may believe she is keeping an inappropriate secret. This particular dilemma of privacy versus secrecy has played out at the societal level in the legal debate over an adolescent's right to make her own decision regarding abortion and the demand for parental notification or consent.

What is kept secret often engenders shame, while truly private matters do not. Secrets are often connected to fear and anxiety regarding disclosure, while privacy implies a certain zone of comfort, free from the unwanted entry of others. Therapy itself is a socially constructed arena where the experience of an umbrella of privacy can often be sufficient to enable the opening of painful secrets.

Secrecy and privacy often exist in a paradoxical relationship with one another, largely because different and sometimes conflicting definitions of secrecy and privacy exist at various levels in a macrosystem. When areas of personal privacy are redefined by government, individuals and families may respond with secret-keeping. For instance, AIDS patients often live with the carefully guarded secret of their illness, while their right to privacy is frequently threatened by proposed legislation, insurance practices, etc., leading directly to intensified secret-keeping (see Black, Chapter 17). For women in North America to gain the right to privacy regarding control of their own bodies, many women had to go public with the previously held secret of their abortions (Brill, 1990). If this right is jeopardized, what is now private will again become corrosively secret.

Karpel (1980) suggested that the distinction between secrecy and privacy be drawn by determining the relevance of the information to the person who does not currently know it. We may broaden this to state that any information that directly affects one's well-being but is being held back, either from oneself or from others who may effect needed protection, takes on the dimension of secrecy, not privacy.

The tensions between secrecy and privacy and who gets to decide for whom leads directly to a discussion of power and powerlessness. Regarding privacy, Brill (1990, p. xviii) states, "Without power, without resources and lots of courage, invasions of privacy are all the more possible and the infringements on it are all the more painful. . . . The more vulnerable you are, the less likely it is that you will feel empowered or enabled to protect your privacy." Such inability to protect one's privacy can lead directly to shame-inducing secrecy. Thus, Sara Green's ultimate privacy, the integrity of her own body, was violated. The societal and family beliefs that blamed women for such violation caused her to hide in painful secrecy for 23 years, keeping the secret of her abuse even from herself. The relationship of power to definitions of secrecy and privacy can be seen in the fact that very dangerous secrets, secrets of violence and abuse, are most often maintained by the more physically and socially powerful person (usually male) using intimidation and invoking the "right to privacy" in the home. It is only very recently that the existence of such a right in the face of abuse has been questioned at the cultural level.

Certain secrets implicitly define hierarchy in relationships. By saying, in effect, "I know what's best for you to know in areas that directly affect your life" and then covering this with a patina of privacy, relationships of power and powerlessness are shaped.

In the therapy room, one often works with shifts from secrecy to privacy and needs to ask which is occurring and which is being invoked at a given moment. Clinically, this becomes particularly important when working with subsystems or individuals during family therapy. Immediately after Sara Green shared what had been her shameful secret, she spoke of feeling like something had lifted, of feeling lighter. At that moment, what had been secret became transformed to that which was private. Decisions about who to tell held no element of secrecy, but rather were her own private decisions, which she made slowly with us over time. We were able to see her with other members of her family, because we were not constrained by a secret alliance with her; rather, we had shared a now private matter that she ultimately decided to tell to her mother, sister, husband, and children. This stands in contrast to those difficult times in therapy when the therapist is told a secret that is, in fact, not private, but directly impinges on another person's right to know the information.[1]

Working with the Location of Secrets

Where a secret is located shapes clinical considerations and intervention possibilities. A secret may be located within one individual, involving thoughts, feelings, or actions that the person has never spoken to another person. Such a secret location often erodes self-esteem and one's capacity to trust other people's responses, because the secret-keeper often feels "If others really knew, they would dislike me, disrespect me, hate me, etc." Sometimes, as in the situation of Sara Green, others may know the secret at its inception and may intimidate the individual into silence. When attempts to tell another are met with mystification and denial, as when Sara tried to tell her aunt of the abuse, the secret is driven further inside an individual, who psychologically begins to "not know" what she knows. The secret becomes denied, repressed, and a secret even from oneself. Conversely, when an individual gives voice to a shameful secret and is met with empathy and receptivity, self-definitions begin to shift dramatically. Thus, Sara Green began to think and speak of herself as "a woman who takes charge" and "a woman of courage."

A secret may be located between two or more people in the family, excluding others and thus shaping triangles in the family and sometimes creating loyalty binds. The issue of who knows a secret in the extended family is particularly important to explore, as one may discover a pervasive secret-keeping pattern, for instance, between a husband and his extended family that excludes a wife and erodes marital trust. It is crucial to determine the position regarding opening the secret of those who are not in the therapy room, but who know the secret and influence decisions of secrecy and openness. For example, grandparents and other relatives generally know when there is a secret regarding parentage. Careful consideration of what they would say and do if a mother and stepfather decide to open the secret to a child that the purported father is really a stepfather needs to be part of any therapeutic work.

A secret may be located between one person in a family and someone outside the family, such as an affair. Secrets that cross the family boundary may also occur between a family member and an outside professional helper (Imber-Black, 1988). For instance, a mother and a school guidance counselor may make a secret regarding a child that excludes the father. Many larger systems are organized to deliver services in ways that create secrets between helpers and family members, with little thought given to the effects on relationships if such secrets are maintained or opened. Effective work with secrets requires making an ecological map of where a secret is located including the larger system level and including interventions that address the macrosystem.

A secret may be located within the boundaries of the nuclear family as something that everyone knows, but extended family and the outside world are kept out. Such secrets may shape a family's entire identity vis-à-vis the outside world and may contribute to a sense of unity. At the same time, the requirement to keep such a secret within the family boundaries may cut the family or individuals off from needed resources.

A secret that the whole family knows may become especially complicated by the injunction "we know, but we pretend not to know," as in George and Carrie's family. Here, there is a whole-family secret, but each family member carries a secret about the secret that operates to distance and divide people. In this case, the intervention of putting the daughters behind the one-way mirror effectively relocated the process of secret-keeping from the previous whole family and individual levels to a subsystem level that, for the first time, included an outsider — the therapist. This was followed by the subsequent relocation of the content of the secret, first from the parents to the therapist and, then, from the parents to their daughters, as they were able to tell their story aloud for the first time.

Finally, a secret or secrets may be located at the larger system level, excluding individuals and families who are directly affected by the information being kept from them. This may include such matters as diagnoses, medical records, dangerous medication side effects, health records of biological parents of children who are adopted, actions within a larger system to cover up mistakes, and government and military secrets kept from the population. The larger context shaped by such secret-keeping certainly affects beliefs and actions in the therapy room whether we realize it or not.

This larger system level may also include community and national secrets that everyone knows but pretends not to know, such as the Holocaust or during reigns of political terror under dictatorships. The issue of both personal and political power reappears in the presence of national secrets. Those who hold power become entitled to keep secrets that, in turn, feed back and amplify positions of power. Those who have little or no power are intimidated into silence. When periods of political terror end, secrets at the national level that found their expression in the daily activities of individuals and ultimately shaped intimate family relationships, must be dealt with, or secrets about the secrets will be generated, preventing genuine healing and obviating the true redistribution of personal and political power.[2]

Once it is determined where a secret is located, therapeutic interventions can be developed that relocate either the process of secret-keeping or the actual content of a secret. An initial relocation of a secret to include the therapist, however, is often just the beginning of the work that needs to be done regarding the personal and relational effects of opening the secret. For example, Sara Green's secret initially was relocated from inside her to between her and our therapy team. While this relocation dramatically eliminated her symptoms of debilitating anxiety and fear and generated a new sense of her own capabilities, several more sessions and much work on her part outside of the therapy room were required to enable her and her family to free themselves from the effects of this toxic secret and to move on.

When working with locating and relocating a secret, it is important to determine if a family or an individual has tried to relocate and open a secret in the past and has failed. For instance, a young woman tried to tell her mother about her stepfather sexually abusing her. Her mother refused to hear this, walked out of the room, and acted as if her daughter had never spoken. Both the sexual abuse and this encounter remained a secret for seven more years, until the daughter spoke to her mother again, in the context of a therapy session, where the mother had already been made to feel safe through a focus on the struggles in her life. When trying a second time to relocate a secret, to shift from secrecy to openness, the therapist needs to know all of the particulars of the first failed attempt in order to make the new attempt a different experience. Often deep shame has attended an initial failed attempt to open a secret. Enabling a family to build a context of strength and courage is required before making a second attempt at opening a toxic secret. Thus, Sara Green had tried 23 years earlier to tell her aunt about the abuse she suffered. She was not only disbelieved, but punished, physically and emotionally. Only when she felt sufficiently safe in a therapy session that focused over and over on stories of her perseverance and survival was she able once again to risk relocating the secret from inside herself to between herself and another.

Direct and Indirect Interventions with Secrets

How directly or indirectly one works with a secret in therapy depends on many factors, including trust and rapport in the therapeutic system, what beliefs pertain regarding the consequences of openness, where the secret is located, and whether danger is attached to either maintaining or opening the secret.

The first requirement for exploring secrets in therapy is constructing a sufficiently safe environment. When George and Carrie came for the session with their daughters behind the mirror, I first secured their permission to conduct the session in this unusual way, and I would not have proceeded without their full consent. When Sara Green intimated that she had a secret she could not discuss, I spent time carefully entering her world. I only returned to the topic after she had led the way by sharing her painful skin color secret with me. After she spoke of being sexually abused, and it was clear that she had not spoken of this since childhood, she remained initially very anxious. When I asked her how she felt about having told me and whether it was all right that she had decided to tell me, she visibly calmed and proclaimed her right to speak to me.

When one first encounters a secret in therapy, as, for instance, when parents tell a therapist a secret they are keeping from a child, it is important to find out who knows the information and what their position would be about opening it. A discussion of the imagined consequences of opening the secret for individuals, relationships, and the whole family is generally useful for the family and informative for the therapist and family who are able to hear predictions of positive and negative outcomes. Often, individuals or a family has never had an opportunity to consider out loud what they imagine the effects of opening a secret would be. Rather, such wonderings, if they have occurred at all, have also remained a secret. Hearing fearful predictions allows the therapist to offer the potential of more positive outcomes, such as ending the constant fear of disclosure, eliminating tension, lifting guilt, and restoring trust and relationship reliability. Once people are able to imagine such positive results, the therapist can make a direct intervention regarding opening the secret. (See Papp, Chapter 4, for an example of directly advising a mother to open a secret regarding a missing father.)

Gathering information about potential negative consequences also allows the therapist to plan subsequent stages of the work, to determine if disclosure should occur in the safety of the therapeutic domain, to consider who should be invited for sessions and in what configurations, and to consider carefully the time that may be necessary to deal with the effects of opening a secret.

Because time to reflect on the consequences of opening a secret is often necessary, tasks can be constructed that ask participants to either think about or talk over the pros and cons of opening a toxic secret. Similar to a discussion in the session, such a task allows people to consider the positive aspects of opening the secret, usually for the first time. In order to obviate against rapid oscillation of positive to negative outcomes, it is often effective to ask people to separate these discussions into distinct time periods (e.g., an hour to consider only the negative consequences and a different hour to consider only the positive outcomes).

When someone has a secret that they cannot yet speak of, using symbols can be an effective means of communication about the unspeakable. Two parents and their 16-year-old daughter came to therapy presenting vague fears about the girl's well-being and future life. These fears had emerged in the last six months, and all three family members felt them but could not explain their origin. When I asked them all to bring symbols of these fears so that I could understand them better, the mother brought a piece of rope. At first she stated that rope represented her fear that her daughter would stay tied to her too long. Then, she began to cry and, for the first time, told her daughter and her husband the story of her own brother's suicide by hanging when he was 17. When her brother killed himself, her own parents insisted that this never be spoken of again. The mother had obeyed this and had not even told her husband that she had a brother. Following this moving session, fears about the daughter dissolved, and the therapy refocused on mourning this terrible unmourned loss and on coaching the mother to open the secret with her parents.

Using the one-way mirror is especially effective when secrets are located within the whole family but cannot be spoken of or acknowledged. Asking part of the family to be behind the mirror to raise questions through the therapist provides a sense of safety regarding secrets.

The existence of the one-way mirror, with members of the family on each side of it who are only able to "see" when lights are turned on, serves as a dramatic metaphor for secrecy and openness in family relationships. "Rules" regarding who knows what and who may speak to whom are repeatedly broken when family members communicate "secretly" on the telephone to the therapist, who, in turn, tells who called and what the message was. The therapist, previously kept outside of the family, can reposition herself between family members.

The effects of a one-way mirror session when secrets pertain are often swift and change-inducing in the direction of openness. Usually, families in which all members know a secret but are enjoined from speaking about it with one another deeply fear the consequences of opening the secret. Because the one-way mirror session provides a repetitive experience of the process of moving from secrecy to openness without any disastrous consequences, dealing with the central secret becomes easier to imagine and actualize.

A similar intervention, which can be used when one does not have a one-way mirror, involves requesting family members to write down questions they would like to have answered, placing them in sealed envelopes, and putting these into a large box. These questions can be directed to an individual, a subsystem, such as the parents or children, the whole family or the therapist. Family members can raise these questions anonymously or put their names on them. The therapist opens each sealed envelope and reads the question, again enacting the process of moving from secrecy to openness. The family wrote meaningless and innocuous questions. At the end of the session, the father said, "Let's do this again next time, and let's work on some *real* questions." In the following session, the father wrote a question to the family, asking why no one noticed how depressed he had been for over a year. In fact, everyone had noticed but had been too afraid to talk about it, fearing he would return to his previous and never-mentioned alcoholic drinking.

It is critical that a therapist be clear about his or her own values and beliefs when intervening in an individual's or a family's secrets. The therapist needs to be able to state his or her own ethical position regarding secrecy and openness to clients.

Working with the Aftermath of Opening a Secret

While the initial opening of a secret in therapy can often have dramatic and positive effects on individual functioning and interpersonal relationships, much work generally remains to be done to restore reliability, heal broken trust, deal with anger, and work on whatever issues may have been kept secret. Opening a secret about a particular symptom, such as alcoholism or an eating disorder is just the beginning of work to alleviate the symptom and alter relationships. When a secret affair is opened in therapy, the hard work of restoring and reconciling the marital relationship can follow, or the work of dealing with marital dissolution. Discovering secrets regarding adoption is usually the start of much longer work, sometimes involving a search for the person's biological parents and therapy involving issues with adoptive parents and an altered sense of self.

When George and Carrie's secret, a secret that everyone knew but could not speak about, was opened, many other relationship issues came to the fore. Their daughters confronted them about the general process of secret-keeping and triangulation that affected nearly all of the small details of family life. The family tendency to make secrets had to be countered over and over again. Planning a party for their anniversary, for the first time in the history of their marriage, was followed by open celebrations of the daughters' birthdays, which became rituals that furthered the family's healing.

Discovering the ways a secret has been maintained informs subsequent work after a secret has been opened. A secret maintained primarily by a motive of protection, such as when a young child is not told that a father is in prison, is a very different secret than one that is maintained by fear and intimidation, such as a secret of abuse. It is usually much easier to restore a sense of trust when protection and subsequent confusion over when the right time has come to open a secret pertains, than when trust has been corroded by an abuse of power and by physical harm.

It is not unusual to find that opening one secret leads to the emergence of other secrets, as the family discovers the relief and new resources that become available through greater openness. Thus, when Sara Green told her secret to her mother, her mother, in turn, felt free to share the secret of her own abuse. Sometimes the dissolution of a secret leads to pressure on other secrets, such as when a mother opened the secret of giving her grown son money for what she believed were his debts, a secret she had kept from her husband, only to discover four months later that her son had been using this money to support a drug habit.

After a secret has been opened, a therapist must be willing to be available for the long haul, and not assume simplistically that openness alone is curative. When certain secrets are opened, therapists must be able to work effectively with the larger systems that may enter a family's life, such as medical, psychiatric, or child welfare systems (Imber-Black, 1988). Creating a therapeutic atmosphere capable of holding all of the differentiated responses to opening a secret is critical, lest a new secret immediately form regarding how family members feel about the content of the secret.

CONCLUSIONS

Working with secrets are part of doing effective therapy. Each therapist needs to develop a position regarding secrets across multiple content areas and relationship configurations, while remaining open to the possibility that this position will be challenged again and again by the endless variety of secrets and secret-keeping that enter the culture and, ultimately, the therapy room. Families have a right to know the therapist's position; it should not remain a secret embedded in the very fabric of the therapy.

When relationships are shaped by toxic or dangerous secrets, an assumed "right to conceal" flows to the illicitly powerful, while the threat of exposure envelopes the vulnerable. Relationship equity, towards which meaningful therapy aims, emerges from the right to know that which affects our lives and the right to give voice to our deepest pain.

NOTES

1. The reader is referred to Karpel (1980) for an informative discussion on "reparative" and "preventive" strategies to use when the therapist is drawn into a secret. See also Walker (1991), Chapter 8 for a thoughtful discussion of this issue when AIDS is involved. The material presented by Walker is a template for this general ethical dilemma.

2. For a moving example of effective therapeutic work in the face of national secrets

regarding political terror, see Kohen, C. (1988). "Political Trauma, Oppression and Rituals" in E. Imber-Black, J. Roberts & R. Whiting (Eds.), *Rituals in Families and Family Therapy*. New York: W. W. Norton. This chapter squarely confronts the therapist's need to deal with political secrets in the therapy room.

REFERENCES

Anderson, C. M., & Stewart S. (1983). *Mastering resistance: A practical guide to family therapy*. New York: Guilford.

Bok, S. (1983). *Secrets: On the ethics of concealment and revelation*. New York: Vintage.

Boscolo, L., Cecchin, G., Hoffman, L., & Penn, P. (1987). *Milan systemic family therapy: Conversations in theory and practice*. New York: Basic.

Bowen, M. (1978). *Family therapy in clinical practice*. Northvale, NJ: Jason Aronson.

Boyd-Franklin, N. (1989). *Black families in therapy: A multisystems approach*. New York: Guilford.

Brill, A. (1990). *Nobody's business: The paradoxes of privacy*. New York: Addison-Wesley.

Friedman, E. H. (1973–74). Secrets and systems. In J. P. Lorio & L. McClenathen (Eds.), *The Georgetown family symposia*, Vol. 2. Washington, DC: Georgetown University Family Center Publishers.

Grolnick, L. (1983). Ibsen's truth, family secrets, and family therapy. *Family Process, 22*, 275–288.

Haley, J. (1976). *Problem-solving therapy*. New York: Jossey-Bass.

Imber-Black, E. (1986). Odysseys of a learner. In D. Efron (Ed.), *Journeys: Expansion of the strategic-systemic therapies*. New York: Brunner/Mazel.

Imber-Black, E. (1988). *Families and larger systems: A family therapist's guide through the labyrinth*. New York: Guilford.

Imber-Coppersmith, E. (1985). "We've got a secret!" A nonmarital marital therapy. In A. Gurman (Ed.), *Casebook of marital therapy* (pp. 369–386). New York: Guilford.

Karpel, M. A. (1980). Family secrets: I. Conceptual and ethical issues in the relational context. II. Ethical and practical considerations in therapeutic management. *Family Process, 19*, 295–306.

Pittman, F. (1989). *Private lies*. New York: W. W. Norton.

Walker, G. (1991). *In the midst of winter: Systemic therapy with families, couples and individuals with AIDS infection*. New York: W. W. Norton.

Wendorf, D. J., & Wendorf, R. J. (1985). A systemic view of family therapy ethics. *Family Process, 24*, 443–453.

2

Shame: Reservoir for Family Secrets

MARILYN J. MASON

IN A RECENT WORKSHOP on family shame, I asked 125 participants to write a family secret on a piece of paper. All but one were able to name at least one secret without much deliberation. They revealed secrets about rape, physical abuse, manic-depressive disorder, affairs, abortions, alcoholism, gambling, children born out of wedlock, transvestitism, promiscuity, finances, adoption, incest, religious practices, suicide, lesbianism and male homosexuality, hunger, and bootlegging. Clearly, not all these named secrets would necessarily be shameful, yet most participants recalled them as sources of shame.

Just what is the relationship between secrets and shame? Some secrets are consciously private; some are wrapped in conscious shame. Still other secrets are buried in the unconscious or in repressed memories. To understand the relationship between shame and secrets, we must first understand how privacy, secrecy, and shame differ.

PRIVACY

Privacy is the right to be let alone, often described as being free from scrutiny — an inviolable right (Brandeis, 1991). The realm of privacy as an individual right is an American value; we often assign to this domain our values around money, politics, religious practices, and sexual behaviors. However, we see a double edge in the protection of our privacy. Often, we see that very private issues, such as reproductive rights and the right to die, are fought for in the *public* arena.

Today, we are ambivalent about privacy even though the private realm can enrich the depth of life. In the United States, our cultural attitudes toward privacy have changed over the years. What was once private is now exploited by the media. Even our courts are ambiguous about the line between the private realm and public display. We see the private lives of the famous and powerful publicly exposed; in fact, "tell-all" biographies have become a late 20th-century American institution (Kaplan, 1991). Radio and television talk shows, magazines, and newspapers thrive on intrusions of privacy.

It is difficult to discern just what to assign to the private domain or to the secret domain. Some say that there is no privacy without shame; many of us contend that a sense of shame can protect us from defiling exposure—that it guards our inner self, our spirit. The bridge between privacy and shame is secrecy.

SECRECY

Some secrets can be private delights: surprises for loved ones or personal covenants we have with others. Through secrecy, we can feel "special." Other secrets cause us to feel burdened and caught in someone else's story; not allowed to tell, we exclude others. When we refer to secrets, we mean hidden information—that is, information that is "owed another." Secrecy protects something by concealing it from view.

Secrets often encompass cultural taboos around money, sex, and illness. Therefore, bankruptcy and theft, incest and sexual abuse, addictions, epilepsy, and AIDS are family secrets. In recent years, the reporting and public exposure of the rising number of violations of cultural taboos have greatly illuminated our private versus public dilemma. While growing up, many of us came to believe that the word "secret" had a negative meaning as we learned about the painful truth enveloped in secrecy. For many, family privacy had long been the hiding place for shameful secrets. Yet we have learned that one person's "right to privacy" is often another person's victimization and shame. Armed with this realization, today's culture sanctions the telling of our secrets.

SHAME

We see our shame reflected in all our systems—ecological, political, family, religious, and, of course, individual. We cannot talk about shame without discussing the larger systems, the cultural context.

A friend from India exclaimed, "You know what your shame is? You have so much!" We live in a culture of abundance, yet we are spiritually impoverished. We recognize that family privacy has protected the fact that the family has become a dangerous hiding place for family violence and sexual abuse. We know that 400,000 cases of father-daughter incest will be reported in the

United States this year; we know that one in four women will be beaten; we know that 38% of women are sexually assaulted by age 18 (Covington, 1986). We know that one of every ten boys is abused. Every six minutes a woman is raped (Covington, 1986). We know that 40% of the people in poverty in this nation are children. Obviously, we live in a sexist, racist, homophobic, ageist, addicted, shamebound culture that touches all of us.

At the same time, we live with a myth of social conformity from which we are not to deviate; we live with an "addiction to social conformity" (Whitaker, 1986). Family members loyal to sociocultural community standards experience a sense of shame when they violate social law or the moral code. We live with a perceived image of some perfect social self, who is to be admired for upholding external social standards. Often, we are admired not for personhood but rather for status and titles and the "image" of success. Our capitalistic culture assures us that consumption conveys an external image of success. Thus, if we have titles and money and the right address and car, we have worth. Yet, paradoxically, we know at some deep level that this cannot eradicate shame.

Shame has been called the most powerful motivator of human progress. Shame becomes the "motor" that drives many to seek perfection, status, and wealth. It is probably no surprise that 38% of American corporate executives grew up in alcoholic families (*EAP Digest*, 1987). Shame often lies at the hub of the cycle of control. In an attempt to move away from the pain of the shame, the "master emotion" (Goleman, 1987), we often are driven to addictive behaviors that give us moments of release by making us feel better or numb. For example, a compulsive shoplifter did not want her spouse to know her painful secret. Once he found out, the couple waited until they were in therapy for almost a year before telling the secret. After some time, she learned that she was running from the pain and shame of her incestuous relationship with her father.

It is not always the secret itself — family suicide, premarital pregnancy, addictions, suicide, or sexual abuse — that determines whether the secret becomes growth-inhibiting. Rather, it is the family process around the event or experience. If a family has a relatively open system — that is, its members are free to comment on what happened and pass it on through family stories — the family is less likely to become bound in shame. Families that are more closed and loyal to the "don't talk, don't trust, don't feel" rules often create family myths or dishonest stories to hide secrets.

Just when does a secret enter the reservoir of shame? By examining the process of shame from the source event down through the family dynamics, we can readily see how secrets become the maintained shame that so many people struggle with in therapy.

Source Events

Often, secrets are related to painful life events, natural and unnatural, that occur outside the sociocultural norms. Many of these secrets may be known consciously—for example, the hiding of ethnicity, learning disabilities, or mental retardation. Many may be unknown, buried secrets. These source events can be behaviors *in the present or from the past*, beliefs and fantasies, or family history (see Table 2.1).

In gathering data on family secrets, I have found that sexual secrets are the most common. I solicit the secrets by asking the question, "What is a family secret that you are carrying? Does it come from your family of origin or from your current family?" At this time, I remind them that they do not have to share this with anyone. I then ask participants to write the secret on a piece of paper, and I collect them. To illustrate the pervasiveness of family secrets and their relationship to shame, I read them aloud. We then discuss what it has been like to carry the secret. In a workshop for 50 women, all secrets reported were sexual except one. Pregnancy, rape, venereal disease, affairs, sex abuse, abortions, promiscuity, and same-sex experiences were listed by the women. In a large workshop with a mixed audience, 56% of the

TABLE 2.1

Source Events

HEALTH	FAMILY HISTORY
Epilepsy	Faked or Denied Ethnicity/Race
Mental Illness	Traumas
Venereal Disease	Holocaust Survivors
AIDS	Physical or Sexual Abuse
Chronic Illness	SELF-DESTRUCTION
FINANCES	Addictions
Theft	Anorexia Nervosa/Bulimia
Embezzlement	Suicide Attempts
Poverty	Mutilation
Bankruptcy	ABUSE
Income Loss	Beatings
RELATIONSHIPS	Rape
Extramarital Affairs	Incest
Adoption Dishonest	SEXUAL
Death	Gay or Lesbian Relationships
	Sexual Identity
	Abortions
	Births for Adoption

secrets revealed were sexual; this same group reported a high incidence of alcoholism in their families of origin. In asking for secrets over the years, what has intrigued me is the finding that it is typically the victim who reports the shame event; only once have I read a secret revealed by a perpetrator. Many factors can affect this. Perhaps when people are in workshop settings, they see themselves as children in their families. Also, another factor could be the way the question is asked. It clearly reflects the shame that is internalized by the victim.

The second most frequent secret expressed is addictions in the family, particularly alcoholism. Fifty percent of incest victims are from alcoholic homes; 74% of women from alcoholic families have been physically, sexually, and emotionally abused (Bass & Davis, 1988). Alcohol and drugs are readily available for numbing and releasing the pain of buried secrets.

Typically we see that an individual's sense of shame is linked to some other family member's behavior—in other words, to violations of the social code. The shame may be consciously known or unconsciously carried in secreted family stories and family myths. Family fidelity holds the secrets and the shame intact, no matter how debilitating.

Case Example: The Invisible Inheritance

Joe sounded stunned when he called for therapy; I asked him to bring his wife with him at least for the first session. In the initial interview, Joe began sobbing as he described opening a letter addressed to his wife, Marsha. The letter was from a lover with whom Marsha had had a relationship for the past year. The secret was out, and both wanted to talk. Marsha was openly worried about Joe; she had never seen him so "emotional." Joe told how he was unable to stop crying; in their fourteen-year marriage Marsha had seen Joe cry once.

History taking revealed that Marsha and Joe were both successful in their careers and in their public lives. Joe, age 37, was a highly respected physician in his community; Marsha was an administrator for an educational institution. Marsha and Joe could be described as a "child-centered" couple: Both focused their energies on the well-being and activities of their children.

Marsha announced that she was not willing to enter into therapy with Joe at this time; she had already been seeing an individual therapist. Joe stayed in therapy, saying he thought he might be going crazy. I assured him that he was "going sane." The initial stages of therapy included a close examination of his family of origin. Joe's family was what we would describe as a "community cultural object"—highly regarded and very public in the community. Joe brought in several newspaper clippings of his "featured" family on different national holidays and began to examine his past.

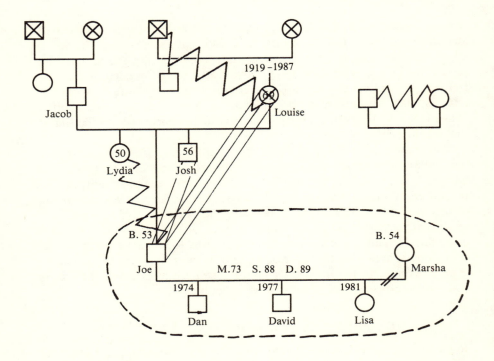

Figure 2.1

While proclaiming how good a childhood he had had, Joe realized he did
not know much about his parents' pasts. His mother had died a year ago.
Family history revealed that his maternal grandfather had died when Joe was
two years old and that Joe, instead of his father, accompanied his mother to
the funeral. Joe was his mother's constant companion as she tended to
community work visiting the sick and homebound. His father worked long
hours away from home.

Joe also brought in childhood photos that reflected the face of a sad little
boy. Yet he could not connect with most of the photographs; he could not
recall how he felt. He began to see that he had been working compulsively to
cover his feelings, avoiding time to be alone with his thoughts. With time,
Joe was flooded by feelings no longer buried. I suggested that, while most of
this flooding was obviously *his* pain, some of it might have been inherited
through the family unconscious.

I explained to Joe that it often requires a dynamic "crisis" for us to
awaken to deeply buried pain. I told him that, in time, he would look quite

differently at the "wake up call" created by his wife's affair. We discussed how the same denial that protected Joe from pain in childhood had also blocked his awareness of pain in his marriage. Joe could then see how his impaired perceptions played a part in not sensing what was going on with Marsha. We agreed to a contract to explore the roots of his denial and to examine his invisible "inheritance."

Inherited Shame: The Family Unconscious

Each of our original pictures of our families is based on radically limited input, as well as on limited internal ways with which to make sense. Like sponges, we receive all that comes into us. What started out as people, places, events, and ways of doing life together—what we call family process—become, over time, internal injunctions or commands for how to be, how to see the self, and how to perceive the world.

A child's position in the family is one of no-choice reactor. First, we have to absorb and make sense out of whatever comes our way, and these data are truly someone else's meaning or order of events, rather than what we are prepared for. Second, we have to deal with a limited ability to make sense of our surroundings. Third, we are dependent upon the need systems of the caregivers in our families; we rely on what they, out of their own struggles and their own energies, are willing to help us comprehend and what they, out of their values, anxieties, secrets, and shame decide children should not know. Our literal dependency as children demands a close adherence to the implicit rules of our family systems regarding what is okay and not okay to be shown and expressed. Both out of our caring and out of our dependency and utter need for the goodwill of our caregivers, we all learn how not to intrude beyond the boundaries of what creates anxiety for those we love and on whom we are dependent. In this regard, we all are potential secret-keepers.

Our fidelity to our families is a major unconscious force that binds us to the process of inherited shame. There are two types of family fidelity. The first is the natural caring we feel for our family members. We understand and appreciate the family group into which we are born. We are loyal to it for creating, sustaining, and supporting our lives—no matter who they are or how they were. The second is "invisible loyalty," which is not overt, not known, and, therefore, not understood (Boszormenyi-Nagy, 1973). This loyalty is a powerful cable of invisible threads that holds us emotionally captive to our families.

Children read parents quite clearly. Sensing our parents' buried pain, we attempt to protect them by burying our own feelings or acting out to draw them away from their pain. Most of this occurs at the *unconscious* level. Clearly, Joe had recognized his parents' pain and unconsciously strived to avoid causing further pain.

For those who have grown up in families with shameful secrets, these invisible interfamilial bonds carry deeply ingrained messages that leave indelible marks on the patterns of our adult relationships. Even the deaths of our parents and siblings fail to sever these bonds; we still carry the relationships within us. This means we must explore how we carry out our loyalty to our families. Part of the process of maturing is to betray our childhood loyalty to our families by breaking the rules and then to create an adult loyalty. Childhood loyalty involves the exercising of the unconsciously taught and learned assignment of how to function within and protect the parameters of family comfort. Family rules, insulators of family pain and discomfort, are taught and learned, *unstated* rules with implicit injunctions about what we can see, hear, feel, and comment on.

"There's nothing going on here — and don't tell anybody" is the injunction many of us lived with in our families. This family rule preserves the shame-filled reservoir for family secrets. When I told Joe this injunction, I said I had a "hunch" there were probably many secrets in his family history. Joe had "normalized" the fact that neither his mother nor his father had ever talked about his mother's childhood. No one ever brought it up. Joe then said, "I should have asked." I reminded Joe that his not asking was vital to the preservation of the secret through his "no-talk" rule and that, unconsciously, he was protecting his mother.

I often remind therapists in training to listen to their own "gut" responses to what they hear and see and to use case consultations when they sense there are "missing pieces" in the stories told.

As Joe took time to focus on his family history, he interviewed relatives and began to reconstruct his life story. He learned that his father's father was depressed (as was his own father) and that his grandparents had always slept in separate bedrooms. In asking his father, aunts, and uncles about his mother, Joe was shocked to learn several family secrets.

First, Joe learned that his mother's father was the town drunk and that he physically abused his son (Joe's uncle). He also learned that his mother's family fled from creditors and had to move almost every three months. When Joe asked his father why his mother had not revealed her past to him and his siblings, he said that they both decided it was best to protect the children from the painful history.

Joe shook his head slowly as he reflected on the mother who had "buckled up," never asked anything for herself, and was always sweet and loving to almost anyone with whom she came in contact. Indeed, mealtimes included visitors from the community as well as interruptive telephone calls. His mother seemed to say yes to everyone; she was very well-liked. Joe began to realize that perhaps some of the pain he was releasing now was his mother's shame. Joe had been loyal to following the rules of shame to maintain his mother's secret. Joe also said he felt his history was invalid. He had never truly known his mother as a person. I reminded Joe that the family rules of shame are powerfully and invisibly binding. I said I would explain what I meant by "family rules."

The Rules of Shame

These rules determine what is allowed and what is not. More importantly, they let us know who decides, who is the authority. Secrets innervate the rules of shame—rules that perpetuate the shame and bind family members in confusion, chaos, and growth-inhibiting relationships. We see these rules played out when we note who can get angry with whom, who can be close to whom, who can talk back, who can sit where—all of which is decided at an unspoken level. We automatically enact the deeply submerged programming in our roles, relationship patterns, and life decisions.

Specific identifiable rules apply to the shame-bound family. These covert rules govern the interactions in the family and perpetuate the shame. The following eight rules illustrate the pattern that ensures the legacy of shame:

1. *Control.* Be in control of all behavior and interactions.
2. *Perfection.* Always be "right." Do the "right" thing.
3. *Blame.* If something doesn't happen as you planned, blame someone (self or other).
4. *Denial.* Deny feelings, especially the negative or vulnerable ones like anxiety, fear, loneliness, grief, rejection, need.
5. *Unreliability.* Don't expect reliability or constancy in relationships. Watch for the unpredictable.
6. *Incompleteness.* Don't bring transactions to resolution or completion because you might have to face what feelings or honest revelations you're protecting.
7. *No talk.* Don't talk openly and directly about shameful, abusive, or compulsive behavior.
8. *Disqualification.* When disrespectful, shameful, abusive, or compulsive behavior occurs, disqualify it, deny it, or disguise it (Fossum & Mason, 1986, pp. 86–7).

These rules not only instill shame, they perpetuate it. The shame-bound family's process is severely galvanized against honest human disclosures.

Family members obey these rules unconsciously and learn not to ask, not to comment. In this way, information that is "owed" to the family becomes a shameful secret. These rules can be both the cause and the result of the secret. These rules organize a family's dynamics; the family becomes shame-bound as children absorb the unexpressed feelings and stories.

> A shame-bound family is a family with a self-sustaining, multigenerational system of interaction with a cast of characters who are (or were in their lifetime) loyal to a set of rules and injunctions demanding control, perfectionism, blame and denial. The pattern inhibits or defeats the development of authentic intimate relationships, promotes secrets and vague personal boundaries, unconsciously instills shame in family members, as well as chaos in their lives, and binds them to perpetuate the shame in themselves and their kin. It does so regardless of the good intentions, wishes, and love that may also be part of the system. (Fossum & Mason, 1986, p. 8)

To go to the heart of any given matter is to move beyond and betray the loyalty to the rules of the system: I'll never see or know, I'll never tell or comment, and I promise to hate (or love) forever.

The task for all of us is to make active choices about how we seek to understand ourselves and our relationships so that we can create our own order of events based on our own system, not that of our parents. As one parent said to an adult child in my office one day, "I know your problems have my fingerprints on them, but the solution is up to you." As long as we are loyal to the unconscious messages, we are committed to maintaining the shame.

Joe was able to recognize his loyalty to the rules of shame in his family. He had been loyal to the rule that he would never ask about his parents' pain. In one of his family sessions, he turned to his stoical father and said, "I saw your outsides when I was a boy, and I felt my insides, and I felt ashamed." He began to recognize that he had become his mother's emotional companion—that he had taken over his father's job. He wrote down his family's rules. As Joe walked through his story and reexamined the photos in the family album, he began to connect with the buried feelings. He began to see how he became the blanket for his mother's unresolved grief, as well as for her secret past. Joe realized his need to talk with his mother at her graveside about the loss of family history and the loss of knowing her as a person. He also realized how superficial his relationship with his father was, how much fathering he had missed, and how angry he was with his father for not encouraging his mother to reveal the family secrets. They began to talk about their losses and to enjoy long conversations together.

Two other secrets were revealed in the therapy process. Joe learned that his mother had told Marsha much of her life history and that Marsha had married him because of his mother's open sharing with her. Indeed, she thought he had the mother she had always wanted. In fact, she had become involved in the affair after the death of Joe's mother. Through his therapy, Joe came to see how his childhood loyalty in the form of denial protected the secrets and family shame; he saw how this prevented him from asking any probing questions that might tap at the secrets. He then recognized fully how he maintained the shame and the secrets.

Maintained Shame

We maintain our shame by adhering to the interpersonal process we learned in our families. Our childhood sense of our families is built not only from limited tools and incomplete data but also from a non-systemic perspective. The child acts as the center of the universe and absorbs events very personally. Each event is experienced and coded with the child—like programming of a computer. Our childhood perceptions are the birthplace of our **process**, that is, how we learn to be in the world, to see ourselves, and to be in relationships. These perceptions are the images we project onto the screen of the mind; they shape our interpretations of our life experiences and the meaning system we live with as adults. We store these perceptions in our memories. Children normalize the behavior patterns they live with; this does not mean, however, that the behaviors are natural. Family therapist Rene Schwartz states this clearly:

> As long as we are content to stay within the confines of the memories, recollections and conclusions about our family formed out of our childhood experiences, we are destined to continue to enact our childhood position of no-choice reactor to the forces—conscious and unconscious—in our families. (Schwartz, 1985)

How do therapists see shame maintained? We see patterns in our clinical work that are clear indicators that family members are engaged in the dynamics of shame. We hear obvious stories that would presume the dynamics of shame—physical and/or sexual abuse, addictions, eating disorders, boundary problems, depression, running away, stealing. All of these violate the social norms and may be expected sources of shame. But many of the sources of shame might be held in secrecy—a compulsive behavior, an extramarital affair, physical disabilities, health concerns, financial mismanagement. Often, the secret is not about behavior in current relationships but what is hidden in the past family history. The shame is masked, but visible in lack or fear of intimacy, perfectionism, self-defeating behaviors, imbalanced relationships where one partner is overresponsible and the other is childlike, and pseudomutual or pseudohostile relationships.

Research informs us that low self-esteem, anxiety, anger, depression, alienation, and feelings of inferiority are symptoms of shame. We have learned that women have much higher scores on shame scales, especially those for inferiority and alienation, than do men (Cook, 1989). Women's socialization as being inferior to men and their responsibility or overresponsibility for relationships clearly underlie their higher scores on the alienation scale. When a relationship ends or dissolves, women often feel alienated because they think it is their responsibility to make relationships work.

Shame can be well-masked and maintained through our loyalty to the family rules; we continue to maintain the cycle of shame and secrets. Shame begets shame.

Joe realized that he had denied the present just as his mother and father had denied their pasts. He began to see how he was continuing the family dynamic of carrying secrets. As he looked back through clearer eyes, he did realize that things had not been quite right with Marsha for a long time. He thought it was "normal" to focus so totally on others. Joe was a natural candidate to maintain his wife's secrets; he spent a lifetime living with secrets and knew when not to ask questions.

I was struck by Joe's commitment to his therapy. At this time, I referred him to a men's group where he could get support from other men for the changes he was making. I reminded him that therapy was about changing his *process*—both in the factual information he had uncovered and *how* he interacted with others. The feedback from the group was most useful to Joe who recognized that his family, while supportive, gave minimal feedback about how he affected others. He realized he had been looking at life through the lens of childhood. Until Joe's "wake up call" he had remained locked in childhood perceptions. He came to see how these had hindered the development of his true self. He had little knowledge about both shame and self. Shame is maintained in the self, and it is more than loss of face or embarrassment.

> Shame is an inner sense of being completely diminished or insufficient as a person. It is the self judging the self. A moment of shame may be humiliation so painful or an indignity so profound that one feels one has been robbed of her or his dignity or exposed as basically inadequate, bad, or worthy of rejection. A pervasive sense of shame is the ongoing premise that one is fundamentally bad, inadequate, defective, unworthy, or not fully valid as a human being. (Fossum & Mason, 1986, p. 5)

Shame is often confused with guilt. However, shame and guilt are at opposite ends of the continuum. Guilt emanates from an integrated conscience and values. The feeling of guilt is a trigger that tells us that we face the possibility of violating a value. Guilt is about behavior; shame is about the self. In other words, guilt relates to what we *do*; shame is about who we *are*: "With guilt I *make* a mistake; with shame I *am* a mistake." With shame, we cannot say, "I'm wrong, I'm sorry, I've made a mistake." Within guilt lies a way back, a way to repair. We are able to look under the guilt and know what value we hold. Our conscience holds our values. Because shame is about the *self* and is internalized deep within us, the possibility of repair is foreclosed. Shame is hidden in the false self, the highly developed role-self that is the substitute for personal boundaries. As we break family rules and find the personhood behind the roles, we see the healing process.

Joe broke his loyalty to the family no-talk rules of secrecy by expressing his feelings to his wife, his father, his brother, and his sister. In family sessions, he shared the painful secrets he had learned about. Together, the family began to talk about their experiences of death and began to grieve. Joe learned how the secrets and the family shame had blocked their very natural family process. In this stage of therapy, I included an empty chair to symbolize the psychological presence of Joe's mother. Joe spoke honestly and directly to his family members and wept when he spoke to his mother's chair.

Joe realized he wanted emotional closeness, which was not included in the implicit marital contract to which he and his wife had nonverbally agreed. Joe and Marsha were divorced while he was in therapy but continued to be effective in their co-parenting.

Joe revealed his reclamation of his feeling awareness in a letter at the conclusion of therapy:

"It was during therapy that I began to feel that my entire life, not just my therapy, was a wonderful, joyful, painful, scary, comforting journey. It is my responsibility as I am journeying to find and stick to my values and to celebrate all of my God-given feelings, not just some of my feelings . . . love, joy, contentment, but all feelings including anger, fear, sadness, and jealousy. . . . There is a kind of wonderful irony here. During my most controlling, illusionary days I could never have imagined that this wonderful but ironic outcome would emerge from a single impulsive moment when I ripped open a letter that was not intended for me. Or was it?"

Joe realized the gift that came from the secret. He now had changed his process in all his relationships and recognized that his parents' desire to protect him had been a barrier to true intimacy. At the time of this writing he has remarried, has another child, and is actively involved with his new blended family. I felt a deep respect for Joe and his willingness to be vulnerable and let himself be "seen." I realized I had finally let go of wondering how the story might have been different if Marsha and Joe had both been in family therapy.

HOW MUCH SECRECY?

Are we entitled to our secrets? With what we know about secrets and the transmission of shame, how do we allow ourselves to hold on to some of our secrets without passing on the shame? When I was consulting on sexuality for a family program in an alcoholism treatment center, one of the therapists there announced proudly, "We are a program with no secrets, absolutely *everything* is told in our family groups. What do you think of that?" I hastened to explain to them that there can be no fixed formula for revealing secrets—that honesty without sensitivity can be brutality. Not every secret has to shared with children; however, it is important that we do share our secrets with someone. In so doing, we allow ourselves to be known to others and allow others to reveal themselves to us. Shameful secrets result in isolation and pain; when we reveal secrets, we can externalize the shame. We begin to separate our self from our shame.

I explained to Joe the importance of recognizing that we *are* our secrets; in our own growth we will reveal those secrets that are painful. Often, our emotional maturity has been blocked by shutdown feelings in childhood; thus, our "affective" age can be quite different from our chronological age. This necessitates focusing on our "affective reconstruction"—finding natural buried feelings from childhood and including them in our life stories.

Joe recognized that he truly had hungered to be known. When people reveal their shameful secrets in therapy, I ask them to tell their secret to at least one other person. This can be a true risk for many. When secrets are revealed, we have less to hide and can be more spontaneous and more vulnerable. Often when there is a shameful secret, there is a sense that something is missing. It is then that I will make a comment that it seems there is a secret somewhere, thus opening the door for the secret-bearer to reveal his or her secret. It may be some weeks or months before a client returns and states, "I don't know how you knew it, but yes, it's true. I do have a secret, and I must tell it now." Of course when we do reveal secrets, we face consequences. We risk the loss of relationship trust; we face feelings of anger, disappointment, hurt, relief, sadness, and rage. Yet, when we risk more of our humanness, we feel our natural human connection. As we learn that shame is learned in relationships, we can develop greater self-empathy and eventually greater other-empathy, as well. We grow in our integrity, and we learn humility.

We all meet life experiences that afford an opportunity for personal growth. While we can never become all of who we can be, when we can experience therapy in a supportive, empathic environment, we can use shameful secrets as catalysts for healing and growing. As we return the truth that is "owed" to a family member or others who matter to us by revealing our secrets, we simultaneously begin to repair the broken interpersonal bridges and heal our shame.

REFERENCES

Bass, E., & Davis, L. (1988). *The courage to heal*. New York: Harper & Row.

Boszormenyi-Nagy, I. (1973). *Invisible loyalties*. New York: Harper & Row.

Brandeis, L. (April, 1991). In A. Brill (Ed.), *Nobody's business: The paradoxes of privacy*. Reading, PA: Addison-Wesley.

Cook, D. (1989). *Internalized shame scale* (unpublished manuscript), pp. 3–4.

Covington, S. (1986). Physical, emotional and sexual abuse. *Focus on Family and Chemical Dependency, 9*(3), 42.

EAP Digest (1987, November–December).

Fossum, M., & Mason, M. (1986). *Facing shame: Families in recovery*. New York: W. W. Norton.

Goleman, D. (1987, September 15). Shame steps out of hiding and into sharper focus. *New York Times*, p. 23.

Kaplan, J. (1991, April 22). Biographies should tell all. *Newsweek*, p. 58.

Schwartz, R. (1985). *Family of origin: A journey home again*. Paper presented at Family Therapy Institute, 15th anniversary, St. Paul, MN.

Whitaker, C. (1986). Foreword. In M. Fossum & M. Mason, *Facing shame: Families in recovery*. New York: W. W. Norton.

II

SECRECY ACROSS
THE FAMILY LIFE CYCLE

3

Secrets of Couples and Couples' Therapy

ROSMARIE WELTER-ENDERLIN

INTRODUCTION

My identity as a family therapist draws on two cultures, European (Swiss) and American. As I tend to combine both worlds in work and life, I will briefly outline a few thoughts of how they merge in my clinical work with secrets of couples and families.

There is an acceptance in European culture of the normalcy of imperfections like extramarital as well as other secretive "affairs" in the life of couples, which is terrible and consoling at the same time. Our readiness to accept things as determined by history as well as the "condition humaine" has, on the one hand, a certain fatalistic and even depressive stance to it. On the other hand, there is a great deal of relief in the idea that you are not entirely responsible for your condition and that nobody promised you a rose garden in the first place. Thus, some of the terror is loosened when looking into the darkness of the closet where the family skeletons are stored.

But, this is completely different from American culture. No wonder Frieda Fromm-Reichmann, a European psychiatrist, shook up her patients in California with the idea that the world did not owe them happiness. Our children used to dislike my quoting Frieda's metaphor (old-fashioned European stuff!) as they grew up in a Midwestern university town in the early 1970's where they were told quite the opposite: You can and should manage to live a happy life. Open communication and family conferences, no secrets, letting all your feelings "hang out" were the prescribed paths to happiness then. "Problems are meant to be fixed and mousetraps can be built better and better . . . " we learned. The blend of the old American dream with the new societal process of individualization and narcissism was exciting. Coming from a culture that did not offer much hope for change of the human species, I loved it. Eager to learn how to implement the American dream as a therapist, I first became a "behavior engineer" and later a strategic family therapist. This experience was a welcome relief from my European socialization as an "understanding" therapist, with little regard for directive interventions and concrete problem-solving.

It took me many years of professional experience as a family therapist to resolve the disequilibrium of seeing the world through two different cultural lenses, the New and the Old World perspectives: understanding the human dilemma as being embedded in the historical and philosophical developments of the culture, on the one hand, and actively instigating change in the here and now of couples' lives, on the other. I still tend to accept the fact that life is not perfect, and moralistic frenzy about its unsavory aspects, like secrets and lies, is not warranted. But, I do not find that this contradicts my willingness to open my eyes to evil in human relationships as well as my cooperating to alleviate guilt and pain.

My clinical approach to secrets represents a blend of these two different cultural lenses. While I tend to normalize spouses' keeping secrets from each other and even find positive aspects in their doing so under certain circumstances, I recognize that the same process may indicate a dangerous power struggle between husband and wife in other situations and needs to be dealt with openly. It has become important to me to differentiate helpful from destructive secret-keeping, and I will distinguish the two kinds as I present my thinking and clinical practice relating to them.

GOOD AND BAD SECRETS AS PART OF MY GROWING UP

Growing up during the silent 1950's in a large rural family, I found out early that keeping secrets from others was one way of evading the fusion of the overwhelming "we" in order to experience a sense of "I" by the demarcation of private spheres. There was hardly any private space in the large house of my childhood shared by family, relatives, and farm workers. Yet, there were plenty of opportunities for us children to look for and to build personal "nests" in which to keep our secrets. When I see some modern family homes where there are no doors or those there are may not be closed, I often wonder where the adults and the children find their nests to hide their secrets from each other.

I also learned early in my childhood how powerlessness can be transformed into power by keeping knowledge secret, that is, by internalizing that which, if externalized, may be labeled deviant. Patients from a nearby psychiatric clinic used to live with us and help in the greenhouses. I especially remember Mrs. V, a schizophrenic in her 40's. That she occasionally heard voices worried nobody as long as she did not talk about them. However, there were times when she got excited and had to tell somebody about her hallucinations. My sister and I listened to her with great interest. We knew that she had invented her stories herself and were not frightened. But we kept reminding her to never tell anyone outside the family or else they would think she was crazy. We knew from the adults' conversations that hearing voices meant danger to Mrs. V and others and immediate return to the Zurich Psychiatric Clinic. I remember feeling quite powerful in helping Mrs. V keep her secret and stay out of the clinic for a long time. One day, however, she forgot and discussed her voices with people at the local store. She never came back to the house afterwards. I learned a great deal from the experience and began to understand the familiar saying that "silence and secrets are worth as much as gold when used in the right way."

There were, of course, also the negative kinds of silence and secrets. Being the oldest of many children and the ideal "go-between," I became the keeper of secrets between my parents early on, especially regarding money, such as when my father secretly told me to go to the drugstore to buy a lottery ticket, hoping for a big win. He was a daydreamer, which left my mother with the opposite role, that of standing with both feet on the ground to manage the family business. Her dreams were concerned with buying the things we lacked in the lean years after the war, a washer or a new dress for herself, for instance. She told me about them but under the condition that I never mention her dreams to Father as he might think of something unrealistic, like buying a lottery ticket to pretend he was making money!

The experience of triangulation obviously influenced my choice of profession. When I am confronted with a couple in treatment who are pulling me into different directions or who are indirectly hinting at the secret deficits of the other, I hear a bell ring from my childhood: "Don't let yourself be dragged into the game, they will not reward you for it." Having broken away from the old triangle with my parents has made me more courageous, as well as more patient, in trying to find out when it is time to let things go and when to confront clients' attempts to pull me into their secret stories and to make me their ally.

I have learned in my clinical practice with couples and families to differentiate between the constructive secrets of individuation and the destructive secrets of lies and injustice as a way of exercising power. In the following section I will deal with constructive secrets as a way of achieving individual spheres of "I" within the couple's "we."

SECRETS AS A WAY OF INDIVIDUATION

"The tyranny of intimacy" (Sennett, 1974) characterizes the way in which many couples attempt to live together, especially those in upwardly mobile milieus. Their relationship ideal reflects the process of individualism and narcissism in modern societies with its emphasis on the continuous verbalization of emotions. They assume this to be the path to reaching intimacy in the face of the erosion of traditions and binding norms. This ideal has also been named the "trend towards heating up the private life as a counterpoint to the coldness of the public life" (Ziehe, 1989). It implies a continuous reflection and control of oneself and the other as the term "homo clausus" (Elias, 1976) suggests. By this term the author means that the individual is closed in him or herself and only allowed to open up within the private world of the couple and the family. The problem with this ideal is, however, that opening one's heart to intimate partners becomes not just an opportunity, but a law. Affect management in the couple's world means, at its extreme, total openness and total control. No secrets, no closed doors! The "I" forever submerged in the "we." I suspect that many secret extramarital affairs may be a reaction to this mandate of permanently disclosing oneself, an idea which I will elaborate on later.

The much desired intimacy that, as the narcissistic ideal suggests, can only be achieved through permanent truthfulness and authenticity often turns against the couple. Their desire for closeness gets subdued by their overemphasis on commonness and "Gemutlichkeit," a feeling inherent in the German romantic culture, but not exclusive to it. Small wonder that under these circumstances, keeping secrets and secret "nests" becomes a major way of gaining a sense of self. Rubin (1983) coined the phrase "intimate strangers" in her research on American couples who, through their claim to total openness and unending nurturance, lose their passion. "Nurturance is not intimacy," she writes as she points out that couples who focus on emotional fusion and total honesty tend to reproduce childhood experiences. Her implication is that only well-differentiated adults may experience passionate intimacy.

Before turning to clinical practice regarding the romantic culture of love with its prohibition of secrets, let us take a brief look at the historical process that led to the culture of "heating up" the private world of husband and wife. By the end of the 18th century, the women of the middle class were forced to retreat into the family and, to a large degree, lost the ability to make friends outside the husband's network of relationships. They were restricted to a "level of concepts of life whose main characteristic is female passivity" (Lorenzer, 1989). The intimacy of the couple and the mother-child bond—especially the one between mother and son—became a substitute for a lost female culture of bonding. As the working class has since adopted this middle-class orientation, the loss of female culture has affected working-class women as well.

No wonder that in the isolation of modern families women become "emotional pursuers," as the clinical term suggests, forever attempting to break into the private spheres of their husbands and children to discover their secrets. Even if women become part of the professional world, they still remain outsiders as long as female culture gets only little recognition. While women's isolation is being reinforced at the workplace and in the family, old expectations are kept alive under the surface of new concepts of equality. Women, "the pursuers," are held responsible for relationships and care; men and children retreat from their "intrusion" through silence and keeping their personal matters secret. This is how the vicious circle is perpetuated. The reduction of female living space to the couple and the mother-child relationship is also reinforced by the historically determined distribution of power between men and women perpetuated by the norms of the work world. The professional success of most men (at least in my country) is still based on their complete regression and regeneration at home: They are silent, self-centered, and use women as "objects" to fulfill their needs. Women are supposed to be available to them and their children around the clock, with neither private space, nor time to themselves. The myth of the perfect wife and mother is based on the assumption of her total availability and, to this day, many of us take it for granted and try to live by it. That women need a room of their own in a real, as well as a metaphorical sense, as a basis for their individuation (and that of their husbands and children as well) is, to most of my clients, still a novel idea.

CLINICAL CONSEQUENCES

It is quite confusing: On the one hand, modern couples experience freedom from the institutionalized aspects of marriage and family, on the other, new constraints appear in their place, for example, the idea of complete frankness in expressing one's feelings, as well as continuous verbal exchange about the subjective state of each partner. The tyranny of intimacy, with its implicit prohibition on maintaining privacy and personal secrets from one another, affects the "dance" of most couples I see in therapy. It is often closely related to a lack of differentiation of the spouses from their families of origin as well as from each other. Whenever the presenting problem is a lack of emotional and sexual intimacy—the most frequent motive for couples coming to my practice, as a recent follow-up study of 40 couples indicates—I assume that there is a lack of private space for both. Too much, not too little togetherness appears to be in the way of individuation as a basis for intimacy.

CONSTRUCTIVE SECRETS AS A BASIS FOR INDIVIDUATION IN COUPLES: LEGITIMIZING ROOMS OF THEIR OWN

When the presenting problem of a couple is intimacy, I direct some of my questions towards the couple's pattern regarding the allocation of private and shared spheres. In this task, I am guided by Virginia Woolf's concept of a "room of one's own" as a precondition of the process of individuation. Normally, I ask couples the following questions during the initial session:

- to the couple:

   When you return home from work—possibly together—is there an opportunity for both of you to take time for yourselves before you turn to each other, to your children, or to housework? Is it possible for you to take "time out" individually before you devote yourselves to common tasks?

   If either of you wants something just for yourself, something personal, something like a private "nest," is there a room for it in your relationship as well as in the organization of your living arrangements? For example, if you want to lock away your diary or some private letters, is there a space in your house that only you have access to?

   If you want to withdraw from your partner into your private sphere—maybe to talk to friends or family members on the phone—how do you go about it?

   What are your arrangements in regard to money? Does each of you have money to spend without having to ask permission of your spouse? Does each of you know how much the other earns, and how do you make decisions in regard to buying things for your family?

- to the wife:

   Is it possible for you to leave home now and then in order to withdraw into your own intimate world without preparing every meal ahead of time? (Many women in my sample have never even thought of such an extravagance, they say.)

- to the husband:

  Are there times for you to go about your own pleasures without combining them with business? (Most men in my practice do not dare to openly claim a trip or go out by themselves if it is not related to business, they say.)

These are only a few examples of questions by which I encourage the legitimacy of private spheres in the physical as well as the metaphorical aspects of relationships. In other words, I assume that the lack of privacy preventing so many couples from individuation is not their personal eccentricity but is part of the general ideal of narcissism in modern societies, which is reflected in their living arrangements. Ours is a culture in which the illusion of the "great couple," with spouses living only through each other still exists under a thin cover of the concept of "individuation by equality" between men and women (Prokop, 1987). Couples' therapy may be one way of questioning the illusion and facilitating equality.

LIES AND SECRETS

"It is not the tragedies that kill us but the messes." I heard this sentence first when I lived with a Jewish family in London as an *au pair*. This family had experienced many losses and also had to cope with the chronic rheumatoid arthritis of the young mother, but they rarely lost their sense of humor. To me, they represented the essence of what I already defined as the European way of accepting the imperfection of the "condition humaine" but without falling into lethargy. They did get excited over the messes, the daily lies of politicians, for instance, as well as my pretending to be happy when I was simply afraid to tell them I felt lonesome and homesick.

Many secrets in people's lives have to do not so much with tragedies but with the messes caused by lies or denial. Whenever I sense an atmosphere of unending tension and anger, which tends to generalize to whatever topic a couple may discuss, I assume there are destructive secrets and lies hidden under the surface. Keeping the lid on Pandora's box for any length of time is quite an effort; it uses up a lot of energy and is a cause for endless strain. Most secrets turn into destructive patterns as each member of the couple uses them to achieve power over the other.

In my early work with couples, I tended to be so eager not to fall in love with tragedy that I would bravely avoid the topic of secrets and lies. As a result of the emphasis on optimism and quick problem-solving, I acquired what I now call a "fear of darkness." The wonderful idea of reframing problems in positive ways in the early models of my family therapy training resulted in my ignoring topics that could not be fixed nicely and easily. If I did not listen to clients' stories of secret shame and grief, they would go away by themselves, I hoped. Eventually, when, as just one example, the secret of incest in one family was reframed positively as "too much love" by some male colleagues, my belief that positive reframings would be the solution to all problems was shaken. The nagging question to me became how the political and social aspects of power were personalized and individualized if the reality of secrets like incest, or a husband's sexual violence towards his wife, were labeled as "their private construction."

Many of the secrets in couples and couples' therapy are related to issues of sexuality, shame, and violence. If we as therapists try to "fix" things simply by offering positive connotations or behavioral prescriptions as I did early in my practice, we may offer relief from immediate pressure. However, if this is all we do, we tend to conspire with a prohibition to put experience into words, which often is part of the problem already. No wonder storytelling has become such an important tool of family therapy. It is a way of empowering clients by breaking the silence and putting events into language, thus achieving structure and directions for change. As far as secrets and lies are concerned, I have come to believe that neither the constructivist ideology, which says that the power generated by secrets exists only in the eyes of the beholder, nor the idea that secrets and lies need to be viewed as clear-cut reality, is the answer. I believe that the key issue in regard to secrets as weapons is the understanding of the cultural and political context in which such strategies are generated, i.e., how power is distributed along gender lines and how a specific couple makes sense of cultural norms according to their personal constructs.

Neither bringing back morals or a sense of tragedy to the scene of couples' therapy, as a traditional view of marital therapy seems to suggest (Pittman, 1987), nor the constructivist idea that power is "just a metaphor" and secrets and lies therefore irrelevant, seem to be the answer. I think both views are essential and complement each other. Custom-tailored therapy means there is a place for both "reality" and "ideas" or the constructs human beings create. The following case vignette illustrates my attempt to balance the two perspectives.

SILVIA'S STORY: INFIDELITY AS A WAY OF BEING TRUE TO HERSELF (BUT WHAT ABOUT HER THERAPIST?)

Silvia is 35, has been married for 12 years, and has two children who are about to take their first steps into the world. She lives with Frank, an ambitious engineer of 40, in their just finished new home. Ten years ago, before the birth of their daughter, Silvia gave up her job as a teacher. Silvia's father is a local conservative politician of some fame; her mother looks in on the young family every day.

When Silvia made an appointment with me for therapy regarding her family of origin, I was rather surprised, as I had often read in the newspaper that her father disapproved of people who rely on the help of others. Silvia, a very attractive woman, her sister, and her brother came to the first session. Neither the parents nor the youngest sister, who is 28, still lives at home, and who was described as "manic-depressive," appeared. In our initial therapy contract we decided on a common course, which would enable these three siblings to cope better with the double-bind imposed by their parents and sister to help them, but under no circumstance to change anything. After five sessions they had disengaged enough from their family of origin to replace their original zigzag course between overinvolvement and distancing with a new definition of their relationship.

As Silvia was leaving she requested an individual session. She began by telling me about a terrible dilemma. After 12 years of a happy marriage with Frank, she had fallen in love "out of the blue" with her husband's boss, a 50-year-old successful, divorced man. She had been meeting him secretly and had experienced sexual passion with him, which had not been possible with Frank. Silvia said she wanted to stay married to Frank because she loved him and knew she had fallen in love with a daydream, but she also said that she simply could not give it up yet. She was upset about holding a secret and lying to Frank, but did not want him to come to therapy at this time.

I did not know Frank yet and, therefore, had no therapeutic bond with him but felt I needed to be fair towards him. Should I insist that Silvia bring him along and ask her to tell him about the affair so that I did not become the secret-keeper? My personal experience, as well as my professional training, urged me to do so, but Silvia asked for time. She first wanted me to help her through her process of separation from her lover. Only in this way could she return to Frank without feeling forced, she said. With feelings of ambivalence, I agreed to enter into her concerns. However, in consultation with an experienced colleague, I was corrected. He told me I had taken part in a typical coalition of two women ("mother-daughter against father") against a deceived husband. Yet, I decided to have another few sessions with Silvia alone. It became more and more obvious to her that the love she gave to and experienced from her lover was a substitute for the love she would have liked to have given to and received from her father, who was both distant and attractive to her. Silvia gradually recognized that she was about to resolve her problems with her father with the "wrong" person and that she was about to start the necessary process of differentiation from her father. Step-by-step she distanced herself from the image of the sweet little girl who tried to reach father by playing Princess to the distant King. By defining her relationship with him for the first time in her life, she took up a dialogue with him as an adult woman. As before, father remained emotionally distant, but he was finally able to tell her how much she meant to him and how proud he was of her.

Silvia told her husband her secret eventually as she prepared to leave her lover eight months after our first session. Frank contacted me immediately, asking to come in with Silvia. On the phone he explained that he had not slept or eaten for the last few days, Silvia's breach of faith had hurt him so much. How would I be able to look him in the face as a keeper of secrets and lies against him? How could I establish a relationship with him that was not tainted by mistrust?

I suggested that Frank ask Silvia about everything he wanted to know at this point and offered to describe our therapeutic process as well. I also told him about my dilemma and was prepared to send the couple to a colleague for therapy. At the end of the first joint session, Frank declared that, in spite of all possible resentments, he wanted to continue in therapy with me, together with Silvia. As a matter of fact, he suggested that he had known that Silvia had a lover and had been a keeper of secrets as well, although for different motives. Frank had not wanted to be confronted with the truth and, therefore, assumed Silvia's infatuation would pass away in time.

In the following sessions with the couple, "being true to oneself" became the central theme. Frank and Silvia both recognized that as adults, they had remained overly loyal to their parents but become disloyal to themselves. As a couple, they had been imprisoned by the rigid norms of their families, which were extinguishing their own vitality. Temporary marital disloyalty by Silvia, which was now connected to her experience of personal autonomy and passion, led to a growing understanding of the meaning of their crisis. Silvia's betrayal was redefined by both as a signal to rediscover their personal concepts of life and become "true to themselves" as a basis for an adult relationship.

Three years later, in a follow-up session of my research project on marital crisis and development, I asked both of them about positive and negative aspects of their crisis, particularly in regard to Silvia's secret and my role as temporary secret-keeper. When I mentioned to Frank the topic of this paper and my uneasiness about the role I had played, he said: "Write that in the Old Testament it says that there is a time for everything. I would have gone crazy or killed my boss if Silvia had told me about her affair when she was still daydreaming and not prepared to give it up. It was good that she took her time to disengage and that you, as her therapist, allowed her that time and kept quiet. I was sometimes extremely angry with you, of course, for I always knew somehow what Silvia was talking to you about. The most important aspect of your handling things was that you described your own dilemma and did not adopt the view of the self-confident expert. I am glad you held and reassured me as I was about to go nuts."

COMMENT

In accordance with Silvia's wish, I chose a route that for a long time meant walking on a tightrope with the permanent danger of falling off. This was in contrast to my original thinking of systemic therapy as always involving people who live together. It also contrasted with my childhood aversion to being the (triangulated) keeper of secrets. There seem to be two reasons for my not falling off the tightrope in this case. First, I followed my hunch that Silvia knew better than I what was good for her, rather than obeying general moral or therapeutic principles. Second, my willingness to discuss my dilemma and insecurity with Frank encouraged him to talk about his own and not hold my secret-keeping against me.

I am not too enthusiastic about the trend of therapeutic "morals" concerning secrets, lies, and affairs (cf. Pittman) as a basis for couples' therapy. Instead of adding to a possible melodrama, I tend to normalize such critical events by connecting them to individual biography as well as sociopolitical aspects of gender and power. It is important for me, however, to discourage couples from keeping secrets in order to perpetuate an unbalanced distribution of power between them. As mentioned in the example of the schizophrenic woman living with my family, powerlessness may be transformed into power by keeping information about oneself secret. Depending on the relational context, this may be a constructive way of individuation or a destructive way of putting others down. If Silvia had exercised power over Frank by not disclosing her secret for an extended period, I would have cancelled my contract with her.

In marital therapy, I find that situations of *temporary secretiveness* nearly always precede a new balance of power and intimacy with a new regulation of who determines closeness and distance and how. My therapeutic experience with couples in this situation very often follows this pattern: An extramarital affair, which is kept secret, at first seems to fulfill the not yet conscious need of one or the other to demarcate a "room of one's own." If things turn out positively, the secret is disclosed and, eventually, a new balance between the "I" and the "we" in the relationship is achieved, with both partners experiencing bonding as well as individual freedom at a new level of differentiation. From a rational point of view there are, of course, easier ways to reach this goal. But sometimes the heart has reasons of which the mind is not aware. For in every love relationship, there are two tendencies and principles. "The first is the principle of loyalty, of staying together through thick and thin. All this takes a lot of cultivation, training of the heart and emotions, tolerance and all that. The contrary principle is passion which is egocentric and does not recognize external arguments and which, of course, finds moralistic principles such as loyalty ridiculous" (Sichtermann, 1982).

SECRETS FROM THE FAMILY OF ORIGIN AS STRAITJACKETS IN THE COUPLE'S RELATIONSHIP

The following case vignette reflects many similar clinical situations in which family secrets and family lies from past generations function as a straitjacket in the relationship of couples.

Monica, 34, a former airline stewardess, and Fritz, 40, a pilot, came for therapy because of problems with sex and intimacy. Due to new regulations at the company, Monica had been forced to quit her job and take on the traditional role of wife and mother, contrary to all former agreements between the spouses. She complained that she now felt totally dependent on Fritz, who "behaves like a captain at home. All he wants is to go to bed with me to recover from work. I feel like an object of regeneration for him." Fritz, in response, said, "I don't know why Monica is so distant and no longer interested in sex. She always wants to talk about feelings first. But, in this respect I am simply different from her. If she slept with me, I might talk to her afterwards. But if she rejects me, I do not know what to say. If I talked, it would result in angry complaints. I hate getting into conflicts at home."

In our early therapeutic process, Monica's anger was related to a work arrangement for which Fritz bore little responsibility. When they realized this, both began to negotiate plans for Monica to have time to herself, with Fritz taking care of the children. I also encouraged them to locate an exclusive space to nurture their relationship. They managed to fly to an island alone and enjoyed being together instead of being absorbed in the ocean of family and work. Upon their return, however, Monica felt that Fritz was simply unable to delve into her and the children's world. Fritz agreed this was true — he felt cold and distant inside as soon as he was with his family.

As a therapist, I was at my wit's end. On a behavioral level, things went well, but I could sense Fritz's emotional distancing and Monica's desperation. At this point, it occurred to me that I knew from his genogram that Fritz's father had died when Fritz was only 15. What kind of father did Fritz have? I asked him, and he seemed wary and tense when he replied briefly: "My father worked too hard in the family business and had little time for us. I hardly knew him." Following my instincts I turned all my attention to Fritz: "Your father obviously had little time for you. Is there anyone else who has acted as a male model for you? Possibly a man who was interested in you, who was warm and emotional yet competent at work like you are?" Tension in the room was growing. Monica was shifting on her chair uneasily. Fritz was sitting as if paralyzed. He did not reply. Then—did I see correctly?—there were tears running down his cheeks. Monica, startled, handed him a handkerchief: "Good God, Fritz, I have never seen you cry." Sobbing and hesitant, Fritz told us that he had had a teacher at vocational school who had become an idol for him. "One day he stood up before us boys and said, with tears in his eyes: 'I want to tell you something. Today is the first day of nearly 50 years in my life that I am without a father. I am sad and yet thankful that I have had him.' All the boys cried with him. And suddenly it became clear to me: Not only did I not have a father I felt close to, but I was also full of anger against him and the lies in our family. For Father was a severe alcoholic, and he drank himself to death. He did not die from overwork as we were told and had to tell others. I think that at this moment with my teacher mourning his father was the last time in my life when I cried." Monica, who heard Fritz's secret for the first time, cried with him. She then said, "If people use all their energy to keep the lid on a powder keg of secrets and lies, all spontaneity is being used up, I guess. Let us never do such a thing to each other or our kids."

Family lies and secrets can function as a straitjacket against sadness, pain, and anger. What a relief when it is all brought out and there is someone like Monica who opens her arms instead of shaming and rejecting you as you had feared! The development of this couple progressed so positively after this turning point that I had little more to do. Looking back at their crisis in the follow-up interview two years later, Monica told me how surprised she was at the depth of Fritz's feelings. Both talked about their personal experiences on the dark side of their life, which before had to be denied in order to preserve the glamour of their jet-set world. Acting on my suggestion, they had since gone to see Fritz's mother. When they had looked through family photos, she depicted an image of her husband that was very different from the time after he had begun to drown his sorrows in drink. As they were leaving, Fritz turned around and asked me, "Do you ask every man in therapy about his father, or did you simply sense my family secret? In any case, for me a heavy burden has been lifted since I was allowed to talk about it."

COMMENT

When I explain a therapeutic process such as I took with Frank to therapists in training, I sometimes get reprimanded: "This is not want I want to learn, how to deal with family history and feelings. I came here for systemic therapy." Explaining that I like to use a double lens, one focusing on behaviors and the other on peoples' biographical motivations for doing as they do, and that these perspectives complement rather than exclude each other, I feel a bit odd about the simplicity of it. It makes me wonder what I or others have been teaching students of systemic family therapy so far. "In the development of family therapy there was a phase in which everybody who dared to look back was threatened by the destiny of Lot" writes a team member of my training institute on this topic (Hildenbrand, 1990). I try to tell students that my attitude is to accept clients' information at face value, naively, and to introduce whatever changes I can think of in the direction desired by them. If things work out and both spouses are satisfied, then so am I. If the same old dance is performed again and again, no matter what the topic of their conversation, I assume we have only touched the tip of the iceberg. I then proceed to search for and effect change in their motivations, calling them the "tunes" to which they perform their painful dance. Very often it is a tune haunted by secrets and lies from their past, well worth uncovering and "recomposing" in the context of desired changes.

SECRETS, GUILT, AND INJUSTICE

Poets know what we scientifically trained therapists often fail to understand. Problem-solving that is based on unresolved guilt and injustice often is not only ineffective, but dangerous. A couple's game can even be life-threatening if they cling to a "myth" often constructed in the early stage of their courtship and frozen since into a secret curse, which may never be questioned again. We owe Eugene O'Neill, one of the great American playwrights, our thanks for this knowledge, which was nearly lost in systems therapy when the emphasis on the positive was carried to the point where lies and injustice were not even to be conceptualized.

In the play, *The Iceman Cometh*, Hickey says to his friends after he has shot his wife:

> And Evelyn always knew about the tarts I'd been with when I came from a trip. She'd kiss me and look in my eyes, and she'd know . . . God, can you picture all I made her suffer, and all the guilt she made me feel, and how I hated myself! If she only hadn't been so damned good—she'd been the same kind of wife I was a husband. . . .
>
> Christ, I loved her so, but I began to hate that pipe dream! I began to be afraid I was going bughouse because sometimes I couldn't forgive her for forgiving me. . . . And then I saw I'd always known that was the only possible way to give her peace and free her from the misery of loving me. . . .
>
> I remember I stood by the bed and suddenly I had to laugh. I couldn't help it, and I knew Evelyn would forgive me. I remember I heard myself speaking to her, as if it was something I'd always wanted to say, 'Well, you know what you can do with your pipe dream now, you damned bitch.'

COMMENT

In my therapeutic experience there is no possibility for constructive development of human relationships skewed by a secret dance of guilt, injustice, and presumed innocence as long as the sources of power are not disclosed and rebalanced. The hidden weapons of innocence can be as strong as those of permanent betrayal. What looks like a complementary relationship on the surface actually is the essence of a symmetrical escalation in the polarization of innocence and guilt characterized by the roles of Evelyn and Hickey. In the drama between them, her motive is to sacrifice herself to save him from evil, and his is to show her that she will never achieve her goal; this seems to be the ultimate reason why he kills her. In a crazy way Hickey prevents Evelyn from having to give up her position of innocence and prevents himself from giving up the role of the villain, true to the secret "myth" they constructed during courtship and reinforced since.

Experiences of secret injustice, which former generations did not disclose and resolve, can easily be postponed and transferred to couples' relationships and individual well-being in the next generation. If such a victim of unresolved family guilt continues the game without knowing its rules, becoming psychotic or committing suicide may be the only way out. With adolescents, I look beyond their present situation for motives to the stories of their parents, especially when their confusion reaches a point where neither I nor their family can make sense of it.

Surely it is no coincidence that, as I wrote this, I received a phone call from a colleague who practices in the former German Democratic Republic. "Do you know," she says, "since the external walls have come down, the internal walls are collapsing, too. Again and again I see women in therapy sessions who were raped but never dared to tell their secret to anyone. This was also true for our society, if you wanted to survive. The same goes for men who, in order to maintain their political position, betrayed their closest friends, but did not talk about it out of fear of losing everything. I am presently seeing a son of such a father who is deeply depressed, even suicidal. . . . If, as a therapist, I had only a range of strategies at hand which stem from the ahistorical "repair models" we used to be taught, I would help to build up new walls and all would have been in vain."

In my opinion, our regard for the positive elements and resources in human relationships should not prevent us from recognizing secret injustice and guilt in their history. It is a basis for ending unfinished business while learning new ways of functioning. "Who enters into league with dark forces, who faces and agrees with them is in touch with the sources and origins of his or her energy" (Hellinger, 1991). Rituals recognizing that injustice was done, and, as Imber-Black (Imber-Black, Roberts, & Whiting, 1988) suggests, rituals reconciling old hurts in order for new perspectives to develop, will allow such energy to emerge and become a new resource in life.

RITUALS TO RESOLVE INJUSTICE AND SECRETS IN COUPLES' LIVES

Encourage the Victim of Secret Injustice to Show Anger

Helen, a young woman, taught me this ritual, which I have since used with other couples. In the first session of marital therapy with Helen and Kurt, she told me how she thought of killing herself when her husband had mentioned to her, out of the blue, that he had fallen in love with a colleague at a business party and had started a passionate relationship with her. This had been going on secretly for months. Kurt replied that he did not know anymore where he stood or with which woman he wanted to live. On the night that Kurt had met the other woman, Helen had remained at home with the baby in order to give her husband a chance to have a good time, which she regarded now as an even greater injustice than his silence about the affair.

After Kurt told Helen his secret, she had not slept and had cried for weeks. Then, one day, she decided to take revenge. Her anger had overcome her desperation. She telephoned all her women friends in the vicinity and asked them to come to her house the following evening as she had to consult with them urgently. Helen suggested to Kurt that he see his woman friend and consult with her about the future. She was going to do the same and, therefore, needed quiet and the support of her friends. Kurt responded with surprise and relief at first. Simultaneously, he felt confused and irritated, but respected Helen's resoluteness. When he returned home at midnight, the women were still talking and drinking wine together. Quite obviously, they were all very much involved in "sorting things out" with Helen, as one of them said. What struck Kurt was the friendly but earnest atmosphere of the group and their nonpunitive reaction to him.

Instead of clinging to the role of the innocent victim, Helen encouraged her friends to tell her in what way they thought she might have contributed to the crisis in her marriage. Some of them believed that she had involved herself too exclusively with the baby and not paid enough attention to Kurt, just as he was starting a new and difficult job. But Helen refused to bear alone the guilt for the injustice she had suffered. Instead of contributing to the usual game of "poor victim, bad villain," she remained angry at Kurt's behavior, even as she tried to understand his motives. Eventually, Kurt suggested martial therapy and arranged for it himself.

Helen's ritual of involving her women's group to help her sort things out allowed her to stay with her anger as a source of energy while, at the same time, questioning her part of the conflict. It was, of course, only the beginning of understanding and resolving the couple's crisis, but I was glad to see two people who had escaped the usual pattern of victim and villain on their own. Whenever I recognize a potential victim in a marital crisis signalling a transitional stage, like that of Helen and Kurt (their dyad having become a triad through the birth of their first child), I remember Helen's "rebalancing ritual" by which she turned a possibly malicious pattern of complementarity into a benevolent pattern of symmetry. Then, I suggest similar rituals to help the potential "victim" achieve a better position without inducing guilt in the potential "villain"; the result is astonishment and curiosity in the partner who "betrayed" as well as a more constructive definition of the crisis for the other.

Suggest an Explicit Ritual of Apology Instead of Allowing Guilt to Accumulate

There are no deadlier secrets of guilt and presumed innocence between two people than those that are never reconciled but silently accumulated in the hidden journals of the spouses, the real as well as metaphorical ones. The more taboo and inexpressible they are, the more dramatic their effect is on the relationship. Here is another example of how therapists can learn, from the clues of their clients, to design rituals of reconciliation for old accounts of guilt and shame.

Arthur, a businessman, came for therapy with Bruna, his wife of many years. They were both in their 50's. Arthur suffered from depression and anxiety attacks. As in the case of Silvia and Frank, the couple's relationship improved on a behavioral level after the first few sessions, and Arthur reported that he felt quite himself, again. However, the atmosphere between the spouses remained poisonous, whether they talked or not, and they let me know that a lot of guilt and anger had accumulated between them for the past decade, since their children left home. I noticed that Arthur carried a black notebook with him to each session and put it visibly next to him on the sofa. Whenever the atmosphere tensed, he would clasp it tightly. Bruna would glance nervously at Arthur's notebook in those instances, but nobody ever talked about it. I finally asked Arthur about his notebook and was told that this is where he had written all the offenses Bruna and others had committed against him over the years. Bruna, he complained, had never even asked to look into it.

I brought in two red and two black notebooks to the next session. I gave each spouse a red and a black book and asked them to use the red one for their memories of three positive actions they had received from each other and the black one for three memories of injustice and insults suffered by the spouse. The rule should be "an eye for an eye, a tooth for a tooth": for each memory in the black notebook came one in the red book. Arthur was encouraged to use his original notebook to remember important incidents. Rather than asking the couple directly what they had written down, I suggested a game of showing me how well they knew each other. They each were to think hard and try to guess the major items in the other's books, but not mention their guesses before our next session.

In the next session, each partner was to tell the "red and black items" of merit and guilt they assumed were hidden in the other's notebook. Of course, each of them kept falling back into talking about their own accumulated merits and disappointments. My task was to make sure that Arthur listened while Bruna talked about her guesses and that Bruna listened while Arthur talked about his. To their amazement, each guessed accurately the three major items of merit as well as of guilt in the other's "secret notebook" and told the associated stories from the spouse's perspective. I congratulated them on their intimate knowledge of one another, which was one way of showing how much they cared for each other, and then suggested the next step in the guessing game: Which of the most hurtful incidents of the past did they assume the partner might want to get an apology for before parting with it forever? The next and final step of the ritual was for each to invent a "good-bye" ritual as a way of absolution, in which Arthur did something important for Bruna and Bruna did something important for Arthur. They came up with some lovely ideas and also put them into action.

When a destructive secret emerges in couples' therapy, sometimes a simple thing like an earnest apology may be all that is needed, for example, "I know that I have hurt you, and I am really sorry." Now and then a more substantial act is required. One may offer a weekend to the other, "just for fun," or an expensive meal. At any rate, it is important that the therapist help formulate the ritual so that it refers to actions, not feelings, the message being: "You don't have to apologize for your feelings, you are only responsible for your behaviors." The major issue of this kind of ritual is, of course, that each "put on the other's shoes temporarily" and get an idea of what it feels like walking in them. It offers people a different way of describing the past and allows for parting with old offenses by balancing them with mutual merits as well as apologies.

CONCLUSION

I have presented some ideas on constructive secrets of individuation as well as destructive ones associated with lies and injustice. In my clinical thinking and practice, I tend to integrate a certain "laissez-faire" tendency from my

European background as well as a respectful "problem-solving" approach from my American training in family therapy, combining behavioral (systemic) with constructivist ideas. Recognizing the meaning of family history and stories and the "tunes" stemming from these, to which couples seem to dance their painful dance, is of particular importance in regard to secret guilt and injustice. Whenever change on the behavioral level does not alleviate a couple's strain, I assume we have only touched the tip of the iceberg and might crash into it if we do not locate its secret parts. As I tend to prefer tailor-made practice to "one-size-fits-all" models of therapy, I have no one way of locating secrets; but I try to create specific techniques drawing from each couple's specific resources. Most important to me is the creation of custom-made rituals of passage reconstructing the past and transforming it into future possibility. My hope is that my case vignettes will stimulate readers in a variety of ways on how to deal with secrets in couples and couples' therapy.

Through the loss of formal structures, such as the ones I described in regard to my traditional family of origin embedded in the village and the church, many necessary rituals of passage regarding secrets, guilt, and reconciliation have been lost. As therapists, we will, now and then, replace what is missing in our culture by becoming the masters of ceremony. For those who deny the burden of injustice, guilt, and fear, are doomed to lose forever part of their history and with it part of themselves.

REFERENCES

Elias, N. (1976). *Ueber den Prozess der Zivilisation*. Frankfurt: Suhrkamp.

Hellinger, B. (1991). Schuld und Unschuld aus systemischer Sicht. *Systhema, 1*, 19–38.

Hildenbrand, B. (1990). Aus der Redaktion. *System Familie, Forschung und Therapie* (p. 195). Heidelberg: Springer Verlag.

Imber-Black, E., Roberts, J., & Whiting, R. (Eds.) (1988). *Rituals in families and family therapy*. New York: W. W. Norton.

Lorenzer, A. (1989). Intimitaet im Zeitalter der instrumentellen Vernunft. In M. B. Buchholz (Ed.), *Intimitat, ueber die Veraenderung des Privaten*. Weinheim/Basel: Psychologie Heute Sachbuch.

O'Neill, E. (1971). *The iceman cometh*. Harmondsworth, NY: Penguin.

Pittman, F. S. (1987). *Turning points: Treating families in transition and crisis*. New York: W. W. Norton.

Prokop, U. (1987). *Lebensentwuerfe im Deutschen Bildungsburgertum 1750-70, Zur Geschichte der Geschlechterkultur*. Frankfurt: Habil-Schrift.

Rubin, L. B. (1983). *Intimate strangers: Men and women together*. New York: Harper & Row.

Sennett, R. (1974). *The fall of public man*. New York: Alfred Knopf.

Sichtermann, B. (1982). *Vorsicht Kind*. Berlin: Verlag Klaus Wagenbach.

Welter-Enderlin, R. (1990). Skelette im Keller und Schaetze auf dem Dachboden. Familientherapiegeschichte(n). *System Familie, Forschung und Therapie*, Bd. 3, Heft 4, pp. 196–205. Heidelberg: Springer Verlag.

Woolf, V. (1929/1979). *A room of one's own*. London: The Women's Press Ltd.

Ziehe, T. (1989). Tyrannei der Selbstsuche. In M. B. Buchholz (Ed.), *Intimitaet, ueber die Veraenderung des Privaten*. Weinheim/Basel: Psychologie Heute Sachbuch.

The Worm in the Bud:
Secrets Between Parents and Children

PEGGY PAPP

"But let concealment, like a worm i' the bud, feed on her damask cheek."

—Shakespeare, *Twelfth Night*

PARENTS ARE CONTINUALLY confronted with decisions concerning how to impart information to their children about the world they live in, including everything from the "facts of life" to the complexities of death. The imparting of such knowledge requires sensitivity on the part of parents and special attention to timing, circumstances, and place. It should take into account the nature of the information, the child's readiness to absorb it, and the integration of the knowledge into the child's life.

Problems arise when the natural sensitivity and judgment of parents is clouded by a particular meaning they bring to an issue, meaning that interferes with their being able to communicate about it. The meaning may involve intense feelings of guilt and shame over some past event, may threaten to expose disguised weaknesses or hidden vulnerabilities, or may trample on sacred generational taboos. The parents may keep the information a secret in order to protect the child or themselves from what they consider to be an unnecessarily painful disclosure. But, although the event itself may be kept secret, the intensity of the feelings surrounding it is difficult to disguise. The very act of keeping the secret generates anxiety in the parent, who must be constantly on guard against disclosure, avoiding particular subjects and distorting information.

Certain topics become taboo, and unspoken rules spring up around forbidden areas that are considered off limits. When children sense information is being withheld they become confused and anxious, they lose their sense of trust and often end up blaming themselves. In searching for a way to explain the inexplicable, they create private beliefs, myths, and fantasies. These often get acted out through symptomatic behavior and become a metaphor for the concealment in the system. The tensions and conflicts produced by secrets remain irresolvable as long as the information necessary for their resolution remains inaccessible.

SECRETS VERSUS PRIVACY

The question arises as to when withheld information becomes a "secret" and when it is simply one of a hundred private things parents never chose to discuss with their children. There is a fine line between secrecy and privacy, and families will draw the line differently depending on their cultural values and personal judgment. Parents should reserve the right to keep certain facts about themselves and their relationship private. Indeed, it would be inappropriate and even destructive to share all the details of their lives with their children. Secrets can serve a healthy as well as unhealthy function in families. They can protect privacy, maintain generational boundaries, promote healthy autonomy in the case of adolescents, and serve to cement age-appropriate alliances with peers and siblings.

One way to distinguish between secrecy and privacy is to determine the relevance of the information for different family members. Karpel (1980) refers to this as "accountability with discretion." For example, an extramarital affair may be highly relevant to the marital relationship but less relevant to the parent/child relationship. The decision regarding whether to tell the children should take into account the age of the children, the degree to which the affair is directly affecting their lives, what they know or don't know, and the impact of the affair on parent/child relationships. If the affair represents a brief resolvable crisis in the marital life of the parents, and they continue to relate to the children in their usual manner, the best decision may be to refrain from burdening the children with upsetting information. If, on the other hand, the children are continually caught in crosscurrents of hostility and suspicion, experience an unpredictable withdrawal of affection from the parents, or witness mysterious and inexplicable events, they are likely to experience an unidentifiable but pervasive guilt and hold themselves responsible for what they don't understand. Under these circumstances, it is better for the parents to demystify the situation by letting the children know where the new tensions in the family are coming from.

In considering children's right to keep secrets from parents, the line be-

tween secrets and privacy becomes even more complicated. Children are
expected to keep some things secret in their lives, and it is considered part of
the normal maturation process for them to do so. Most parents can recall
with a sense of amusement and delight the secrets they kept from their own
parents: the tricks they played, the stories they told, the risks they took, and
the limits they tested. Some childhood secrets are relatively benign and call
for a different level of concern than, for example, hiding drugs under a
mattress or writing suicide notes in a diary. Because the information is being
kept secret, parents are confronted with deciding if they are being intrusive
in seeking information or if they are simply being responsible parents. The
answer should be based on the nature of the suspected secret and whether or
not it endangers the child's health and safety. Of course, children and parents are likely to disagree about this, especially if the children are teenagers.
In most cases, it is better for parents to err on the side of intrusion when a
harmful secret is suspected. By expressing their concern openly, the issue is
at least laid out on the table where it can be discussed.

SECRET ALLIANCES AND COALITIONS

Among the most harmful kinds of secrets are those that involve hidden
alliances and coalitions in families. For example, if one parent discovers a
secret about a child and doesn't tell the other parent an "unholy alliance" is
formed with that child. Secrets can become powerful weapons in the politics
of the family, used to create boundaries or alliances in order to manipulate
relationships. One parent may reveal something extremely personal to a
child, such as an affair or a financial loss and ask the child to keep it a secret
from the other parent. The child is then caught in a devastating loyalty bind,
having to betray either one parent or the other. The same kind of bind is
created if a parent requests a child to keep certain information a secret from
another sibling or to spy on a sibling and report back to the parent.

Estrangement can be created through various subsystems of the family
according to who knows, who doesn't know, and who doesn't know who
knows. If a parent tells two siblings a secret about a third sibling, a secret
alliance is formed between the two siblings and the parent, estranging the
third child. If the parent tells the first two siblings a secret about a third
sibling and doesn't tell either that the other one knows, a barrier is formed
among all three siblings.

It is not uncommon for family members to blackmail one another by
threatening to expose secret information. One sibling may say to another,
"Unless you do what I say I'll tell on you." Or a parent may threaten a child
with, "I'll tell your father about your smoking if you don't behave." One

person is held hostage by another until the secret is exposed and loses its power.

EVALUATING SECRETS

The following questions are helpful in evaluating whether or not secrets are having a benign or damaging effect on relationships.

1. Is the secret interfering with any family member's current functioning? If a family member is showing signs of depression, anxiety, or psychosomatic symptoms as a result of either keeping a secret or having a secret kept from him or her, it is an indication that a destructive and unstable tension is being created that needs to be dealt with openly.

2. Is the withheld information interfering with direct and open communication between family members? If the secret-keeping is confined to a small circumscribed area of a person's life that has little relevancy to current relationships, it will probably have little effect on communication among family members. However, if the secret requires pretense, deception, or evasion on a daily basis, it is bound to inhibit communication and create emotional distancing. Other family members may then experience what Pauline Boss (1991) describes as "ambiguous loss," in which the person is physically but not emotionally present.

3. Would it be devastating if the unaware person found out about the secret accidentally or through someone else? For example, when a secret involves a child's identity (such as an adoption or a date of birth), there is always the danger that someone outside the family may reveal the information in a derogatory manner, or the secret may be blurted out inside the family during a heated argument and have a lasting effect on the child's ability to integrate it.

4. Who should reveal the secret, to whom, and under what circumstances? Who else in the family knows about the secret? These questions should be given careful thought by the therapist and family. In most cases, it is best for the person who has the secret to reveal it directly to the person it most concerns, rather than allowing it to be conveyed through a third person. At the time of the revelation, the person should also be told who else in the family knows abut it in order to prevent further pretense and deception.

5. What will be the effects of disclosure? The time, place, and circum-

stances should be considered so that time is allowed for absorption
and reaction to the new knowledge. The therapist should anticipate
and be prepared to help the family deal with the aftermath of
disclosure. Sometimes the revelation of new information is a relief
but often it is a shock, even when suspected, and family members
need a safe place to express their thoughts and feelings.

Shared Secrets

The issue of secrecy versus privacy involves not only internal family secrets
but those that are shared among family members and kept from the outside
world. In these situations, children are instructed not to let the neighbors
know about "our private business." This can include anything from trivial
matters, such as the price of their newest car to more pernicious secrets
involving alcoholism, suicide, incest, or unemployment.

Shared secrets are perhaps the most difficult kind to deal with in family
therapy, as all family members are pledged to secrecy and are compelled to
practice deception out of a sense of loyalty to the family. The family hides
behind a wall of pretense that isolates them from the outside world and most
of their resources go into protecting this wall. In some cases, the wall can
only be penetrated through the intervention of outside agencies. It is generally a child who alerts the outside agencies through some form of socially
unacceptable behavior that brings the family to the attention of a community facility.

The Whistle Blower

An example of the need for outside intervention was seen in the case of
Gregory Richards, age 16, who was hospitalized for violent and uncontrolla-
ble behavior exhibited as a reaction to the deception required of him to keep
his father's secret.

The Richards family was referred to the Ackerman Institute after Gregory's three-week hospital stay. Eight months previous to his hospitalization, Mr. Richards had been fired from a prestigious white-collar job after
20 years because of heavy drinking. Rather than looking for another job in
his field of expertise, Mr. Richards sank into a deep rut of apathy and
depression, drank more heavily and turned to driving a cab as a means of
earning a living. Both Mr. and Mrs. Richards were so ashamed and humiliated by this sudden loss of status, income, and prestige that they kept it a
secret not only from their son, Gregory, but from the rest of the world. This
required an extraordinary amount of pretense and duplicity. Every morning,
Mr. Richards dressed in his business suit and left the house at his usual hour,

pretending to go to his office. He then went to the cab station, changed his clothes and spent the day driving a taxi, returning in the evening at his accustomed hour.

One day on his way to a friend's house, Gregory spotted his father sitting in a parked cab waiting for a customer. Upon seeing his son, Mr. Richards quickly slid over into the customer's seat and told Gregory he was waiting for the driver. Gregory knew he was covering something up as he was dressed in old clothes.

Upon confronting his father that evening, Gregory learned that his mother had known about the situation for some time and was an accomplice in keeping the secret. The parents explained to Gregory that there was no need for anyone outside the family to know about his father's change of employment, as it was probably only temporary. Sensing their embarrassment and deep humiliation, Gregory reluctantly joined his parents in playing the cover-up game. This required him to lie when teachers or friends asked, "What does your father do?" and he was forbidden to bring friends home. He invented lies to tell relatives and learned to be evasive with neighbors.

On one occasion, Gregory and his friends happened to hail his father's cab on their way home from a party, and Gregory and his father pretended not to know one another. After this incident, Gregory stopped going to school and the tension between him and his parents steadily increased. When his father fell into his drunken stupor every evening, Gregory began provoking him, calling him a liar and a quitter. If he failed to get a response to his verbal taunts, he sorted to hitting and punching his father. Mrs. Richards then rushed in to protect her husband, and all three ended up in a physical fight. After several such fights, the parents had Gregory hospitalized for violent behavior.

The social worker at the hospital gathered the above information and referred the family to our Institute. In my one and only session with them, Gregory told the family story, but the parents colluded against any outside help. They insisted the only problem was Gregory's violence, saw no reason for them to be involved in family therapy, and did not return for a second session.

Fortunately, the story did not end there. Six months later, I received a call from a probation officer in another borough, where the family had since moved. The parents had taken out a PINS petition, and the court was considering placing Gregory. The probation officer asked for my recommendation, and I sent a report of my session and recommended family therapy rather than placement. The court followed my recommendation and the parents complied with the mandatory ruling.

In following up on the case, I learned from the social worker and probation officer that the veil of secrecy was lifted slowly from the family, and the parents had finally been able to allow their friends and relatives to know the truth about their situation. As soon as Gregory was able to tell his friends what his father did for a living, he returned to school and stopped his violent behavior. This occurred despite the fact that many other other issues in the family remained unresolved. The disappearance of Gregory's symptomatic behavior seemed to be an indication that he no longer felt the need to send an SOS signal to the outside world.

"PROTECTIVE" SECRETS

Children Protecting Parents

One of the most common reasons for keeping secrets both on the part of children and parents is "protection." Unfortunately, many secrets that are meant to protect instead end up alienating or undermining trust. Children often keep secrets in order to protect their parents from unnecessary worry or to protect themselves or a sibling from punishment. They are extremely attuned to their parents' emotional sensitivities, know what will upset them, and learn to keep these things to themselves. This can lead to lying or evasiveness around certain issues, which then creates even more anxiety and mistrust in the parents. In order to stop this escalating cycle, the child must feel the parent can deal directly and rationally with the material that is being kept secret.

It is not uncommon for one parent and a child to team up together to protect another parent from knowledge that might distress him or her. The parent tells the child, "Don't tell your father about this. He has too many other worries to tend to" or "No need to worry your mother. You know how excited she gets." Often, the parent is protecting him or herself from dealing with the other parent's reaction. Not only is the child taught to deceive one parent, he or she is given the message that the other parent is incapable of dealing with serious issues, thus creating a fixed distance between the parent and child.

The important question to ask is: who is being protected from what and for what reasons? Facing secrets involves each person taking responsibility for his or her own actions and reactions and holding others responsible for theirs.

Parents Protecting Children

Parents may have the best intentions in withholding information about themselves or others; often, they don't want to tarnish a child's cherished image or create disillusionment. Parents may be reluctant to reveal some humiliating or traumatic event in their past, such as a jail record, a secret affair, a drinking problem, an abortion, or psychiatric hospitalization. Under certain circumstances, it may be wise to be discreet, but if the information is causing the secret-bearer great mental and emotional distress, the child will experience the distress without any way of decoding it.

Parents generally underestimate the ability of children to handle sensitive information, especially when it is presented in a direct manner in a safe atmosphere. Most parents are surprised at how often their children already know or have guessed at what they are telling them.

Deep Are the Roots

The following case, which was treated by Olga Silverstein, is an example of the consequences of a mother's effort to protect her daughter from a painful secret related to the mother's past. I served as the consultant on the case, observing from behind a one-way mirror.

Mrs. Grothe, a single mother, brought her 14-year-old daughter, Sonya, to our clinic because of her involvement with abusive boyfriends over the past several years. These relationships, besides endangering her physical well-being, absorbed her to the point of interfering with her schooling. Her current boyfriend, who was extremely possessive, hit her when he became jealous and had recently threatened to kill her if he ever saw her with her previous boyfriend. Mrs. Grothe constantly worried about Sonya's safety and could not understand why she continued to carry on relationships with violent men.

As more information emerged it became clear that Mrs. Grothe herself had a history of abusive relationships with men that often placed her in danger. After many years of being physically abused by an alcoholic husband, she finally left him, but still maintained a relationship with him and allowed him to rent a room in her two-story house. The ex-husband spied on all her activities and tried to interfere with any new relationships she formed. He was jealous of her current suitor, who had also abused her physically, on occasion. Frequently, all three ended up in violent confrontations.

Mrs. Grothe spoke with a heavy foreign accent and inquiries into her background revealed she was born and raised in Germany, where she lived with her family during the war years. In the first telling of her life story, she described how a bomb had fallen on their home during a bombing raid, killing her mother and father. She and her brother survived and were placed in an orphanage. Two years later, at age eight, she was adopted by an American couple and brought to the United States, where she had lived ever since.

Several sessions later she retold the story, revealing a long-buried secret.

The impetus for this revelation came from Olga's puzzling over why such bright, talented women had so little respect for themselves as to allow men to abuse them. This struck a sensitive chord with Mrs. Grothe and, taking a deep breath, she said, "Listen, I'm going to tell you something I've never told anyone before — not even my daughter." She then proceeded to tell the real story of what happened to her parents. Her father killed her mother in the midst of a heated argument, and she and her brother witnessed it. The headlines in all the newspapers described it as an "act of passion," and her father was sent to prison. She had no communication with him after the police took him away. She saved the newspaper clippings and had reread them year after year trying to understand the calamity. When she was adopted, she tried to gain more information from her adoptive parents about the details of the trial, but they refused to discuss it saying she must forget about it. The adoptive parents had since died, and her brother had been killed in an accident. She had carried the awful secret alone and, until now, had not trusted anyone enough to share it. When Sonya was born, she decided the truth was too terrible for her to bear and so made up the story about the bomb.

Although Sonya did not know about the real event, she had experienced the emotional aftermath of it through her mother's moods and behavior. She had sensed a dark shadow over her mother's life, experienced her deep moods of despair, and witnessed her feelings of unworthiness being acted out with men. She had credited this to her mother having lost her parents at an early age, but she had no way of understanding the true nature of her mother's tragic legacy.

As a result of being able to speak about this unspeakable event, Mrs. Grothe was able to explore the effects of it on her life and to see the way in which she was unwittingly recreating a scenario similar to that of her parents. During this process, she admitted something she had been afraid to admit even to herself — that, on some level, she believed her mother must have provoked her father and that she deserved her fate. In her own life, this was translated into the belief that "women deserve to be punished at the hands of men."

Olga challenged Mrs. Grothe's harsh judgment of her own mother and placed the event within the context of the extreme patriarchy of wartime Germany, in which women were expected to serve men and the state. Eventually, Mrs. Grothe was able to replace her old belief with the new belief that "women deserve respect and should protect themselves and each other." She acted upon this new belief by evicting her ex-husband so he could no longer harass her. She stopped seeing her current male friend, as she decided she no longer wanted to be intimidated by him. Within a short period of time, Sonya, following her mother's example, lost interest in her abusive boyfriend. However, it was not easy to break off her relationship with him. He refused to stop seeing her, followed her around, and sent her threatening letters. At this point, mother took steps to protect her daughter by reporting him to the police, who intervened and stopped him.

At the end of therapy, Sonya had returned to school, had a part-time job, and was too busy for anything but occasional dating. She no longer needed to act out her mother's unspoken messages concerning the rights of men to possess and dominate women. Instead, once this deeply ingrained belief became accessible through the revelation of the secret, she and her mother were able to join together as two allies against the abusive men in their lives.

KNOW AND TELL

The ability of family secrets to affect not only the feelings and behavior of children, but their cognitive functioning and academic performance, is graphically documented by Donovan and McIntyre (1990): "It is very difficult to develop the cognitive blinders necessary for secret-keeping without having the process generalize to other areas, especially those specifically related to knowing and telling."

As the authors point out, school is a place where children tell adults what they know, but family secrets represent knowledge of which children cannot even be aware that they are aware. This bizarre situation in which children cannot allow themselves to know what they know or to tell what they know often leads to "cognitive blinders" and academic failure.

In their book, *Healing the Hurt Child*, Donovan and McIntyre give an example of a ten-year-old girl, Gina, who was placed in a special education program because of a "selective math disability." In gathering the family history, the therapist learned she was an adopted child who had never been told about her adoption because of her father's difficulty in accepting himself as an adoptive parent. For many years she had scrutinized her parents' wedding picture and wondered why the flowers in front of the church, which only bloomed in the fall, were blooming in the spring. When the therapist asked her how long it took to make a baby, she was able to figure out that she had been 15 months old when her parents were married. Once she was permitted to add up the facts of her life and compute the arithmetic of her birth, her math disability disappeared.

In a similar case that I treated, an 11-year-old boy named Billy developed a learning block in history. Although Billy's grades were consistently high in all other subjects, he could not remember dates or places and refused to learn them. The school was puzzled as to why his "learning deficit" was relegated to this particular area.

In therapy sessions, we discovered that Billy Hardy had been prohibited from learning about his own history, which was filled with chaos, confusion, and mystery, because asking questions about it upset his mother. Therefore, Billy had stifled such questions about why he and his mother suddenly left his father, why his father kept disappearing and reappearing during his early childhood, and why the family kept moving from one place to another. The past was dangerous territory, not to be talked about or even thought about. Billy had globalized this prohibition against knowledge of his personal past to a prohibition against knowledge of the world's past.

This prohibition had been created by Mrs. Hardy's desire to protect Billy from learning that his father was an alcoholic who went on periodic binges, during which he disappeared for days at a time and lost many jobs requiring many different moves.

When Billy was no longer compelled to split off the knowledge of his past from his present, his "learning block" disappeared, and he was able to remember historical dates and places.

SECRET FEARS AND BELIEFS

One of the most fertile grounds for the flourishing of secret fears in a parent is centered around real or imagined inherited traits in their child. It is not unusual for parents to harbor a secret belief that their child has inherited certain unacceptable characteristics from a relative in the family. Parents naturally observe family likenesses in their children and compare certain physical, temperamental, and emotional attributes. If parents feel positively about these qualities, the comparison can serve as a source of love and pride. Problems develop when parents begin to see the emergence of what they consider to be reprehensible mannerisms or behavior and, rather than dealing with these behaviors on their own terms, view them as being genetic and unchangeable. The child, unaware of the secret fear, only experiences the accompanying anxiety, anger, or disgust. The child's response often takes the form of a symptom that mirrors the very trait that is dreaded.

Footsteps

The Macnamara case graphically illustrated this process. (Evan Imber-Black served as my consultant on this case.) Fifteen-year-old Kevin and his family were referred to our Institute by his school, because his grades had suddenly plummeted, and he was looking "alarmingly depressed." His depression coincided with Mrs. Macnamara deciding to completely withdraw from him, because she couldn't deal with his provocative behavior. She and Kevin were in constant conflict with one another. Their arguments, which seemed to stem from ordinary teenage rebellion, would suddenly and inexplicably escalate into violence.

From the beginning, the case had an air of mystery. The ferocity of the fighting was puzzling given such minor provocations. A clue to the intensity of their relationship was provided in the second session, when Mrs. Macnamara described what she considered to be the real problem. She appeared without Kevin, saying she wanted to talk about something without his being present because "he gets crazy if I mention this thing and we get nowhere." The "thing" she was alluding to turned out to be "compulsive stealing and lying since he was 9 years old."

Tracing the theme of lying in the system, I asked if anyone else in the family lied or stole, and Mrs. Macnamara reported that Kevin's paternal grandmother was a "compulsive liar" and stole from everyone. She dreaded her mother-in-law's visits when she was married to Kevin's father, as her jewelry was always missing afterwards. No one ever confronted her mother-in-law, and the situation was never discussed. For years, Mrs. Macnamara had harbored the secret fear that Kevin's lying and stealing was genetic and the he had inherited it from his grandmother.

Still another secret was uncovered in this session when questions were asked about Kevin's father. He had abandoned the family when Kevin was a baby, and Mrs. Macnamara had recently learned from people in the neighborhood that he was now a drug dealer. Kevin never asked about his father, and Mrs. Macnamara never mentioned him, but she lived in fear that one day he would ask to visit him. She was terrified that if Kevin learned the truth he would surely follow in his footsteps. "Every time he does something wrong, my mind goes back to his father. He even looks like him and has his mannerisms."

Thus, the father's presence was kept alive in the home through Mrs. Macnamara's secret fears. One can speculate that she must have monitored Kevin's every move and mood over the years, tense and on guard in her efforts to protect him from the truth, watching for signs of the dread characteristics of grandmother and father to emerge, and then reacting to them by trying to stamp them out.

The first step in releasing mother and son from this legacy of secrets and deception was to dispel the mythology of inheritance surrounding the father and grandmother.

First, using a purely educational approach, I debunked the myth that lying and stealing were genetic, telling her there was no scientific evidence to support her belief and that, so far, no one had isolated a "lying" gene. I then offered a counter belief by proposing that Kevin was being loyal to the tradition of secrecy in the family by being secretive and that the best way to deal with hidden loyalties was to puncture them with the clear light of exposure. I suggested she tell Kevin the truth about his father and grandmother and about her fears of his following in their footsteps. Framed in this way, it made sense to her to break the rule of secrecy.

When she told Kevin about his father, he broke down and cried and asked why she hadn't told him before. For the first time, they talked about their history together and about her fears that had propelled her to react so intensely to everything that reminded her either of his grandmother or of his father. This served to clear the air between them and made it possible for them to begin to relate to each other in a new way.

After this, Kevin stole and lied only once during the course of the therapy, and both he and his mother reacted to the incident quite differently. Mrs. Macnamara calmly told Kevin he must pay back the money, and he agreed to do so, apologizing and promising never to do it again.

In exploring with the family what they thought had brought about the change, Mrs. Macnamara said, "I think what helped a lot was when you told us to be honest, not to have any—what should I call it?—secrets—and letting things out into the open, not trying to hide anything from him. I don't think I ever realized that a child is so attuned to your own—how shall I put it?—that he was somehow knowing I was keeping something from him, and he felt there was an emotional tug-of-war there because as long as I had a secret he wasn't going to fully tell the truth to me."

Kevin's lying and stealing was a metaphorical comment on the cover-up in the system. What initially appeared to be a tug-of-war around chores and homework was actually a tug-of-war around deception and honesty.

SECRETS AND THERAPEUTIC IMPASSE

Secrets are one of the most common causes of therapeutic impasse, as they can block a therapist from knowledge that is essential to understanding and resolving the core problem. The therapist may sense something is missing and pursue many false leads in the course of searching for clues. Various kinds of interventions may be tried based on what appear to be "sensible" solutions, but these are usually doomed to failure if they go against some powerful emotional currents in the family. There are many different reasons why families withhold information. They may be unaware of its relevance to the presenting problem; they may need to feel they can trust the therapist before sharing such private and painful material; or they may need to feel they have the permission of other family members to reveal it.

The following case points up the fallacy of pursing "logical" solutions while the family is reading and acting on subliminal messages of which the therapist has no knowledge. It was not until I pressed Mrs. Arnold to make a critical decision that she revealed the secret that had blocked the therapy.

The Long Shadow

Mrs. Arnold had been widowed for two years when she brought her 20-year-old son, Rick, to our clinic. Rick had dropped out of two colleges during the first semesters and had run away from a third while in the process of registering. He stayed at home all day, refused to work or attend school, had no friends, and spent a great deal of time alone in his room.

Mrs. Arnold stated that, after her husband's death, she and her 17-year-old daughter, Louise, had moved on with their lives. Louise had left home to attend college, and Mrs. Arnold had taken over her husband's business and was busy running the company. But Rick remained with his two feet firmly planted in the home. This situation pre-dated Mr. Arnold's death, and both parents had been concerned about Rick's inability to leave home since he graduated from high school.

Rick, who accompanied mother reluctantly to the sessions, retreated into silence whenever the subject of his leaving home was raised. Mrs. Arnold said emphatically she was now at the end of her rope. She admitted she may have been too soft on him in the past, but now realized how detrimental this was, and wanted to change her ways. She stated she was willing to do anything that was necessary to get him to function on his own.

My first thought was that Rick might feel he needed to stay home to fill in for his father and keep his mother company after Louise left home. This thought had also occurred to Mrs. Arnold, and she stated she had tried in every way to assure him this was not necessary. She led a very active social life, had many friends, was dating several men, and was looking forward to living alone. Rick emphatically denied any worries about his mother's well-being.

My second thought was that Rick might have some unresolved issues regarding his father's death, which were immobilizing him, but this did not seem to be the case. He was reported to have had a good relationship with his father, had participated with the rest of the family in taking care of him during his illness, and had openly expressed grief at his death.

I then shifted to focusing on a practical plan of action. Capitalizing on Mrs. Arnold's stated desire to be more firm with Rick, I helped her to lay down specific rules for his conduct, to plan time schedules, to discuss financial arrangements, to decide on future plans, and to inform Rick on when, where, and how these plans would be put into action. Among the decisions Mrs. Arnold made was to give Rick one month in which to find a job or enroll in a school of his choice. At this point, Rick stated vehemently that he preferred to go back to college, and we discussed how he would go about doing this. He agreed to send for catalogues, fill out applications, and make visits to campuses.

Rick followed through on his agreement. Mrs. Arnold drove him around to visit different colleges, and he was accepted at two. He participated actively with his mother in discussing financial and living arrangements away from home. It was, therefore, a big shock to her when she learned Rick had not answered the letters of acceptance he received from the two colleges. She said, in a bewildered tone, "I don't know what's holding him back. I can't get him to talk to me about it. When I try to bring it up, he walks away. I think all along he wasn't serious about going to college. He was only trying to appease me."

When asked for his response, Rick stated, "You could say it was appeasement." I questioned him further, "So you had no intention of following through on the plans?" After a long pause, he replied, "I did what she asked me to do, but I was not interested in going to those places." He would say no more.

I asked Mrs. Arnold if she was prepared to take the next step she had decided on, which was to put him out of the house. She replied hesitantly, "I'm not sure." She then began to cry and revealed information she had withheld when initially discussing her family of origin, "I had a brother who didn't make it. We weren't available, and he didn't make it."

She then told the story of her schizophrenic brother, Jim, who stayed with different family members in between hospitalizations and half-way houses, until they found him impossible to deal with and threw him out. He had lived with Mrs. Arnold and her husband when the children were young, but he interfered in their lives to such an extent that they finally asked him to leave. "Everybody kept telling us for years, 'stand back—stand back, don't allow him to get you involved again.' Well, we did stand back, and he committed suicide. I felt responsible. I don't think I could ever again turn anyone out. It's as simple as that. I don't want to carry something like that around with me for the rest of my life. I don't think that would happen to Rick, but if it's going to take him a couple of years, then all right, he can stay."

In light of this revelation, Rick's inability to leave home took on a new meaning and opened up a different direction for exploration and intervention. The idea of separation and leaving home held an ominous meaning for mother and was loaded with guilt, shame, and regret. Separation was equated with death. She had tried to cover over these feelings and act in a "sensible" way. However, her dread of making the same mistake twice continually undermined her conscious intentions to give Rick a firm, consistent message and caused her to waver at critical moments. Rick responded to her wavering by signaling that he couldn't function on his own, and mother then became preoccupied with his psychic well-being.

Now that this subtext had been brought into the open, it was possible to begin to separate the reality of Rick's life from the memory of Jim's death. This was the separation that needed to be made before Rick could leave home.

Rick had never been told about his uncle's suicide, and his response upon hearing about it for the first time was one of astonishment. He suddenly lost his stoic pose and became intensely interested, asking his mother why she had never told him before. Mother replied that she hadn't wanted him to know because she was afraid it would "put ideas into your head." Rick stuttered in disbelief, "You — you — what? I — I — can't believe what you're saying. I never even thought of such a thing. And I'm nothing like my uncle. I hardly even knew him."

I said I thought it was time he got to know this man whom he had not been permitted to know, but who had indirectly had such a powerful influence on his life. He would then be able to make a conscious decision as to whether he wanted to continue to behave like him.

The next phase of therapy dealt with the separation of fact from fantasy and fear from reality. This was done through a series of tasks centered around comparing the similarities and differences between Rick and Jim. Photograph albums, family stories, school records, and psychiatric reports were brought into the session and used as a source for these comparisons. Mrs. Arnold and Rick were asked to note the differences in their appearance, personalities, talents, life experiences, relationships, and behavior. All of this further opened and detoxified the old secret. The more Mrs. Arnold compared Rick with Jim, the more essential the differences she found. Rick felt he had only one thing in common with Jim, that they both liked baseball.

Now that Jim's suicide was an open topic between Mrs. Arnold and Rick, I encouraged Mrs. Arnold to discuss it with her daughter, Louise, who knew nothing about it, and with her family of origin where it remained a taboo subject. Although all members of her extended family had been involved in the saga of Jim's life and death, no one ever talked about it. This is understandable because a suicide in a family is one of the most difficult deaths with which to deal. The societal, legal, and religious sanctions against it lead to feelings of humiliation and disgrace that promote secretiveness both inside and outside the family. As family members search for a way to explain the tragedy, they are haunted by terrible questions. Rather than sharing these questions with one another, the tendency is to keep them secret. And yet, in cases of suicide, more than any other kind of death, it is of the upmost importance that these anguishing questions be named and shared so that family members are not left to deal with them alone.

With some coaching from me, Mrs. Arnold was able to discuss Jim's suicide separately with each family member and finally to invite them all to attend a family session. During this meeting, it became clear the family had been caught in all the complexities of a disjointed, confusing, and inadequate mental health system in which they were given contradictory messages regarding diagnosis, care, and treatment. Hearing that her brothers and sisters had been as confused, frustrated, and conflicted as she helped to dissipate a great deal of Mrs. Arnold's guilt. She no longer felt that she alone bore the responsibility for Jim's death. Rather, she saw it as the tragic culmination of a long series of historical events, biological circumstances, and clinical incompetence over which she had no control.

After the family session, therapy was interrupted for two months because of summer vacations. At the beginning of September, Mrs. Arnold called to tell me the following story: In the middle of a family party, Rick surprised everyone by announcing he had to leave the party early. When Mrs. Arnold asked why, he said, "Because I'm leaving for college." Unbeknownst to Mrs. Arnold, he had selected a college on his own, driven there for the admission interview, been accepted, had his physical exam, packed his bags, and was ready to leave. He telephoned his mother a week later to say he liked the school and intended to major in psychology. Mrs. Arnold said laughingly, "He certainly made a quick getaway. I guess he got fed up with talking about Jim."

HOW NOT TO REVEAL A SECRET

> As lightning to the children eased,
> with explanation kind,
> the truth must dazzle gradually,
> or every man be blind.
>   Emily Dickinson

Ibsen's play, *The Wild Duck*, is a classic example of the devastating effects on a family of the "truth" being revealed in the wrong way for the wrong reasons. In this play, Gregers returns to his hometown after many years away, with the mission of freeing his old friend, Hjalmar "from all the lies and evasions that are smothering him." In a fit of "moralistic fever" he brutally reveals to Hjalmar that his adored daughter, Hedvig, is not his own but the result of a liaison between his wife, Gina, and Gregers' father, Werle. Werle, an old roue, impregnated Gina when she worked as his maid many years ago. Before she began to "show," Werle conspired to have Hjalmar meet and marry her, and Hedvig was raised as their daughter. Gregers' motivation for revealing this information is cloaked in a moralist position concerning "truth" that hides his vindictive feelings towards his father. Hjalmar is totally unprepared for this shock. Rather than sorting out the situation with his wife, Hjalmar turns on his daughter, Hedvig, and suddenly and ruthlessly rejects her, crying, "Don't come near me — I can't bear seeing you." Hedvig, to whom the secret is not revealed, is so distraught by her father's inexplicable rejection, she kills herself.

This is a tragic example of the truth being revealed in such a way as to divide and shatter a family.

Fallout from Truth

The Nelson family story is a clinical example of the devastating effect of an impulsive act of truth-telling without any follow-up to help the family integrate the new information. Here, the reckless opening of a couple's secret resulted in a severe symptom in their child.

Mr. and Mrs. Nelson initially came to our institute because their 14-year-old daughter, Heather, had suddenly become anorexic. In gathering information in the first session, it became clear that Heather was worried about her mother, who was obviously depressed and highly distraught. The focus gradually shifted from a discussion of Heather's symptoms to a discussion of Mrs. Nelson's depressed state. Heather expressed her alarm about the marked change that had taken place in her mother and was concerned about her having a nervous breakdown. Mr. Nelson agreed his wife was very upset.

Mrs. Nelson first blamed her strain on pressures at work, but then conceded it was related to a problem between her and her husband.

I dismissed Heather for the next several sessions, telling her I would try to help her parents with some private issues and, in the meantime, she should get on with her life.

The couple told me of having attended a marriage encounter group several months earlier in which they were encouraged to "open up and share everything" with each other. Following the "tell all" session, there was a "forgiveness" session in which they were supposed to "forgive" each other for all their past grievances. In this atmosphere of "share and forgive," Mrs. Nelson told her husband of a very brief affair she had had ten years earlier. Instead of the forgiveness she was hoping for, Mr. Nelson was enraged. He became obsessed with what he considered to be the ultimate betrayal and felt he no longer knew or could trust his wife. There followed nightmarish weeks for both of them, in which he berated her unmercifully for hours on end, called her names, asked endless questions, and threatened to leave. His obsession grew to the point where he found it difficult to concentrate on his work and became worried about his mental state.

Mrs. Nelson was consumed with guilt, shame, and humiliation. She cried for hours and withdrew from Heather except to become extremely preoccupied with her budding sexuality. She began spying on her, questioning her, cautioning her, and setting strict limits on her hours. Heather responded to her mother's covert message that sexuality was dangerous and forbidden by starving herself and preventing the development of womanly curves.

In working with the parents, I changed the context of the problem from questions of morality, which invariably led to a dead end, to the history of their relationship and what preceded the affair. Mrs. Nelson then revealed another secret that was more relevant to their relationship than the first. At the time of the affair, she was seriously contemplating suicide. She had gone so far as to buy the pills and plan all the details of her death. She described herself as being in a deep state of depression due to the sudden death of her father. She felt she had no place to turn with her grief, as her husband was preoccupied with starting a new business and seemed completely "walled off." She briefly turned to another man to ease her loneliness and pain.

As Mr. Nelson listened to his wife's story, his mood slowly changed from one of rage and condemnation to one of dismay and disbelief that he could have been so unaware of what his wife was going through. He kept asking why she hadn't let him know, and she said she had repeatedly tried, but he was "tuned out."

The rest of the therapy consisted of helping the couple to reexamine both past and present aspects of their relationship and to use their new knowledge of each other to build a new relationship.

Heather's symptoms disappeared as the tension between her parents eased, and her mother was no longer depressed. I saw her for only one more session to confirm the parents' report that she was eating, dating, and acting like a typical teenager.

It was not necessary for Heather to know what was discussed in the sessions with her parents. These were intimate and private issues to be resolved between the two of them. It was not the secret in and of itself, but the parents' inability to come to terms with it that destabilized the family. When the parents were able to face their issue, Heather stopped receiving the covert messages that prohibited her from maturing into womanhood.

One can argue that the revelation of Mrs. Nelson's secret ultimately had a beneficial effect on the couple's relationship. But, had there been preparation for its telling and forethought as to its consequences, each family member would have been spared unnecessary distress and pain.

CONCLUSION

Secrets between parents and children present the clinician with complex issues and dilemmas, which require special therapeutic considerations in eliciting and disclosing them. Certain secrets can have a pernicious effect on family interaction, destroying trust and communication and creating symptomatic behavior. Other secrets can serve to protect privacy and promote independence and autonomy. It is part of our work as therapists to assist families in discovering the difference.

REFERENCES

Boss, P. (1991). Ambiguous loss. In F. Walsh & M. McGoldrick (Eds.), *Living beyond loss*. New York: W. W. Norton.
Donovan, D., & McIntyre, D. (1990). *Healing the hurt child*. New York: W. W. Norton.
Grolnick, L. (1983). Ibsen's truth, family secrets and family therapy. *Family Process, 22*, 275–288.
Karpel, M. (1980). Family secrets. *Family Process, 19*, 295–306.

5

Secrecy in Adoption

ANN HARTMAN

> "From my earliest years, I felt there was a mystery surrounding my life—and, like any secret you know exists but cannot fathom, that mystery haunted me."
>
> —Fisher, 1974, p. 19

THUS WROTE Florence Fisher in her autobiography, a testament that broke all the rules of silence, secrecy, and shame that had subjugated the voices of millions of adoptees. As Florence Fisher (1974), Jane Paton (1968), Betty Jean Lifton (1975), Rod McKuen (1976), and others searched for their birth families and told their stories, the world of adoption was challenged, the secrecy that had characterized adoption for a generation began to be questioned, and adoptees, birth parents, and adoptive parents organized themselves across the country in self-help, support, and political action groups to share their stories, to help each other search, and to change the legal and social structure that defines adoption.

Adoption touches the lives of many Americans, and it is unlikely that any therapist does not see at least one person in his or her practice in the course of a week who is an adoptee, a birth parent, an adoptive parent, or the spouse, son, or daughter of an adoptee. Currently, according to the American Adoption Congress, there are an estimated six million adoptees. And, of course, each of these adoptees has birth parents, adoptive parents, and, in all likelihood, other close familial associations. It is, thus, that every therapist, whether he or she is aware of it or not, provides post-adoption services. It is essential that all therapists have an understanding of the many issues in adoption and be able to translate this awareness into practice.

This chapter will focus on one of the major issues in adoption: secrecy. The historical and sociolegal context of secrecy in adoption and the impact of secrecy on all those involved in adoption will be explored. The implications for practice will then be considered.

SECRECY IN ADOPTION

Adoption is a social construction and has developed differently in different cultures and different lands. Historically in this country, the guiding principle that has shaped traditional adoption has been that adoption should be, insofar as possible, exactly like building a family biologically. "The adopted child is brought into the family of his adoptive parents as completely as by the process of birth. The purpose of [the adoption status] is to effectuate a complete substitution of the adoptive family for the natural in every respect except the biological" (Lee, 1963, p. 223). This view of adoption was built on a denial of the fact that adoption was, indeed, different from biological parenting, a view defined by David Kirk in his early research on adoption as "rejection of difference" (1964).

In order to construct adoption in this way, and to support this denial, anything that makes adoption different must be denied or minimized. The greatest threat to the denial of difference is the existence of the biological family and, thus, this connection must be totally and permanently broken. Although adoptive parents were advised to tell a child he or she was adopted, little information about the child's background was given to the family or to the child. The denial of the realities of adoption and the cloak of secrecy were reinforced by other social and personal attitudes. Most children who were adopted were born to unmarried parents and, thus, the effort was to protect the child from "shameful" facts of his or her birth. Often, false and more socially acceptable explanations were given, and members of adoptee groups share with considerable ironic humor stories about the large numbers of couples that seem to have perished in automobile accidents leaving no kin. The connection, however, between secrecy and stigma (Tefft, 1980) is intuitively known by children and, as an adoptee wrote, "an important aspect of secrecy is the easily made assumption that if one is not allowed to know something, especially about ourself, it must be bad" (Partridge, 1991, p. 202). The recursive relationship between secrecy and stigma is clear. A stigmatized person is protected by secrecy but secrecy also promotes stigmatization.

It was also felt that the stigmatized birth mother, who had been guilty of sexual misconduct, was protected through denial and secrecy. The mother was told "you will forget," "go on with your life." As soon as she signed the relinquishment, she ceased to exist. She not only carried a secret, but *was* a secret. She was assured that her identity would be protected—but it was also made clear to her that she could never have any contact with her relinquished child. Nor would she ever have news of the child. She must "put this all behind her."

Adoptive parents participate in the denial of difference, not only to protect themselves and their child from any intrusion from the past, but also because they are stigmatized by being infertile, unable to bear children. Until fairly recently, parents had to prove to the adoption agency that they were unable to conceive in order to be eligible to adopt. If adoptive families are able to deny the difference between biological and adoptive parenthood, they can finally suppress the loss and the grief about being unable to give birth.

Secrecy and denial have thus been at the core of traditional adoption practice. Although this is now being challenged, the institution has been slow to change, and adult adoptees as well as many younger adoptees and their birth and adoptive families exist in this world of denial and secrecy. The resistance of the institution to change is dramatically illustrated by the fact that the publication, almost 30 years ago, of David Kirk's research, which demonstrated that acceptance of difference in adoptive families was strongly associated with successful adoption, had very little effect on adoption practice.

THE SOCIAL, LEGAL, AND PROFESSIONAL CONSTRUCTION OF SECRECY IN ADOPTION

Secrecy in adoption is a matter of law. There is no other situation in which the law of the land reaches into the private lives of people so intimately to limit the right of association. In 47 states, adoption records are sealed by law, with Alabama, Alaska, and Kansas the only exceptions. Interestingly enough, the sealing of adoption records is a fairly recent phenomenon, which was not completed in this country until the late 1930's and is primarily characteristic of the English-speaking industrialized countries. Although England and Scotland have opened the records to adult adoptees, Australia and Canada join the United States in maintaining closed records. Efforts to open records in this country have been met with strong opposition from some adoptive parents, professionals, and others. Some states—for example, Pennsylvania—where adoptees' original birth certificates were available have now closed access.

The movement to seal records began as an effort by reformers to free children from the stigma of illegitimacy. Adopted children had suffered with birth certificates stating "father unknown" or stamped "illegitimate." The new laws provided that a new legal birth certificate be created with the names of the adoptive parents inserted and that the original birth certificate be sealed. What started, however, as an effort to protect children from painful stigmatization quickly became an impenetrable wall between adoptees and their birth families. Before long, not only were records sealed, but laws were passed forbidding agencies to give identifying information to adoptees, birth parents, or adoptive parents. As arguments rage over this crucial policy, those who defend closed records do so on the grounds that this: (a) protects the child from the stigma of his or her adopted status and illegitimacy; (b) protects the adoptive family and the child from future intrusion into their lives by birth parents; (c) protects the birth parents from future intrusion into their lives by the adopted child, and (d) reassures birth parents that records will be confidential so they will place the child. Of particular concern is the fact that the birth mother may not have told her husband, should she be married.

Those who favor opening the records, at least to adult adoptees, do so on the grounds that every human being has a right to know his or her biological relatives. Depriving adoptees of this right as a special group denies them equal protection under the law. Finally, they argue that while, in most situations involving children, the guiding principle is "the best interest of the child," in this situation, the rights of the birth and adoptive parents are placed above the rights of the adoptee (Cole & Donley, 1990). Many argue, with good reason, that records should be open so that adoptees may obtain a full health history. Certainly, the awareness of possible vulnerabilities, such as a family history of diabetes or heart disease or other hereditary diseases, can signal the need for preventive care.

Karpel (1980) points out that when there is a secret, one must always ask who is being protected by whom and from what. It is also important to inquire whether the person wants protection. For example, although secrecy around adoption is supposed to protect the birth mother, evidence is mounting that this is not her wish. For example, since 1980, Michigan has given birth mothers the opportunity to choose whether or not identifying information about them can be made available to their relinquished children when they reach 18. Over 98% of the mothers have chosen to make this information available (American Adoption Congress, 1990).

As adult adoptees and many birth parents fight to open adoption records, much of the force to maintain this wall of secrecy comes from an influential group of adoptive parents and some traditional adoption agencies, which have been strongly supported and influenced by adoptive families.

Until recently, traditional adoption practice has not only supported the legal cut-off between adoptees and their birth parents, it has gone even farther to promote secrecy in the adoption situation. For example, a rather typical instruction to adoptive parents given by one adoption expert was "it is best always to be indefinite about the biological parents, to try to keep them somewhat shadowy figures in your child's thoughts" (Raymond, 1955, p. 81). Adoptive parents further were instructed to tell the child early of the adoption, to minimize the difference between adopted and biological relationships, to give minimal and only positive information, and to emphasize that the child was chosen (Kowal & Schilling, 1985, p. 356).

Almost universally, adoptees reflecting on the communication from their adoptive parents about their origins report that they were told they were adopted but given very little information about their birth parents or the circumstances of their adoption. Further, these exchanges generally were accompanied by an atmosphere of tension and secrecy, which communicated to the adoptee that the subject was not to be explored. Most adoptees learned early to keep their questions to themselves.

The whole field of adoption has been going through a major revolution in the past 15 years. The availability of more adequate birth control measures and of abortion and the major values change that makes it possible for young unmarried women to keep their children has sharply reduced the number of infants available for adoption. Traditional adoption has largely been replaced by international adoption and by the adoption of older children and children with special needs who, not long ago, would have been considered unadoptable. Children are entering adoption with clear memories of their pre-adoption life. Although the issue of loss remains salient, as does difficulty around sharing information and talking about pre-adoptive relationships and experiences, secrecy is less of an issue. Very different children are moving into adoption and very diverse families are adopting: single parents, families with biological children, older parents, and gay and lesbian couples.

Traditional or infant adoption is also changing, with many professionals and agencies moving to varying degrees of open adoption, from anonymity but a full exchange of information, to the adoptive mother acting as Lamaze coach for the biological mother.

But, despite this revolution, adoption records remain sealed, and many professional workers in adoptive agencies continue to favor this or, if they consider that searches and reunion of adoptees and birth parents are sometimes appropriate, they feel they should be mediated by the adoption agency (Auth & Zaret, 1986). One agency describes a rather typical program, "The service consists of two or more interviews of the adoptee who wishes to search with a trained social worker to explore the adoptee's motivation, expectations, coping abilities, attitudes toward adoption, present circumstances and other related issues" (Depp, 1982, p. 115). After such a screening, the agency makes a recommendation concerning whether a search should proceed.

This is clearly a disempowering procedure, which repeats the adoptee's early experience of being helpless in the hands of a social worker who makes major life decisions for the adoptee. Evident in the professional's position of insisting on an intermediary is a lack of confidence in the adoptee's ability to handle his or her own life and important relationships with sensitivity and good judgment. In fact, in research on adoptee-birth parent reunions it was discovered that "the success of the reunion had little to do with the presence of an agency as intermediary. Those adoptees and birth parents who were left to their own devices were able to work out a meeting that respected their various needs and was productive as well" (Campbell, Silverman, & Patti, 1991, p. 334).

As with any social revolution, change in adoption laws is uneven and inconsistent. Agency policies and adoption practice principles are enormously diverse. Some agencies continue to practice adoption exactly as it was practiced in the 1950's, dedicated to the total replacement of the biological family, to closed adoption, and to the "minimization" of difference. Other adoption agencies are equally dedicated to special needs adoption, open adoption, adoption reform advocacy, and facilitating reunions. Thus, it is important for all therapists not only to discover which of their clients have been touched by adoption but also to explore their particular experiences. Adopted adults are likely to have been adopted through a public or private child welfare or adoption agency operating under the guidelines and standards described as "traditional adoption" (Child Welfare League of America, 1968).

THE IMPACT OF SECRECY

It has been from those who have lived through the adoption experience that professionals have come to really understand adoption and the impact of secrecy and denial on the lives of adoptees, birth parents, and adoptive parents. Adoptees were the first to be heard as they began to tell their stories. The voices of Jane Paton and Florence Fisher have been joined by the thousands of adoptees who, through their writing and their testimony, have taught us.

Several common themes emerge. Adoptees commonly speak of experiencing a void, a vacuum. "Adoptees . . . typically refer to spaces within themselves which represent a painful and disturbing/vacuum" (Bertocci & Schechter, 1991). This is expressed in many ways. Writes an adoptee, "most of us who have had the experience of an early separation from our natural parents appear to possess a sort of vacuum in our life for which we can find no substitute" (Sorosky, Baran, & Pannor, 1978, p. 13). Another writes, "Because I was adopted I grew up with a part of me missing. In place of ancestors, I had a void" (p. 133).

This was dramatically demonstrated by an adoptee who, when it was her turn in a family-of-origin group to put her genogram on the chalkboard, went up to the empty board and said, "There's my genogram." The sense of emptiness may be related to lost people but is often expressed in terms of the impact of secrecy, of a lack of knowledge. Penny Partridge writes about grieving the loss of information. "The lack of knowledge about our origins makes us feel that we, ourselves, are unreal too" (1991, p. 200). Kowal and Schilling's findings were that "the most commonly mentioned need [to know] was to find some resolution of confusion or a sense of emptiness. Repeatedly the word 'void' appeared. One adoptee expressed that she wished to search out the truth because 'It will fill a void in my life.' Lack of knowledge meant too much room for speculation and confusion" (Kowal & Schilling, 1985). Comments another adoptee, "Everyone should search and find. We have a deep and compelling need to know the truth, not mere curiosity or absolution of guilt" (Silverman, Campbell, Patti, & Style, 1988, p. 527).

Another adoptee writes, "I have no natural parents, no nationality. I feel like a test tube baby. I have asked my adoptive parents what is my background, who am I? All I get is two hurt people that I love very much. So I no longer question them on the subject. Isn't it natural for me to wonder about my past? I feel that it couldn't harm me to know. My adoption seems like a highly guarded secret. Even secrets are told to people with the need to know. I have the need to know" (Sorosky et al., 1978, pp. 133–34). Although more women have been involved in the search movement than have men, and it has been assumed that men have less interest in connecting with their birth families, one study that compared male and female searchers discovered that "In general males presented their 'need to know' in more intense, emotional tones and were more committed to searching than were females" (Kowal & Schilling, 1985).

Finally, difficulties in the establishment of identity have been related to secrecy. One young male adoptee summed it up, "I'm tired of not knowing who I really am" (Bertocci & Schechter, 1991, p. 185). Another commented, "I have built many false identities with an underlying theme of ruse and insecurity" (Kowal & Schilling, 1985, p. 360). Many adoptees physicalize their quest for identity, reporting the powerful need to see a face that looks like their own. "Someday I will have a baby and then I will look at someone I am biologically related to whose face will look a little bit like mine, then I will see someone who will tell me a little bit about what I look like . . . until

I saw a picture of my birth mother, I don't think that I was able to have a picture in my mind of my own face" (Hartman, 1979).

Many students of adoption have emphasized the identity issues for adoptees resulting, in part, from lack of information. Sants (Bertocci & Schechter, 1991) has referred to this as "genealogical bewilderment." Most research reports that the willingness and ability of adoptive parents to discuss adoption comfortably and openly and to share information produces more secure adults with a firmer sense of self (Hooper, 1990). This supports Kirk's view that the "acceptance of difference" is a major variable in predicting a successful adoption (Kirk, 1964).

Birth parents' voices are also beginning to be heard through their joining adoption groups, identifying themselves to researchers so that they can tell their stories, and through joining their voices together in their own organization, Concerned United Birth Parents (CUB). These voices have taught us that birth parents do not "forget and put all this behind them" as social workers assured them they would. In fact, not only has this not been the case, but the very process of relinquishment and the necessary grieving process has been constrained by this assumption. A large majority of birth parents in the largest study undertaken (a sample of 334) report that the surrender of their child had a continuing negative effect on their lives (Deykin, Campbell, & Patti, 1984).

In an extensive review of the existing literature, while acknowledging the sampling problems in the studies, Brodzinsky concludes "the considerable anecdotal data gathered by each of these investigators is consistent with previous professional documentation of profound and protracted grief reactions, depression, and an enduring preoccupation with and worry about the welfare of the child among these women" (1990). Not only does the birth mother deal with loss, but issues of secrecy and cut-off make her situation more difficult. Many women, particularly in the last generation, kept the existence of the child a secret from their husbands, friends, and relatives. This not only cut them off from comfort and support but also made them vulnerable to exposure and shame. Betty Jean Lifton's description of her mother portrays the burdens of secrecy and shame, "She had lived with the hope that she would one day hear her daughter had fared well and was successful, perhaps that would redeem her sin. But she had also been living in fear with this secret, fear that the phone would ring one day, or the knock would come at the door which would expose her to the world" (1975, p. 134).

Almost unheard, however, have been the voices of birth fathers. In fact, in most adoption literature, the birth fathers are never mentioned. They had no rights as fathers until 1972 when, in the landmark decision in Stanley vs. Illinois, the Supreme Court recognized the rights of birth fathers in regard to the future of the child (Stanley vs. Illinois, 405 U.S. 645, 1972) (Deykin, Patti, & Ryan, 1988). Some of the reasons for their exclusion from the adoption process probably can be found in deeply held cultural attitudes and gender stereotypes. First, children in our culture have clearly belonged to and been the responsibility of women. The fact that women have been favored in custody disputes and that noncustodial fathers rarely are pursued actively for child support express these views. Mothers' pensions, one of the first major social interventions into family life, supported widows in caring for children but were not available to men.

Further, in the situation of children born out of marriage, the stereotypical view of the male who takes his pleasure, casts his seed but has no thought of or interest in his offspring or the mother, is widespread and is shown in the hostility toward men that subtly has permeated adoption practice. Such attitudes and expectations have probably become self-fulfilling prophecies.

Of course, the relationship between the father and the child is very different from that between the mother and the child until birth. Further, motherhood is self-evident, whereas fatherhood must be either claimed or proved.

The fact is, we know almost nothing about the birth fathers of adopted infants and young children. Their silence is, in part, self-imposed. For example, when Silverman et al. advertised widely to develop a sample of birth parents for study, 246 women, but only five men, responded (Silverman et al., 1988). Only one study of birth fathers has appeared in the adoption literature (Deykin, Patti, & Ryan, 1988). The sample was selected from among self-identified birth fathers who were active in the adoption search movement or were members of support groups. Their voices, as they describe the unresolved pain and loss, sound very similar to the voices of similarly selected birth mothers. For example, one man volunteered, "No one thinks of the birth fathers! I hurt every day. I can't go any place without wondering. Every 15-year-old girl I see, I wonder, is she my daughter? For the last 15 years I have been living in hell. I would do anything to find her" (pp. 244–45).

This group of self-identified birth fathers challenges the stereotypes of the uncaring male and must lead us to question our assumptions about the select and unknown birth fathers who have come forward.

The voices of adoptive parents have also been heard, most frequently in organized testimony against the opening of adoption records. Many adoptive parents are fearful that the biological family will disrupt the security of their family, will threaten their relationship with their adopted children. However, other adoptive parents have been active partners in the adoptee self-help movement, have supported their son or daughter's need to search, and have found that, rather than straining the relationship, sharing this experience has brought them closer. Some adoptive parents are aware of the impact of secrecy on their families. Robert Jay Lifton, psychiatrist and adoption advocate, in a court appearance on the sealed record issues testified, "I think that continued secrecy about the information concerning one's natural parents poisons the relationship between the adoptive parents and the adoptive person. What it does is build an aura of guilt and conflict over that very natural, healthy, and inevitable curiosity. Both of them get locked into that aura of guilt and conflict concerning the whole subject" (Sorosky, Baran, & Pannor, 1978, pp. 137–8).

An interesting indication of adoptive families' interest in having more information emerged when adoption records in Pennsylvania were sealed after having been open. During the brief grace period between the enactment of the law and the actual sealing of the records of the 4,000 applications, people applied to the Bureau of Vital Statistics for a pre-adoption birth certificate; 1,000 requests came from adoptive parents (Partridge & Heller, 1988).

FROM EXPERIENCE TO THEORY TO PRACTICE

How can we, as professionals, understand the voices of those who tell us of the impact of secrecy in adoption? What theories help us place these personal statements in an interpretative framework that can then move us to therapeutic models that will be effective in helping individuals and families?

Three bodies of explanatory and practice theory appear to be particularly clarifying in thinking about secrets in adoption: one is narrative theory and social constructivism, the second is Bowen family-of-origin theory and practice, and the third is family systems theory, particularly as it relates to secrets in the family and communication, coalitions, and loyalty.

Individual and family therapists have been turning to constructivism and to narrative as a way of understanding the self and as a therapeutic model. Human beings define themselves through developing a narrative, a life story that has coherence, that takes one from the past through the present and into the future. "The development of these self-defining narratives takes place in a social and local context involving conversation with others including oneself" (Anderson & Goolishian, 1991). This social context for constructing the adoption narrative, for filling in the adoptee's story, is not available to adoptees who grew up in families that excluded anything about the adoption from family conversation. Joan Laird writes, "The self-narrative is an individual's account of the relationship among self-relevant events across time, a way of connecting coherently the events in one's own life. One's identity, then, is built on the sense one can make of one's own life story" (Laird, 1989, pp. 430–31).

The importance of the adoption story is demonstrated by the popularity of the book, *The Chosen Baby* (Wasson, 1939), written for adoptive parents to read to their children. This fictional construction is, of course, not the child's own story but was used to fill the vacuum created by the secrecy and lack of information about the adoptee's origins.

Adoptees are struggling to make sense of their life stories, to fill in the gaps, to put faces on the shadowy figures, to discover their motives, to resolve somehow the dissonance and confusion created by incomplete and contradictory information. This perspective suggests a powerful and effective therapeutic model. Adoptees need to have an opportunity to restory their lives. Interestingly enough, this therapeutic model follows the model of storying that has spontaneously developed in the adoptee self-help movement, which has made central use of narrative. An important part of their work together and of adoptee group meetings is the sharing of life stories, adoption stories, search stories.

Family-of-origin theory and practice adds another dimension to our understanding the adoption situation and extends the possibilities for intervention. First, Bowen's (1978) emphasis on the importance of the family of origin and particularly on the destructive effects of cut-offs throws light on the immense power many adoptees and birth parents have in each other's lives. He suggests that the more complete the cut-off, the more intense the involvement with the absent figure. The therapeutic method in intergenerational work of coaching clients to reconnect with important members of the family system, to move across family cut-offs and meet forbidden people, to expose secrets helps facilitate the healing potential of the adoption search process.

Finally, family systems theory informs our thinking about the devastating effect the presence of secrets in the heart of the family has on trust, on family communication, on the family's anxiety level (Karpel, 1980). Issues of origin and of identity do lie in the heart of the family. The effect of secrets on the adoptive family is similar to their effects on other families discussed elsewhere in this volume. Of particular importance in adoptive families is the constraint that loyalty places on adoptees, who experience curiosity about their origins as disloyalty to their adoptive families. "It is nearly impossible to overemphasize the significance of loyalty dynamics in the creation and maintenance of secrets," writes Karpel (p. 296). Nothing demonstrates that more dramatically and painfully than the conflict experienced by adoptees who struggle with the disloyal wish to learn of their origins. Adoptees suffer a great deal if they are unable to receive their adoptive parents' blessing, or even permission, as they explore their origins. The co-construction of the adoptee's life story, in conversation with the adoptive family in family therapy sessions can get beyond the guilt and loyalty issues, the mysteries, the fears of abandonment and betrayal.

IMPLICATION FOR PRACTICE: THE CONSTRUCTION OF THE ADOPTION STORY

Obviously, the first requirement in working with someone who has been touched by adoption is for the therapist to discover that fact. Too often, the issue is never raised. Not unusual is the story told by one birth mother: "It was pushed back into the unconscious where it proceeded to wreck havoc. My son's loss was so well repressed that 11 years later, suffering from severe and unexplained depression . . . I hadn't even mentioned to my therapist that I had surrendered a child for adoption" (Silverman, Campbell, Patti, & Style, 1988, p. 526). A careful genogram will generally expose the adoption history, wherever it exists in the family. If the therapist is sensitive to adoption issues, he or she will ask if any family members were adopted. Further, in order to discover relinquished children, it is important to ask, "Were there any other pregnancies or births?" It is important to expose information about adoption wherever it exists in the genogram. Adoption in the family may well have significance that resonates through the generations. For example, my own experience suggests that adoption and the shadowy and mysterious figure of the birth grandparents has considerable significance for the first-born child of an adoptee.

An Intergenerational Adoption Situation

Janet, a 40-year-old first-born daughter in a large family, sought help around relationship problems, identity and vocational issues, and self-esteem. Family-of-origin work first focused on her complex relationship with her father, who had died when she was 20.

As attention turned to her relationship with her mother, it became evident that there was considerable distance between them and that her mother felt very ambivalent toward her daughter. She was, apparently, much closer to and more comfortable with the other children. Janet felt that she was somehow different from her siblings. She felt as if she were an outsider. She knew that her mother had been adopted as an infant, but this was never discussed in the family.

In time, Janet got up the courage to talk to her mother about the adoption, and the two of them began to work together on getting some information about the mother's origins. It appeared that Janet's mother had unconsciously identified this first-born daughter with her birth mother, a figure shrouded in secrecy. This is understandable, because when adoptees who were relinquished in infancy have a child, it may be the first time they have seen the face of a biologically related person since they were separated from their mothers. Although Janet and her mother could actually gain very little information, talking together about the adoption and the attention to the mother's birth mother as a real person began to help the mother differentiate Janet from the lost and mysterious birth mother, diminishing the identification. Further, discussing together this crucial but forbidden topic created a new kind of closeness and sharing in the mother-daughter relationship.

It is not only important for therapists to expose the adoption history, it is also important that they don't collude in ignoring its significance. One birth mother, who relinquished a child 17 years previously, had had extensive experiences in therapy with three different therapists and, although she told each one about the child, it was never explored or considered important. Frequently, therapists join the adoptive family in denying the fact that the family is one of adoption. Some adoptees may keep the importance of adoption secret even from themselves, will resist exploration of the issues. In the face of this denial and resistance, it is important for the therapist to continue to gently challenge the adoptee and validate the right to want to know about his or her origins.

Once the adoption history has emerged as part of assessment, treatment, while it may be slow and while there may be many obstacles in the way, is not complicated. The task is to both deconstruct and reconstruct the adoption story (Hartman & Laird, 1990). This may be done through the client's gathering information, or through an actual search and the establishment of some personal contact between the adoptee and birth parents. In the long run, narrative takes place and is shared, as Anderson and Goolishian suggest, in a social context, in conversation with others.

An Adolescent Adoptee with Identity Issues

Sharon, age 14, and her family came to the Family Center for help because of her parents' alarm about Sharon's precocious sexual acting out. In the initial session, Sharon angrily refused to participate, while the loving and desperately concerned parents told of their worries about Sharon's behavior and their confusion. Everything had been wonderful until just a few months earlier, and they couldn't understand what had happened. They mentioned that Sharon was adopted but were sure that had nothing to do with the problem.

After listening to the parents' concern, I asked Sharon how old her birth mother had been when she was born. Sharon looked uneasily at her adoptive mother and responded that she didn't know. Her adoptive mother answered for her, "Nineteen." I responded to Sharon, "What's your hurry? You have five years." Although at first the parents were shocked, they then laughed and Sharon smiled a private smile.

The adoption clearly had a great deal to do with the problem. It could be said that the sexual acting out was Sharon's solution to her problem of alienation from her origins, loss, her identity struggles, and possible concerns about sexuality and fertility.

In the ensuing weeks, the primary focus was on the co-construction of the adoption story in every detail. The adoptive parents were amazed that, although they had given Sharon what information they had when she was little, she was aware of knowing nothing except that she was adopted and she came from the Southwest. By the end of the five-session contact, every step of the adoption had been recounted: the parents' discovery that they were infertile, their decision to adopt, their search for a baby, their trip to an agency in another state where Sharon was adopted, every detail of their time at the agency, and their first few days with their new daughter. They brought photograph albums, which pictured Sharon's first days and weeks with them. Sharon's adoptive mother became tense and tearful when she talked about discovering that they couldn't conceive. The parents had kept their infertility problem secret from Sharon. They "didn't want Sharon to think they were disappointed about having to adopt—disappointed in her."

They shared everything they knew about Sharon's birth parents and, most importantly to Sharon, told her that her mother, in the face of agency disapproval, took care of her infant daughter the first few days of her life. Sharon responded with considerable feeling, "You mean she held me? She really knew me?" The family talked together about the possibility of trying to find Sharon's mother. Sharon said she didn't want to do this now, but perhaps she would when she was older. The adoptive parents assured her they would do what they could to help if she ever wanted to search. The family planned to take a trip to the agency the following summer to see the adoption worker who was still on the staff, not only to fill in more details about the birth parents but also to connect with someone connected with the birth mother. The co-construction of this story in the therapeutic sessions with the adoptive parents and Sharon challenged all the secrets, eliminated tension, and improved the quality of family communication. Sharon's acting out ceased.

An Adoptee Suffering from Acute and Chronic Depression

Claire's work in therapy also illustrates the importance of constructing a coherent narrative. Claire sought help almost three years after the sudden death of her husband. A successful professional woman in her early 40's, she was severely depressed and had been unable to move beyond the loss. She was embarrassed and apologetic about seeking help. She thought she ought to be feeling better, but if anything, she was worse.

The first three sessions focused on her husband, the marriage, and her grieving. She seemed totally caught in the mourning process. In the fourth session, I realized, much to my surprise, that I had failed to get any family history. This was very different from my general way of working, and I recognized that something about the client had "warned me off" my usual path. I proceeded to ask about Claire's family and learned, after some discussion, that she was adopted. Claire was very disinterested in talking about her origins, maintaining that it was entirely irrelevant to her current grief and her situation. At this point, it would have been easy to accept her position that the adoption was without consequence.

I persisted, however, and over the next months, the story began to unfold. Claire really knew little about her beginnings except that hers was a private adoption through a cousin of her father. She supposed her birth mother was unmarried but was not sure. She thought she was about 18 months old when she was adopted and did not know where she had spent the first year and a half of her life. She was always described by her family as "sober sides," and she had seen many pictures in family albums of a grave, unsmiling toddler and child. Although Claire continued to feel this was all beside the point, I continued to turn the focus to her origins and, finally, Claire did begin to allow herself to become more curious about her past. The turning point came when, quite unexpectedly, she decided to call the cousin who had originally told her adoptive parents about her. Thus, she began to fashion a new and more complete adoption story.

She learned that her birth mother had been a good friend of the cousin. She discovered that her mother, a self-supporting working woman in her early 30's, had tried to keep her. This was long before this was an acceptable thing to do. Her mother had continued to work but kept her daughter with her in her small apartment and arranged for sitters. She had little support, except from Claire's future adoptive parents' cousin and another friend. Finally, after 18 months, she arranged the private adoption through her friend, who knew that Claire's adoptive parents were seeking a child. The fact that her birth mother had tried to keep her, against all odds, had great meaning to her. Claire began to make sense of her life story. She now understood the loss she experienced as a toddler and realized how depressed she was as a young child.

Interestingly enough, these explorations made her feel closer to her adoptive parents. For the first time she talked about the adoption with her mother and father and arranged to spend her vacation with them, something she had not done in many years. Her depression slowly abated as the original loss was discovered, explored, and validated. She began to consider searching for her birth mother.

The importance of the adoption story in a person's life is well illustrated in this case. When Claire came to therapy, her adoption was largely unstoried, secretive, and full of gaps. It carried a strong implication of rejection by her mother. She had never, within memory, talked about the adoption with her parents. The lack of information about where she had spent the first 18 months of life exaggerated her sense of discontinuity. She was ashamed of being called "sober sides," feeling it reflected her adoptive parents' disappointment in her. This shame was not unlike the shame she now felt about not being able to deal better with her husband's death. Although connections continued to be made to her current situation, the most powerful part of her work was slowly developing a new adoption story, which, in turn, gave her a very different view of herself; she constructed a new meaning, not only of her adoption but of her life.

It may also be considered that, for this client, the loss of her birth mother and her adoption was, in Daniel Stern's (1985) terms, the narrative point of origin, "the potent life-experienced that provides the key therapeutic metaphor for understanding and changing the patient's life" (p. 257).

The primary task in therapy, according to Stern, is to find the narrative point and to reconstruct that narrative. Although Claire was a mature, well-functioning woman, there was always about her the deep sense of being a lost child seeking a home. She had found a home with her husband in a fairly late marriage. His death powerfully revived the central metaphor of her life and its associated affects.

TO SEARCH OR NOT TO SEARCH

The decision of whether to search or not is one that can only be made by the adoptee or birth parent him or herself. When a search is undertaken, it is usually after a long period of consideration and of struggle with all of the intense feelings even considering a search will raise. To get to the point of making a search, adoptees must face and deal with feelings of disloyalty to the adoptive parents, as well as the fear of what they will find. The secrets around their origins have been so carefully guarded, even by law, that it can be experienced as very dangerous to dare to unlock them. Adoptees must also come to feel they have a right to search if they so desire, that their right to know their origins supersedes their birth mother's right to privacy and their adoptive parents right to cut off the birth family from the child. Birth parents also must struggle with the issue of rights. They ask themselves, do I have a right to intrude into my child's life? It is hard for many birth parents—who feel so guilty, not simply about the birth but about the relinquishment—to claim that right. Many want to leave the decision up to the child and simply try to make themselves available should the son or daughter wish to search, through giving information about their whereabouts and their willingness to be "found" to the adoption agency, or through register-ing in the adoption search computer system.[1]

It is important to help all of those who are considering a search to sort out distinctions between secrecy and privacy. Secrecy involves the withhold-ing of information from those who have a considerable and legitimate per-sonal stake in the situation. Violations of privacy, on the other hand, occur through the intrusion into the life of a person without an important reason or the communication of information about a person to those who have no major personal interest. Thus, adoptees must be helped to proceed with a search in such a way that the birth parents' privacy is protected.

For most adoptees, whether they want to try to find their birth parents or not, referral to an adoptee group can be very helpful. This, in itself, helps the adoptee feel connected, feel less different, less like a secret. As one adoptee said, "Finding other adoptees was like finding my brothers and sisters." Through participation in such groups, the meaning of being an adoptee and the individual's identity as an adoptee is clarified and elaborat-ed. Further, adoptees who have been disempowered in the adoption become empowered through joining with others in advocating for their rights and for the reform of adoption practice.

For those who wish to search, the support and help of their fellow adop-tees is crucial. Beginning a search can be a frustrating, disappointing, and disempowering experience. It takes enormous ingenuity, creativity, and dog-ged detective work to overcome the many obstacles to the search. In fact, sharing stories of the search process and of how the obstacles were overcome is very much a part of adoptee groups. The search story is, in a sense, another chapter of the adoption story, but the search story is one of power rather than helplessness, of acting in one's own behalf, of taking charge.

Although social agencies and social workers in states where there is some access to information about adoptees' origins, recommend that the adoption agency act as a mediator in the search process, many adoptees feel this is not a satisfactory approach because the search itself, going through all the work, is an important part of the healing process. Adoptees' view that they should do their own search is supported by family therapists' experience in family-of-origin work. The value lies, at least in part, in the fact that the person is doing this for him or herself. As one adoptee said after she com-pleted her search, "I feel so wonderful that I have done this for myself. It is like giving myself a gift, a wonderful gift" (Hartman, 1979).

---

[1]Many search registries have been developed under both governmental and private auspices. State-operated registries tend to limit participation. The largest, most suc-cessful, and free service, supported by the American Adoption Congress, is Interna-tional Soundex Reunion Registry in Carson City, Nevada.

The outcomes of the searches are obviously varied. Some searchers never find their birth families or children. Of those who do, a few are turned away. Some have a brief reunion but do not build a relationship, and some are able to develop a meaningful continuing connection.

Bertocci and Schechter, in their reviews of existing research on reunions, find a consensus that a completed search is perceived by most adoptees to have been of psychological benefit to them and to have improved their relationships with their adoptive families (1991). But even when the reunion does not meet the expectations of the searcher, most are glad they searched. In fact, Campbell, Silverman, and Patti (1991) found that 100% of the searchers studied (N = 114) reported they would search again.

One birth mother, reflecting on her experience, commented "On bad days, I count my reunion as another of my failures in life, but on good days, it is one of my successes — a triumph over the 'forces of secrecy'" (Silverman et al., 1988, p. 527). The meaning of the search is perhaps best summarized in the words of Robin R. Heller, President of the Adoption Forum of Philadelphia: "For all, the search is a personal journey of validity and empowerment. It is an enormously political act which flies in the face of passivity. It is the refusal to accept silence. It requires harrowing commitment to truth. It is simply one added journey adoptees take in answering the question, 'Who am I?'" (Partridge & Heller, 1988).

CONCLUSION

Adoptees, birth parents, and adoptive parents have been teaching adoption and mental health professionals about the meaning of secrecy in their lives. They have taught us how it is to *be* a secret and to have those around them keep vital, even crucial information from them. They have shown us how disempowering it is to have the law of the land deny them access to their origins. And they will teach us how to be helpful if we but listen.

Some social agencies and birth and adoptive parents are experimenting with open adoption. Open adoption has, of course, been the norm in most other countries and other times. The outcomes of open adoptions in this country will only be known as a generation of children grow up knowing their birth parents. It is essential that these children be followed and that we learn though actual experience not only how the placements turn out for all involved but also what particular strategies and arrangements predict the most positive outcomes.

Our theory would tell us that an open adoption, without secrecy and cutoffs, is better for the child's development. However, it is also more complex and more challenging. Sometimes birth parents will disrupt adoptive homes; sometimes they will abandon the child who will experience loss and disappointment; sometimes the child will feel caught between two families. We must not abandon openness in adoption because of these possibilities, but rather develop ways of helping all of the members of the adoption triangle with these relationships.

As the world changes, as adoptive parents are seeking children in foreign lands, and as scientific technology enables children to be born through sperm donorship, in vitro fertilization, and other even more dramatic methods, technology has once again outstripped our ability to understand and deal with the implications of scientific achievements. The identity, continuity, and secrecy issues in international adoption and for the growing number of children born through technological intervention, with genetic heritages other than those of one or both of their parents, challenge policymakers to clarify and protect the rights of the child.

These new circumstances will also challenge therapists who will meet these children and their families in years to come. The basic principles we have learned from adoptees and their birth and adoptive families can offer us guidance in devising ways of helping and empowering clients to deal with the consequences of these new ways of creating a family.

REFERENCES

American Adoption Congress (1990). Suggested questions and answers about open adoption records. Washington, DC. Unpublished brochure.

Anderson, H., & Goolishian, H. (In press). *The client is the expert: A not-knowing approach to therapy*. In K. Gergen & S. McNamee (eds.), *Inquiries in social construction*. Newbury, CA: Sage.

Auth, R. J., & Zaret, S. (1986). The search in adoption: A service and a process. *Social Casework, 67*, 560–68.

Bertocci, D., & Schechter, M. (1991). Adopted adults perception of their need to search: Implications for clinical practice. *Smith College Studies in Social Work, 61*(2), 169–96.

Bowen, M. (1978). *Family therapy in clinical practice*. New York: Jason Aronson.

Brodzinsky, A. B. (1990). Surrendering an infant for adoption: The birth mother's experience. In D. M. Brodzinsky & M. D. Schechter (Eds.), *Psychology of adoption*. New York: Oxford University Press.

Campbell, L. H., Silverman, P. R., & Patti, P. (1991). Reunions between adoptees and birth parents: The adoptees' experience. *Social Work, 36*(4), 329–38.

Child Welfare League of America (1968). *Child Welfare League of America standards for adoption service* (rev.). New York: Author.

Cole, E. S., & Donley, K. S. (1990). History, values, and placement policy issues in adoption. In D. M. Brodzinsky & M. D. Schechter (Eds.), *Psychology of adoption*. New York: Oxford University Press.

Depp, C. H. (1982). After reunion: Perceptions of adult adoptees, adoptive parents, and birth parents. *Child Welfare, 61*, 115–19.

Deykin, E. Y., Campbell, L., & Patti, P. (1984). The post-adoption experience of surrendering parents. *Ortho, 54*, 271–80.

Deykin, E. Y., Patti, P., & Ryan, J. (1988). Fathers of adopted children: A study of the impact of child surrender on birth fathers. *American Journal of Orthopsychiatry, 58*, 240–48.

Fisher, Florence (1974). *The search for Anna Fisher*. New York: Fawcett Crest.

Hartman, A. (1979). *Making connections* [video]. Taped at Eastern Michigan University.

Hartman, A., & Laird, J. (1990). Making connections: Family treatment after adoption. In D. M. Brodzinsky & M. D. Schechter (eds.), *Psychology of adoption*, pp. 221-239. New York: Oxford University Press.

Hooper, J. L. (1990). Adoption and identity formation. In D. M. Brodzinsky & M. D. Schechter (Eds.), *Psychology of adoption*. New York: Oxford University Press.

Karpel, M. (1980). Family secrets: 1. Conceptual and ethical issues in the relational context. 2. Ethical and practical considerations in therapeutic management. *Family Process, 19*, 295-306.

Kirk, D. (1964). *Shared fate: A theory of adoption and mental health*. New York: Free Press.

Kowal, K. A., & Schilling, K. M. (1985). Adoption through the eyes of adult adoptees. *Ortho, 55*, 354-62.

Laird, J. (1989). Women and stories: Restorying women's self constructions. In M. McGoldrick, C. M. Anderson, & F. Walsh (Eds.), *Women in families: A framework for family therapy*. New York: W. W. Norton.

Lee, R. (1963). North Carolina Family Law, Volume 3, Charlottesville, VA.

Lifton, B. J. (1975). *Twice born: Memoirs of an adoptive daughter*. New York: McGraw-Hill.

McKuen, R. (1976). *Finding my father*. New York: Coward, McCann & Geoghegan.

Partridge, P., & Heller, R. R. (Eds.) (1988). *Fifteen years of shared experiences: Fifteen questions about the search*. Philadelphia: Adoption Forum.

Partridge, P. C. (1991). The particular challenges of being adopted. *Smith College Studies in Social Work, 61*(2), 197-208.

Paton, J. (1968). *Orphan voyage*. New York: Vintage.

Raymond, L. (1955). *Adoption and after*. New York: Harper & Row.

Silverman, P., Campbell, L., Patti, P., & Style, C. (1988). Reunions between adoptees and birth parents: The birth parents' experience. *Social Work, 33*(6), 523-30.

Sorosky, A., Baran, A., & Pannor, R. (1978). *The adoption triangle*. Garden City, NY: Anchor/Doubleday.

Stern, D. (1985). *The interpersonal world of the infant*. New York: Basic.

Tefft, S. K. (1980). *Secrecy: A cross-cultural perspective*. New York: Human Sciences Press.

Wasson, V. P. (1939). *The chosen baby*. Philadelphia: Lippincott.

6

Infertility:
Private Pain and Secret Stigma

JUDITH A. SCHAFFER
RONNY DIAMOND

> Reproductive technologies make it technically possible for a child to have a total of five "parents," three types of mothers (genetic, gestational and rearing) and two types of fathers (genetic and rearing).
> — U.S. Department of Commerce, 1988, p. 213

"DON'T WORRY, SOON YOU WILL FORGET"

Charlie recently requested counseling for himself and his wife, Susan, about how to tell their preschool children, conceived by donor insemination, that they are not his genetic children, and that they have other fathers. He and Susan were seen for three sessions.

Charlie and Susan married when they were in their late 20's. They began trying to conceive a child almost immediately. When Susan did not become pregnant during the first year, they sought medical help. After a brief medical evaluation, they were told that Charlie was sterile. They were shocked by the news, for, like most couples, they assumed that becoming parents was only a matter of deciding when. Remaining childless was never an option for either of them.

Susan needed to talk to friends and family about their situation, although she felt guilty about sharing Charlie's secret. Charlie, on the other hand, kept his feelings to himself. These two styles, while often characteristic of the different ways in which men and women handle difficulties, were also related to their families of origin and their different ethnic backgrounds.

Susan was from a traditional Jewish family that she describes as open and expressive. Charlie's Irish Catholic family was one in which no one ever asked questions and feelings were rarely discussed. His family had been disrupted by the early divorce of his parents. When he was five, his mother abandoned him, and he was raised by his paternal grandmother. He didn't see his father again until he was 12.

The couple eliminated adoption as a possibility almost immediately. Although Charlie would have considered it, Susan was against adoption because she had an adopted relative "who didn't turn out so well." Because Susan wanted to experience pregnancy and birth, the option available to them was to use donated sperm (donor insemination or DI).

They approached a major medical center, "window shopping," as Charlie expressed it, to learn more about DI. He was concerned and confused about whether one could love a child conceived in this way. They were told not to worry, were advised not to tell anybody about the donor insemination, not even the child, and were assured "that soon they would forget" that the child hadn't been conceived by both of them. Susan was eager to become a parent, ready to take this step, and confident it was right for them.

In retrospect, both Charlie and Susan agree that the personnel at the medical center "conspired not to hear ambivalence." Charlie felt they were being treated as part of a research project. All that was needed for the DI to take place was a copy of their marriage certificate and money for the inseminations. He wasn't even expected to be present. No one ever mentioned or offered counseling, which they both agree they would have embraced.

Susan became pregnant almost immediately. Charlie felt increasingly alienated from the whole experience. He felt like a fraud, acting like the father. He was worried that they had told too many people of their situation. "I don't mind spreading the word about being sterile, the manhood thing isn't such a big deal, but it feels private." When he was given a baby shower at his job, he felt like he didn't deserve it. He found himself feeling resentful towards Susan and showing it in funny ways like coming late for their Lamaze method birth preparation classes, being "uncommunicative," or "forgetting" to do certain things for his wife. He feared he would be estranged from his children as he had been from his own father. "I know fathers always feel a little out of it, but I felt cheated, handicapped. . . . "

Charlie secretly hoped their first born would be a girl, so that when he looked at her he wouldn't envision the donor. When their daughter Maureen was born, Charlie said, "God, I hope I love this baby. God, I hope this baby loves me." When their son, also conceived through DI, was born two and a

half years later, Charlie felt ready for a son, but acknowledges that sometimes when he looks at Sean, who doesn't look at all like him, he "wonders
where the biological father is."

Charlie and Susan eventually sought out the advice of a counselor, as
they wanted to tell their children of their origins in the "best way possible."
Charlie worries about the impact this will have on the children, but Susan
feels they will do fine. When asked for their explanation of why Charlie is
the worrier, he immediately responds that he feels a heavier burden "because
it is because of my condition we are where we are."

Although Charlie and Susan both believe that they have a relatively good
marriage and that their children are doing well, they are convinced that the
doctors were wrong, they haven't "just forgotten." They believe that counseling prior to DI would have allowed Charlie to express his feeling of being left
out of the decision and allowed him to be more open about his reservations.
Charlie admits now that his reservations were so strong that such an open
discussion would have led to postponing DI. They both would have had to
think about living as a couple without children, and Susan would have had
to reconsider adoption. Susan related that she was well aware of Charlie's
reservations, especially with her second DI, but assumed that Charlie would
accept the child once it was born. In joining a support group of families like
themselves and seeking treatment, Charlie and Susan are exploring the many
complex issues associated with infertility and donor insemination that had
interfered with their relationship and with Charlie's relationship with his
children. They decided, through the therapy, to tell the children by the time
they reach early adolescence. Because there are no visible role models for
openness in families such as theirs, it is difficult for them to determine just
what the right age should be. Although we encourage early disclosure for
adoptive parents, it is difficult to do so with donor insemination. Here, the
stigma and risk of cruel responses from peers and others may still be too
great a burden for young children, who usually find it difficult to keep
secrets that protect family privacy.

INVOLUNTARY CHILDLESSNESS

Newspaper headlines describing advances in infertility treatment report on
methods of conception and childbearing that are nothing short of remark-
able. The most recent report concerns a woman pregnant with twins, conceived from her daughter's eggs and her son-in-law's sperm, a surrogate
mother pregnant with her own grandchildren. The social, moral, ethical,
and legal implications of these technological advances are currently under
study by ethicists, lawyers, and social scientists.

Today, it is possible for a baby to be conceived by a woman alone using a turkey baster and donated sperm, in a doctor's office, in a medical laboratory, or in an operating room. Assisted reproduction can occur using the couple's own ova and sperm (gametes) or with donated gametes and embryos. Embryos are now being created by joining sperm and ova in a petri dish and then implanting the embryo in a woman's womb (in vitro fertilization or IVF) or her fallopian tube (gamete intrafallopian transfer or GIFT). Motherhood and fatherhood can be broken down into components—genetic, gestational, and social.

While scholars investigate the meaning of these technological advances for child and adult development, identity formation, self-concept, family interaction, and society as a whole, a therapist may be confronted with clients who need immediate help. Couples may come for assistance in making decisions about infertility treatments, when they disagree about treatment, when they are having difficulty with their relationships with each other, with other family members, or with friends because of infertility, or when they must decide who to tell when a child is born from donated gametes.

WHY SECRECY?

Usually, people undergoing prolonged infertility treatment feel isolated from others as they walk a fine line between maintaining their privacy while undergoing traditional treatment or being more secretive when more controversial treatments are undertaken. It is important to remember that major religious groups, such as the Roman Catholic Church, strongly oppose noncoital methods of reproduction. Neither surrogacy nor the use of donated gametes are wholly accepted by the society. Couples rarely have an opportunity to reflect on the moral implications of what they are doing while they are undergoing fertility treatment. It is only after a child is born that the impact of what they have done may surface and cause them to question the entire process of infertility treatment in their lives. In addition, infertility specialists, as a rule, counsel their patients to be secretive, not to tell anyone, even the child (Mahlstedt & Greenfeld, 1989). For these and other reasons, couples may follow their doctors' advice and live with a profound secret.

In working with secrets, we, as clinicians, do not take the stance of openness for its own sake but are interested in understanding the function of the secret to the larger system. With secrets about parentage, the question arises of the "relevance of the information for the unaware" (Karpel, 1980, p. 298). It is the political, moral, and ethical position of the authors that people are entitled to know who are or are not their biological parents or children. When families present with a secret of that magnitude, the therapist can decide that the family's presence in her office is a request for help with disclosure.

How and when this information is shared with children and whether or not it should be shared with others is far from simple. The literature in this field is not an adequate guide because it is based almost solely on anecdotal reports, studies of clinical populations, and authors' hunches. There are no studies available on family relationships over time when children have been conceived with donated gametes and/or a surrogate has been employed. So, families are faced with a dilemma. Some will follow their doctor's orders, and others, like Charlie and Susan, will question it and seek counseling and group support in order to bring their family "out of the closet."

THE INFERTILE

We assume, as a society, that a major biological and social function of marriage is to have children. Nearly all young couples in the U.S. and Canada say that they expect to give birth to their own genetic children at some time during their childbearing years (Matthews & Matthews, 1986). An inability to do so because of infertility continues to be seen as a shameful defect and a social stigma, in spite of advances in medical diagnosis and treatment.

For couples who desperately want to have children and are unable to do so, infertility is a painful and often devastating experience. The ways in which a couple deal with this incapacity can influence their family's past, present, and future across the generations. Newspaper columnist Mona Charen recently wrote about her personal experience with infertility:

> After a while, when infertility begins to feel permanent, it robs the couple of the sense that they are participants in life. The roundness of being born, growing up, getting married, having children, then grandchildren, seems to get warped. One feels thwarted, stunted and sometimes punished. (Charen, 1991, p. 86)

Infertility is commonly defined as the inability to achieve either a pregnancy or a live birth after a year of regular sexual relations. It is widespread. Depending on the source, this significant medical and psychosocial conditions affects between 8.5% (U.S. Dept. Commerce, 1988) and 20% of couples of childbearing age. Infertility is increasing, up 10% from 20 years ago (Burns, 1987). Couples between the ages of 20 and 24 account for the greatest increase. The rate tripled between 1960 and 1977 because of the physiological effects of sexually transmitted diseases. Infertility also increases with age. One in every four couples older than 35 years old will suffer from infertility.

The infertile are an unstudied population, who seek treatment in order to achieve a pregnancy and perhaps are evaluated by adoption agencies when these efforts have failed. Sometimes, they seek counseling for marital tensions exacerbated by the stress of infertility treatment or around questions about disclosure or nondisclosure (openness or secrecy) when children have been produced through adoption or new reproductive technology. In these situations the relationship between the presenting problem and infertility seems clear. We need to wonder how often clinicians see couples and families with dysfunctional patterns of interaction where the connection to a history of infertility has neither been inquired about nor revealed.

Infertility can have a significant influence on all levels of family life. Whether a couple pursues infertility treatment, as about half of infertile couples do, or decides to remain childless; whether they undertake traditional infertility treatment or pursue new reproductive technologies where a pregnancy occurs outside of sexual intercourse; whether they will consider adoption; whether they will consider conceiving a child with donated sperm or ova, all are influenced by and influence all levels of family life. Of course many couples don't have an opportunity to make these choices. They simply can't afford to do very much about infertility. Most infertility treatment is not covered by medical insurance. Sophisticated treatment and adoption of healthy infants are provided privately and are expensive. There are waiting lists and criteria for selection. Often, these services are routinely denied to unmarried couples and individuals as a matter of course.

THE CHANGING FACE OF INFERTILITY

During the past two decades, the relationship between sex and reproduction has undergone great change. We have been able to control reproduction since the 1970's through birth control, sterilization, and legal abortion, and we have, therefore, become accustomed to seeing reproduction as separate from sexual relations. With the advent of the new reproductive technologies it is now possible to have reproduction without sexual intercourse. Herz states "sex without reproduction was a severe blow to the highly regarded societal belief in parenting as the epitome of life goals. Reproduction without sex, through various technically feasible collaborative means, further jolts fundamental traditional values and mandates their re-evaluation" (1989, p. 129). Such re-evaluation requires engaging the issues of secrecy, privacy, and openness within the usually intimate domain of a couple's sexual relationship.

In her review of the psychological literature on infertility, Burns (1987, p. 359) states that "historically, studies of infertility have focused primarily on the woman who was thought to be either hostile and overly dependent on her mother, or who aggressively initiated the male role. It was also held that infertile women were conflicted or ambivalent about motherhood, which resulted in their inability to conceive."

Even as recently as 20 years ago, the 40 to 50% of cases of unexplained infertility were routinely attributed to the emotional condition of the woman. With improved medical diagnosis, we now know that male and female biological factors contribute almost equally to infertility. Yet, women who have been studied report that they feel both guilty and responsible even when the husband is the infertile partner (Berger, 1980).

The new reproductive technologies, including IVF, GIFT, and surrogacy, have added possibility and complexity to the world of the infertile. The pattern of secrecy as it relates to many of the assisted reproductive techniques is due to a number of factors including religious and moral objections, legal questions associated with clarifying the child's parentage, and continued stigma. The Catholic Church and other orthodox religious groups morally proscribe procreation outside of sexual intercourse between husband and wife. Surrogacy is morally questionable or strictly prohibited by most major religious groups. State courts are currently considering cases of legal parentage of children born to surrogate mothers. States individually regulate the "legitimacy" of children conceived by donor insemination. Although they vary, most laws make clear that the children are to be treated as "the legal offspring of the consenting husband for legitimacy, inheritance, and support purposes" (U.S. Dept. of Commerce, 1988, p. 244).

Prior to 1975, the legitimacy of children conceived from donated sperm was not clear. Lineage and legitimacy were so problematic a woman was often inseminated by a physician other than her own, so that the delivering obstetrician could record the husband as the legal father on the birth certificate. All in all, secrecy was seen by many as a logical way of protecting the child from stigma and from feeling different. Karpel (1980) suggests that we question who, in fact, is being protected by secrecy. Although secrecy is counseled to protect the child from feeling different, it seems more likely to us that the parents are being sheltered from openly acknowledging both their infertility and the child's heritage; the physician is being protected from the complex task of counseling and educating the couple about raising a child with a different genetic parent; and our society is being helped to avoid the complex social, moral, and ethical implications of the new reproductive technologies.

In spite of the American Fertility Society recommendation that couples seek psychological services to sort out their feelings regarding infertility, few actually do (Berg & Wilson, 1990). It has been suggested that therapy is often less attractive to this stigmatized population and that support groups offer more empowerment (Berg & Wilson, 1990; Menning, 1980; U.S. Dept. of Commerce, 1988). While the medical profession still opts for secrecy, and the majority of couples are following their "doctor's orders" (Mahlstedt & Greenfeld, 1989), an increasing minority of couples are interested in openness. Resolve, Inc., a nationwide support group for the infertile, was developed to provide them with information about medical options, support, and an opportunity to *openly* share with others in similar situations.

INFERTILITY TREATMENT

Because of the rapid proliferation of treatment techniques, this is both the best and worst of times to be infertile. While there is more hope for couples about the possibility of conception, the treatments are often quite experimental, are only occasionally successful, and are very costly. In 1987, Americans spent $1 billion on infertility treatment. In 1988, the U.S. Department of Commerce reported that, while the amounts vary by state, average costs for certain treatments were as follows: initial diagnosis and fertility drug treatment, $3,668; a more complete evaluation, $2,055; tubal surgery, $7,118; in vitro fertilization, $9,376; and other individual medical treatments, more than $22,000. These costs are beyond the range of low-income families and can amount to 62% of the before-tax income of moderate-income families (U.S. Dept. of Commerce, 1988). Infertility treatment is rarely covered directly through medical insurance. Perhaps one secret regarding infertility is the societal secret that only the economically well-off can have access to treatment.

Connected to the technology of infertility treatment, but largely left unattended, are the enormous psychological and interactional issues. When is a couple to decide they have done "all they can" towards their dream of conceiving a biological child? Will they have an adequate opportunity to explore the complex emotional questions associated with raising a child not genetically related to one or both of them before making a decision to conceive in this way? When such services are not offered, stigma and secrecy are supported, albeit by omission.

ETHICAL CONCERNS

Paul Lauritzen, a professor of Religious Ethics (1990) and himself infertile, raises the dilemma of whether the choice to have children, particularly biologically related children, is really a free choice. Given the cultural milieu in the United States, the mere existence of reproductive technology may be "inescapably coercive" for infertile couples. They appear to decide freely to pursue these treatments, yet this freedom may be illusory. Lauritzen (1990) believes that genetic linkages are so important for our society, especially for men, that women are virtually required to bear or provide children for their husbands in order to experience their womanhood fully. To meet societal expectations of marriage, women must pursue treatments and procedures that, at best, are embarrassing and uncomfortable and, at worst, are humiliating, exceedingly painful, and dangerous, whether or not they wish to do so. And, to protect their husbands' infertility, they are further required to keep this secret from those who could provide them with support.

Traditionally, our culture, and physicians as its representatives, have assured couples that donor insemination is "the same as having your own," "that nobody needs to know," and "once you have your child, you'll forget how it happened." Reassurance can provide temporary comfort for an infertile couple. Secrecy and the indirect sanction of denial can interfere also with a couple's acknowledging and discussing sensitive, complex psychological issues as it did for Charlie and Susan. Discussion of the "implications of unresolved infertility, secrecy and multiple 'parents' on families can be effectively inhibited" (Mahlstedt & Greenfeld, 1989, p. 909). We question the morality and ethics, as well, of counseling a couple to deny their child's genetic and biological identity.

A SENSE OF SHAME

Couples' decisions about openness or secrecy regarding their child are made within the context of a society that views infertility and children conceived with donated gametes with suspicion, stigma, and scorn. Many couples bring to this their own sense of shame at not being able to reproduce "like everyone else." The sense of shame promotes the protective response of secrecy, which, in turn, works to maintain and prolong the sense of shame. This cycle is easily activated and difficult to interrupt, particularly without outside intervention such as support groups or therapy.

At a recent meeting, a young woman, who is being treated for infertility and is a member of Resolve, Inc., described how shame and secrecy associated with infertility had created unbearable problems for her in her social relationships. She lived in fear that strangers, friends, and colleagues would ask her "whether she had children" or "when she and her husband were going to have children." She avoided answering the questions or just made up lies. Her hidden secret made her feel "dishonest and inferior." Now, she responds with the truth, that she is infertile. She sometimes describes the precise nature of her problem and the remedies she and her husband are pursuing. She has come to believe that her previous secrecy had imprisoned her. Now, she feels like an "equal" in her relationships with others. She also believes that her honesty make it possible for other people to be sensitive and empathetic. She is convinced that her secretive and protective response to infertility created problems for her that were as damaging as the infertility itself.

Marriage usually provides a private world, yet for the infertile, these barriers are constantly being transgressed, by the "well-intentioned" questions of family and friends or the medical interventions of specialists. Infertility, as a life crisis, can sometimes go on for years, leaving couples in a state of "suspended animation." According to Burns (1987), for certain couples, this kind of "boundary ambiguity" may complicate the normal life-cycle transitions families undergo. Because of the "fantasy child" who is psychologically present, but physically absent, such couples may defer important decisions such as career changes, home purchases, and travel. Women undergoing long-term infertility treatment often report that they are frustrated by being able to neither experience parenthood, nor pursue alternative sources of satisfaction actively (Slade, 1981). It is important for the clinician to understand that these difficulties are a possible, but not necessary, response to infertility. A number of studies of couples undergoing long-term infertility treatment report that, although they are frustrated by infertility, their marital and other relationships are affectionate, strong, and supportive (Callen, 1987; Humphrey, 1975; Kipper et al., 1977).

Until only recently, textbooks on family life defined life-cycle stages by parenthood. Childbirth of the first born is often seen as the couple's rite of passage into adulthood. For some couples, infertility can prevent a shift in loyalty from the family of origin to the new family. In failing to differentiate, the families may remain enmeshed. Just as couples are frustrated in their efforts to become parents, their own parents may be frustrated in their efforts to become grandparents and mentors, and their siblings may be frustrated in their desire to become aunts and uncles. Often, emotions and thoughts regarding the intergenerational pain of a couple's infertility remain secret and unspoken.

"MARRIAGE MEANS HAVING CHILDREN"

Linda and John are a young couple in their late 20's, who have been married for four years and who have been trying to give birth to a child for three years. They both come from large Italian-American, Roman Catholic families, and all of their brothers and sisters have several children. They both assumed that they would have children as well. A marriage without children was something that neither of them had ever even contemplated. Linda has had several miscarriages, and it has become more and more likely that she will be unable to carry a child to term.

When they first decided to have children, they were so excited they told "just about everyone we talked to," Linda recalled. It was after her first miscarriage, when they had to call everyone back to report the bad news, that they decided to keep things more to themselves. Increasingly, they found the "well-intentioned questions of family and friends" to be insensitive and hurtful. "People are always asking us what's new," says John. Because nothing is new, they have begun to avoid family events especially when pregnant relatives or babies will be present. They stopped even telling people when Linda was pregnant and then when she miscarried. Neither of them has told anybody that childbirth is likely to be impossible for Linda.

They came into couples' therapy, because Linda was growing more and more depressed and isolated from others and having trouble leaving the house. John reported that he "walks on egg shells," never sure that what he says will be interpreted as he means it. They were fighting all of the time. Although John said that he tries to be available to Linda, his work schedule had increased over the years, and he was rarely at home. John wants therapy to "leave no stone unturned." Both think they are headed for divorce.

Linda and John had become isolated from their extended network of supports as well as from one another. They described themselves as separate individuals within a marriage. He, like many men in conflict over infertility, reacted with transient impotence and withdrawal. Linda felt hopeless, defective, guilty, and angry.

When couples such as Linda and John seek therapy, they have often lost a sense of perspective, and feel isolated, hopeless, and uniquely impaired. The secrecy they have imposed has forced them to rely exclusively on each other for support and understanding, placing a great strain on their marriage. They have no idea about a "healthy" way of being an infertile couple together or in relationship to their families and their friends. John and Linda believed that living as a couple without children would only be a brief transitional stage in their marriage.

Their individual experiences of infertility were both different and similar. John couldn't begin to understand how Linda felt month after month and year after year as she waited to see if she were pregnant and, when she conceived, if she could maintain the pregnancy. Each month she was on an emotional rollercoaster going from elation to depression. John was uncomfortable talking about his own sadness, because he worried that Linda would feel guilty, and so he kept his feelings secret and distanced from her. Linda knew that John could have a child in a different relationship and worried that she would lose him.

Normalizing a couple's experiences regarding the impact of infertility is very useful and can be done in a number of direct and indirect ways. Storytelling can be a powerful way of universalizing experiences and, in so doing, options can be indirectly offered. With Linda and John, the notion was seeded that some couples find it helpful to put medical treatments on hold, so as to be able to recapture what they liked about each other before they became vehicles for creating a baby. Linda and John were also reminded that their different ways of responding to this crisis were characteristic of the ways men and women often respond to difficult life events. Books and articles were suggested describing personal experiences with infertility. As a normalizing intervention, they were referred to Resolve, Inc., so that they could meet other couples like themselves.

Reframing interventions were useful and productive. We reframed their fighting as their way of protecting one another from the terrible pain of not being able to give birth to a biological child. We further reframed their isolation from their families and friends as their way of being "private" rather than keeping secrets. We acknowledged that they felt guilty, as though they were keeping secrets. To address their feelings of disloyalty to their well-intentioned families and friends, and to allow them more contact with those who could be supportive, we helped them to redefine their privacy by deciding themselves who they would talk to regarding their situation.

A final intervention involved a mourning ritual around the loss of their wished-for biological baby. Not knowing how to mourn for the babies who had miscarried kept the couple suspended in time, with no hope for the future. Linda and John were instructed to talk together periodically about their baby and what she or he would have been like. Whose characteristics would the baby have, whose eyes, hair, smile, etc? When they had really allowed their baby to come alive, we helped them devise a symbolic funeral, so they could let the baby "rest in peace." They were to decide whether to include family and friends, and which ones. In this way, their grief was framed as "private" rather than shameful and secret. As Imber-Black et al. (1988) suggest, rituals are important markers for families, and yet, with infertility or miscarriage there are no socially sanctioned ways to mourn and hence to move on.

PUTTING A LIE AT THE CENTER OF THE MOST BASIC RELATIONSHIP

The adoption world has been slow to accept the importance of telling children of their origins in spite of the public nature of that event, and the real risk of revelation. For adoptive families of today the question isn't "Do we tell?" but "When do we tell?" The dilemma for families whose children have been conceived by donated gametes is not only that their secret is very secure, but that secrecy is sanctioned at all levels of society.

Secrecy can affect a child's sense of belonging to a family (Kramer, 1982), family members' feelings of entitlement to one another (Hartman, 1984), and parents' feelings of competence (Kral et al., 1989; Schaffer & Lindstrom, 1991). Secrecy can affect communication, trust, and cognition, and create tension around the possibility of unanticipated disclosure. Secrecy also has been implicated in the failure of some families to negotiate life-cycle transitions successfully (Talen & Lehr, 1984). Mahlstedt and Greenfeld (1989) caution

> Since the parent-child relationship is probably the most powerful of human bonds, clarity about the meaning of biological and social parent is essential especially for the social parents. The reality in the use of donor gametes is that there are more than two "parents" involved in the conception. Though this reality may be kept secret from others, it can not be changed nor denied by the couple nor, in some cases, by the (known) donor. Therefore, when discussing donor conception, couples must acknowledge that there is a third "parent" whose "presence" will always represent a unique loss to each of them, but whose psychological significance isn't really understood. (p. 912)

As clinicians who have worked with hundreds of adoptees and their families over the past 20 years, we have treated families who have kept the "secret" of adoption from their children for many years. It has been our experience that "the secret" organizes the family into those who know (the parents and perhaps others) and the child, who is mystified. One adult adoptee, who learned, when she was 25 years old, that she was adopted, described her childhood as "always feeling just on the outside of the family looking in, and never knowing why." Adoption research clearly indicates that when families can openly acknowledge adoption, family interactions are likely to be healthier (see Hartman in this volume, Chapter 5).

While similar in some ways to adoption, infertility and its remedies pose different moral as well as psychological issues for decisions regarding secrecy and openness. Should a couple create a child through a process that they believe is shameful? What are the implications for parenting? Would such shame maintain if couples were counseled about openness rather than encouraged to be secretive with their children? A child should be able to trust that her parents will accept how she came to them and tell her important truths. What does it mean to the parent/child relationship when a lie is at the center of it?

There are virtually no studies on the effects on parenting after infertility or on the effects on parenting of conception with the use of donated gametes. Secrecy is thus replicated at the level of scholarly research. Burns (1987) postulates certain dysfunctional adjustments to infertility, usually associated with shame and secrecy, such as triangulation, parental overprotection, child-centered marriages, enmeshment, marginal person status, and self-defeating, obsessive behaviors. In 1990, she suggested that couples with a history of problems in infertility are likely to have more marital, individual, parenting, and child problems, as reported to her by a small volunteer sample of parents who had been infertile. She hypothesized that the parental attitudes towards infertility, *not* the way the children joined the families, accounted for these difficulties. Mahlstedt and Greenfeld (1989, p. 910) propose that when parents have to lie to their children while they are growing up, "the lies are harder to maintain and require energy which takes away from resolving personal struggles and building trust."

CLINICAL CONCERNS

From our clinical experiences in working with secrecy and infertility, two broad categories of families emerge. The first are those couples, like Linda and John, whose dysfunctional adjustment, including secret-keeping, to reproductive failure has escalated into intense marital discord and disharmony. They come into therapy for help with the marriage. The clinician helps them to sort out the interrelationship between the infertility and their relationship to one another and the outside world. We have certainly seen many adoptive families like this, as well. The second category of couples are those, like Susan and Charlie, who have conceived through donated gametes or other new birth technologies. Their struggle is over the fine line between privacy and secrecy and whose rights are to be protected—the parents' rights to privacy or the child's rights to know his or her genetic heritage.

With couples like Linda and John, the most effective therapeutic techniques are those that are direct, respectful, and build on the strengths of the system regardless of which model the therapist chooses to use. Brief, solution-focused therapy and Milan systemic models have both been employed by the authors and been successful in working with these kinds of problems.

Couples like Charlie and Susan benefit most from an educational approach. This allows the family to acknowledge that their form of family building, although different, is normal. These couples may need help to define the boundaries around their private world and to decide who they will tell and who they won't tell about their infertility. This is a population that has been pathologized and stigmatized. Normalizing their experiences with infertility helps them to avoid the perception of pathology.

In summary, Mahlstedt and Greenfeld (1989) insist that secrecy about one's beginnings is particularly difficult to justify, as it places a lie at the center of the most basic of relationships—the one between parent and child. We fully endorse this position.

REFERENCES

Berg, B. J., & Wilson, J. F. (1990). Psychiatric morbidity in the infertile population: A recon-ceptualization. *Fertility and Sterility, 53*(4), 654–61.

Berger, D. M. (1980). Couples' reactions to make infertility and donor insemination. *American Journal of Psychiatry, 137*(9), 1047–49.

Burns, L. H. (1990). An exploratory study of perceptions of parenting after infertility. *Family Systems Medicine, 8*(2), 177–89.

Burns, L. H. (1987). Infertility as boundary ambiguity: One theoretical perspective. *Family Process, 26*, 359–72.

Callen, V. J. (1987). The personal and marital adjustment of mothers and of voluntarily and involuntarily childless wives. *Journal of Marriage and the Family, 49*, 847–56.

Charen, Mona (1991, July 17). Adoption's not easy, but it works. *New York Newsday*, p. 86.

Grolnick, L. (1983). Ibsen's truth, family secrets, and family therapy. *Family Process, 22*, 275–88.

Hartman, A. (1984). *Women with adopted families*. New York: Child Welfare League.

Herz, E. K. (1989). Infertility and bioethical issues of the new reproductive technologies. *Psychiatric Clinics of North America, 12*(1), 117–31.

Humphrey, M. (1975). The effect of children on the marriage relationship. *British Journal of Medical Psychology, 48*, 273–79.

Imber-Black, E., Roberts, J., & Whiting, R. (1988). *Rituals in families and family therapy*. New York: W. W. Norton.

Karpel, M. A. (1980). Family secrets: I. Conceptual and ethical issues in the relational context. II. Ethical and practical considerations in therapeutic management. *Family Process, 19*, 295–306.

Kipper, D. J., Zigler-Shani, D., Serr, D. M., & Insler, V. (1977). Psychogenic infertility, neuroti-cism and the feminine role: A methodological inquiry. *Journal of Psychosomatic Research, 21*, 353–58.

Kral, R., Schaffer, J., & de Shazer, S. (1989). Adoptive families: more of the same and different. *Journal of Systemic and Strategic Therapies, 8*(1), 36–49.

Kramer, D. (1982). The adopted child in family therapy. *American Journal of Family Therapy, 10*, 70–73.

Lauritzen, P. (1990). What price parenthood? *Hastings Center Report*, March/April, 38–46.

Mahlstedt, P. P., & Greenfeld, D. A. (1989). Assisted reproductive technology with donor gametes: The need for patient preparation. *Fertility and Sterility, 52*(6), 908–14.

Matthews, R., & Matthews, A. M. (1986). Infertility and involuntary childlessness: The transi-tion to nonparenthood. *Journal of Marriage and the Family, 48*, 641–49.

Menning, B. E. (1980). The emotional needs of infertile couples. *Fertility and Sterility, 34*, 313–19.

Schaffer, J., & Lindstrom, C. (1991). *How to raise an adopted child*. New York: Plume.

Slade, P. (1981). Sexual attitudes and social role orientations in infertile women. *Journal of Psychosomatic Research, 25*(3), 183–86.

Talen, M., & Lehr, M. (1984). A structural and developmental analysis of symptomatic adopted children and their families. *Journal of Marital and Family Therapy, 10*, 381–91.

U.S. Department of Commerce, National Technical Information Service (1988). *Infertility: Medical and social choices*. Washington, DC: U.S. Government Printing Office.

Wendorf, D. J., & Wendorf, R. J. (1985). A systemic view of family therapy ethics. *Family Process, 24*, 443–53.

7

Death: The Most Troublesome Family Secret of All

LORRAINE M. WRIGHT
JANE NAGY

"The only thing that really dies is death."

—Anonymous

"Let us accustom ourselves to regard death as a form of life which we do not yet understand."

—Maurice Maeterlinck

DEATH IS THE MOST troublesome family secret of all. Death does not elude any family member of any race, color, or creed. Death shows no mercy for age. Death can come suddenly, unexpectedly, or after long anticipation. But death never gives the hour of its arrival; it is always a secret. Death invites family members to keep its secret hidden; to live as if dying is not part of living. Death challenges and confronts every belief about life. But death is weak in its ability to prevent humankind from mourning, grieving, and fearing its arrival. Such is the experience of families facing a life-shortening illness. A life-shortening illness invites families to live being afraid of dying rather than to live being united against the secret of death.

How can health-care professionals deal with the secret and mystery of death with families who are experiencing a life-shortening illness? This chapter presents one approach, namely Systemic Belief Therapy, to dealing with the deadly secret of death.

CONTEXT FOR CLINICAL PRACTICE

Family Nursing Unit

The context for the clinical work that is described in this chapter is the Family Nursing Unit (FNU), Faculty of Nursing, University of Calgary. The FNU is an outpatient education and research unit devoted to the interactional study and treatment of families experiencing difficulties with health problems (Wright, Watson, & Bell, 1990). Families experiencing difficulties coping with a life-shortening illness are often part of our clinical practice. Therefore, we have had a variety of experiences dealing with the secret of death. We wish to emphasize that working with families experiencing impending death has not become easier over the years. However, through the process of working with these families, we have developed greater respect and appreciation for what it means to live with the knowledge of impending death. We attempt, within our own clinical nursing team and with the families with whom we work, to deal openly with the mystery and secret of death. In doing so, we have witnessed some very courageous efforts by families to stand up to death, expose it, and deal with the secret of never knowing when death will come.

SYSTEMIC BELIEF THERAPY

The Therapy Model

Systemic Belief Therapy, conceived, developed, and practiced at the Family Nursing Unit, focuses on the interaction between the health problem and family members' beliefs about the health problem (Wright & Simpson, 1991; Wright & Watson, 1988; Wright, Luckhurst, & Amundson, 1990; Wright, Watson, & Bell, 1990). One main assumption underlying all our clinical work is that *the belief about the problem is the problem.* This assumption is very similar to the first-century philosopher, Epictetus. He wrote that "men are disturbed not by things, but by the views which they take of things. Thus death is nothing terrible, but the terror consists in our notion of death, that it is terrible. When, therefore, we are hindered or disturbed, or grieved, let us never impute it to others, but to ourselves—that is, to our own views" (Higginson, 1948, p. 19).

When families present at the FNU, efforts are made to invite new beliefs or views of the health problem, in order to broaden the range of solution options. Distinctions that both families and health care professionals make about "health" and "illness" are believed to be subjective judgments made by observers about this adaptation (Maturana & Varela, 1992). We are concerned with understanding the recursive interactions between health/illness and family beliefs. We respect that each family should function the way that they desire and in a way that they determine is most effective. As part of a larger system, however, the FNU team members recognize that they are bound by moral, legal, cultural, and societal norms that require them to act in accordance with those norms regarding illegal and/or dangerous behaviors.

Through the medium of therapeutic conversations with families, we draw forth beliefs through the asking of questions by *both* client and interviewer (Wright, 1990). Families coevolve an ecology of beliefs, which helps each of the individuals to define cognitions, behaviors, and emotions. During the assessment phase, we attempt to elicit each family member's beliefs about the etiology, treatment, and prognosis of the illness. In addition, we assess their beliefs about control of the symptoms associated with the illness. Beliefs shape the way families adapt to life-shortening illness. Following the assessment, the therapist makes distinctions between constraining and facilitative family beliefs.

Constraining beliefs arise from social, interactional, and cultural contexts. Constraining beliefs inhibit the autonomy of the individual and the family by restricting options for alternate solutions to problems. Constraining beliefs may be challenged by health-care professionals introducing new connections between beliefs and behaviors, which may draw forth facilitative beliefs from family members. Change occurs when there is a shift in the constraining beliefs. The family's ability to change depends upon their ability to alter their beliefs about the problem.

Efforts are made also to assess any constraining beliefs held by the therapist that may hinder a family's ability to deal with the secret of death. Health-care professionals are confronted about their own beliefs about immortality when a life-shortening illness presents itself. Impending death also challenges our professional beliefs about our ability to alleviate suffering and grieving. In both the family and treatment systems, the "meaning" assigned to death becomes paramount. Prior to middle adulthood, few people think about their own deaths. Pattison (1977) suggests that serious consideration of death constitutes projection of "a trajectory of our life." A life-threatening diagnosis, a "crisis knowledge of death," changes the family life trajectory. As this life trajectory is changed, our innermost beliefs about life and death are confronted and challenged.

BELIEFS ABOUT DIAGNOSIS

Both the nursing and medical professions have been given the privileged power of making diagnoses. However, a diagnosis only becomes meaningful in an interactional context. A diagnosis is an interactional event that occurs when one person (the medical or nursing professional) assigns a classification to another (the identified patient) (Glenn, 1984). At the time of diagnosis, the patient, family, and health-care system enter into a contract regarding the health problem. Among the most powerful implications of a life-shortening diagnosis are the patient's and family's beliefs about it. Unfortunately, health-care professionals too often do not seize the time of diagnosis as an opportunity to begin a discussion about death. Frequently, health-care professionals have colluded amongst themselves and made decisions that families should not be informed about the possibility or inevitability of death. This presumptuous behavior is based, in our opinion, on health-care professionals' belief that families will find it too emotionally burdensome to deal with the knowledge of impending death. In our clinical practice we have experienced quite the opposite. Families find it *less* troublesome to deal with the knowledge of a life-shortening illness and consequently *impending* death when we deal more frankly about our inability to predict the *time* of death. Unfortunately, impending death often invites health-care professionals to behave as if they know death's secret, i.e., when the time of death will occur.

However, there does exist a trend by health-care professionals to be less constrained and to inform families of the prognosis of impending death. Perhaps to be even more helpful as health-care professionals, we need to give our professional judgment regarding prognosis in a manner that focuses on living rather than on trying to ascertain the time of death.

Our clinical team has witnessed both small and major miracles with families experiencing life-shortening illness as they deal more openly with the prognosis of *impending* death and the inability to *predict* the hour of death. By being more explicit about the secret of death, that is, that *no one* can predict the time and hour of death, we begin to demystify death. We must emphasize to our clients and their families that they are entitled to life as long as they are living. We must also emphasize that prognosis is based on clinical expertise and medical science; it is not based on an objective knowledge of when death will occur. When the secret of death is no longer kept hidden in family conversations, new and different interactions may take place between family members, which may facilitate the healing of wounded relationships. When families engage in new conversational experiences, they may find they appreciate a "quick" death when there has been great physical pain, or they may be thankful for a slow death when there has been emotional pain, in order for emotional healing to occur.

Just as each person's grief is unique, so is each person's *anticipation* of loss. The anticipation of loss is a functional response, usually related to how other family members are preparing for it. Thus, one family member's denial may be more a relational than an intrapsychic phenomenon.

To appreciate more fully our clinical approach to assisting families who are confronting death, we present the following narrative:

ONE FAMILY CONFRONTS THE DEADLY SECRET OF DEATH

Frank, the grandfather in the Watt Family, called the FNU to make the first appointment and identified that the presenting problem was the experience of sexual abuse of his grandson, John. From age three to 11, John was sexually abused by his stepfather's cousin. McGoldrick (1991) suggests that it is not surprising, because of denial of death in our society, that many clinical cases involve loss even when it is not the presenting problem. John is presently living with his grandparents, Alice and Frank. John's mother, Anne, is a 37-year-old homemaker married to Bob, who is 35 years old and unemployed. Anne and Bob have been married for 12 years and have one child from their union, Kevin, age 12. Anne has two children from previous relationships, Peter, age 20, and John, age 16. John and Peter have minimal contact with their biological fathers.

Our Clinical Work: The Beginning of the Story

John attended the first session with his grandparents, Alice and Frank. Alice inquired if the sessions were confidential as, "John's parents don't

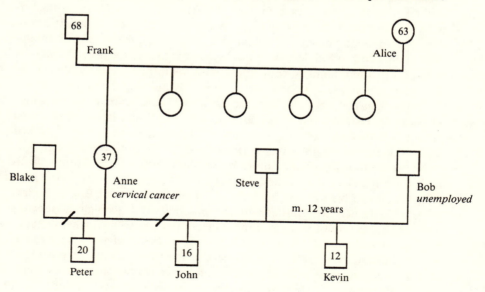

Figure 7.1

know that we are here." John added that he wanted to keep the sessions a secret from his mother and stepfather because "they won't feel like they are part of my life and besides I don't want mom to worry." Our clinical nursing team then learned that John's mother, Anne, was diagnosed seven years ago with cervical cancer. Anne recently had a re-occurrence of the cancer and had been extremely ill. Several significant beliefs surfaced regarding the impact of Anne's illness on the family. John stated that: "Mom's cancer and her pain has destroyed our family." The prognosis of Anne's illness, which had not been discussed among family members or with health-care professionals, emerged as another "secret" in the family.

In our clinical work with families, the phenomenon of health-care professionals not discussing the prognosis with the patient and/or family members is a common occurrence. Family members have their own beliefs, which may have been influenced by the medical system about the length of life, but death remains the ultimate secret. By asking circular questions, the interviewer sought to explore the impact on John of his mother's illness (Tomm, 1988). John related that he frequently felt sick to his stomach and found it difficult to concentrate at school.

In families experiencing a life-shortening illness, there is an increased likelihood of emotional and/or physical symptom development when family members are unable to openly discuss the impending death (Herz Brown, 1989). Even though parental roles are much less differentiated than in past decades, a mother's terminal illness at this stage of the family life cycle has different implications than a father's. "Disturbance of archetypal nurturance and security relationships with the mother creates deep anxiety about future satisfaction and care in the family" (Bahnson, 1987, p. 38). Terminally ill mothers often feel despair at not being able to care for their children. It is important that families with terminally ill mothers develop alternative nurturant resources. This is important not only because the mother cannot fill that role as fully, but also because she herself needs care or "mothering." These shifts in roles tend to be easier in less traditional families, but each family discovers its own unique solution. However, when the prognosis of impending death remains a secret, these resources cannot be generated.

Based on this significant information about Anne's life-shortening illness, our clinical team hypothesized that the extensive involvement of John's grandparents in his life had inadvertently invited Anne and Bob to be less involved in his life. We wrestled with the possibility that keeping the sessions a secret between John and his grandparents might serve to further distance his mother and stepfather from his life. Karpel (1980) refers to this type of secret as an internal family secret where at least two people keep a secret from at least one other person. Internal family secrets can create or strengthen boundaries and alliances within the family between secret-holders. Our clinical team decided that as the Watt family had firm beliefs that were organizing their behavior in regards to who presented at the family sessions, our clinical team would be less directive and invested in who attended sessions. Through Systemic Belief Therapy, we hoped to challenge some of their beliefs in an effort to influence the other key family members to participate in the sessions.

In exploring the circumstances of how John had come to live with his grandparents, it was revealed that Anne and Bob had had an abusive and violent relationship throughout their marriage. John believed that his mother's illness was related to the continual marital conflict between his mother and stepfather.

This belief of John's is also held by our clinical research team (Wright, Watson, & Bell, 1990) through our study of the relationship between illness and family dynamics (Watson, Wright, & Bell, in press; Wright, Bell, & Rock, 1989). We believe that our ontogenic history (all of the past structural changes that occur throughout our history of interactions) is as equally significant as our phylogenic history (genetic or evolutionary history) (Maturana & Varela, 1992). However, it is within the domain of family interactions that we have an opportunity to intervene by facilitating conversations of affirmation and affection among family members (Wright, 1991). Maturana (personal communication, October, 1988) offered the following poignant comment about this connection: "The only thing that I know is that love is a fundamental emotion in human beings. And I consider the most human diseases, most human suffering arises from interference with these fundamental emotions."

John's grandparents believed that their grandson did not need confrontations with his parents on a daily basis and that their daughter was too sick to be a mother to him. John's move to live with his grandparents was viewed by our clinical team as an attempt to distance himself from the emotionally charged situation of his mother's life-shortening illness and his parents' constant fighting. We also wondered if John and his grandparents were attempting to protect Anne and preserve her strength because she was presently very ill.

Herz (1980) suggests that when facing a life-shortening illness, families will attempt to reduce emotional tension. In the Watt family, the lack of discussion regarding Anne's prognosis was creating emotional and even physical distance between John and his mother. Herz (1980) believes that the degree of disruption to the family system dealing with a life-shortening illness is affected by four major factors: "1) the timing of the serious illness in the life cycle; 2) the nature of the serious illness; 3) the openness of the family system; and 4) the family position of the seriously ill family member" (p. 224). Applying Herz's perspective to the Watt family would indicate a high degree of disruption. The life-shortening illness of John's mother is occurring at a time in the life cycle that does not follow the normative course of life. "The timing is off; it is out of sync" (Herz Brown, 1989, p. 464). When a serious illness occurs in family members who are in the prime of their lives, the experience can be *the* most disruptive to the family (Herz Brown, 1989; Rolland, 1990; Wright & Leahey, 1987).

During the first session, the therapeutic conversation also centered around John's experience of sexual abuse. John had disclosed his "secret" to his grandfather in the week before their first therapy meeting. John had previously received treatment for the sexual abuse when he was 12 years old, but Frank believed that treatment had been inadequate. Frank was also very concerned and upset that he had not been told earlier about the sexual abuse that John had experienced as a child. He could not understand why John had kept this secret from him for so long. During the session, it was learned that Alice had always known about the sexual abuse, but had never shared the secret with Frank.

At the end of the first session, it is a routine part of our practice to ask each family member the "one question question" (Wright, 1990) i.e., "If you could have only one question answered through our work together, what would that one question be?" John responded by asking: "Who am I? Once I tear down the wall I have built up, how do I keep it down?" Alice and Frank responded with, "What can we do to help?" We believe that soliciting questions from clients often reveals their constraining or facilitative beliefs and their most pressing concerns that may otherwise go overlooked. As therapists, we can only ask what we know to ask. By inviting clients to ask questions of us as therapists, we are taken into another domain of clients' belief systems.

At the end of the first session, Alice and Frank were commended by our clinical team for the caring, respectful, and nonjudgmental attitude that existed among the three of them. John also was commended for his openness and was told that, in the opinion of the team, he had been both tyrannized by illness and betrayed by an adult. We agreed with the family that there were many issues to pursue; betrayal by an adult in the form of sexual abuse and the impact of a life-shortening illness on the family.

The Middle of the Story

In the third session, John came by himself. He informed us that, after our last session, he had initiated a talk with his mother about his strained relationship with his stepfather. John stated: "I started to think about the situation from my dad's perspective." The therapeutic conversation from the previous session appeared to have influenced John to consider a new view.

We explored John's new perspective about his stepfather by asking, "What will this new view of Bob invite you to think or do differently?" John responded that he would talk differently to him and go over and visit more. Very quickly, John proceeded to discuss the issue most pressing for him: "Everyone believes I have so many problems. My only problem is having everyone worry about me. Grandpa drives me crazy because there is always something about me that he wants to fix. Ever since I told grandpa about the sexual abuse, suddenly I became a teenager that really needed help." John had a desire to live with his grandparents, but to lead his own life.

In the next session, Alice wanted to come on her own. Again, although our clinical team believes that systemic work can be accomplished with only one family member present, we struggled with the family's desire to have members seen individually. We were concerned that the pattern of seeing family members individually might serve to increase the potency of the secrets. However, our clinical team decided to let the family direct both the pace and direction of change (Wright, Watson, & Bell, 1990), of which one aspect was who would come to sessions.

Alice relayed the news that her husband, Frank, had been hospitalized for a cardiac condition and that Anne, her daughter, was receiving radiotherapy to shrink the tumour in her pelvis. Alice listed a great many things that John did with which she and Frank did not agree. The impact of John's behavior on Frank and Alice's life was explored. Alice stated that she thinks it is "too big a job to look after John" and that she is "too old for this." Alice expressed that they rarely showed their anger or disappointment in John's behavior, because they did not want their home to resemble the hostile environment that he experienced at his parent's house. It is interesting to note that the fact that his grandparents were not pleased with John's behavior was kept a secret from John. The team introduced the idea that it seemed that there were many different people interested in parenting John. Distinctions of parenting and grandparenting were made by our clinical team. We offered the opinion that "we would recommend taking a holiday from parenting for the next few weeks and focus on grandparenting. This may help you get through the next difficult weeks with both Frank and Anne in the hospital." Our clinical team hoped that our opinion would serve to promote Alice's facilitative belief of becoming more of a grandmother to John and less of a mother. Alice responded that she had been thinking about being more like a grandparent to John and less of a mother. It is this alternative view which may shift a family's outlook and increase the variety of responses possible in a situation.

In session five, Alice and John arrived at the session together looking relaxed and happy. John reported being left more on his own to make his own decisions. Alice reported that she had felt more like a grandmother, but that she was not in agreement with some of the decisions that John had made. She believed that a 16-year-old was just too young to have free rein.

Frank, who had recently been discharged from hospital, came to the sixth session with two main concerns. First, he was concerned about the relationship between John and his daughter, Anne. Mother and son were fighting a lot, and John appeared to be angry with his mother much of the time. The therapist focused on exploring Anne's role in John's life and the family's beliefs about that relationship. Frank believed that John thought his mother was going to die shortly. Frank believed also that Anne would like to be more involved in John's life. The interviewer asked Frank, "Is there a belief in the family that Anne is too sick to deal with concerns about John?" Frank stated that was indeed the case. However, he further stated that Anne had a lot of insight and empathy for John. The team hypothesized that John's belief that his mother was going to die soon perpetuated his desire for distance from the family. The increased conflict between John and his mother enabled them to keep distant from one another. We believed that it was not only the knowledge of impending death but also the secret of the actual *time* of death that propelled the need for more distance. Recursively, the more difficulties that John experienced, the more Anne attempted to be close to him. Her behavior may also been driven by her beliefs that she might not have long to live and that John needed her help.

Herz Brown (1989) suggests that the intensity of long-term illness is hard to deal with on a continuing basis because of the difficulty in maintaining a balance between living and dying. Often, when the family and the dying individual attempt to protect each other from anxiety, they stop communicating. The lack of communication creates tension and distance, which can be manifested in a variety of symptoms. "The longer and more intense the family stress is, the more difficult it is for the family relationships to remain open and the more likely it is that dysfunction will develop" (Herz Brown, 1989, p. 473).

In this session, the reflecting team (Andersen, 1987) was utilized to offer the idea that it would be beneficial to include Anne in John's life and in our sessions. Frank commented that he could now "see" that Anne had been a missing part of the sessions and that he would approach his daughter and ask her to attend the next session. Finally, the team would have the opportunity to meet John's mother who, despite her absence, had been a powerful presence.

The Turning Point of the Story

In the seventh session, the team had the opportunity to meet Anne. She came by herself to the session, and our clinical nursing team was immediately struck by her frail appearance and her tremendous desire to help her son.

She eagerly reported that "I wanted to be in on this counselling because our family needs help, John needs help, and I need help in helping John." We now felt that with the presence of Anne in the sessions, a context for change had finally been created.

Anne expressed concern that her son had lost interest in everything. Anne believed that John must be angry at her for being sick for so long. She also believed that not knowing *when* she was going to die was the most difficult thing for John to handle. While Anne was explaining her perspective she became tearyeyed. When the therapist explored her related affect, she replied, "I am feeling worried and guilty about John because of my husband and I — we have really messed him up." At the end of the session, our clinical team commended Anne for her concern, insight, and empathy for John. The team validated Anne's perspective as being valuable and offered the opinion that John could be experiencing extreme fear and grief in response to Anne's impending death. Anne felt that she would like to return with John for a session the following week.

The Climax of the Story

Indeed, mother and son came to the next session together. During this session, we learned that one of John's school friends had been killed in a car accident. As well, he had recently left high school because he found it too difficult to concentrate. John described his friend's death as the "straw that broke the camel's back." He told the team how depressed and hopeless he felt when his friend died. "His death showed me that I could lose everyone. But I am feeling much better now because I realize that I have supportive friends who care about me and that I like myself. I also know mom is worried about me, but I just want her to know that I'm okay."

Providing an opportunity to discuss an impending family member's death can be a significant intervention when working with families experiencing a life-shortening illness. The discussion may facilitate the release of new information into the family system helping the family to face the impending family member's death (Wright & Leahey, 1987). Herz Brown (1989) believes that the life-threatening illness of one family member can allow the family, if the system remains open, to resolve significant relationship issues.

In exploring John's understanding of Anne's prognosis, the team learned that John had found the secret of not knowing his mother's prognosis was the most difficult aspect for him to handle. "When you have no clue, you feel like your life is being played with. I'd rather mom died, I could accept that." The uncertainty and the secret nature of the time of death is, for many families, more difficult than the death itself. Toward the end of a long illness, it is not unusual for the dying individual and the family to wish for death (Herz Brown, 1989; Rolland, 1990).

Anne raised her concern that she did not feel a part of John's life. The therapist sought to understand if John believed that his mother was too ill and would feel too burdened if he shared more of the stresses of his life with her. John agreed that he thought his mother was too ill to handle his problems. His stepfather had recently reinforced this belief by telling John not to worry his mother because she was "too sick to cope."

The therapist explored ways that Anne could be more involved as a mother in John's life. The conversation quickly deteriorated into one of accusations and recriminations (Wright, 1991).

JOHN: I know you want me to move home, but I can't, it's like an emotional holocaust. There's problems everywhere, between you and Dad; you are sick; Dad feels guilty because you are sick, and no one is happy with me and who I am. I don't want you involved in my life.

ANNE: (sobbing) I realize that it's too late to have the kind of family that I always wanted. There's too much bitterness, anger, and hatred. I had just hoped that we could work on putting our family back together.

JOHN: I feel totally guilty.

Suddenly, John asked to leave the room. While he was out of the room, the therapist took the opportunity to inquire whether Anne was feeling as worried as she had been at the last session about John's behavior. Anne reported that, from her perspective, John's behavior had improved.

When John returned to the session, the urgency he felt to tell his story was evident. The conversation gradually shifted to one of mutual affirmation and affection.

JOHN: What am I supposed to do? You are sick and I know that you want to have the family that you've dreamed about. But should I put myself back into an emotional holocaust? I don't want to get messed up again. But, at the same time, my mom is sick, and I love you. What if you die, how can I live for the rest of my life knowing that the one thing my mom wanted never came to be?

ANNE: You are right John, I don't think you should come home. I'm crying because of my own personal guilt about the past, not because our family isn't together and you won't come home. I don't blame you.

As the session progressed, John and Anne began to bridge the emotional and physical distance that had existed between them. John shared with his mother how pleased he was about the reduced conflict between him and his stepfather and that he felt closer to his family now than ever before. John also wanted his mother to know that "I am fine, and I've turned out well."

The therapist then asked Anne if there was anything that she would like to say to John. Anne told John how impressed she was with his thinking and that he knew a lot more about what he was doing than she had previously realized. John tenderly responded by reaching out and taking her hand.

A major transition occurred in the session when John spontaneously reframed their past sorrows.

JOHN: Another way to think about our life, Mom, is that if none of this had happened, we would not be the same people that we are today.

ANNE: I hope that we can use all the garbage that's gone on to our benefit rather than let it destroy us.

JOHN: The way I look at it, Mom, I am like a piece of coal, and through all the pressure it becomes a diamond.

The therapist entered the conversation, again by asking John and Anne what they had come to appreciate about each other and what their hopes were for the future. John commented that he appreciated his mother's strength and the way that "she really fought for our family." John hoped that, in the future, Anne would remember that he loved her and that he was okay. Anne also expressed that she hoped John would know how much she loved him. She also hoped that they would be able to have a better relationship in the future because of all that they had learned about each other during this session.

Reflections on Our Clinical Work

In the first several sessions, John's grandparents believed that John's problems were related to his early childhood experience of sexual abuse. However, as the sessions progressed, it became apparent that John's primary concern was the lack of control over his life related to his mother's illness and prognosis. The uncertainty of his mother's chances of survival produced his fear of impending death. Once the inability to predict the secret of death was verbalized, it allowed a healing process to begin between mother and son.

The underlying beliefs that were driving particular family members' behaviors took time to identify and conceptualize. The other secrets that were operating within the family had to be addressed before the secret of death could be confronted. Change, which Bateson (1972) describes as "difference which occurs across time" (p. 452), happened very gradually throughout the sessions. From our previous clinical experience of working with families experiencing a life-shortening illness, this is not an uncommon occurrence.

To stand up to the secret of death takes tremendous courage and tenaciousness. A dramatic story was unfolding.

A significant transition point in our clinical work was the use of a reflecting team (Andersen, 1987), which challenged the constraining belief that
Anne was too sick to be involved directly in John's life. The reflecting team
is a powerful intervention as it allows family members to assume a meta-
position to their situation and provides them with a reflection of their
beliefs. If the alternate perspectives, beliefs, and opinions offered by the
team are relevant for the family, they will select an idea that can influence
them to view their situation in a different way. The idea offered by the
reflecting team fortunately influenced Frank to entertain the possibility of
Anne being involved in further sessions. Our clinical team believed that
Anne was the critical missing family member. Once Anne became involved
in sessions, a significant turning point had been reached and a context for
change was created.

We view health problems as interactional dilemmas derived from family
beliefs. Family beliefs organize family behavior. Anne's belief that she was
responsible for John's problems, and John's belief that his mother was going
to die and his emotional turmoil resulting from not knowing *when* she
would die, created an interactional dilemma of mother and son inadvertently distancing from each other. The secret nature of Anne's prognosis, and
the fact that the family had not discussed it, intensified the interactional
dilemma between mother and son. The life-cycle stage of this family also
contributed to the interactional dilemma as the primary developmental task
of adolescent separation conflicted with the anticipated loss, which requires
families to move emotionally closer to support one another (McGoldrick
& Walsh, 1991). The poignant and beautiful healing session with mother
and son was facilitated by the therapist providing a context in which conversations of accusations and recriminations were altered to conversations
of affirmation and affection (Wright, 1991). As the conversation between
Anne and John shifted to one of affirmation and affection, it was evident
that Anne was entertaining a new belief about her son, that he was "okay."
As well, John's recognition of the pain and guilt that his mother felt about
the past, as well as the love she had for him invited new facilitative beliefs
about his mother. By altering Anne and John's beliefs about each other, new
stories were created about their relationship and themselves. When new
stories are created, old beliefs are refuted.

John's metaphor of the coal becoming a diamond was a poignant vehicle
through which he was able to express what was previously inexpressible. By
making the implicit explicit, John and his mother were able to begin the
healing process. Further, John's metaphor about himself was hopeful as it
implied that he was beginning to answer his question from the first session,
"Who am I?" It was the team's hope that the open communication that had

been re-established between John and his mother would help him to keep down the wall he had built around himself.

Rolland (1990) suggests that making peace with self and family is a fundamental task in coping with threatened loss. Unresolved issues of blame, shame, or guilt can seriously compromise movement towards healing relationships. "Threatened loss, by emphasizing life's fragility and preciousness, provides families with an opportunity to heal unresolved issues and develop more immediate, caring relationships" (Rolland, 1990, p. 242). However, we feel that the secret of death is *the* controlling factor in a family's ability to face the impending loss of a family member. Once family members can stand up to death, then there is the opportunity to be united against its secret.

With regard to the future, the team wondered if the change in the relationship between John and his mother would influence other relationships in the family. Also, now that Anne had come to believe that John was all right, would her death come more quickly? At the time of the writing of this chapter, Anne continues her courageous effort towards surviving. Her time of death continues to be a secret.

CONCLUSION

A life-shortening illness of a family member is a highly emotional and challenging experience. Our clinical work with the courageous family described in this chapter indicates the role of constraining beliefs surrounding the interaction between family members and their secrets, uncertainty and loss of control around a life-shortening illness, and more importantly beliefs about death. Systemic Belief Therapy focused on identifying those beliefs that were constraining and providing alternate facilitative beliefs for the family's consideration. Alternate beliefs were introduced in the form of interventive questions by the therapist *and* family members, opinions of the clinical nursing team, and the use of a reflecting team. With the caring context provided by our clinical nursing team, mother and son were able to stand up to the secret of death and begin to heal their relationship. Through assisting families to unite against the secret of death, we have observed immeasurable courage and faith in families as they face one of life's greatest challenges: the challenge of living with the knowledge of dying.

> Who never mourned hath never know,
> What treasures grief reveal,
> The sympathies that humanize,
> The tenderness that heals.
> — Anonymous

Postscript

Anne's time of death is no longer a secret. She died "peacefully" three months after the completion of our clinical work.

REFERENCES

Andersen, T. (1987). The reflecting team: Dialogue and meta-dialogue in clinical work. *Family Process, 26*, 415–428.

Bahnson, C. B. (1987). The impact of life-threatening illness on the family and the impact of the family on illness: An overview. In M. Leahey & L. M. Wright (Eds.), *Families and life-threatening illness*. Springhouse, PA: Springhouse Corporation.

Bateson, G. (1972). *Steps to an ecology of mind*. New York: Ballantine Books.

Glenn, M. L. (1984). *On diagnosis: A systemic approach*. New York: Brunner/Mazel.

Herz, F. (1980). The impact of death and serious illness on the family cycle. In E. A. Carter & M. McGoldrick (Eds.), *The family life cycle: A framework for family therapy*. New York: Gardner.

Herz Brown, F. (1989). The impact of death and serious illness on the family life cycle. In B. Carter & M. McGoldrick (Eds.), *The changing family life cycle: A framework for family therapy* (2nd ed.). Toronto: Allyn & Bacon.

Higginson, J. W. (1948). *Epictetus, the enchiridion*. New York: Macmillan.

Karpel, M. A. (1980). Family secrets: I. Conceptual and ethical issues in the relational context. II. Ethical and practical considerations in therapeutic management. *Family Process, 19*, 295–306.

Maturana, H. R., & Varela, F. J. (1992). *The tree of knowledge: The biological roots of human understanding*. Boston: New Science Library.

McGoldrick, M. (1991). Echoes from the past: Helping families mourn their losses. In F. Walsh & M. McGoldrick (Eds.), *Living beyond loss: Death in the family*. New York: W. W. Norton.

McGoldrick, M., & Walsh, F. (1991). A time to mourn: Death and the family life cycle. In F. Walsh & M. McGoldrick (Eds.), *Living beyond loss: Death in the family*. New York: W. W. Norton.

Pattison, E. M. (1977). *The experience of dying*. Englewood Cliffs, NJ: Prentice-Hall.

Rolland, J. S. (1990). Anticipatory loss: A family systems developmental framework. *Family Process, 29*(3), 229–244.

Tomm, K. (1988). Interventive interviewing: Part III. Intending to ask lineal, circular, strategic or reflexive questions? *Family Process, 27*, 1–15.

Watson, W. L., Wright, L. M., & Bell, J. M. (in press). Osteophytes and marital fights: A systemic approach to chronic pain. *Family Systems Medicine*.

Wright, L. M. (1991). *Therapeutic conversations: From accusations to affirmation*. Unpublished manuscript.

Wright, L. (1990). When clients ask questions: Enriching the therapeutic conversation. *Family Therapy Networker, 13*(6), 15–16.

Wright, L. M., Bell, J. M., & Rock, B. L. (1989). Smoking behavior and spouses: A case report. *Family Systems Medicine, 7*(2), 158–171.

Wright, L. M., & Leahey, M. (1987). *Families and life-threatening illness*. Springhouse, PA: Springhouse Corporation.

Wright, L. M., Luckhurst, P., & Amundson, J. (1990). Family therapy supervision as counter-induction. *Journal of Family Psychotherapy, 1*(3), 65–74.

Wright, L. M., & Simpson, P. (1991). A systemic belief approach to epileptic seizures: A case of being spellbound. *Contemporary Family Therapy: An International Journal, 13*(2), 165–181.

Wright, L. M., & Watson, W. L. (1988). Systemic family therapy and family development. In

C. J. Falicov (Ed.), *Family transitions: Continuity and change over the life cycle* (pp. 407–430). New York: Guilford.

Wright, L. M., Watson, W. L., & Bell, J. M. (1990). The Family Nursing Unit: A unique integration of research, education and clinical practice. In J. M. Bell, W. L. Watson, & L. M. Wright (Eds.), *The cutting edge of family nursing*. Calgary, Canada: Family Nursing Unit Publications.

III

SECRECY AND SYMPTOMS

8

On Lies, Secrets, and Silence: The Multiple Levels of Denial in Addictive Families

JO-ANN KRESTAN
CLAUDIA BEPKO

A SECRET IS SOMETHING hidden or concealed. The keeping of a secret blocks the flow of information between people, and in this sense, it deprives them of knowledge of what is true. Sisela Bok speaks of the outcome of secretive behavior: "To keep a secret from someone . . . is to block information about it or evidence of it from reaching that person and thus from possessing it, making use of it, or revealing it" (1983, pp. 5–6).

Sometimes we keep secrets as a way of having fun, with the intention to later surprise and delight another. But more often, secrets create a breakdown of relatedness. They undermine intimacy, they confuse and distort, they create difficult and unnecessary tensions.

The complex nature of secrecy in an addictive family is, in fact, at the heart of the problem. Dysfunctional behavior, such as drinking or drug taking, sooner or later may become absolutely overt. The best-kept secret, however, is the concealment of the meaning and consequence of that behavior. The failure to name the problem as a problem — in short, denial — has the same effects Bok speaks of when she refers to keeping secrets: the blocking of evidence that prevents a person from possessing information, revealing it, or *making use of it*. It's in this conundrum that the addictive family system is stalled; there is an inability to share or make use of the secret that everybody knows.

LEVELS OF DENIAL

Denial as a form of secretive behavior operates at many levels in the addictive family. At its core, denial begins in the form of a lie: "No, I don't drink," "I only had a couple," "No, I never use drugs," "I didn't go to the party where everybody was drinking, I was at my friend's house," "No, I never tried cocaine."

In some instances, the *fact* of alcohol or drug use is acknowledged, but its problematic nature is denied. Ultimately, the lie moves from creating an interactional distortion of reality to creating an internal one: "My drinking isn't a problem. I'm not losing my job because of my drinking, it's because my boss hates me. So, I get a few speeding tickets, so what. So, I 'borrowed' some money from the savings account, I'll put it back next month." Eventually the person engaged in the process of denial begins himself to believe the lies he tells others.

This basic lie, "I'm not doing what I'm doing," or "What I'm doing doesn't have the consequences it appears to have," eventually leads to more profound forms of secret-keeping. One begins to tell lies to cover up other lies. The drinker may hide extramarital affairs, other forms of sexual acting out, illegal behaviors perpetrated in the interests of financing drug use; he may deny health problems related to drug use; he may go to extraordinary lengths to hide and manipulate financial debt; he may even secretly gamble in an attempt to raise money or to cover debts.

As lies and secrets deepen, so does the distortion of affect. The deepest and most complex level of secrecy in the addictive family manifests as silence—the absence of all forms of direct communication about feeling. Secrecy ultimately demands a withdrawal of emotional "presence" from the relational context. The secret keeper is "missing in action"—his or her physical presence in the family belies the fact that his or her emotional presence has been either withdrawn totally or completely distorted by misrepresentation, defensiveness, or extreme reactivity that functions to protect the secret.

Lies create secrets, silence maintains secrets, and secrecy feeds denial. The three concepts are inextricably linked in describing the process of increasing distortion and invalidation of experience that occurs within the family system. As an outgrowth of lying, secretiveness, and silence, denial lies at the core of any discussion of addictive process.

THE ROOTS OF DENIAL

The concept of denial is an entrenched part of the folk wisdom of the twelve-step programs of Alcoholics Anonymous and Al-Anon. The alcoholism treatment community has reified and generally embraced denial both as a behavioral characteristic of the alcoholic and as a diagnostic indicator of alcoholism. The statement, "he's still in denial," conveys a clear message to all who speak the language of addiction. It means, "he's still keeping his problem a secret from himself and, hence, the first stage of healing is being blocked."

Theoretical literature on the nature of denial is sparse, but denial is generally defined in psychodynamic terms as a mechanism of defense (Bean, 1981; Forrest, 1985; Nace, 1987; Royce, 1981; Wallace, 1977). As Bean says, "Denial has its origins in early attempts of the organism to obtain relief from painful external stimuli or the painful affects generated by them" (Bean, 1981, p. 73). She points out that denial, as a defense mechanism, may be both adaptive and pathological.

Nace (1987) outlines in detail the "adjunctive defenses" that support or enhance denial: rationalization, projection, minimizing, avoidance, and delaying. Nace contends that the process of denial must be understood as having four important characteristics: It is largely unconscious and, in this sense, differs from lying or deliberate deceit, it protects the option to drink (or drug), which is experienced as a life and death necessity, it prevents a fragile sense of self from being overwhelmed by reality, and it equally protects the ego from an overwhelming sense of hopelessness and despair.

Forrest (1985) believes that the defensive structure of the addicted person functions to help him avoid intimate human encounters as well as intimate contact with his own feelings. Understanding the protective power of the denial system, John Wallace warns against a premature dismantling of it: ". . . denial is there for a purpose. It is the glue that holds an already shattered self-esteem system together. And it is the tactic through which otherwise overwhelming anxiety can be contained" (Wallace, 1977, p. 15).

From this perspective, the secrecy or denial of the addict can be seen as not so much a deliberate behavior but as a functional one, a protective mechanism employed in the face of massive fears of breakdown, of "coming apart" in response to the pressures of reality. Nace points out that the physiological effects of alcohol on memory tend to reinforce denial. Blackouts, "euphoric recall," and memory lapses related to chronic intoxication all aid in the process of "forgetting" and, thus, maintaining the secret.

DENIAL IN THE FAMILY

From this perspective, it becomes equally clear that the corresponding denial that evolves within the family system is motivated by the family's need to maintain itself in the face of deepening fears of "coming apart." Secrecy begets secrecy and denial operates as well at the level of lies, secrets, and silence for other family members. "No, my husband doesn't drink," "No, my child would never take drugs," "Yes, of course he drinks, but it isn't a problem." Hangovers may be dismissed as a "virus." More insidiously, the inadequate functioning of the alcoholic is met with "benign" disregard, and others in the family simply do more to "hide" its impact. When the reality of alcohol or drug use is acknowledged, spouses or children deny or rationalize that it has impact or meaning for the others in the family.

Eventually, family members adopt their own "secretive" behaviors. They hide bottles, empty them, or mark levels so they can monitor the progress of the drinking. When their fears of alcoholism are confirmed, however, they may keep the evidence to themselves and suffer alone, keeping from anyone else the secret they've uncovered. A mother fails to tell her husband about their son's drug use. A daughter doesn't tell her mother that she saw her father drinking at a local bar. In other words, one response to the alcoholic's secretiveness is a reciprocal engagement in secretive behavior on the part of other family members. Children in the family may begin to act out secretly; they may stay away from home or refuse to tell anyone where they've been. Spouses hide money, find devious ways of protecting the alcoholic from the consequences of the drinking. They make excuses for the alcoholic's behavior, they intervene with bill collectors, with extended family members. They may engage in furtive relationships with friends or extramarital partners and essentially develop hidden "lives of their own" to protect themselves from the deep anxiety they experience because of the alcoholic or drug user's behavior. They may secretly begin to use drugs or alcohol themselves.

Children may keep lethal secrets having to do with incest or sexual abuse. As the family progresses to deeper levels of dysfunction, the necessity of maintaining secrecy becomes more compelling because the threat of "coming apart" becomes more ominous. Most significantly, family members know that they must never reveal the "secret" of the problem to anyone outside or even anyone else *inside* the family.

Maintaining these secrets feeds denial: What is hidden doesn't really exist and doesn't have to be discussed. Family members, along with the addict, begin to believe their own lies, so that when one says, "This didn't happen," or "I didn't drink too much," the protective veil of secrecy permits the person to believe that the denial actually represents truth. Addiction becomes a secret that everyone keeps from themselves and from one another. Communication and interaction in the family takes on a highly "crazy" and distorted quality. The resulting tension results in increased drinking, drugging, or compulsive behavior on the parts of other family members.

Ultimately, silence rules family life. Emotional secrecy between and within family members becomes the norm. Claudia Black (1981) commented on this dynamic when she first referred to the messages not to "talk, trust, or feel" that dominate an addictive family. Secrecy or denial is maintained by silence. All members of the family withdraw from one another emotionally.

In the process, capacities for mutual need satisfaction and nurturing go undeveloped. The family oscillates between extremes of deep silence and lack of engagement and periods of extreme reactivity that mask authentic emotion. One emotion is expressed as something else: Anger becomes violence, sadness becomes anger, fear becomes anger, despair becomes a deep need to control, dependency becomes shame. Real feelings remain hidden and unexpressed.

FACTORS THAT MAINTAIN DENIAL

Families develop the denial process both internally and interactionally and the secret is maintained in many "locations" and by many different dynamics. Drug abuse may be denied by the user, by one or more family members, and it may also be denied and maintained by the larger "helping" and medical care system. Ultimately, though this may be less the case currently, denial in a family can be affected by our culture's more general failure to acknowledge the reality of the ongoing impact of addiction.

Internal states of shame and fear are among the dynamic processes that maintain denial, as are the physiological impact of the drug use, the general adaptive patterns within the family that include over- and underresponsible behavior, triangulation and loyalty to intergenerational patterns, and larger systems dynamics that include professional denial.

Denial as a Form of Adaptation

In 1954, Joan Jackson described the phases that evolve in the family in response to abusive drinking. Hers was the first work to acknowledge that the behavior of other family members in the face of the "crisis" of alcoholism has an adaptive rather than a causative function. Specifically, her phases detail the evolution of secrecy and denial and their defensive counterparts: minimization, avoidance, overresponsibility, and emotional withdrawal. In her paradigm, denial and avoidance constitute the first phases of adaptation. Marital interaction becomes strained as a result of drinking and, gradually, most other problems "go underground"—they are avoided or denied. As the family struggles to keep the problem a secret, increasing social isolation occurs. Self-esteem in the family is eroded, and a developing atmosphere of shame and fear contribute to greater silence. Eventually, attempts to control the problem are abandoned, and the spouse and children reorganize as a unit from which the drinker is excluded. The spouse or one or more children take on almost total functional responsibility. The problem is never discussed, or is acknowledged only between certain dyads in the family with the result that intense triangles form, further eroding family stability.

The degree to which the family retreats into silence about addictive behavior can be extreme. One client tells the story of being lined up with her 10
siblings in the backyard to be interrogated about a broken vase. Their alcoholic mother proceeded to beat each of them with a strap. What was most
amazing to the client was that, even though she and her siblings suffered
through many such abusive incidents together, they never mentioned to one
another their awareness of their mother's drinking.

This story demonstrates a point that Mark Karpel (1980) made in an early
paper on secrecy: Secrets deprive family members of relational resources.
While the stance is maintained that no one can talk about the problem
behavior, family members deprive the drug user of appropriate reality-based
feedback about the effects of his behavior. As Ruth Maxwell (1976) says,
"Without a message from reality the alcoholic has *no other choice* but to
continue drinking. As long as he believes he *can* drink, he *cannot stop
drinking*."

But more significantly, family members fail to find any relief from their
own and one another's fear and shame. They become increasingly disconnected from one another and the developing closed system becomes insulat-
ed against feedback that would address the distortion of reality taking place
within it. In other words, just as it does for the alcoholic, the secrecy deprives the family of information that would allow them to take action.

In some families, the mandate to secrecy is an extension of intergenerational rules or patterns and can be affected by ethnic or cultural norms.
People hide information because they feel it would be disloyal or a betrayal
to expose it. Some families have strong injunctions against "airing dirty
laundry in public." In WASP or Irish families, for instance, where, as a
general rule, emotionality is often tightly contained, the presence of a
shameful secret only intensifies silence.

One client came to treatment because her whole early life had been literally "shrouded in secrecy." She experienced intense conflict to the point of cut
off in her relationship with her father. She did suspect, or had been convinced by friends, that alcoholism might be a factor in their relationship.
But more important was the generally "secret" nature of their family life.
Her father had worked for the CIA and was considered an expert at "covert"
operations. At various points during her childhood he had disappeared,
having been captured for a time by the enemy. When he returned, his behavior would be changed dramatically, he would refuse to talk about what had
happened and, ultimately, he and his wife divorced. The client lived with a
total mystery: What had happened to her father, was he mentally ill, alcoholic, what had been done to him, did the problem have something to do
with her? No believable explanation was ever provided for her, and, as an
adult, it had never occurred to her to ask him directly. Other family mem-

bers seemed equally deprived of information and could only speculate and concoct plausible stories about him.

When her father finally came for a family session, much of the mystery was cleared. He did have a problem with drinking, the exact events of his career with the CIA were discussed, but, most significantly, he described an almost identical history of secrecy and "cover up" in his own family. Various family members had apparently been mentally ill and hospitalized, but this was never discussed. He had come to learn that one did not talk about such things, least of all feelings, and that secrecy was a norm. He had many of his own mysteries still to uncover. It had never occurred to him to talk to either his children or his wife about his experiences early in their marriage.

While the "covert operations" in this family seriously deprived this client of relational information that was crucial to her own sense of herself, a more interactional impact was the intensity of the triangle that ultimately evolved among her, her mother, and her father. Having essentially been abandoned first by her father's silence and then by his withdrawal from the family, she became closely allied with her mother. In the face of the devastating impact of denial and secrecy, she may have had little choice. But nevertheless, triangles also deprive one of relational resources. This client's struggles with a sense of loyalty to her mother were to have a deep impact on her later ability to relate to her father as well as to her husband.

In many ways in this family, the impact of alcoholism was perhaps less significant than the impact of secrecy surrounding it. In the absence of clear and authentic communication, this client could only guess at the truth about herself and the nature of relationships within the family. Essentially she made up "stories" about what might be true. Such vagueness left her with poor measures for testing reality and poor skills for understanding or experiencing meaningful connection with others. It lead to impoverishment of a core sense of herself. As processes that maintained the addiction, secrecy and denial were more damaging to the relational process than the drinking itself. And in the face of a serious breakdown of connection, the drinking was bound to intensify.

Finally, on the level of interactional adaptation, overresponsible behavior (Bepko with Krestan, 1985) is a major factor in maintaining denial. Over-responsibility protects the alcoholic from the consequences of his under-responsibility, and it equally protects the family from truly acknowledging the extent of the problem. If he can't pay the mortgage and she works two jobs to make up for it, they don't lose the house and family stability appears to be maintained. What the family gains in short-term relief from the deep fear and anxiety that they experience is undercut by the longer-term devastation that will develop as drinking or drug use progresses. The family settles for sustained crisis rather than facing the real crisis of change.

Overresponsible behavior is damaging on one level because it maintains underfunctioning and all the concrete and emotional consequences that such imbalance entails. But the more damaging impact of overfunctioning is that it helps to maintain the secret and thus prevents the family from acquiring information that would help them take action.

Ashamed, Afraid, Drunk

The interactional dynamics that maintain secrecy and denial both create and arise from negative internal experiences of shame and fear. Shame is inextricably linked with the maintenance of secrets and is always a characteristic of addictive systems. *Drug or alcohol use may function as a defense against shame and anxiety, and denial arises as a secondary system of defense against the shame and anxiety generated by the drug use.* More shame generates more drug use generates more shame in a circular process that increasingly rigidifies the need to deny.

Interactions between family members in addictive systems become dominated by shame-based, defensive operations geared towards protection of each member's very fragile sense of self. Shame is the experience that one's self is inadequate and insufficient, somehow "less than" or bad. Fossum and Mason (1986, p. 8) write, " . . . a shame-bound family is a family . . . with a cast of characters who are (or were in their lifetime) loyal to a set of rules and injunctions demanding control, perfectionism, blame and denial. The pattern inhibits or defeats the development of authentic intimate relationships, promotes secrets and vague interpersonal boundaries, unconsciously instills shame in the family members, as well as chaos in their lives, and binds them to perpetuate the shame in themselves and their kin." When one feels shame, one is equally frightened that the shameful secret will be revealed. Anxiety about acknowledging alcohol or drug use can operate on this emotional level and on a very practical level as well. Female spouses often fear that saying their husband is alcoholic means they must leave. Economically, this may not be a realistic option. Children and spouses often fear physical violence if they speak the "truth" about drinking behavior. The husband of the alcoholic wife often worries about the difficulty of finding adequate child care if he leaves his wife or if she needs to get treatment for her problem.

Fear is a powerful motivator, and the primary fear is often anxiety about separation and change. Denial and secrecy are supported by the larger fear of change. But the physiological characteristics of drug use tend to aid in the ongoing denial process precisely because they allow for the intermittent relief of anxiety. The drug user relieves anxiety by ingesting the drug. The corresponding memory loss, sense of euphoria, and blackouts, all help him forget that he was frightened or that there was any negative or painful consequence or antecedent to his drug taking.

The family experiences heightened anxiety when the drinker drinks. But, one day later, the drinking binge is over. These time lapses between incidents of drunkenness or drug-induced crisis permit anxiety levels to relax to more normal levels. At this point, the more pervasive fear of change along with rationalization and minimalization set in: "It really wasn't so bad," "He doesn't have that big a problem," "He hit me yesterday, but today he's being sweet." One easily "forgets" the despair of the day before in the relief generated by the passing of the immediate crisis. This selective "forgetting" maintains denial and secrecy.

Denial in the Professional

Attitudes toward addiction and alcoholism have undergone a radical revision in recent years as we gain more knowledge and as the problem gains more visibility. In effect, this grave social "secret" has been exposed. But, until very recently, it was not unusual for professionals to hold some highly dysfunctional attitudes themselves towards alcoholics. Among those attitudes were beliefs that alcoholics were sociopathic, incapable of responsibility, or untreatable. Professionals also persistently ignored the existence of alcoholism and focused on other symptomatology. Given the shaming and denial around this problem that were pervasive in the mental health community itself, it's not unusual that a family or individual's denial could easily be maintained by a health-care system that often failed to diagnose addiction, proceeding often, like the family, to call it something else.

In spite of the explosion of attention to addictions that has been generated in the wake of the Adult Children of Alcoholics movement, family therapists are still vulnerable to certain forms of denial. Misdiagnosis, failure to look carefully for addiction in all families and to suspect it until it is explicitly ruled out, and erroneous assumptions that family therapy is adequate in itself as a treatment for addiction are all forms of therapeutic denial. The latter form of denial can arise from our tendency to therapeutic arrogance and our denial that we need to make use of other resources across a continuum of treatment. Such arrogance may be supported by our failure to thoroughly understand the dynamics of addiction.

But the continuing tendency to misdiagnose is frequently a function of denial of our own problems with alcohol and drug use. The "impaired professional" continues to be a major problem in the provision of services to addictive families specifically and all families in general (Bratter, 1985).

Our professional roles often become protective veils of secrecy for our own problems, particularly with alcohol and drug use. Within our work settings or within professional organizations, out of a kind of misguided loyalty to "one of our own," we tend not to confront colleagues, we maintain the "secret" by not discussing the problem with others or by speaking about it in derogatory ways, and we deny in our colleagues or in ourselves the impact of behavior we might easily diagnose in our clients. This secrecy becomes grist for triangulation, gossip, and indirect exclusionary behavior. It creates relational breakdown at a professional systems level, and that breakdown ultimately affects our work with clients.

As professionals, we should commit ourselves to openness when we become aware of the addictive problem of another medical or mental health worker. We need to encourage clients to confront their own suspicions about us or other professionals directly. We must be willing to make use of helping networks available for impaired colleagues.

CLINICAL APPROACHES TO DENIAL AND SECRECY

In most cases the treatment of addiction *is* the treatment of secrecy and denial. Treatment of addiction is always phase related and, in general, it may be useful to conceptualize those phases as addressing the three levels of denial outlined in this paper: lies, the outright denial of drug use or abuse; secrets, the hiding of dysfunctional behavior related to the drug use; and, finally, silence, the emotional distortion and withdrawal that evolves in response to shame and fear. These phases apply to treatment of the individual addict, treatment of the family system of the addict, or both. When addressing the first phase, in which lying is the operative form of secrecy, it is critical to remember that this behavior is a defense against overwhelming feelings of shame and fear.

The Stance of the Therapist

Many different approaches to working with denial in the addictive system may be effective if they assume that a primary goal is to break through denial. But therapists often fail to successfully deal directly with the secrecy that pervades the family dynamic because they are trained to respect the client's presenting problem and "start where the client is." Therapists who are highly respectful of the family's own pace of change may be comfortable with a constructivist approach, which gently introduces the subject of problem drinking into the conversation, but they may be uncomfortable with using their position as an "expert" to directly encourage disclosure. Bowen family systems practitioners may view tracking the problem drinking through three generations as equivalent to diagnosing and addressing the alcoholism; they may assume that talking about the problem effectively prepares the family to take action about it. Inexperienced systemic therapists often restrain alcoholics from change in a way that really countenances the continuation of drinking and associated domestic violence or serious family dysfunction.

These outcomes represent pitfalls to be avoided in various approaches. It's important to examine the ways that different models of therapy and of clinical practice help to maintain secrecy and to minimize the impact of addiction within the family. As Michael Elkin (1984, p. 79) says, "When dealing with alcoholic families, it is important to understand that they are suffering from a condition that is not only dangerous to their own physical and emotional well-being, but that of others. They are teaching their children patterns that may be taken up by following generations. It is important that the counselor feel responsible to intervene whether or not any or all of the family members 'seek help.'"

Our own stance is always a direct one: to state that the family seems to have a problem with alcohol or drug abuse and that it needs to be addressed before other family problems can improve (Bepko with Krestan, 1985). Essentially, we take responsibility for exposing the lie or unearthing the secret and work with the inevitable resistance that will follow. Our goal is to make information accessible that will allow the family to take a different action.

What follows then is a summary discussion of interventions based on the premise that the family therapist is responsible for diagnosing the addiction and for treating the family's denial of it. If in doubt, the therapist is responsible for arranging a consultation with an addiction professional for the purpose of establishing that diagnosis.

Providing the Family with New Information

On rare occasions, an alcoholic will seek treatment for his alcoholism directly, but denial surfaces when it is suggested that he needs additional help from the self-help community or an addiction treatment program. Frequently, the addict asks for help with his addiction but then minimizes and rationalizes its scope or impact as the therapist pursues a more detailed discussion of it. But more commonly, the therapist hears a different presenting problem and must take the initiative in suggesting that alcoholism or drug abuse is part of the picture.

Spouses and other family members more often define the problem as one of addiction but may start treatment with concerns about an acting-out adolescent, learning problems in younger children, marital problems, or the full range of symptomatology and suffering that any family presents. Here, too, the therapist must take the initiative in assessing for and then targeting the addiction as a focus of treatment.

Denial is maintained on a purely cognitive level in the family by lack of information and by long-held myths about alcoholism and addiction. The family simply may not have enough information about the problem to motivate them to address it. One way to gain access to the defended fortress of denial in the family is to suggest ways to obtain new information. Such information can relieve fear and help to lessen shame.

Whether with the alcoholic or with the spouse, it is often our first recommendation that people attend six A.A. or Al-Anon meetings for the purpose of self-diagnosis. Attendance at an educational series on alcoholism provides an alternative to A.A. or Al-Anon. Such programs are frequently offered by local alcoholism treatment centers. Education is a relatively nonthreatening intervention and is easily justified without the need to engage the addict or family in fruitless arguments about whether you or they are "right" about the nature of the problem. Our rationale to the family might look something like this: "If you thought someone you loved had cancer, the first thing you would do is find out as much as you could about cancer from people who are experts. This problem could be as serious and as life-threatening. We recommend that you get as much information as possible about alcoholism so that you will have the knowledge to make your own assessment as to whether drinking is a problem in this family."

Often addicts or family members resist even exposing themselves to education. There are many techniques to break through this level of resistance. Following are two powerful examples of interventions that were used with cases that were highly resistant to treatment.

Case Example: Intervening with Individual Denial

Miriam was a highly visible professional woman, assistant to the state commissioner for human services. She had divorced two husbands and lived alone. Despite her high level of professional visibility she was relatively isolated socially, due, in part, to her need to keep her alcoholism a secret. She acknowledged her alcoholism but her denial took the form of minimizing the degree to which it was affecting her life, particularly the degree to which it might be a contributor to her chronic depression. She took tremendous pride in her self-sufficiency, and this pride also prevented her from going to A.A. despite repeated suggestions that she do so. Despite her resistance, or perhaps because of it, it was clear that she longed for closer human contact and was probably deeply distressed about her inability to stop drinking.

After months of futile confrontation, and because there was no real social support system that could be involved in the treatment, Miriam was asked if she would be willing to look at the impact of her drinking by allowing herself to be videotaped while drunk so that she could see her own behavior. She agreed. It was negotiated that a professional colleague of hers, a highly responsible woman, would drive her to and from the session. Miriam was to start drinking a couple of hours before the session and was to bring the bottle with her to continue drinking while she talked and the session was filmed.

The results of this intervention were dramatic. Rather than being defensive about the intervention itself, Miriam, while drinking, expressed how cared for she felt that the friend would take the time to drive her while she was inebriated and that anyone would be willing to see her in that state. She expressed a great deal of vulnerability while drinking. She also had trouble standing by the end of the session, so the film recorded her in a highly intoxicated state.

In the few days directly following the videotaped session Miriam started attending A.A. regularly and acknowledged her need for help. Because she might have felt shamed by seeing the videotape, it was not played back for her until she was sober several months. The intervention had accomplished its goal without a playback: Miriam felt "seen" and accepted being both drunk and vulnerable, and she felt that she didn't have to be so ashamed. Her deeper secret was not so much the alcoholism as the need for acceptance and connection. The session was processed shortly afterwards and Miriam was given this feedback. She was also given support for the courage it would take for her to go to A.A. Her isolation addressed, the relief of giving up drinking was greater than her pain at doing so.

Discussion

An intervention like this is risky and should not be undertaken unless the therapist is extremely knowledgeable about alcoholism and unless the relationship with the client is trusting enough to permit it. It is also critical to arrange transportation in a way that insures physical safety. The "secret" revealed to Miriam by the intervention was the reality of her loneliness and need for others and the ways that drinking protected her from facing that. The poignancy of the denial process is that it helps the addict maintain a deeper "secret" from himself: the pain of emotional emptiness and difficulty with connection. Need and dependency are experienced as shameful and must be pushed out of consciousness. Because the "secret" crept out anyway when she drank, it was suggested to Miriam that she might as well make it overt by asking directly for help with her life through the support and fellowship of A.A.

Case Example: Intervening with Family Denial

A similar videotaped intervention was arranged with the Smith family. Pat sought help for her depression. Although she and John both acknowledged that John drank, Pat wasn't aware that drinking affected her depression. John admitted the alcoholism but minimized it. Neither was aware of the part alcoholism had played in their families of origin nor did they realize that it contributed to their marital difficulties.

Pat agreed to a reformulation of the problem as alcoholism. She examined her own drinking and briefly attended A.A., finally deciding she wasn't a problem drinker herself. But she resisted attending Al-Anon and her minimization of the effects of John's drinking persisted. John was unwilling either to stop drinking or to attend A.A.

A family session was held with Pat and her three children, Johnny, age 20 (home on college vacation), Susan, 21, and Betsey, 16. John, Sr. was invited to the session but declined. He and the family were advised that the session would be videotaped and made available for him to watch. The purpose of this session was to break through the family's denial and prepare them to talk with John in a modified "intervention." Its purpose was also to help them disclose the "secrets" each was holding about their worry about John's drinking. No one in the family had previously talked about their fear or their sense of hopelessness that things could get better especially because Pat refused to go to Al-Anon or take a firm position with John about his drinking.

By the end of the session, Pat had agreed to attend Al-Anon with Susan. The children's frank discussion of their father's alcoholism and her son's hopelessness about his father's possible recovery were critical to her change of attitude. Following the session, the family confronted John on his alcoholism. He immediately started attending A.A. and stopped drinking shortly thereafter. In a follow-up session with him, he was shown the videotape, and he wept at the recognition of his family's love for him.

Discussion

While the use of video was an important component of these two interventions, the goal of breaking through denial so that family members could take action was ironically accomplished before the tapes were played back. The awareness that the truths that had emerged in those sessions were recorded and not open to argument or distortion was a powerful factor in blocking the family from slipping back into denial. The evidence, the secrets, were now "visible" and the emotional "breakthrough" of people in the session could be recaptured should they have a need to distort it or claim it hadn't happened.

The above two examples of the use of videotape in breaking through the alcoholic's and the family's denial are actually modifications of an approach developed by Vernon Johnson (1973) and subsequently elaborated and refined by other alcoholism professionals such as Ruth Maxwell (1976). Intervention is a confrontation technique designed to break through the denial of the alcoholic by presenting reality to him. " . . . in a receivable form" (Johnson, p. 49). The assumption is that an alcoholic whose alcoholism is well advanced cannot perceive reality on his own without intervention from significant others. As Maxwell says, "Without outside intervention, most alcoholics die of their disease. Their shield against reality is go great that *they are unable* to perceive their own sickness" (pp. 96–7).

The intervention, although developed by chemical dependency professionals and not family therapists, is actually similar to a family network session. On one level, the power of intervention is related to the factual confrontation of the denial of the alcoholic, who is then presented with a forced choice situation: One choice is to accept treatment, the other is to accept whatever consequence, or "bottom line," the spouse and other family members have decided best meets their needs. *But the intervention also functions to reveal the secrets that have maintained family members in isolated subsystem coalitions.* It returns family members to one another as resources and gives them the information they need, practically and emotionally, to take action. No longer, for instance, is a daughter holding the secret of her father's inappropriate sexual remarks to her from her brother, who is holding the secret of his shame about bringing his friends home from school. No longer is a wife pretending to the employer that her husband has the flu every Monday when he loses time from work. And no longer are any of them holding the secret of their love and concern for the alcoholic. Breaking secrets has to do, most directly and importantly, with the simple rendering of the truth.

COMPOUND, COMPLEX SECRETS

Lying, denial, and secrecy are problems that may be compounded in addictive families in the presence of other difficult issues that are typically hidden because of social censure or disapproval. In these situations, the addiction heightens the difficulties of disclosure, and the difficulties of disclosure increase the likelihood of progressive addiction.

AIDS, for instance, has become a major health concern and it is common for those who are infected with the HIV virus to not disclose this fact to other family members or, more problematically, to their sexual partners. AIDS is often connected to other difficult secrets, a homosexual orientation, IV drug use, or both. Since the AIDS virus is spread most frequently either through homosexual contact or through IV drug use, all three issues are highly toxic ones around which lying and secrecy have become almost social norms. While on the level of public health and social policy, government and social service agencies struggle to develop guidelines for determining how to protect public safety and to require disclosure while maintaining the individual's right to privacy, in families, the struggle is to respond to the reality that to disclose one secret is often to automatically disclose the other as well.

A family affected by addiction already experiences serious deficits in its capacity to respond to crisis or to the individual needs of its members. Disclosure of other major hidden issues such as these seriously strains the already limited resources of the family. Yet nondisclosure heightens the shame and cut off from relational resources that originally fans the fires of addiction.

It would be ideal if therapists were always able to help families deal first with the denial around addiction and then proceed to facilitate the disclosure of other difficult secrets. But it's often "coming out," or a crisis around a health problem like AIDS or an unwanted pregnancy, for instance, that brings the family to treatment. The disclosure of the larger secret can be used effectively as leverage, essentially to say to the family: "This is a crisis (or a very difficult issue for any family to handle), and you will handle it better if drinking or drug use isn't getting in the way." The clinician then has the tactical dilemma of disrupting the denial of addiction with some of the techniques described above and, at the same time, keeping the system open to dealing with the more toxic "secret."

It is generally the case that secrets having to do with sexuality or health-related issues are more toxic to families than secrets involving addiction. One client tells the story of being confronted by her mother: "Are you a lesbian?" the mother demanded. The client replied, "Yes." "Do you have a drinking problem?" "Yes," the client said. The mother proceeded to slap her across the face and scream, "You are from a good Christian family and Christians don't drink!" The lesbianism went undiscussed.

ANONYMITY VERSUS SECRECY

A final connection between the issues of addiction and secrecy involves the current widespread disclosure of personal problems with alcoholism and drug abuse by people in the media. More and more the "secret" of addiction is being publicly disclosed with the effect that our growing awareness of the problem lessens the possibility of denial. Self-disclosure has become a new social norm. Celebrities such as Betty Ford have done a great deal to remove the stigma of alcoholism by their courage in making their own addiction problems public.

Yet Alcoholics Anonymous and its related programs, some of the most effective forms of treatment available to addicts, are based on a tradition of anonymity. The program of Alcoholics Anonymous is based not only on twelve steps but on twelve traditions. Four of these traditions have particular relevance to a discussion of secrecy. Tradition Six states, "An A.A. group ought never endorse, finance, or lend the A.A. name to any related facility or outside enterprise, lest problems of money, property, and prestige divert us from our primary purpose." Tradition Eight states, "Alcoholics Anonymous should remain forever non-professional, but our service centers may employ special workers." Tradition Eleven states, "Our public relations policy is based on attraction rather than promotion; we need always maintain personal anonymity at the level of press, radio, and films." And Tradition Twelve states, "Anonymity is the spiritual foundation of our traditions, ever reminding us to place principles before personalities" (Alcoholics Anonymous World Services, 1952, pp. 11–13).

The point of A.A.'s maintaining anonymity as a basis of its healing has to do with the necessity of not allowing the identification of oneself as an alcoholic or addict to be contaminated by conflicts of interest with other individuals, professionals, or groups. The traditions of anonymity and of separation of volunteer and professional interests have actually been concepts with an evolving significance and meaning within Alcoholics Anonymous. Anonymity has been broken and tested at various points in A.A.'s history at junctures when it appeared that more publicity about the program would be helpful.

One particular incident marks a kind of turning point in the evolution of the traditions. Kurtz (1979), in his history of Alcoholics Anonymous, talks about the crisis that faced A.A. when Bill Wilson, co-founder of A.A., and others met with John D. Rockefeller in the hopes of winning his financial support. The ensuing publicity, as Kurtz describes it, confronted these early members of A.A. with their own personality difficulties. What they realized as a result of the "Rockefeller dinner" and its results (Rockefeller wisely pointed out that mixing A.A. and money would destroy A.A.) was that grandiosity is the heart of addiction and that it is fostered by too much publicity. Kurtz continues describing their insight: "and insofar as this marked a retraction of 'surrender,' forgetfulness of 'bottom,' the attempt again to take control over their lives and wills, it gave warning of, if not a return to active alcoholism, at least a kind of dry hangover that could render sobriety itself almost too painful to bear" (Kurtz, 1979, pp. 94–5).

Bateson (1972), too, writes of alcoholic "hubris" as the heart of the problem. Paradoxically, alcoholic "grandiosity or hubris" can lead both to the keeping of the secret of alcoholism and to the arrogant broadcasting of the triumph of recovery and sometimes the misuse of that recovery for personal profit.

As the traditions evolved and the founders of A.A., through their resolution of the various developmental crises that faced the organization, began to understand the nature of addiction more clearly, recovery came to be viewed as a spiritual process that takes place within oneself, with the support of the larger group. One conceivably might attend meetings for 20 years and never know the last names of the other members. This "secrecy," which is really a form of privacy, protects the individual as well as the program from political, financial, or professional identifications that might undermine the essentially private nature of recovery within the program.

The zeal to destroy the stigma of addiction and to bring "the secret" out of the closet on a larger societal level has come perilously close to breaking the anonymity on which the success of Alcoholics Anonymous has rested. The recovery movement has created a seemingly insatiable appetite for workshops, books, games, healing meditations, and other supposed "tools for recovery" that depend frequently on the personal disclosure of the individuals who market them. The concept of anonymity has been gravely compromised. There is no question that many of these offerings are extraordinarily helpful to many people. But often the breaking of secrecy has come to be used as a technique of personal gain. Clients need to be helped to distinguish personal disclosure that is helpful and therapeutic, from disclosure that violates twelve-step traditions, as well as concepts of healthy limit-setting and privacy. The therapist helping the client to make those distinctions must fully understand the traditions of A.A.

SUMMARY

The life-style of the addict is one of lying, secrecy, and finally silence — a painful withdrawal from contact and engagement with the self and with a larger community. The real tragedy of addiction is this power to destroy connection. Yet, it may also be the case that a painful sense of alienation sets the stage for the first drink, the first pill, the first snort of cocaine. The drug relieves pain, and the secrecy of denial is an adaptation that protects the process of pain relief and further insulates one from shame and fear. Not only is the addict's life-style one of withdrawal, but all family relationships become dominated by lying and secrecy.

As we move clinically to disrupt denial and secrecy at their many levels, it's important to remember, as John Wallace suggests, that denial is there for a reason. The human capacity for maintaining secrecy deserves to be respected, the underlying wisdom of it as an adaptation to very painful realities understood. Once we can feel compassion for the shame and anxiety that denial protects, we become more effective healers in replacing secrecy with the truth.

REFERENCES

Alcoholics Anonymous World Services, Inc. (1952). *Twelve steps and twelve traditions*. New York: Author.

Bateson, G. (1972). *Steps to an ecology of mind*. New York: Chandler Publishing.

Bean, M. (1981). Denial and the psychological complications of alcoholism. In M. Bean & N. Zinberg (Eds.), *Dynamic approaches to the understanding and treatment of alcoholism*. New York: Free Press.

Bepko, C., with Krestan, J. (1985). *The responsibility trap: A blueprint for treating the alcoholic family*. New York: Free Press.

Black, C. (1981). *It will never happen to me*. Denver, CO: MAC.

Bok, S. (1984). *Secrets: On the ethics of concealment and revelation*. New York: Vintage.

Bratter, T. (1985). Special clinical psychotherapeutic concerns for alcoholics and drug-addicted individuals. In T. Bratter & G. Forrest (Eds.), *Alcoholism and substance abuse: Strategies for clinical intervention*. New York: Free Press.

Elkin, M. (1984). *Families under the influence: Changing alcoholic patterns*. New York: W. W. Norton.

Forrest, G. (1985). Psychodynamically oriented treatment of alcoholism and substance abuse. In T. Bratter & G. Forrest (Eds.), *Alcoholism and substance abuse: Strategies for clinical intervention*. New York: Free Press.

Fossum, M., & Mason, M. (1986). *Facing shame: Families in recovery*. New York: W. W. Norton.

Jackson, J. (1954). The adjustment of the family to the crisis of alcoholism. *Quarterly Journal of Studies on Alcohol, 15*(4), 562–586.

Johnson, V. (1973). *I'll quit tomorrow*. New York: Harper & Row.

Karpel, M. (1980). Family secrets: I. Conceptual and ethical issues in the relational context. II. Ethical and practical considerations in therapeutic management. *Family Process, 19*, 295–306.

Kurtz, E. (1979). *Not-God: A history of Alcoholics Anonymous*. Center City, MN: Hazelden.

Maxwell, R. (1976). *The booze battle*. New York: Ballentine.

Nace, E. (1987). *The treatment of alcoholism*. New York: Brunner/Mazel.

Royce, J. (1981). *Alcohol problems and alcoholism*. New York: Free Press.

Wallace, J. (1977). Between Scylla and Charybdis: Issues in alcoholism therapy. *Alcohol Health and Research World*, Summer issue.

9

Eating Disorders as Family Secrets

LAURA GIAT ROBERTO

The Bonwit family requested consultation for a daughter, Lena, age 15. Mr. Bonwit, Lena's father, had only recently received her into his home; he was divorced from Lena's mother, and she had remained in her mother's custody since the age of five. In the interview, he revealed that Lena had come to live with him following a three-year battle with anorexia nervosa, after which she became bulimic.

The divorced parents decided (without the participation of Lena's stepparents) that perhaps her symptoms would improve if she "made a fresh start." Lena said that she had no idea what propelled her to starve earlier, or to starve and make herself vomit now. Mr. Bonwit was mystified and requested individual therapy "to improve Lena's self-esteem." In passing, he mentioned that he and Lena's mother "had issues" but that they were in complete accord regarding the importance of treatment. Despite the "fresh start," Lena was vomiting daily, had social phobias, and remained underweight. Neither parent had any idea how to help, and Lena became progressively dehydrated and depressed.

Of all secrets that are harbored in marriages and families, the "secret" of psychosomatic illness is perhaps the most paradoxical and difficult to treat. When a family member shows physiological symptoms and experiences him- or herself as "out of control" of the symptoms, families mobilize in anxiety and fear. But with psychosomatic illness, the family is faced with a situation in which the symptom-bearer has no explanation for the problem, no apparent disease, and very few clear ideas about the problem or its solution.

Psychosomatic symptoms are stress-related: They intensify in stressful life circumstances. *Thus, they are a metaphor* for the symptom-bearer's distress about some undefined personal issue. Nowhere is this mystifying, metaphorical communication process seen more clearly than in the case of eating disorders—anorexia nervosa and bulimia nervosa.[1] This chapter will explore eating disorders as "open family secrets," which fulfill the same functions as do other more concrete, less metaphorical family secrets. I will also offer an interpretation of the "secret" family dysfunctions accompanying eating disorders and give reasons why dysfunction in the family is kept covert and metaphorical rather than made overt.

To the observer, these families are obviously symptomatic. In their interactional patterns, which are the bedrock for the formation of starving, binging, and purging, individuals with eating disorders show tremendous confusion about the acceptability of their appearance, their own self-worth, their importance to others, and the significance of personal needs, goals, and motivations. The *sine qua non* of families presenting with eating disorders is a chronic difficulty in tolerating, promoting, and integrating individual differences within the nuclear family as a whole.

The process by which the underlying, covert dysfunctions in these families become overt and are treated in therapy can be best understood in the context of their dynamics surrounding differentiation, separation, conflict, and self-expression. Medical symptoms and self-destructive eating come to affect cohesion, conflict resolution, individuation, and intimacy in self-perpetuating cycles. There are repercussions in the family's outside relationship with caregivers, such as a primary-care physician or school officials. The clinician has to possess an armamentarium of techniques for "translating" medical symptoms into metaphorical messages and then, later, into direct communications. The techniques I will introduce derive from work with several hundred couples and families who have come to our team at the Center for Eating Disorders, between 1981 and 1991, in an effort to come to terms with their own physical and emotional secrets.

DEFICIT OR DECEPTION?

Accounts of self-starvation (anorexia nervosa) and binge-purging (bulimia nervosa) have been present in the medical literature since the 1600's. Analytic psychiatrists began to produce case studies of eating disordered individuals in the 1950's. Otto Fenichel, the prominent Freudian analyst, commented on a number of cases published about these disorders (1945). These analytic case studies involved clients, mainly women, who appeared anxious, starved, binged, vomited or used purgatives, and were preoccupied by tensions with their families of origin.*

Psychoanalytic formulations of these women focused upon fears regarding sexuality, intimacy, and control, which were viewed as causing them to withdraw emotionally from intimate relationships, especially with men, and to cope with their fears indirectly by self-destructive eating. They were described as having intensely close and conflictual relationships with their mothers. A self-critical and punitive attitude toward the body, a distorted and desexualized body image, and direction of anger against the self were also targets for intervention by both Freudian and object-relations psychoanalysts.

In contrast, the problem of psychosomatic symptoms and eating disorders remained of little interest to family therapists until the late 1970's, when two groups of theorists each produced a book on the subject. Salvador Minuchin, together with Bernice Rosman and Lester Baker at the Children's Hospital of the University of Pennsylvania, produced *Psychosomatic Families*, a seminal book that has been reviewed, debated, and re-reviewed since its controversial appearance in 1978. On the other side of the Atlantic, in Milan, Italy, Mara Selvini Palazzoli produced a personal account of her shift from psychoanalysis to family therapy with anorexics in *Self-Starvation*. The revised English version also appeared in 1978. Both groups of theorists were interested in the specific, repetitive cycles of symptoms and relational problems that seemed to characterize the families of anorexic children and teens. Minuchin's group created a *deficit theory* to explain anorexia. They described boundary problems, poor conflict management, and poor decision-making in the parental dyads and family units of young adolescent children. This was consistent with Minuchin's structural model, which links inadequate or inconsistent family hierarchies with emotional disorders. Palazzoli, who was chiefly influenced by early general systems theory at the time of her publication, posited a *deception theory*: paradoxical and indirect communications that obscured individual differences and prevented clear position-taking and constructive conflict.

The commentaries provided by both these groups of clinicians stimulated a great wave of interest in eating disorders among family therapists. This interest is partly explained by the fact that, in Minuchin and colleagues' observations of young anorexics and their parents, the majority of families showed severe enmeshment between a parent or parents and child. Thus, there seemed to be an entire population of families that could increase our understanding of the effects of enmeshed relationships upon emotional

---

*Because almost 90% of reported anorexics and bulimics are female, it is customary to predominantly use the pronoun "she."

individuation in offspring. A debate ensued in the literature, which has never been well addressed, regarding whether families of anorexics/bulimics suffer from *deficits* in their internal structure and organization, or *mutual deceptiveness* in the way that they understand and present themselves to one another and the world.

Palazzoli's work excited interest in the families of anorexics because she felt that the communication in these families provided a model for psychotically disordered families. The commonalities that she noticed included the absence of clearly defined positions on important family conflicts; the indirect but powerful effects of the symptom-bearer's suffering on family-wide functioning; and the way in which the anorexic daughter seemed equally close and equally protective of both, rather than one of her parents. Accustomed to viewing enmeshment as a dyadic process, family therapists seemed fascinated that enmeshment could be a triadic phenomenon rather than a coalition of two against one.

It is evident that these two independent groups of clinicians chiefly utilized anorexic subjects and very few bulimic subjects, although some of their cases did involve "purging anorexics" (that is, adolescents and adults who are 15% or more underweight and also use purging techniques to control their weight). Bulimic clients and their families were not investigated as a separate group, but were later included in generalizations as if their internal processes were identical to anorexic families. In the 1980's, a number of clinicians and researchers took exception to these generalizations, based upon their findings that in families of bulimics, other family patterns appeared (explosive, disorganized, addictive). However, none of these clinicians or researchers expanded on the idea of conflicting, deceptive *content* and *metaphor* in self-starvation and purging.

Thus, one of the richest and most powerful observations of early clinical observers was largely overlooked. The Milan team claimed that, by becoming ill through eating poorly, without having a concrete disease, and by seeming helpless and confused, anorexics actually engage their families in a *confusing double bind*, a mystifying process, which no one can decode or master. I believe that the bind consists of giving one message on the content level, "I am ill and need help," and another on the metaphorical level, "I alone know what I am doing and must be left alone." Which message is real, and which is deceptive? Significant others and, at times, therapists become caught up in this double bind and experience the anorexic client as having a secret.

In my view, it is *the relational meanings behind self-starvation and purging, the story beneath the deceptive and elusive "illness,"* that contains the key to treating starvation and bulimia. It is true that, in the last decade, writers within psychology, psychiatry, and social work have looked beyond family interaction to the social context of self-starvation in a consumer-oriented, wealthy, and patriarchal culture. In such cultures, which include most industrialized and high-technology societies, young women are confronted with complex and even impossible tasks in order to gain social approval (for example, they are told to utilize their advanced educations in a meaningful way, while refraining from competing with their peers and with men in the job market). Culturally, it can be said that eating disorders represent a "secret" communication about women's discontent with their social options for self-expression and meaningful work.

Since this discontent *does* contribute to anorexia, which has a prevalence rate of 0.1% of the population, or to bulimia, which has a prevalence rate of roughly 15%, then it bears close scrutiny by those choosing to treat these disorders. Yet, within mainstream family therapy, few writers have expanded upon Palazzoli's classic view of eating disorder symptoms as covert strategies — strategies that serve to divert one's family and oneself from admitting discontent. Physically expressed, self-contained, nonverbal, internally damaging eating behaviors are powerful mechanisms for altering a person's state of consciousness and for propelling his or her family into certain areas of awareness rather than others.

ANOREXIA AND BULIMIA AS SELF-DECEPTION

The first observation one makes in an initial interview with an anorexic or bulimic client and spouse or family is that the symptomatic man or woman has difficulty describing the cause of his or her bouts of starving or purging or personal distress generally. We refer to these causal incidents or ideas as "triggers." Although no one life event or critical incident actually causes an eating disorder, clients do experience specific painful events as "causing" them to want to avoid a meal or to purge.

This apparent difficulty describing the "triggers" for a binge or for a period of starvation does not necessarily improve when the spouse or family is not present. At times, the inability to describe her internal state before, during, or after eating disordered behavior seems to represent a real lack of language to share her internal, affective world. This inability has been termed "alexithymia."

Alexithymia has been thought to reflect greatly delayed individuation and self-awareness and was examined at length by Bruch (1978). Her position was that eating disordered women often *literally do not know how they feel* about specific events or issues. Other theorists have speculated that such women show a lack of trust in the validity and reliability of their feelings. Dynamic psychotherapists reduce the context of alexithymia, literally mood-related absence of words to an active internal conflict between her emotional reactions and her learned beliefs that those reactions are inappropriate, unacceptable, or unjustified (Garner & Bemis, 1985).

There are other clients who do verbalize thoughts and feelings, but avoid doing so unless pressed in the most persistent way. These clients suppress controversial ideas and reactions but can easily discuss issues that involve other people or are not emotionally loaded (for example, concerns of the husband or siblings; stresses in the workplace). I think of all these clients — those who "do not know" and those who "will not say" — as *keeping a secret from themselves*. It is as if they themselves pose a threat to established relationships and social expectations should they "rock the boat." Many feminists writers relate this suppression of self and initiative to the oppressive socialization of young girls (Orbach, 1985).

I believe that there is a complex interaction that occurs among a woman's efforts to *deceive herself*, a larger deception *in her family* (and marriage), and rampant *social deception* about the competence of women. We can thus conceive of *three levels of secrets* that underlie anorexia and bulimia: cultural secrets, relational secrets, and internal secrets.

CULTURAL SECRETS

Since the 1960's, with the advent of fashion model Twiggy, the fashion, entertainment, and media industries in America and her economic partners have advocated an ideal feminine image that is emaciated. Lovers of ballet will notice that, in the past three decades, the body weight of the prima ballerina has decreased continuously. While this pattern has persisted for over 25 years, it has never been acknowledged by the media that this body type is impossible to achieve by a healthy postpubertal woman. The fantastically high frequency of illness in women athletes, dancers, entertainers, and media personalities — all highly visible women — is an "open secret" that their young protégées know but do not discuss. Jane Fonda's admission that she was bulimic in the late 1980's was reported widely and greeted with shock by the media — and then buried in a series of videotapes for the exercise-obsessed.

Given that a young teenage girl must have approximately 13% body fat to reach menarche, in order to maintain an emaciated state (15% underweight or more) she will at least lose her reproductive functioning. Those who cannot deny themselves food, and purge or fast to lose weight, will deplete their bodies of electrolytes and fluid necessary for normal heart, kidney, and liver function. Despite over ten years of documentation in the popular literature that anorexia nervosa and bulimia carry a high mortality rate, it also remains an "open secret" that rapid weight loss can mean metabolic collapse and/or sudden death. Only recently, for example, have studies following people on fasting or liquid ("very low calorie") diets published accounts of sudden crisis and death.

RELATIONAL SECRETS

It is difficult to imagine that a young woman can become severely underweight or use invasive purging techniques like persistent vomiting and laxative abuse without creating high anxiety in her partner or family. Yet, the coping strategies that she and her intimates develop over time, in mutual accommodation, actually allow her behavior to occur without intervention. The result is that the family acts as if the behavior were invisible, despite the fact that the anorexic's eating can be highly ritualistic, obvious, and extremely disturbing.

> Susan was unwilling to eat dinner with her family, except under unusual conditions, despite her day-long fasting. No one food was allowed to touch another on her plate, or the whole dinner must be thrown away. She was disgusted if the gravy from the meat touched her vegetables, and she peeled potatoes, peas, and grapes to "cut the calories." Her parents and brother watched this behavior on the nights when Susan was willing to come to the table, avoiding any mention of her fetishes.

Eating disorders become a relational secret, because the family is trying to avoid what they believe will be a worsening of the tensions and the symptoms. Family harmony is, in fact, held together purely through avoidance. This reflects the fact that when the symptom-bearer's sense of competence comes only through pleasing, helpful, or compliant behavior, the degree of relational tension created is considerable. Because it takes so much effort to hold back negative emotions and conflictual opinions, the symptom-bearer comes to possess an air of aloofness and "brittleness" in intimate relationships. This tension tends to encourage withdrawal by partners, the "walking on eggshells" phenomenon that we see in addictions. Family members report that they fear increasing her stress (and, therefore, starving or purging) if they inform her that they are concerned. Further, because the symptomatic member tries to preserve her self-esteem through self-control and self-denial, others tend to want to reinforce her sense of self-esteem, even if it means letting her go on harming herself.

> Ursula, 20, and her husband sought counseling three months after their wedding, because between their engagement and the marriage

she had lost weight until she was only 80 pounds. Although Paul accompanied her to buy her wedding dress and knew that the size 4 dress was too big for her and that she was weak and exhausted, he felt that "talking about it all the time just made her angry and frustrated him." Ursula's mother and grandmother, who resided in the same town, also knew that she had stopped eating and was quite wasted. However, they both noted that she became defensive and upset when they challenged her: "All she does is get upset and lock herself in her room, so we've given up."

INTERNAL SECRETS

To the extent that a distressed individual suppresses personal differences out of his or her awareness, it becomes less probable that there will be relational conflict. For women particularly, who are socialized to provide relationship maintenance and nurture family, children, and friends, the psychological defense of suppression (or even repression) removes resistances or ambivalence around fulfilling this role. In families where the father or both parents are emotionally abusive, even sons are vulnerable to adopting this defensive strategy and developing psychosomatic symptoms.

A woman who has experienced success at pleasing her employer, her children, and her husband by maintaining a calm demeanor and giving them all her attention and energies can find it very aversive to discover that her own internal stress is building into a compulsive desire to diet and get thin. If she admits to herself (or them) that her compulsion is a manifestation of anxiety and stress, she will also have to admit the possibility that her family role may not be meeting her own adult need for autonomy, competence, and self-worth. Yet, these "selfless" behaviors, in which she has engaged with husband and family, are taught and rewarded by a consumer-oriented society that depends upon women to provide nurturance, education, and relationship maintenance for men and children (Goldner, 1985; Walters et al., 1988).

The act of identifying and examining a woman's own discontent in a social context that still bypasses her individual needs in favor of family well-being, is therefore very threatening. This is especially true for both young and older women who have been successful in the eyes of parents, community, religion, and society. And it is a consistent finding in almost all industrialized, Western societies that girls and women with eating disorders are intelligent, high-functioning women within the middle and upper economic strata.

Therefore, to the extent that a woman is unaware of her internal stress, she is not forced to examine alternatives or to initiate conflictual changes in important family relationships. Unless she is prepared to undergo criticism, lack of support, and even loss of relationships, she may prefer to avoid awareness of negative feelings, memories, and beliefs. Even in family relationships that are more egalitarian, and in a culture with feminist role models, social pressures are such that such girls and women *create a secret within themselves of their own unhappiness.*

> Anika, a 25-year-old museum curator, was engaged to marry at the time her parents sought therapy for her. Anika's fiancé was well-established in a family business and had well-to-do parents, who were very pleased with their son's choice of mate. Anika's parents, professional people, also approved of her marital choice. The young couple planned to marry after a six-month engagement, during which Anika and her mother had intended to plan a lavish and impressive wedding for the friends of the couple's parents, as well as for the younger generation. Anika experienced severe anxiety about her weight, vomited multiple times daily in an effort to control her weight, and felt quite depressed.
>
> When asked about her relationship with her fiancé, Anika described it as one with considerable distance and frequent disagreements around his work schedule, which occupied him continuously. She had little comment about her own plans for work or social life after the wedding and was preoccupied with meeting her new mother-in-law's expectations for furnishing their new home. In the area of personal concerns regarding the courtship, the marriage, or her mood, Anika had no complaints nor any ideas about why she was depressed.

The negative and self-punitive judgements that anorexic and bulimic women direct at their bodies stems from their *complete induction into (and introjection of) externally imposed expectations for self-sacrificial behavior.* Because a compliant, pleasing daughter or wife is successful in garnering acceptance or favor, she becomes dependent on the initiatives and opinions of her intimates rather than on her own. The "secret"—that underneath the helpless, self-critical introjects there is anger, hopelessness, mistrust, or insecurity—reflects a basic helplessness about asserting herself. Rather than facing the helplessness and reconsidering the value of asserting her own needs, she finds it less threatening to redirect the anxiety against herself, her weight, and her own body image.

The internal secret can be highly resistant to disclosure. As we saw in the case of Lena, the client may feel she has a great deal at stake if she chooses to stop hiding her displeasure. Her social standing may suffer if she alienates her husband. She may lose needed financial aid or child care from her family. If she has made her identity one of raising her children, her self-esteem may be at stake if she sets limits with them. At times, the most crucial phase of individual and family therapy consists of creating a context where the client feels there is more to lose in keeping the secret so that he or she becomes ready to acknowledge suppressed negative affects.

DECEPTION AND DISENGAGEMENT

Gradual withdrawal and deceptiveness "feed forward" into future family functioning. Twelve- to thirteen-year-old children who are just beginning to obsess about body weight are in radically different positions with their families than are 25-year-old marrieds who are still starving or using laxatives and other purgatives. Minuchin's group (1978) focused specifically on young starvers and noted family patterns of conflict avoidance, overfocusing on the child's symptoms, and emotional distancing, although there was an overtly benign atmosphere. Although these findings have been widely disputed in the literature, and were poorly documented, the notion that there is poor conflict resolution and poor communication in these families has been generally supported.

Five years later, when the child is 18, there is an extremely different scenario. There is often considerable and violent conflict around episodes of food restriction and/or purging, an attempt by parents or significant others to "get away" from discussing the child's symptoms, explosive arguing or repetitive unresolved conflicts, and family coalitions "against" the child (Roberto, 1987). Several writers have noted a distinct family pattern in bulimic families of explosive conflict or "chaos" (Root, Fallon, & Friedrich, 1986).

It is my belief that this pattern of explosive interaction is a *transitional state, which evolves over time as a counterpoint to the fusion that occurs earlier in the illness.* The angry disengagement is part of a larger, cyclic pattern because family members cannot become sufficiently autonomous while the ill member is in danger. One outcome of the explosive fights and disengagements is that, where formerly the spouse or parent may have been too patronizing, subsequently he or she may become aloof and unavailable during real crises.

Clark, a 19-year-old youth, was admitted to the hospital for starvation. Although he was six feet tall, he weighed only 115 pounds. His parents stated that previous attempts at individual psychotherapy with several professionals had not made an impact upon his food restriction. He was not willing to openly discuss his hostile family

relationships in therapy and was interested only in starving and purging. Clark was also quite angry at doctors for insisting that he gain
weight and made it clear that no circumstances could compel him to
eat.

Although Clark's parents had been extremely involved in his problem, escorting him from doctor to doctor and supervising his frequent leaves of absence from college, they stated that they were
"burned out" from attempts to discover the sources of his anger.
They felt that they had made themselves available in every way, and
received no explanations, apologies, or clarifications of his intentions for the future. They were not willing to participate in family
meetings, left town twice on vacation while he was hospitalized, and
returned only after Clark had to be transferred to a secure facility for
partially slitting his throat with a piece of glass.

What a dilemma results from the rebelliousness, the secrecy, and the
withdrawal of a young adult who is risking death! The family and the
treating therapists begin to experience intense power struggles around eating
and decision-making. Susie Orbach (1986) describes this stage of disengagement and conflict well:

> . . . the rebellion the anoretic [and binging/purging] woman is expressing rever-
> berates and we can feel the strength that is bound up in the refusal and rejection
> of food. There is a force propelling that refusal, a force that one wishes to
> overpower, a resilience which calls forth an equally belligerent response—a desire
> on the part of the observer to control. (p. 99)

By attempting to gain power over herself, by saying "no" to help, she actually *loses her power* by being labelled as out of control, ill, and in need of
help. As the atmosphere of resentment, mistrust, threats, and dissension
increase, the symptomatic member's sense of self-confidence and self-awareness is submerged deeper and deeper under a load of family recriminations.

Families with eating disordered members have difficulty assessing the
extent to which they feel they can trust one another. At the beginning of
the self-destructive behavior, family members may see it as temporary self-
punishment, which warrants understanding and consideration. Spouses and
families can actually advance their symptomatic member "too much trust"
for long periods, during which she becomes quite ill with little comment
from others.

Later, as her symptoms cause repeated alarms and perhaps medical and
emotional crises, her intimates may move to the opposite extreme and advance her no trust or consideration, even when she is trying to get control of
her eating. The perception is often, "I listened to her anxieties and offered

support and was rejected, therefore, she is deliberately manipulating me and deserves no more help." In this fashion, parents or spouses swing from one pole to the other, from offering unrealistic hope and trust to offering no trust.

Ironically, as Helm Stierlin has pointed out, the symptom-bearer tends to feel betrayed by her family from the start. Her perception is that others respond not to her inner turmoil, but to her appearance, weight, and compliant behavior. Her experience is that others wish only to control her and hinder her independence, a reflection also of her own belief that her own opinions are unimportant in relationships. The whole family's tendency to stress perfectionism, appearance, status, social standing, and self-control, betray their common human need for self-disclosure and mutual honesty. Her starving or purging is only one metaphor for the secrecy, deceptiveness, and evasiveness of the whole family.

WORKING CLINICALLY WITH DECEPTION AND SECRETS

Our experience has been that, the less that an anorexic or bulimic individual reveals of the eating disorder, the more severe the symptoms become. The submerged turmoil literally "eats her alive." This is understandable in the sense that, the more she keeps personal positions secret from others, the less she can challenge others to take seriously her desires and needs. Because others are not challenged, she denies herself the experience of influencing those outside herself. Without the experience of personal influence and power in her relationships, her belief that she is helpless and ineffective increases. Thus, her use of starving, or binging and purging, increases as a (useless) way of proving to herself that she is powerful and decisive.

For this reason, in the therapy of eating disorders, we begin with insisting on early disclosure of the starvation or binging and purging techniques she has used. The client is encouraged to assume that she may collapse at any time without warning and is asked whether she has thought of the position that this collapse will put her husband, parents, or children in, especially because they do not know her condition. I am quite graphic in discussing how a husband will locate her in an emergency room, who will care for her children if she does not come home, where her parents will look for her. These clients are not used to being taken seriously by their significant others. Typically, no one has talked with them about how they will be affected if she is hospitalized or dies.

At first glance, it might appear that such a confrontive, "life or death" conversation with a client who comes for help is a form of coercion or guilt induction. However, my belief is that such a conversation removes the patina of deception and evasion that she has lived with before. It recognizes her pain, acknowledges the danger she is in, and admits that crucial decisions are hers to make. If the client is an adolescent, the parents are asked these questions in front of her. Frequently, as the dialogue leaves the level of food intake and moves to the level of negotiating mutual trust, the client shows relief and opens up for the first time about her degree of self-starvation or purging.

There are situations where the spouse or parents do not wish to accompany the client to therapy or try to leave the room as discussion begins. A frequent rationale is that "she will be more comfortable alone with the therapist, she does not trust the family." I do not force family members to stay in the room, which only creates one more level of power struggle to distract from the secret. There are several alternatives available: The client can be asked to report home all that has been discussed in the session, a task that many are willing to do because the therapist has empowered it; or, the couple or family can be called in for a consultation, in which the seriousness of the client's condition is laid out by the therapist with the client observing silently. In this case, the therapist is actually placing him- or herself in the position of the client, enjoining the pressures to avoid conflict and modelling for the client. In essence, the therapist exposes the client's secret for her, with her prior permission.

There are a few eating disordered clients who refuse to disclose their behavior even when there is a trustworthy and respectful therapist available. I advise these clients that I am as helpless as they, because I do not know their reality and, therefore, cannot give understanding. Admission of helplessness diffuses the extremely negative transference that these clients possess and can diffuse the mistrust that binds them to silence.

In contrast to other secrets, which can create severe emotional pain for the family (for example, extramarital affairs, incest, or abuse), this secret is, in reality, less threatening to a parent or partner. In fact, it takes a great deal of work in order to make spouses and families aware that they play any part at all in the maintenance of an apparently psychosomatic illness. If the therapist is willing, disclosure can proceed satisfactorily during the first several interviews with the spouse or family present. He or she can then predict and manage the protectiveness and pressure from the family and the guilt and defensiveness of the symptom-bearer as therapy progresses with the symptoms "out in the open."

The secretiveness that surrounds episodes of starving and severe binge-purge behavior does not end with the client's initial admission. I find that, throughout the course of therapy, clients will avoid discussing severe episodes unless I ask specifically how they are eating. The process of withholding, questioning, and disclosure is like a reenactment of the initial interchanges, in which the client tests to see whether her distress will be acknowledged and explored. If the therapist assumes that she is now "behaving," she will stop disclosing. Through the middle phase of therapy, the therapist must take the stance that the client is in danger, is in pain, and will be tempted to hurt herself if stressed. When the spouse or family begins to mirror that degree of acceptance and understanding and gives up their need to control appearances, the eating disorder is no longer as necessary.

Case Example: Elsa: "Eating My Feelings"

Elsa, a 35-year-old married homemaker, called in a considerable state of agitation to request consultation for herself and her husband, Phil. Phil, also 35, was a salesman who often travelled on business but had agreed to attend a meeting. In the initial interview, the couple centered their discussion on Elsa's temper outbursts, which seemed to "come from nowhere" and involved screaming, crying, or throwing kitchen towels or newspapers at her husband. The couple had been married for five years and had a three-year-old son whom Elsa had had difficulty conceiving due to the fact that she weighed 220 pounds and was not ovulating properly. There was no mention of an eating disorder, and the couple defined their problem as marital stress due to Elsa's temper.

The history of their marriage, and their experiences with their families of origin, showed that Elsa had a painfully conflictual relationship with her mother, an anorexic, who constantly commented on Elsa's weight and had humiliated and belittled her while she was growing up. Elsa did not turn to her father at all. He had been frighteningly strict and physically abusive at times. Phil was almost completely cut off from his family, who had blamed him for forcing his father into drug rehabilitation against his will by taking out a petition for commitment years earlier. Phil was an emotionally constricted, almost robotlike man, whose emotional life was restricted to reacting to Elsa's temper. It was after revealing her mother's starvation that Elsa described a pattern of binge-eating followed by eight-hour fasts. She stated that during her binges she was "eating her feelings." Her binges had never occurred in front of Phil, making this the first secret that Elsa revealed in therapy. Phil responded with disgust, much as he had when he recalled his father's chronic heroin habit. However, the tensions between them could not be discussed unless Elsa blew up, at which point all she felt able to say was that they "weren't close enough."

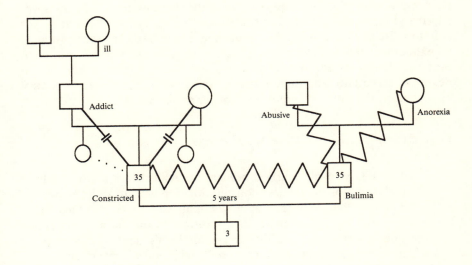

Figure 9.1

In marital therapy, Elsa's binging and fasting were defined as a way of trying to calm her turmoil without troubling Phil. Knowing that he was not comfortable with intense emotion and that he expected her to show contentment and provide companionship in the marriage, Elsa would try to stave off unproductive confrontations by trying to eat, instead. Further, her resulting obesity was a medical problem, which she could acknowledge as hers alone, further "taking heat off" her easily frustrated husband. Phil gained a wife who, although overweight and overanxious, was at home for him and their son and focused her thoughts and goals solely on the marriage. As the metaphorical value of "eating her feelings" was explored, Elsa became willing and able to control her intake and began to lose weight.

Thus, the second secret revealed in therapy was that Elsa appeared to be in control of her intake and was choosing to overeat and fast in response to her views about important family issues, including her marriage. Elsa's willingness to control her intake stemmed from the therapist's insistence that the binging and temper outbursts were a message of some kind, a message meant for Phil and possibly others, a metaphorical message underlying her obesity. Her husband's availability for marital therapy was his first step in changing his constricted stance, a problem that the therapist considered as serious as Elsa's symptoms. The therapist stated openly that Elsa's underlying desire to lose weight was a secret and that she must have believed previously that Phil could not be trusted to know her deepest needs. Phil was able to admit that he had not been encouraging with Elsa.

As Elsa's weight dropped, she became more interested than she had been in two specific problems: her continuing power struggles with her parents and her phobia about looking for work outside the home (she had been a highly successful fashion photographer when she met Phil). She planned more family visits and informed her mother for the first time that criticism was driving them apart rather than together. She informed her parents of her bulimia and explained that she herself wished to control her intake and lose weight. She asked them not to comment on her weight but, rather, to ask after her progress. She applied for several jobs, although when she was not hired immediately she became severely demoralized. In contrast, Phil seemed to withdraw further into his job, stated that he did not know what Elsa wanted from him, and criticized her for obtaining child care for their son. He began making longer business trips and failed to call home. Elsa started to relapse, overeating at meals and raging at Phil for failing to call home. Her relapse once again made her look confused and undecisive, "taking the heat off" Phil and allowing him to withdraw "until she could calm down." Once again, marital sessions focused on Elsa's efforts to "eat her feelings" rather than tell Phil exactly what she expected from the marriage in terms of cooperation, co-parenting, and involvement. It was after this point that the couple began to discuss, for the first time, Phil's refusal to lower his guard with his wife or family or to discuss personal concerns and reactions of his own.

During this phase of therapy, the therapist took the stance that, in order to increase his own trustworthiness in his marriage, Phil would have to address his emotional constrictedness and his anger. She pointed out that if he continued to avoid meaningful reflection, Elsa could not approach him further and would need to keep her secrets from him. She suggested that he work on an alliance with his own family members. Phil elected to contact his older sister, with whom he had been close during his childhood, in order to begin reestablishing a personal connection. Although he refused to visit his parents, he called and talked to his father about his paternal grandmother's failing health. This is as far as he would go in reopening the wound that had been inflicted when he tried to save his father from drug-related death. The contacts resulted in an ongoing conversation with the sister he had trusted. However, Phil used his sister's support to push Elsa, telling her that his newfound ability to get along with her pointed out that the marital tensions were Elsa's fault. This time, Elsa did not relapse. She began taking advanced photography classes while looking for work. When her weight dropped to 170 pounds, she admitted her third secret: that she feared substantial weight loss would make her look as attractive as she had been when single and that she might want to leave her marriage.

This third secret became the focus of the remaining marital sessions. Because Elsa could now admit that she was ambivalent about her marriage, the therapist moved to the most challenging issues in the therapy: whether the marriage could exist without mutuality or trust. The last several months of marital therapy were spent on discussing whether the couple would split up. Phil tended to handle Elsa's ambivalence by seeming to dare her, i.e., "If you want to leave, leave." Despite this behavior, Elsa did not take the bait and, instead, obtained half-time child care without asking Phil's permission. Relieved of many home responsibilities, she was able to socialize with other professionals and no longer felt as strong a need for a response from Phil. As her autonomy grew, and she was able to communicate her new direction to her own parents, Phil slowly began to treat her with more attention. The mutuality that had been lacking evolved slowly from the autonomy that Elsa had achieved through disclosing her secrets within the context of the marriage. The couple terminated treatment, with Elsa at 150 pounds and working on her photography portfolio.

CONCLUSION

The appearance of eating disorder symptoms, whether starving, starving and purging, or binge-eating and purging, serves as a way of making secret and metaphorical communications to a spouse or family without arousing conflict. The secrets inherent in the disorder include the presence of family dysfunction in the area of autonomy and self-expression; the symptom-bearer's dissatisfaction with or alienation from the family of origin; the use of ritualized, self-destructive acts to immobilize or "numb out" his or her own impulses and goals; and the existence of opinions and values that may be radically different from those of the spouse or family. As I have stated, these secrets are kept not only from the spouse or family but frequently also from the anorexic or bulimic member him- or herself. Such self-deception insures that he or she will never be in danger of stirring up conflict in areas that are sensitive or threatening to the family's values or her values, emphasizing cohesion at all costs.

A therapy that focuses on the metaphorical value of these somatic symptoms and treats the starving or binging and purging as relational secrets empowers the affected member and her intimates to begin examining the most sensitive, covert aspects of their relationship. In the process, space is opened up for each of them to begin taking individual stances on important family problems and events, so that self-expression can be integrated into the marital and family attachments. When this is achieved, the secrets of anorexia and bulimia are no longer useful and are replaced by relationships based on mutuality and trust.

NOTE

[1] At the present time, the diagnosis of an eating disorder depends upon the presence of self-starvation, starvation and self-induced purging, binge-eating and self-induced purging, or binge-eating. Simple self-starvation involves severe restriction of food intake and is termed *anorexia nervosa*. This diagnosis also applies to starvers who may purge whenever food is eaten, out of a fear that they may gain weight or "become fat." Starvation is diagnosed at 15% below an expected body weight, using standard pediatric and adult height/weight tables. *Bulimia nervosa* pertains to taking in large quantities of high-calorie foods, often in a very brief time period (e.g., 15 minutes), and afterward eliminating it from the gastrointestinal tract using self-induced vomiting, ipecac ingestion, laxatives, or fasting periods. Another purging equivalent is compulsive exercise. "Atypical eating disorder not otherwise specified" is the nonspecific category reserved for those who binge but do not purge—these individuals are informally called "compulsive overeaters" and become obese (American Psychiatric Association, 1980).

REFERENCES

American Psychiatric Association (1980). *Diagnostic and statistical manual* (3rd ed., rev.). Washington, DC: Author.

Bruch, H. (1978). *The golden cage: The enigma of anorexia nervosa*. Cambridge, MA: Harvard University Press.

Fenichel, O. (1945). *The psychoanalytic theory of neurosis*. New York: W. W. Norton.

Garner, D. M., & Bemis, K. M. (1985). Cognitive therapy for anorexia nervosa. In D. M. Garner & P. E. Garfinkel (Eds.), *Handbook of psychotherapy for anorexia nervosa and bulimia* (pp. 107–146). New York: Guilford.

Goldner, V. (1985). Feminism and family therapy. *Family Process, 24,* 31–47.

Minuchin, S., Rosman, B. L., & Baker, L. (1978). *Psychosomatic families: Anorexia nervosa in context*. Cambridge, MA: Harvard University Press.

Orbach, S. (1985). Feminist psychoanalytic treatment. In D. M. Garner & P. E. Garfinkel (Eds.), *Handbook of psychotherapy for anorexia nervosa and bulimia* (pp. 83–104). New York: Guilford.

Orbach, S. (1986). *Hunger strike: The anoretic's struggle as a metaphor for our age*. New York: W. W. Norton.

Roberto, L. Giat. (1987). Bulimia: Transgenerational family therapy. In J. E. Harkaway (Ed.), *Eating disorders* (pp. 1–11). Rockville, MD: Aspen.

Root, M. P., Fallon, P., & Friedrich, W. N. (1986). *Bulimia: A systems approach to treatment*. New York: W. W. Norton.

Selvini Palazzoli, M. (1974). *Self-starvation: From individual to family therapy in the treatment of anorexia nervosa*. New York: Jason Aronson.

Walters, M., Carter, B., Papp, P., & Silverstein, O. (1988). *The invisible web: Gender patterns in family relationships*. New York: Guilford.

IV

SECRETS OF VIOLENCE
AND ABUSE

10

Incest: The Heart of Darkness

DUSTY MILLER

ADULT SEXUAL ABUSE of children embodies the darkest forces of human nature. Incest is a story of misused power, exploitation, and the betrayal of innocence. Society recognizes incest as a breach of faith with the community of humanity; the individual who has been a victim of incest understands incest's legacy of madness. No wonder, then, that incest has been "the best kept secret" (Rush, 1980) in the history of humankind.

Still, the enduring human impulse to tell about our experience compels us to transcend even our most entrenched denial about incest. The 1990's find us listening to victims of incest tell their secrets in the privacy of their therapist's office as well as in the legion of recovery groups. Surprisingly, victims of incest are also broadcasting their stories through the media.

There is, of course, a good argument for breaking the bondage of dangerous silence and secrets. The incest secret, left to fester within the wounded individual, distorts his or her experience of living and often leads to the anguish of remorseless emotional illness and psychic pain. We see the symptoms in our clients' substance abuse, eating disorders, self-mutilation, and broken relationships.

But those who promote the importance of disclosing the secret too soon or in unsafe situations fail to recognize how fraught with danger telling the story of incest can be. Those who insist upon immediate disclosure fail to understand that keeping the secret often serves as a protective function for the victim. For various psychologically intricate reasons, the victim often needs to protect the incest relationship. In our well-meaning but misguided

I gratefully acknowledge my collaboration with Dr. Michelle Loris, on the developmental and articulation of many ideas presented in this chapter.

attempts to aid the victim, too often we ignore, or are unaware of, the complex and contradictory interplay of hatred, lust, loyalty, fear, desire, and love that is inherent in the incest relationship.

Yet, if we are to help heal or empower individuals we need to learn how best to approach the secrets that are held deep within. We must carefully and methodically enable incest victims to transform their experiences of pain and wretchedness into stories of healing and wholeness.

For the disclosure of the incest secret to be healing, we must provide the context of a meaningful, therapeutic relationship that allows for the power of telling a story to one who listens with knowledge, skill, and empathy, *and* that emphasizes a relationship of mutuality between client and therapist. Telling the incest secret can be healing or it can repeat the exploitation and betrayal. And, we, as therapists, need to know the difference.

HISTORY OF ATTITUDES TOWARD THE TREATMENT OF ABUSE/INCEST

The history of societal attitudes towards child abuse shows us that we have not always understood how best to help incest victims. For example, we know that since the days of man/boy "love" in ancient Greece, children have been sexually used and abused by adults (Rush, 1980).

Historically, children were considered the property of adults and subject to physical and sexual abuse. This practice prevailed through the end of the Victorian era. It was during this time that Freud developed and later recanted his now controversial "seduction theory."

Freud initially believed his female patients when they disclosed their memories of childhood incest and abuse. He believed patients who were diagnosed with "hysteria" were victims of childhood sexual abuse. This theory shocked his colleagues because of the undeniable implications of wide-spread incest perpetrated by "respectable" family men. Frightened by his cohorts' negative response, he abandoned the seduction theory and, in its place, created the myth-based Oedipus complex, which transformed the disclosures of incest into the child's fantasies of sexual longing for the cross-gender parent (Masson, 1984). *Thus, the father of psychoanalysis was the first to create psychological dogma that protected the dark secret of incest.*

Twentieth-century attitudes and laws have become more respectful and protective of children, thereby creating new possibilities for incest to become recognized and named. Since the 1970's, we have witnessed how the women's movement has created a new awareness in the public sector about abuse and incest. As a result of the efforts of this powerful movement, we have seen shelters set up at a grass roots level to provide a haven for abused women and children. Social and legal structures, too, have responded to the growing awareness of incest and abuse: Medical systems, child protective services, schools, and legal systems are more likely to intervene in situations involving incest; the law mandates reporting child sexual abuse not only in known (or substantiated) cases, but in any instance in which child sexual abuse is *suspected*.

Most significantly, both traditional psychodynamic therapy and contemporary systemic therapy have responded to feminism's powerful influence. In light of the realities of child sexual abuse versus the fantasy of the child desiring sexual union with the parent, psychotherapy was challenged to reformulate its theories and therefore hypotheses, diagnoses, and interventions regarding the classic Oedipal triangle. Post-Freudian psychoanalytic thinkers have been forced to consider their role in inadvertently perpetrating the denial of incest. Developmental theory has been challenged to reexamine psychosexual development in light of the pervasive existence of child abuse. For example, it is no longer possible to assume that children's sexual preoccupations with the cross-gender parent is simply a normal part of developing autonomy. Instead, it must be explored as a possible response to sexual activities initiated by adult caretakers.

Family therapy also has begun to move from its "neutral" position regarding "dysfunctional families." Power and control issues, deemphasized by constructivists, have been explored by feminist family therapists (MacKinnon & Miller, 1987), especially as these pertain to the sexual abuse of women and children.

The twelve-step recovery movement has also played a central role in elevating the disclosure of traumatic and shameful incest experiences. Abuse and addiction specialists insist on confronting the client to disclose incest material and related addiction problems at the outset of therapy. According to this way of thinking, telling the secret becomes the central feature of the healing. More recently, sharing the shameful secret of incest has become appropriated by talk show hosts who encourage and promote incest victims to tell their secret to millions of viewers and listeners.

THE PROS AND CONS
OF DISCLOSING THE SECRET

There are, of course, good arguments for confronting the history of dangerous silences and secrets. One reason is that the anger and fear attached to the untold incest secret will distort the person's sense of wholeness and cohesiveness. Another powerful reason for telling the story is because it connects us with each other, breaking the silence of shame and suffering.

The ritual of group storying legitimates both the person and the story, connecting self to a larger community (Miller, 1990b).

Adrienne Rich, the poet and feminist writer, offers this from *On Lies, Secrets and Silence* (1979):

> . . . In every life there are experiences, painful and at first disorienting, which by their very intensity throw a sudden floodlight on the ways we have been living, the forces that control our lives, the *hypocrisies* that have allowed us to collaborate with those forces, the harsh but liberating facts we have been enjoined from recognizing. Some people allow such illuminations only the brevity of a flash of sheet-lightening, that throws a whole landscape into sharp relief, after which the darkness of denial closes in again. For others, these clarifications provide a motive and impulse toward a more enduring lucidity, a search for greater honesty and recognition of larger issues of which our personal suffering is a symptom, a specific example. (Rich, 1979, p. 215)

While the telling of these toxic secrets may be immediately frightening, it is sometimes the act of breaking the silence that breaks the chronic fear:

> And of course I am afraid, because the transformation of silence into language and action is an act of self-revelation, and that always seems fraught with danger. But my daughter, when I told her of our topic and my difficulty with it, said, "Tell them about how you're never really a whole person if you remain silent, because there's always that one little piece inside you that wants to be spoken out, and if you keep ignoring it, it gets madder and madder and hotter and hotter, and it you don't speak it out one day it will just up and punch you in the mouth from the inside." (Lorde, 1984, p. 42)

Most important, telling the secret of incest allows the victim to get protection and support from a variety of sources. In the case of ongoing incest, the child's telling the secret should lead to acts of protection on the part of the professional/social system and the family. For the adult, telling the secret can allow the victim to connect with important resources, including mental health professionals, peer support resources, family, significant others, and, in some cases, the abuser.

The question of disclosure in situations of incest, however, is complex and very intricate. As the public and professional communities have become actively involved in the reporting of incest and the separation of children from incest perpetrators, the epidemic proportions of the problem have surfaced. This has, in turn, raised questions about disclosure: When can telling the secret be unsafe or not in the best interests of the child or adult victim?

Clinicians working with protective services and/or the school system can recount seemingly endless tales of disastrous reporting instances. The classic situation is that of the professional hearing about incest from the victim or strongly suspecting incest from indirect behaviors, collateral reports, or other forms of oblique communication. The professional files the mandatory report of disclosed (or strongly suspected) incest, and the machinery of protective services goes into motion. Unfortunately, as often as not, something goes wrong. The child may recant, experiencing or at least fearing reprisals. This of course, puts the child at great risk, and the family as a whole may simply disappear from view in relation to professional involvement. Or, there may be no safe home for the child and/or no way to remove the offending adult from the family. Or, the child may be placed in an inadequate or abusive foster home.

Whatever happens, the child inevitably feels confusing guilt, fear, and also, quite frequently, the loss of connection with the offending adult and other central family members. Attempts to build a relationship context within which the child can experience a sense of safety and love, even while disclosing the incest, seem thwarted by the laws and belief systems that mandate immediate disclosure.

Adults, too, may be injured by unsafe disclosure of their long-hidden incest secrets. For instance, disclosure often extends beyond individual psychotherapy to include the sharing of traumatic experiences in twelve-step recovery groups. Those groups identified specifically as "incest survivor" groups and those dealing with the addiction patterns often related to incest, i.e., Alcoholics Anonymous, Narcotics Anonymous, Overeaters Anonymous, etc., become forums for painful self-disclosure. The incest secrets shared in such groups may create a sense of relief and connection to a community of others. Unfortunately, this format may also constrict the telling of the story so that the complex interplay of loyalty, fear, and love inherent in the incest relationship becomes oversimplified. When this occurs, the incest victim may be overwhelmed with feelings of isolation and frightened by the experience of cognitive dissonance.

Research on incest produces another arena of concern. In gathering research data on the problem of incest, another level of secret-extraction occurs. In her book, *The Secret Trauma*, Diana Russell (1986) reports on the various problems surrounding the reporting of facts and feelings about incest:

> Repression is a common protective mechanism employed by victims of all ages, but particularly victims of childhood traumas. In addition, unlike some other traumas, like major medical illnesses, accidents, or loss of a loved one, the incest trauma is often kept a total secret. Even when incest is known to others, it is rarely reminisced about or shared with others. (Russell, 1986, p. 34)

If Russell is right, then the researcher may be among the first to hear the secret. When the researcher questions the subject on the experience of incest, he or she may be unaware of how the memory has been distorted, occluded, or completely repressed. Perhaps even more disturbing is the sharing of these secrets in the absence of a meaningful relationship context. The subject does not have knowledge of whether or not the researcher understands, judges, or accepts her traumatic secrets.

Disclosure of the incest secret is not simple nor is it always curative. One of the problems affecting both children and adults who are forced into premature disclosure of the incest secret is the threat to the relationship between victim and abuser. Incest is undeniably an abuse of adult power; the physical violation is often painful and frightening for the child. The abuser often perpetrates the violation without any empathic awareness of the victim's experience. Often, the abuser is in a state of rage or sexual arousal, which has nothing to do with the relationship with the victim.

For the incest victim, however, the relationship may be more primary than even the trauma of the physical violence or violation. The perpetrator is not only a powerful caregiver figure in the child's world but, paradoxically, may be more present, tender, and loving than anyone else in the child's life. This is frequently the case in the lives of neglected children who may experience the attention (and sometimes the post-sexual remorse) as a way of being "special" to the adult.

Another aspect of secret-keeping for the child is the coercion exercised by the abusive parent. While the adult is *entitled* to keep the secret, the child is *required* to do so. The child may fear direct repercussions, such as violence inflicted on the mother, siblings, pets, property, and most likely, herself. She may be convinced that if she tells the secret, her primary relationship to the seemingly omnipotent and often beloved abuser may be threatened.

Children, and later adults, seem to "take in" the abusive parent as a result of frequent or chronic abuse. This concept of the child identifying with or internalizing the abuser or aggressor has its roots in early psychoanalytic theory (Ferenczi, 1933). It also is part of various object-relations theories, including Fairbairn's concept of the "internal sabateur" (Fairbairn, 1952). In psychoanalytic terms, this means that the child, who cannot tolerate "badness" in the omnipotent parent, takes in the "badness" and incorporates it as part of the self. This splitting allows the parent to be seen as "good." This internalization of the abuser, who, for the child, is often both perpetrator and lover, becomes part of the victim's psychic self. Thus, when the risk of disclosure occurs, the child (and later the adult victim) is, in fact, risking a part of herself.

CASE EXAMPLE:
LEARNING FROM MISTAKES

The following two case vignettes illustrate the development of my ideas about working with the incest secret. First, I have reviewed my "mistakes" and my growing awareness of problems in disclosure. Later, I go on to use the same cases to demonstrate the multimodal treatment model I have developed.

The Wounded Warrior Within

Laura, a 26-year-old, white, self-referred heroin addict, who had been "clean" for one year, began her first session with me by disclosing paternal incest. Despite her nervousness, which indicated that she didn't feel safe with me, Laura insisted on telling me as much of her childhood incest history as she could squeeze into the session. She came to me straight from inpatient and half-way house "recovery" treatment and had learned that self-disclosure was the recommended path to recovery.

I learned from my mistake in allowing Laura's premature disclosure: What I observed was that telling the story of childhood trauma was *not* initially healing. It was, in fact, dangerous. Laura did not begin using drugs again; instead, a series of other dangerous and painful behaviors emerged. The more of her incest story she told, the more compelled she was to commit acts of self-mutilation and other seriously dangerous behaviors, such as running out in the path of cars at night, or going into non-white inner-city neighborhoods where she would taunt residents with racial epithets, thus provoking violent attacks.

One problem with Laura's disclosure was that it was not framed within a relationship. I was as disconnected to her as if I had been watching her tell her story on *Oprah*. Thus, the tales of sadistic abuse served only to stimulate her feelings of guilt, shame, and violation, leading again and again to self-punishing behavior. I was a helpless bystander, witnessing the excruciating reenactment of traumatic abuse, this time by her own hand.

Another issue, that of complex loyalty, was prominent in this case. Although Laura spoke of her father with scorn and rage, it became increasingly clear in our work that she had internalized her relationship with him to such an extent that his "voice" was often indistinguishable from hers. For example, he had convinced her that he was teaching her to be an invincible warrior through the vehicle of his sadistic behavior. As an adult, she had developed a belief that only through her self-inflicted torture could she remain safe or inviolable.

His voice became the voice of this isolated young woman who feared closeness of any sort with any other humans. By letting me get close enough to hear her painful story, she had broken "his" rule. She therefore punished herself for this by increasing dangerous self-abusive behavior.

Fortunately, Laura's story does not end in disaster. Despite the premature disclosure of this complex incest relationship, Laura and I together managed to create a meaningful and real enough relationship to allow for the untangling of the internalized father from the healthier parts of herself.

Working with the Offender's Victim Within

In another case, I had the knowledge gleaned from Laura's suffering to help me approach the situation differently: Rick was referred to me by a therapist who did not find his attitude acceptable for a therapy group of male sex-abuse perpetrators. Rick had failed to convince the group leader that he was sufficiently accepting of his culpability in the sexual abuse of his 13-year-old stepdaughter. The case had gone through the court system: Rick had admitted guilt, had served time in prison, and had participated in one and a half years of court-ordered group therapy for perpetrators. Upon release, his parole conditions specified two years of continuing outpatient therapy.

Rick was not, initially, an easy client to like. He was coldly angry and somewhat sarcastic, and he made it clear to me that he was contemptuous of all mental health professionals, myself included. Rick had learned all the "rules" about what he was required to disclose. He went through his disclosure with an air of indifference, having told it many times before. It was easy to see why his attitude bothered the group therapist as well as other professionals whose reports I received.

Rick had not been able to talk about the secrets surrounding his own childhood humiliations and probable abuse. Each time he was asked to disclose the story of abusing his stepdaughter, he was, without realizing it, reexperiencing the traumas of his childhood humiliations.

Our work together became productive after I postponed reading the reports from previous therapists and listening to Rick's coerced "confessions." We worked on his experiences of being in jail, in mandated treatment, and even before the involvement of the courts, his attempts to tell his uneasy secrets to a therapist he had sought help from on his own.

The next step was to agree to Rick's request for marital work. He and the mother of the abused daughter had divorced during the several years of trial and incarceration, and he had married a woman friend from his church. In our first meeting, Rick's wife had disclosed her own history as an incest victim.

Rick's wife felt cherished by the perpetrator of the incest (her uncle). In her adult memory of herself as an awkward, neglected child, she experienced her uncle as "comforting" and "present." She was resistant to any educational input from me regarding the "fact" or "truth" that adult sexual use of a child is an abuse of power and not in the best interests of the child. She was fiercely protective of Rick, just as she was protective of her relationship with her uncle.

Her willingness to disclose complex feelings about her incest treatment helped me to begin to understand Rick's detachment from his own abuse history, both as perpetrator and as victim. The central insight I had was that, for Rick and his wife, protection of the abusing adult was motivated by believing that incest equals connectedness.

As I got to know this couple better, they began to allow me to know more about Rick's childhood. Rick's childhood miseries had, like his wife's, been somewhat mitigated by a relationship with an adult male relative. After more than a year of marital therapy, Rick finally asked to meet with me alone. He wept when he talked about the kindness of his childhood protector, implying, then denying, sexual involvement with this adult.

Despite the careful relationship-building work we had accomplished, Rick was distressed enough by the disclosure of this long-held secret that he refused to see me alone for several months, requesting instead that we resume couples' therapy.

Working with Rick taught me the importance of developing a strong therapeutic relationship based on mutual trust and relative acceptance of each other's beliefs about the themes of loyalty, protection, and secrets. It became clear that this kind of relationship has to be carefully constructed before moving to the traumatic and complex memories of childhood incest and before confronting the secrets of the adult's abusive behavior. I also learned the necessity of involving significant and supportive others in the therapy process.

In Rick's case, it was important to include his wife in therapy. This served several purposes: (1) It diffused the apparently frightening intensity of one-to-one meetings in which Rick might have felt trapped and forced to share more than he was ready to; (2) it allowed me to work with the couple regarding beliefs that kept them both stuck in dysfunctional patterns of protecting the internalized incest relationship; (3) it allowed me to probe necessary areas of current functioning, i.e., I asked Rick's wife to assess Rick's potential for depression and self-harm; (4) it allowed the secrets in Rick's past to emerge more as reflections or responses to his wife's story. This allowed him to feel more in control of the material because he was participating in the construction of his partner's story as well as his own; this helped us to avoid the dynamics of blaming and shaming so common in working with male perpetrators of incest.

I learned from Rick the importance of doing this work very carefully, of allowing him to disclose secrets at *his* own pace. The resulting awareness, both for Rick and his wife, was that sexual involvement between children and adults is harmful on many levels. This gradual shift in perception was achieved by working from the premises that: (1) *Disclosure of shame and trauma is healing only within the context of a noncoercive, carefully constructed relationship*, and (2) *the incest relationship is a complicated one for both the child and the abuser, varying greatly from one client to another.*

A final note on Rick's story as a representation of the abuser's secrets and shame: If we are groping for language to express the pain and loyalty of the abuse victim's story, we are almost mute when it comes to the secrets of those who commit incest. Part of the problem is that we are angry, frightened, and judgmental towards those who inflict violence on children or women. We don't *want* to listen to the story of the "perpetrator." We prefer to view him as "criminal," and we relegate him to behavior modification. He is viewed as someone who will contain his behavior only through the use of deterrents, be they educational, behavioral, legal, or social.

Obviously, the situation is even more complicated if the "perpetrator" of sexual abuse is a woman. When she has a history of childhood abuse, we view her as a victim as well as a perpetrator. But can we tolerate the use of that "double description" when it is a man who both abuses and was abused? One of the most problematic aspects of disclosure for male victims of sexual abuse is that it puts the male in a "female" position. If he has been sexually victimized, he is "like a woman" as sex object. This obviously triggers the anxiety of having participated, willingly or not, in a homosexual act or relationship. It is for these reasons that many male victims of sexual abuse do not disclose and would even prefer to be identified as perpetrators rather than be viewed through the more compassionate lens the label "victim" evokes.

My strong feeling is that we have to hear the full depth and complexity of the abuser's story, whether we are listening to a man or a woman. Otherwise, we silence the "wounded child within" once again, just as he or she was silenced in childhood. It is in this silence that we replicate old family behaviors and then misinterpret client responses as pathologic.

HOW I WORK WITH VIOLENCE AND ABUSE

In learning from clients like Laura and Rick, I have developed an integrated treatment model (Miller, 1990b). It is narrative-centered and illustrates the centrality of relationship in developing stages of self-disclosure.

The careful unfolding of the abuse secret is central to all stages of the model. This model provides an integrated approach to conceptualizing and treating victims (both children and adults) of abuse and violence. It integrates systematic and intrapsychic levels and moves sequentially through three major stages of treatment: the outer, middle, and inner "circles of conversation." Moving from the "outer" (or systemic) circle, the therapist gathers information about family rules, myths, beliefs, and sequences, which provide information necessary to construct a new, more useful narrative about the family and context of the traumas and secrets (Miller, 1989).

In the "middle" circle, the problematic behaviors are addressed more directly. Clients are helped to connect with relevant peer support resources, like the twelve-step recovery groups and other supportive professional systems such as hospitals, legal systems, school personnel, and the like.

When the client is already involved in such "middle circle" peer support groups or professional systems, the work of the outer circle begins. The gathering of information in the earlier stage of therapy serves both to help the therapist support or alter the client's "larger system" involvement and also helps the client to get a sense of how the therapist will position herself in relation to other professionals or recovery programs.* Then, within the "inner," or intrapsychic, circle, the therapist can work with the client on reconfiguring the internalized trauma narrative or repetition patterns. The

---

*My understanding of and respect for this interface is primarily due to the teaching and writings of my graduate and postgraduate mentor, Dr. Evan Imber-Black.

use of sequential circles or stages of therapy also allows the *client* time to observe the *therapist* and to engage in therapy at her own pace.

An important part of the inner circle work is my conceptualization of the "tripartite self-system." The theory is that the child's internalized self-other relational system includes three introjects oscillating between concept of self and concept of other:

- the victim, an image reinforced constantly in experience
- the internalized abuser
- the non-protecting parent or bystander

This tripartite self-system manifests in the adult client as an ambivalent, rapidly oscillating, often unconscious set of relational beliefs and patterns frequently enacted in self-abusive behaviors and relationships.

Treatment involves helping the client to make conscious and to clearly identify these parts of the self, both in relation to the current self-injurious patterns (or abusive relationship) and to the historical dynamics being re-enacted. Having learned to separate and externalize these voices, the client is then able to develop her own "protective presence" in place of the "non-protecting bystander," and eventually to feel in control of the "internalized abuser" and, with that, of the self-abusive behavior or the abusive relationship.

The work with self-abusive behaviors and/or abuse histories goes far beyond the behaviors themselves. Focusing only on the behaviors can leave clients feeling as silenced as they have been in their families (Miller, 1990a). Evaluation of outcome is based on more global manifestations: the management of relationships, the development of a bounded self (for example, the capacity to define a distinction between the client's needs versus the needs of her partner), the ability to defend against abuse and neglect, and, eventually, the elimination of self-abusive behaviors.

The same theory of the tripartite self-system can apply to patterns of abusive *relationships* as well. The tendency to move towards abusive patterns and the feelings of powerlessness to stop the abuse dynamics stem from the same internalized or introjected presence of the abuser and the same absence of an internalized soothing and protecting presence.

The final stages of the therapeutic work may involve members of the client's current support system, including family, supportive members of the family of origin, friends, and also face-to-face meetings with the abusive and/or non-protecting parents. The goal at this stage is to work through past unresolved relationships, to confront the past abuse, and to build connections to the people in the client's life.

Laura's story and Rick's story both illustrate the following clinical approaches to the incest secret, using this model.

1. How to Manage Secrets Told Prematurely

Laura posed an immediate problem for me by telling me her story before we had even begun to create a meaningful relationship. She was acting on the commonly held belief that the first step in healing the incest wound is to disclose shameful painful secrets.

In the "outer circle" stage of the treatment model, I suggest slowing down or even blocking the client from premature disclosure. Among the reasons for doing this is the central issue of the client's past failures to gain help or protection from those in parental or authority roles.

Laura, for example, had experienced years of a tortured childhood, knowing that neither her mother nor concerned teachers at school could (or would) intervene to protect her. She had also internalized her father's paranoid commands to protect their secret relationship. It was, therefore, very risky for Laura, as an adult, to break the silence and to ask for protection.

It was important for me to explain to Laura why we needed some time to develop mutual trust before she told me the details of her abuse. I explained to her what I needed to understand about her relationship not only with her father but with her mother, her siblings, and other adults who were significant in her childhood. We had to establish a mutual conviction that by telling me her story, neither she nor I would be overwhelmed.

I began by trying to learn the meanings of her symptoms (what she was reenacting) and the beliefs she held about family loyalty and alliances. It was difficult to do so, but I frequently blocked her early attempts to disclose the abuse stories. I always explained why I was doing this by framing it as an attempt to protect her in ways she was not accustomed to being protected.

2. How to Work with Telling the Secrets to Various Family Members

The secret of Rick's incestuous relationship with his stepdaughter had been exposed by the child and then by the criminal justice system. Because so much of that story had been coerced, he had developed an almost dissociated recital of these secrets in his narrative. I think the first genuine disclosures occurred in the empathic relationship of his current marriage.

Generally, our approach, in working both with adults and children, is to try to involve nonabusing members of the client's (current) family in the process of disclosing incest material. For Rick it was helpful to tell the shameful secrets in presence of his wife.

3. Sharing the Incest Secret with Other Siblings and with the Nonabusing Parent (or Parental Figures)

This is often critical for adult clients, just as it is for children. For this to happen in a supportive context, it is usually important for the client to have established a nonfamilial support network in the "middle circle" stage of the work. In my model, the therapist's job is to help the client determine a hierarchy of safety, i.e., who would be the most accepting person to tell first? I help the client to determine what kind of network support (i.e., an Al-Anon group) she or he can count on if and when the disclosure process becomes painful or enraging.

4. How to Deal with Incest Secrets That Have Already Been Disclosed in an Unsafe Context

Both Rick's and Laura's stories represent damaging effects of premature, unsafe disclosures. The "outer circle" in the model is the stage where this can be remedied. Laura, for example, was fixed on her idea that if she didn't "share" her story in twelve-step meetings, she was being cowardly and/or not trying hard enough. I made an effort to understand the negative associations specific to her childhood experiences of disclosure and, then, to protect her by waiting until we had developed a relationship before I really *heard* and *held* her secret shame and suffering.

There is a major emphasis, throughout the treatment phases of this model, on the power of self-disclosure, or storytelling, *and* on the mutuality established between client and therapist. The client is continually encouraged to seek self-determination, to view herself as "expert" in her own healing process. Clients are also encouraged to work collaboratively in a variety of healing relationships, including family, friends, partners, peers in recovery, and therapists.

CONCLUSION

The secrets attached to the incest relationship are complex and tenacious. In this chapter the intention has been to approach these secrets carefully and methodically. Like the naturalist who successfully enters the habitat of the wild creature by both observing *and being observed*, professionals in this field must find ways to create a relatively safe environment in which the incest secret can be disclosed as part of a genuine relationship.

It is suggested that this work be done in stages, moving from the gathering of relevant systemic information, to a middle stage of networking with peer support groups and other professional systems, to finally entering a one-to-one relationship in which the secret can open. Secrets serve protective as well as toxic functions. Each incest experience is different. A multimodal approach can allow the various levels of complexity to be brought forth and healed.

REFERENCES

Davidson, J., Lax, W., Lussardi, D., Miller, D., & Ratheau, M. (1988). The reflecting team. *Family Therapy Networker* (Sept./Oct.) 44–46, 76–77.

Fairbairn, W. R. D. (1952). Endopsychic structure considered in terms of object relationships. In W. R. D. Fairbairn (Ed.), *Psychoanalytic studies of the personality*. London: Routledge & Kegan Paul.

Ferenczi, S. (1933). Confusion of tongues between adults and the child. *International Journal of Psychoanalysis, 30:*225–30.

Gelinas, D. (1983). The persisting negative effects of incest. *Psychiatry, 46:*312–32.

Hoffman, L. (1990). Constructing realities: An art of lenses. *Family Process, 29:*1–12.

Jordan, J. (1987). *Clarity in connection: Empathic knowing, desire, and sexuality.* Wellesley, MA: Stone Center Working Papers Series.

Krestan, J., & Bepko, C. (1990). Codependency: The social reconstruction of female experience. *Smith College Studies in Social Work, 60:*216–32.

Laird, J. (1989). Women and stories: Restoring women's self-constructions. In M. McGoldrick, C. Anderson, & F. Walsh (Eds.), *Women in families: A framework for family therapy.* New York: W. W. Norton.

Lorde, A. (1984). *Sister outsider.* Freedom, CA: Crossing Press.

MacKinnon, L., & Miller, D. (1987). The new epistemology and the Milan approach: Feminist and sociopolitical considerations. *Journal of Marriage and Family Therapy, 13:*2.

Masson, J. (1984). *The assault on truth: Freud's suppression of the seduction theory.* New York: Farrar, Straus & Giroux.

Miller, D. (1988a). Special section on gender. *Journal of Strategic and Systematic Therapies, 7:*2.

Miller, D. (1988b). Interrupting deadly struggles. *Journal of Strategic and Systematic Therapies, 7:*2.

Miller, D. (1989). Family violence and the helping system. In L. Combrinck-Graham (Ed.), *Children in family contexts.* New York: Guilford.

Miller, D. (1990a). Women in pain: Substance abuse/self-medication. In M. Mirkin (Ed.), *Social and political contexts of family therapy.* Boston, MA: Allyn & Bacon.

Miller, D. (1990b). The trauma of interpersonal violence. *Smith College Studies in Social Work, 61:*6–26.

Miller, D. (in press). *Women in pain.* New York: HarperCollins.

Rich, A. (1979). *On lies, secrets, and silence.* New York: W. W. Norton.

Rush, F. (1980). *The best kept secret: Sexual abuse of children.* Englewood Cliffs, NJ: Prentice-Hall.

Russell, D. (1986). *The secret trauma: Incest in the lives of girls and women.* New York: Basic Books.

White, M., & Epston, D. (1990). *Narrative means to therapeutic ends.* New York: W. W. Norton.

11

The Mysterious Disappearance of Battered Women in Family Therapists' Offices: Male Privilege Colluding with Male Violence

GUS KAUFMAN, JR.

VIOLENCE WILL OCCUR at least once in two-thirds of all marriages (Roy, 1982)—that is one of the best-kept secrets in America today. Family therapists have been part of the secret-keeping system; most of us received no training in how to ferret out this secret, much less how to intervene to stop the violence. I don't remember battering being brought up in my training as a family therapist. That I now write about battering and family therapy is not because I saw through the secret on my own, but because of my contact with the battered women's movement. It was this movement that only 20 years ago began to expose the ugly secret of men abusing the women they say they love. My own exposure to those truths has been through my work for an organization—Men Stopping Violence, in Atlanta, Georgia—that is governed at every level by battered women's reality.

An earlier version of this chapter was delivered as a Presidential Plenary Address to the American Family Therapy Association Annual Meeting in San Diego, California on June 20, 1991. The plenary, entitled "Abuse and Violence: The Dark Side of the Family," was published in *The Journal of Marital and Family Therapy*, July, 1992, *18*, 3.

Kathleen Carlin, M.S.W., Executive Director of Men Stopping Violence, Inc., has been my primary mentor in this work for nine years—the overall framework of analysis and many of the specific examples here are based on her work.

This approach is very different from the ordinary conditions of family therapy, under which battered women's reality is usually invisible. In this chapter, I will be advocating an understanding of wife abuse as an issue of oppression of a class of people, not as a matter of individual or couples psychopathology or dynamics. I will point out how family therapists, when lacking this understanding, fail to recognize when the husband of a couple they are seeing is abusing the wife. Finally, I will argue that couples therapy is not an appropriate intervention in situations where a man has abused a woman.

In an effort to begin to render the invisible—battered women's reality— visible, Men Stopping Violence staffers sometimes show a brief video of one of our batterers' groups. In the excerpt from that video presented here, two men, Ernest and Dallas, tell what they did in their worst incidents of violence toward a woman. Each man follows this with an account of the effects of that abuse on the woman, both physically and emotionally. Each also describes any abusive or controlling behaviors he has used since the last meeting, their effects, and what efforts he has made toward working with other men to be nonabusive.

Following are the men's words*:

ERNEST: My name's Ernest, and I'm here because I'm a batterer. My goals are to become nonabusive in all aspects.

My worst incident of violence towards a woman, towards my wife, Leslie, happened about a few years ago. We were discussing a phone number that I didn't recognize, and she was trying to tell me—well, she didn't recognize it. Anyway, I had—we got in a fight, and I beat Leslie real bad. I punched her, hit her, kicked her; I took an object, some type of wood, and hit her across the head with it. And after I beat her, I had sex with her.

Then my other incident was towards my girlfriend, Jackie. I caught her in bed with another man. I lost it, and I slapped Jackie. I was punching her; she said I kicked her—I don't remember. The only time that I got control of myself was when I saw blood coming down her mouth and nose, and she made a statement about, "What about the kids?" and it kind of like snapped me back to reality.

The effects on both of these women: first with Leslie. She had to go to the hospital. Her arm was in a sling. She had bruises all over her body. Emotionally, she doesn't trust me. She won't even let me talk to the kids now; I haven't seen my kids in two years. There's no trust between—she doesn't trust me. And I understand why she doesn't.

---

*Some names have been changed in the transcript by the author.

Since I've been in the program I can see a lot of things more clearly than before I was in the program.

With Jackie, she had to go to the hospital, also. She was emotionally upset. Her self-esteem was low. She didn't know if she was coming or going; she didn't know what was going on. Her children were very petrified of me. She said that they were having nightmares at night. I believe she told me that she had to take her kids to a psychiatrist.

Since the last meeting I haven't used any type of physical, psychological, or any type of controlling behavior. Right now I'm somewhat tired but I'm in good spirits. This week I've contacted—I have several friends that I have known for five years and I talk with them about—normally it'll be about their problems, their marital difficulties, and sometimes I get to express my problems with them. So I have a lot of good contacts with other men not affiliated with M.S.V. And with my experience in the tools that M.S.V. has given me I've been passing them on to other men. I've started to see that other men have a tendency to blame the woman for the problem, and I see myself now as telling them, "Hey, take a look at yourself. Look at the man in the mirror first before you start saying it's the woman's fault." So I've been getting that message across to all of my friends, and it's been good with me. I feel good about myself. They respect me because they see I'm honest, and I'm not telling them what they want to hear. I've been honest with them; I tell them practically the opposite of what they want to hear. But they appreciate that; that's what friendship is about.

DALLAS: My name's Dallas, and I'm a wife abuser as well as a child abuser. I'm here to learn to develop a better way of life for myself, as well as for my family, by using the tools that I pick up at these meetings and through this organization called Men Stopping Violence.

It's been a while since I've been here. It's been just a little over three years ago I got started with M.S.V. At that time, when I first got in contact, my family was split up. And all I can say is, happily today, through some work of mine, as well as the balance of the family, we're back together and seem to be happy today; in fact we *are* happy. Why tell a lie, we *are* happy.

The worst incident of violence towards my wife, Rosalind, occurred after a Christmas party. This goes back about, oh, I'd say about five years ago. Like other people who've shared here, I drank heavily at that Christmas party—to the point where I was more than intoxicated. I couldn't even walk, hardly—but yet I insisted on driving the car. Rosalind's insistence that she drive just angered the heck out of me. In fact I was to the point of being furious. And needless to say, she made the decision and announced that if I were driving she was walking, and therefore I surrendered the keys to the car.

Well, on the way back home from the party, I got verbally abusive in the car. Several times I reached over and just simply turned the ignition off. Of course, with it being a late model car, when you turn the ignition off, the steering wheel locks. But that was something that wasn't in my consciousness at the time. There were other moments in that particular trip home where I had Rosalind by the throat, and I was shaking her. I had a good hold on her throat; it was tight. After we got home, this particular incident continued to the point where I knocked her to the floor and straddled her and then hit her about the face.

The effects of this on her: Top of the list has got to be fear. I myself, I've been in a vehicle when the engine just simply stopped and the steering got difficult — let alone locked. Today, I can look back and say that she had to be horrified. As far as at home, this disturbance woke the children. At that time there were the four boys there: Mark's the oldest, and then there's Ricky, Alan, and then Bill. And the sitter up there asleep was disturbed by this.

My violence towards the children primarily focused at my stepson, but at times it came through towards the other children as well. Usually it was coupled with the use of alcohol. I was — at this time I *am* a recovering alcoholic — and I've been in the fellowship of A.A. just as long as I've been involved with the M.S.V. group.

As far as my violence, abusiveness, and controlling behavior since last meeting, it hasn't been of a physical nature, but there has been some of the emotional trips, like the withdrawing. And even though it's been a long time since there was active violence in the home, the fear of reoccurring violence is still present in the children. And there are some times I capitalize on that fear. To the point where, if the children are becoming unruly, or what I determine unruly, or they're not listening, I'll raise my voice. And I've seen where all of a sudden they get the stone-cold fear in their eyes, and in their face, that they used to have when the violence was active in the home. I try not to use that. But I'm human, and every once in a while I tend to forget.

Like I say, it's been a long time since I started. On looking back from this side, this is by far a better way to live — for all of us. The principles and some of the tools I've picked up here, I not only take them home, but I take them to work. And when I do that, life — the home situation as well as the work situation — is less stressful on me. I don't seem to be so taxed when I come in from work or when I come home off the road. But don't get me wrong: This is not a bed of roses, yet, and I doubt that it ever will be. But it's by far the better way of life.

Ernest, I liked the way you checked in. Let's put it this way. With what you shared with us, it's difficult to keep any secrets. I mean you laid it all out there. All I can say is I can identify with where you've been.

Hearing men describe their violent, abusive, and controlling behaviors without blaming or making a plea for sympathy is unusual for family therapists. It is a hard-won achievement for these men. After each "check in," each man receives feedback — confrontation, suggestions, support — from other men, including the instructors. Men listen to the feedback without rebutting or even responding until the end of class. Thus, we practice listening without interrupting, a "skill" many men lack.

LANGUAGE, OWNERSHIP, AND COVER-UP

In spite of the positive changes illustrated above, these men and the M.S.V. program are not success stories in certain significant ways. The men still partially deny and minimize what they have done and its devastating effects. Such denial and minimization must be confronted, for the effect of keeping aspects of his abusive behavior a secret is to preserve a man's ability to get away with it. For example, Dallas refers to the time "when the violence was active in the home." In "Acts Without Agents," Sharon Lamb outlines how family therapists' language in writing about male violence toward women (use of the passive voice, terms without agents like "domestic violence," etc.) tends to obscure who did what to whom, and who is responsible (Lamb, 1991).

In feedback, one of the leaders pointed out to Ernest that "we don't lose it, lose control, we move to take control of the other person when we don't like what they're doing." All the men are encouraged to stop saying "my wife" or "my wife, Jane" as this subtly reinforces the mode of possession. The instructors pointed out to everyone in the group that they did not adequately portray the *effects* of their violence on others or the horror and the destruction of others' lives they had created.

One of the leaders spoke of the difficulty and necessity of facing these effects and pointed out that no man mentioned the *rage* of the abused person. It is illustrative of why we tape our regular sessions and are supervised on them by Kathleen Carlin, Executive Director of M.S.V. and former director of a YWCA battered women's and rape crisis center that, though we heard Ernest say, "I beat Leslie up and then had sex with her," none of us said to him, as Kathleen said to us, "That was rape."

What *is* unusual about this tape is that it is an instance of men responding to a situation in which they feel called, at least in some degree, to speak the truth of their abuse. I discuss below why family therapy is not such a situation, nor can it be.

WHO BATTERS AND WHY

That our society is hierarchical, heterosexist, and white-male dominated is clear to anyone who is willing to look at the abundantly available evidence. What is equally evident, though constantly obscured, is how that social organization is maintained. For what should be obvious is that *all oppressed people struggle to rise.* All want to escape bondage and participate equally in life. This means that the relations society deems appropriate—i.e., white, heterosexual male dominance and the concomitant subordination of women, people of color, homosexuals, and the poor—can only be maintained by constant assertion and enforcement of that regime. This is the true perspective from which we must look at the otherwise incredible information that between 25 and 66% of men in relationships have used violence toward "their wives." When behavior is that widespread, you can't very well call it pathology unless you want to say the perpetrator's whole class (i.e. males) is sick.

When we began M.S.V., we expected to see some real monsters. However, we found we were meeting with men who seemed like nice guys. Some were unemployed, others were doctors, lawyers, therapists; we saw a professor of theology and a professional mediator. These men who had battered were of various races and religions. We found that relatively few batterers felt good about what they had done, "but what was I supposed to do when she just kept on and on, wouldn't stop?" We saw that battering is considered necessary in order to maintain the status quo in what has historically been a hierarchical institution, the family. Men had to batter because to listen rather than speak, to take the woman's position seriously rather than silence her, would upset the appropriate order of things.

What we do to maintain that order is the reality of the battering and rape of women and children and of all the forms of male violence toward women. Constructivists and systems theorists who are enamored of speaking of the recursive sequences and the arbitrariness of punctuation in relationships, of cybernetic, Heisenbergian, and other new physical explanatory systems, should realize this violence follows the old Newtonian physical laws of mass, velocity, momentum, and inertia—as in a fist hitting a face breaking bones.[1]

That's what battering is—the use of force or the threat of force to get someone to do something they don't want to do or to stop them from doing something they want to do. A battered woman's advocate tells of giving a talk and, afterwards, a woman in the audience coming up and telling her, "I never knew I was a battered woman. My husband and I were married in the fall and were having his family over for Thanksgiving. That morning he got

---

[1] I am indebted to Rich Vodde, M.S.W., formerly of Men Stopping Violence, Inc., for this insight.

angry at me and smashed all my grandmother's china and broke my nose. We were married ten years, and he never hit me again, but if I did something he didn't like, he'd get a certain look in his eye and say, 'Remember Thanksgiving'" (Carlin, 1989b).

For women who survive the physical assaults that are such common events in female lives, there is really no question about the punctuation of sequences. Life is forever divided into before and after. That is the usual reality of battering, the reality of a woman who "walks on eggshells," "lives in fear," who suffers episodic assaults and underlying menace, all designed to break her resistance.

HOW THE SECRET OF WIFE BATTERING IS MAINTAINED

How is it so many family therapists don't know this? The answer is that it's a story we never hear. We don't hear because an aspect of the silencing is the batterer's denial, rationalization, and blaming. We don't hear because we never ask the right questions in the right context of the right people. We are like Red Cross workers visiting a P.O.W. camp and asking, "How are they treating you?" as the guards stand by. She is a prisoner, he is a guard, and we—the well-meaning helpers—won't be there to insure her safety after the visit (Carlin, 1989a).

One hundred percent of batterers deny, minimize, justify, and blame. And women who are abused deny and minimize, too. When a man calls M.S.V., he usually says, "I don't think I'm a violent man but. . . . " The same is true when a woman calls the shelter. And, of course, we family therapists do it, too. We don't want to believe, nor does the woman, that this man she's loved and cast her lot with, this good man did that to her, and surely, we and she don't want to have to admit that he could do it again. She *wants* to forgive and forget as he so urgently requests. She is ashamed of having been so treated, she is fearful of his anger, and she wants him to get help without retaliating against her. All this is why we never hear.

And *too often we collude in the cover-up*, especially if we never ask, "What happens when you fight? Has he ever hit, shoved, or grabbed you?" or, if hearing her answer, we "forget Thanksgiving," forget the climate of terror *one* violent act creates. If our silence is combined with the reality that a woman may have convinced her partner to come for help but that he has insisted that she accompany him to therapy (as hostage), she is going to feel powerfully pulled toward being an agent of her own destruction either by keeping quiet to keep him there, or by sending only the smallest, most tentative of signals. Will you and I learn, as we are learning with addiction and incest, to pick up those signals, to take them seriously, and to act?

The woman is in a hellish bind: If she tells the truth, she knows she faces his wrath/punishment and threat to drop out of treatment when they return home. If she keeps quiet, she betrays herself. And, if therapy is based on honest communication, what have we here? What battered women tell over and over in shelter support groups is "It never came up" or "The therapist blamed me, asked what was my part in it. My husband knew he had an ally, then." For it is virtually essential to battering that it never be seen, never be named for the crime that it is. It is secret behavior, framed as a private, in-the-family matter, a notion unconsciously reinforced by the family therapist. It is not criminal behavior, not a public concern. The first popular book on wife abuse was Erin Pizzey's (1974) *Scream Quietly Or The Neighbors Will Hear*; another early text was *Behind Closed Doors* (Straus et al., 1980). These titles indicate how essential secrecy masquerading as privacy is to abuse.

Juxtaposing "privacy" (a word that we tend to construe positively as a near constitutional right) with "secrecy" (which we tend to see as destructive), we expose a dilemma for family therapists and our culture. Sayings like "A man's home is his castle" point to the basis of this dilemma—that historically the standard has been, and is patriarchal. "The family" originally consisted of a male head of household and his chattel and possessions. "Privacy" pertained to his absolute rights regarding management of his possessions. Hopefully, knowing this can alert us to the reality that, when we "protect the privacy" of clients (by the routine extension of confidentiality, for example), we may be supporting a deadly secret status quo.

Abusive men silence women in a variety of ways. We use combinations of violence, economic controls, criticism, logic, and "gas lighting" (what we now call "mind games"). For example, after he has abused a woman, a man may say, "What are you getting so upset for? I can't talk to you when you're like this. You're hysterical." Over the years, a woman may be so broken down by this regime that she turns to alcohol, pills, or self-destruction, or becomes seriously depressed, at which point she has a "treatable and diagnosable condition," one that doctors can deal with without having to confront the reality of the relationship's power structure.

I've been talking mainly about battered women and batterers. Many of us don't identify with either of those categories. Aren't we the good guys, the helpers? We'd like to think the therapist is the "good guy," the healthy one, the non-client. If a male, we are a nonabuser; if female, we are not abused. But these distinctions are suspect in a world where male dominance and sexism is the norm. A document we reprint in our batterers' program manual, "The Continuum of Male Controls Over Women" (Adams, 1988), diagrams the network or combinations of overt, covert, institutional, and social controls whereby the system of male supremacy is maintained. Basic to the idea of the continuum is that, in general, men living in this society (a) grow up learning that to control others, especially women, is essential to manhood and (b) that men benefit from a system set up that way. All women in varying degrees experience being the objects controlled. Of course, there are important variations of class, race, and individual family experience. Because of this set up some of us—the Pope, the President, and other white males of privilege—don't necessarily have to use hands-on violence to get our way; but the potential for violence in the system is essential to our position of power.

After nine and a half years of doing this work, I no longer believe in the good guy/bad guy split. And I don't believe the problem is male anger or poor impulse control. Anger is a signal to a woman that she's gone too far, that she'd better back down and take it back. Michele Bograd has written about how women therapists are not immune to that signal (1990). By writing about this, she overcame the natural impulse of men and women therapists to disassociate themselves from female clients. We don't see her reality, but instead we say to her, "Here's what you should do." We identify with the oppressor because he controls the information flow and because it's safer. Think what it means to put yourself in opposition to the prevailing power structure. I wonder if women with privileged positions, like therapists, ever feel like Jews who were mayors of ghettos or trustees in the concentration camps, who cooperated with their oppressors believing they could save their own lives and the lives of some others. This sounds extreme, but there is surely a war against women going on. It has been waged for millennia and the dead and damaged are beyond counting. There is no monument to those who have been killed; it is a silent, secret war (Zavala, 1986).

What of male therapists? Are we the good guys? Some of us have had sex with our clients, students, or trainees, to their great detriment. In a recent study, quoted by Rutter in *Sex in the Forbidden Zone* (1989), 17% of female graduate students in psychology had become sexually intimate with a professor during their training, and an additional 30% turned away unwelcome advances. Hopefully, most of us haven't made such advances. It's hard to know, of course. We don't tell those stories. Rutter points out that almost all women have such stories of harassment. I haven't had sex with a client or trainee, but I hit each of the two women I have been in serious relationships with, and I played the good guy so skillfully that I succeeded in getting them to take the blame. I told no one about these episodes of violence and expected that same "loyalty" from my wife and from my other partner, too. It wasn't until I was in a batterers' group, years later, that I first acknowledged and took responsibility for this abuse.

MEN'S RESPONSIBILITY FOR CHANGE

I believe with John Stoltenberg, author of *Refusing to Be a Man* (1989), that men must begin this revolutionary truth-telling, must become accountable for their actions. To batter, sexually abuse, harass, or use women and then to benefit from a set up that implicitly approves of or keeps silent about our actions makes us, at best, good Germans, comfortable white Southerners, who enjoy the power and privilege of keeping a class of cheap laborers or subjects.

THE ROLE OF THERAPY IN MAINTAINING SECRECY

What is the role of therapy in our current social organization? All too often, therapy serves the status quo. I don't necessarily exclude batterers' groups from this indictment, for women are more likely to stay with a man who attends a batterers' group, and, in reality, his attending may not make her safer. Ellen Pence of the Domestic Abuse Intervention Project once observed that when Martin Luther King, Jr., and the civil rights movement set out to end segregation, they didn't start by setting up encounter groups for Klan members.

The radical therapy movement of the early days of my involvement as a therapist had a formula:

Alienation = Oppression + Mystification

To me, this formula explains much about our arguments on this issue. The term "battered women" is a political term, one that demystifies oppression. Most of us grew up in a time before that term existed. Before it, says Gloria Steinem, the term was life, as in, "That's life." The term "battered woman" was and is taken by women in defiance of men, including therapists. They assert their right to name the reality of what has happened to them. By asserting that they were being battered and that they didn't have to take it anymore, women created the first safe house networks and battered women's shelters only 20 years ago. The location of these shelters had to be kept secret, speaking to the fact that society is not a safe place for women. They are part of an underground railroad that has no North. They hold up a mirror to society that says, "We are not the problem, there's something wrong with a society where we have no safety in our homes" (Carlin, 1989b). The effort to make them "take it back" is fierce: Shelters, like abortion clinics, are constantly under attack, not so much with bombs and pickets, as

with efforts to make them tone down their message, stop being "political,"
stop telling their stories, *keep the secret.*

Therapy, much of it with the best intentions, is part of this reprivatizing
context, this mystification of oppression, when we agree to keep his crimes
confidential, and when we explain "the situation" via intrapsychic or intergenerational or couples' dynamics. The term "battered woman" is not one
most women hear from a therapist as possibly describing themselves. And,
if battered women frequently "disappear" in therapy, the nonappearance of
the batterer is even more complete. The fact that a crime has been committed is never discussed, much less that he has committed it. Family therapists
say they don't want to be agents of social control. What this means in our
society is that family therapists don't want to challenge the patriarchal norm
for fear of being attacked or of losing some of our heterosexist and class
privilege.

Our fears are not so much of assault but that we will be seen as "going too
far." Women fear, rightly, that it will be said that they are taking sides, that
they are too serious, too angry. They fear being called a man hater, a castrat-
ing bitch, a lesbian. (Homophobia and misogyny are faces of the same
coin.) We men often simply never see or hear, for the dominant group never
has to see the reality of the subordinate. We rest on our privilege, rather than
step out and risk being a traitor to our class. At least these are some of the
answers I come up with when I ask myself why it is that people of good will,
people who want to help, can be blind to what it means for a battered
woman to sit in a room with a therapist and her batterer. I think that partly
it's that women have never been free to speak the truth. Partly it's an economic issue: This is our livelihood. And we believe in ourselves, our ability
to help these people. All of this rides along with our need to not know about
the true horrors, to distance, to disassociate.

Therapy has not been good for battered women. At a forum on battered
women and therapy at the National Coalition Against Domestic Violence
Conference in St. Louis, I heard one shelter worker say, "In two years of
crisis counseling, I never heard a woman in couples counseling say the
battering stopped." For this reason, state coalitions of battered women's
shelters have issued statements condemning couples' counseling as an intervention when a man has been violent to a woman in a relationship. But state
coalitions and battered women's shelters, as representatives of battered
women, are under relentless attack, multiple pressures to take it back, make
nice, don't rock the boat. The co-option and destruction of what, a few
years ago, was called perhaps the largest grass roots social change movement
in this country is well advanced. It has been accomplished through the
carrot and the stick, seduction and punishment, lesbian baiting (those angry
women), United Way funding followed by fears of loss of that funding.

Divide and conquer has been used, too. Those with a bit of power have often become agents controlling those with less power—straights against lesbians, professionals taking power from "nonprofessionals," whites and those who will serve their interests against "angry, demanding" blacks. How women can be turned on one another to help destroy their own rights is aptly delineated in Margaret Atwood's *The Handmaid's Tale* (1986).

Women have not been trained to fight for rights, as Carol Gilligan (1982) points out, but to care for others. In their concern for others and avoidance of conflict, they come to be used as agents of their own destruction. William Grier and Price Cobbs, in their classic text *Black Rage* (1968), wrote about the rage oppressed people feel and how they hold it in and turn it on themselves. Women, black and white, have been socialized, taught, and punished to get them not to show anger. After all, wife abuse is the only crime where the victim is expected to go to bed with the assailant, if not the night of the crime, then very soon after. But women need their anger to stand up and force change. Frederick Douglass, the great abolitionist and former slave, instructs us:

> The whole history of the progress of human liberty shows us that all concessions yet made to her august claims have been born of earnest struggle. . . . If there is no struggle, there is no progress. Those who profess to favor freedom, and yet deprecate agitation, are men who want crops without plowing the ground, they want rain without thunder and lightning. They want the ocean without the awful roar of its many waters. (Blassingame, 1976)

I'd like to propose a corrective for us—the George Bush standard. Let's ask ourselves, if he had done to George Bush what he has done to her, what would happen to him? And let's consider her as much a citizen with as many rights in this democracy as George Bush. Some of us have used "no violence" contracts; what if he had beaten George Bush, would we expect him to still be at large and free to negotiate with George so long as he didn't attack him again? Will we agree that he can physically attack *us*, and we'll meet with him after that, as long as he promises not to do it again?

WHY MEN BATTER: MYTHS AND MISSTEPS

If we're going to open the secret of wife abuse and confront batterers, we need to be clear about why men batter. One popular mental health theory is that "insecurity" causes men to batter. David Adams' "Treatment Models of Men Who Batter: A Profeminist Perspective" (Yllo & Bograd, 1988) quotes a dialogue with a man interviewing for the EMERGE batterers' program. The counselor says, "A lot of people feel insecure but they are not violent.

What I'm interested in finding out is how do you make the decision to hit your wife—and to break the law—even if you are feeling insecure?" The client (who has been in therapy) reports being "dumbfounded" by the idea that hitting is a decision. The counselor asks, " . . . are you waiting to stop feeling insecure before you stop being violent?" Explaining battering as resulting from insecurity or loss of control ignores the power dimension— that battering is a tool for maintaining power over someone. Otherwise, those who are more insecure—the oppressed—would be the primary batterers!

Another popular theory is that "the warrior is hard-wired" (Bly, 1990), he is genetically programmed to be a male. The idea that men are inherently violent has several problems. One is that it would seem to cast men who don't fight as being somehow defective. Popularly, such men are labeled wimp, sissy, womanish. The contemporary men's movement, through its back-to-the-warrior ideology, may be, perhaps unwittingly, contributing to the mystification around battering.

This movement has not presented a clear challenge to male violence, in part because it has not confronted male or class privilege. While men with less money go to basic training and recently to Saudi Arabia with Desert Storm, some of us with more privilege have headed to the country on "Wild Man" weekends. Certainly, there is much of value to be found in this new men's movement. The way our fathers were abusive and/or absent *is* worth grieving. But we need to acknowledge that we're also the fathers who take power and control when we are around and we are free to go to these weekends. We don't seem to note that women missed having nurturing, supportive, nonabusive fathers, too, or that when we say "It's a privilege to be here," that's literally true.

I think many women and people of color rightly see the mythopoetic men's movement as, in many ways, an effort to shore up and consolidate white male hegemony and power. This movement never seems to challenge male privilege; it has no interest in that (Bathrick, 1991; Kaufman, 1991). Men in this movement don't seem to acknowledge that they are perpetrators, especially against women, they see themselves only as victims. In its emphasis on male bonding and "finding the deep masculine," this movement seems determined to strengthen what John Stoltenberg calls "the male sex-class." Stoltenberg says the idea of the male sex-class is like the idea of the Aryan race. The tactics of control, as in Germany or in the South, an array backed by violence, are the very forces that create and maintain the differences.

But our belief in the primacy of gender is deeply instilled. Most of us reject the notion of inherited Jewish or African-American character traits, yet we still may be committed to the idea of profoundly different feminine and masculine traits that are basic and genetic. Brilliant studies by Broverman et al. (1972) and Gilligan (1982) have shown that our idea of what those traits are and how we value them amount to a belief that qualities we consider healthy in an adult (e.g., logic, rationality, assertiveness), we consider pathological in a female, i.e., what is female is unhealthy.

The Wisconsin Department of Health and Social Services commissioned a study report on programs for batterers, which states:

> As programs for battered women developed and grew, researchers and program staff began analyzing batterers. They found that batterers are not out of control when they abuse, are not angry, nasty men, and do not suffer from lower self-esteem than non-batterers. (Brandl, 1990, p. 6)

I believe, and the experiences of battered women teaches us, the true reasons we batter and use other power and control tactics are (a) we've learned to, (b) it works, and (c) we can. The implications of this are that for us to stop we'll have to (a) learn differently and (b) not be able to get away with it.

How can that come about? Last year, a group of us from batterers' programs met with Paulo Freire, author of *Pedagogy of the Oppressed*, who works in South America creating educational practices that are liberating and demystifying. We came together to examine the question "Can there be a liberatory pedagogy for the oppressor?" I would like to think there can be—that Ernest and Dallas are examples of change in that direction. But Ernest has hit his wife again, and Dallas says his kids still "get that stone-cold look of fear in their eyes." Last year, M.S.V. marched in the Martin Luther King Day parade in Atlanta; 16 or 17 of us were behind a big banner saying "Men Stopping Violence Against Women." As we rounded the corner from Peachtree Street onto Auburn Avenue, a woman in the crowd saw our sign and yelled out, "Oh, I really feel safe now!"

Our efforts so far *are* puny.

TOWARDS SAFETY AND JUSTICE: CHALLENGING THE SECRECY

What finally stopped lynching was when it was treated as a crime, when the perpetrators were unmasked, prosecuted, and punished. We therapists influence how behavior is viewed; we need to advocate for battering being identified and treated as a crime. Twenty years ago, my supervisor Jean Harsch told me the most powerful people in a system have the most room to move and change. As a change agent, she said, you need to throw your weight on the side of the less powerful.

What I don't remember Jean telling me is how the powerful react when you challenge their power. When we label violent acts as criminal, when we stop the collusion, challenge the secrecy, and put it all out in the open, we can expect a reaction. If we throw our weight on the side of consequences for abusing, he will label that as "making it worse for him." He may increase his efforts to control and intimidate us and her. She knows that, and like other hostages, may exhibit Stockholm syndrome, whereby the captor's interests become paramount. There is no easy way out of these binds.

With that in mind I, nonetheless, want to offer a few practical suggestions for what we can do in our clinical settings towards establishing safety and justice for battered women.

1. Be sure there's a woman therapist in the room. (I don't see any couples without a woman co-therapist anymore, since I've realized I don't know what I don't know.) Ideally, the woman therapist will have been through volunteer training at a battered women's shelter.

2. Ask the questions: "What happens when you argue?" "Has he ever hit you? Shoved you?" "Are you afraid of what he might do if you didn't back down?" Before you decide that the man's level of controlling behavior was not so high as to make couples therapy untenable, ask yourself, "What if he'd done that to me?"

3. If either of you suspects violence, *separate* the couple, with the man seeing the man and the woman seeing the woman. The women can work on a safety plan for her, what she can do to maximize her safety. That should always go along with a fourth step:

4. Refer her to the nearest battered women's shelter. It can be located by calling 1-800-333-SAFE, the National Coalition Against Domestic Violence Hotline. Shelters have legal advocacy and battered women's support groups. There, she'll hear other women tell their stories; she won't feel isolated and crazy anymore. The staff won't tell her what to do; they work on the principle of empowering her to make her own choices. Even if she doesn't go now, she'll have the number for the next time.

5. If she gives you the okay, tell the abusing man *why* you won't do couples' therapy, that you don't believe it would be safe for his partner, and you won't go along to keep him from feeling upset, controlled, or uncomfortable. Tell him that what he has done is a crime and that this is a criminal matter, not a therapy issue, (even though they undoubtedly have other individual and couples' problems). Tell him you believe it's his job to stop endangering her and to do what is necessary for her to feel safe, though she may never feel safe around him again. Find ways to support that position and the law—her basic rights.

6. Get supervision by battered women's advocates. (Pay for it.) Build in listening to women in a variety of contexts where they are free and empowered to speak the truth. Read feminist and battered women's books; there, we can't intimidate or interrupt, we can't force a book to placate us.

Sitting down in a room with the couple implies that this is the place and the unit that can fix the problem. When the problem is battery, that isn't so. In fact, as long as she's there, he blames her. What will fix it is a society that has so many sanctions against male violence that it becomes too costly, too unthinkable, that it is no longer an option. In the short term, she can meet with other women to get practical help and verbal confirmation that she isn't crazy, isn't at fault for his behavior, and has a right to her say. He can go to work with other men on what he'll do instead of battering.

That sort of men's work must be based on accountability to battered women. At Men Stopping Violence, our principles of having battered women's advocates on our board, having leaders "check in" on their abusiveness, supervision by advocates, having a safety check with women, in which we take as reality what they say about how they've been treated — all arise from this accountability. It's not easy for men or women. I used to get headaches in the supervision sessions. The shelter women advocates had to rehearse before we came to their offices to feel able to confront us as male therapists. What this has led to, though, is a structure that goes a long way towards holding men accountable for their actions. To enter an M.S.V. class, a man must sign a contract that requires not only the usual stipulations of payment and no alcohol or drug abuse, but also no firearms, no confidentiality, no pre-trial diversion — he must plead guilty to any crimes with which he is charged and that he committed, if he wants to get into our program. If he abuses again, there are negative consequences — he may be required to move out, if he has not already, he may have to give us and the abused woman a signed confession of his violent acts, which she can use in court, and we may require a variety of other measures in the direction of justice and safety for her.

Our efforts or your efforts alone can't insure this. If the cause is patriarchy, how can the cure be family therapy *or* batterers' groups? The cure must be change at every level. We can give our testimony, and refuse to go along doing couples' therapy on her back. She has so little room to move if there are children, if she has a job and a stable community she'll have to leave, if leaving means poverty and feeling she has failed as a wife, and if there is a real possibility that he'll track her down and kill her. The shelters work at helping her see that she has choices and what those choices are. They're underfunded, under-respected, under pressure to conform. We are not in danger, we do not have so much to lose. So, let's experiment with standing up to him and saying no.

REFERENCES

Adams, D. (1988). The continuum of male controls over women. Reprinted and modified in D. Bathrick, K. Carlin, G. Kaufman, & R. Vodde, *Men stopping violence: A program for change*. Atlanta, GA: Men Stopping Violence, Inc.

Atwood, M. (1986). *The handmaid's tale*. Boston, MA: Houghton Mifflin.

Bathrick, D. (1991). Being a man: How we go about our fathers' business. *Working together* (newsletter of the Center for the Prevention of Sexual and Domestic Violence, Seattle, WA), 2, 3.

Blassingame, J. W. (1976). *Frederick Douglass: The clarion voice*. Washington, DC: Division of Publications, National Park Service, U.S. Department of the Interior.

Bly, R. (1990). *Iron John*. Reading, MA: Addison Wesley.

Bograd, M. (1990). Women treating men: Confronting our gender assumptions. *Family Therapy Networker, 14*, 54–58.

Brandl, B. (1990). *Programs for batterers: A discussion paper*. Madison: Wisconsin Department of Health and Human Services.

Broverman, I., Vogel, S., Broverman, D., Clarkson, F., & Rosenkrantz, P. (1972). Sex-role stereotypes: A current appraisal. *Journal of Social Issues, 28*, 59–78.

Carlin, K. (1988, May). Family violence issues. Third Annual Social Work Futures Conference, University of Houston School of Social Work, Houston, TX.

Carlin, K. (1989a, March). Wife battering/spouse abuse/couples' violence. American Orthopsychiatric Association Institute, New York, NY.

Carlin, K. (1989b, October). Family violence: An issue of social justice. The American Medical Association Conference on Family Violence and Victimization, Chicago, IL.

Freire, P. (1989). *Pedagogy of the oppressed*. New York: Continuum.

Gilligan, C. (1982). *In a different voice: Psychological theory and women's development*. Cambridge, MA: Harvard University Press.

Grier, W. H., & Cobbs, P. M. (1968). *Black rage*. New York: Basic.

Kaufman, G. (1991). Healing the pain by misplacing blame: Some thoughts on the men's movement. *Working Together, 2, 3*.

Lamb, S. (1991). Acts without agents: An analysis of linguistic avoidance in journal articles on men who batter women. *American Journal of Orthopsychiatry, 61*, 250–257.

Pizzey, E. (1974). *Scream quietly or the neighbors will hear*. London: Penguin.

Roy, M. (Ed.) (1982). *The abusive partner*. New York: Van Nostrand Reinhold.

Rutter, P. (1989). *Sex in the forbidden zone: When men in power—therapists, doctors, clergy, teachers, and others—betray women's trust*. Los Angeles: Tarcher.

Stoltenberg, J. (1989). *Refusing to be a man: Essays on sex and justice*. New York: Penguin/Meridian.

Straus, M., Gelles, R. J., & Steinmetz, S. K. (1980). *Behind closed doors: Violence in the American family*. Garden City, NY: Anchor.

Yllo, K., & Bograd, M. (Eds.) (1988). *Feminist perspectives on wife abuse*. Newbury Park, CA: Sage.

Zavala, M. (1986, June). Keynote address to the National Coalition Against Domestic Violence conference, St. Louis, MO.

V

LEARNING TO HEAR THE
VOICE OF SILENCE

12

The Love That Dares to Speak Its Name: From Secrecy to Openness in Gay and Lesbian Affiliations

GARY L. SANDERS

All trials are trials for one's life, just as all sentences are sentences of death.

—Oscar Wilde, *Profundis*

Experience is the name everyone gives to their mistakes.

—Oscar Wilde, *Lady Windemere's Fan*

The yellow slip identifying a request for consultation rested in my letter box in the doctors' lounge of the General Hospital. I picked it up, scanned the name of patient, his age, and the unit where he was an inpatient. A neurologist was asking me to see a 32-year-old man diagnosed with atypical *grand mal* epilepsy. The fellow was currently in the hospital for further investigation and medication stabilization. Intrigued by this information, I glanced down to see the reason for consultation and saw a simple yet curious phrase: "issues of sexual orientation." So began a four-year long, rich therapeutic relationship with Jonathan Whiteson.[1]

My first meeting with Jonathan surprised me a bit because he seemed so much younger than his recorded age. He had sandy hair, a

[1] All names have been changed.

slight build, and was lying in a hospital bed, obviously under the influence of medication. He looked at me languorously as I walked in, sat beside him, and introduced myself. At the mention of my being a psychiatrist with an interest in the area of sexuality, his face became instantly guarded. I explained that his physician had asked me to see him.

After setting Jonathan at ease, I discovered that he was an only child, that his parents were in their 50's, and that he was working for a trust company as an accountant. I asked him how it was that he came to be in the hospital. He told me that since the age of 18 he had been struggling with a form of epilepsy diagnosed as *grand mal*. Following an attack, he would be left unconscious, his memory would be blank, and often he would be unable to interact effectively for as long as two days. He described how he would shake uncontrollably, often would weep emotionally, but would end up with total amnesia for the actual epileptic event itself. His response to these events had traditionally been one of increasing his isolation and rest, and taking time off work to remain at home. His parents, with whom he continued to live, would help nurse him during these post-attack times. He said that he would suffer attacks about once every four to six weeks. Jonathan had been on long-term antiepileptic medication for a number of years, which had decreased the frequency, but not the severity of the episodes.

This current hospitalization was his first for a complete investigation which included continual monitoring of his EEG or brain waves. One attack was observed by hospital staff but without any supporting EEG evidence of an epileptic seizure having actually occurred. When his physician asked him more personal questions, he discovered that Jonathan had sexual concerns but refused to speak to his doctor about them, saying they were too private. His doctor suggested a specialist consultation, to which Jonathan agreed. The consultation request had then come to me.

The story that he hesitantly told, with much self-recrimination and occasional tears, was of a young man who, at the age of 17, had discovered himself to be passionately in love with his best friend. This friendship had lasted for two years and had been quite intimate: They had discussed the meaning of life, the extent of the universe, and the place of human beings, like themselves, in all of this. They had played sports together, worked on their projects together, attended school together, and talked of going to the same university together. They even had occasions to double-date. However, once, when the two were camping together, Jonathan disclosed to his friend the depth of his feelings for him. His friend indicated that he felt similarly and, with that, Jonathan reached out to begin a first hesitant, sexual interaction. But, Jonathan said, it had gone no further than a few caresses when his friend jumped angrily to his feet saying that he was no "fag" and then moved silently to the opposite side of the tent. This event was never spoken of again, but their friendship quickly waned. Jonathan was left confused, isolated, hurt, and extremely lonely. Only a few months after this incident, at the end of his last year of school, Jonathan had his first "epileptic" seizure. He and his best friend had always planned to double-date on graduation and had looked forward to attending university together in the fall. Jonathan was unable to attend graduation because of his attack.

What followed that first attack was an increasing frequency of such seizures, to the point where significant medications were used to try to decrease them. Unfortunately, the medications seemed to have little or no effect on his attacks, but did sedate him and quiet his sense of worry and anxiety. Due to the nature and frequency of his symptoms (he and his parents were afraid he would hurt himself during an attack), Jonathan remained at home and attended a local university rather than going to the same university as his former friend. He also gave up many of his social interactions, except for casual friendships, and stopped dating entirely. He had spoken to no one about the experience with his best friend until the day of our talk, 15 years later, in a sterile hospital room.

Jonathan, having discovered that his intensely felt love for his best friend was unacceptable, decided to keep secret this difference from what was expected and seemingly accepted by society. He experienced many toxic effects from keeping this secret. He suffered years of disability as an "epileptic." He was often heavily medicated and frequently unable to complete his work effectively due to side effects of the medication. What, I wondered, would be so troubling as to actually erase itself from conscious memory (he had amnesia for the few days before an attack) and require him to be nursed along by family? Careful reflection on Jonathan's experiences leading up to an attack revealed that he had invariably experienced being in a position of choosing between self-affirmation (but at the risk of personal rejection) or self-erasure through social conformity. Ever since his first painful attempts at choosing self-affirmation with his adolescent friend, he had always chosen social conformity with its tyrannizing side effect of self-erasure. When these "choices" were of great importance, he would suffer an attack, losing conscious memory for the decision and the issue. He would be ill and dependent in such a way that his family could not reject him. He also considered himself (and his sexual orientation) as being ill. Additionally, he appeared to suffer chronic sadness and loneliness. He tried to overcompensate for his difference by becoming "stereotypically similar" to what he was "supposed" to be—dressing in the proper manner, dating the proper women, even attending the church of his parents' choice, although he felt no affiliation to that particular view of God. In the end, he even began to act in a political direction that was commensurate with what Tripp (1975) has called, "Trying to slay the dragon within by slaying it without." He became anti-gay himself, seeing gay and lesbian people as inferior, weaker, sicker than others, and less able to have a fulfilling life.

My work with Jonathan was based on the notion of externalizing the tyranny of secrecy and then helping him see the damaging effects of being victimized by such a tyranny. For Jonathan, self-erasing secrecy, as we came to call the tyranny, caused such damaging effects as social isolation, preoccupation with a sense of personal inadequacy, fear of his parents' rejection if he were not close enough to monitor their views of him, a continued avoidance of any situations that could include intimacy, and, of course, his "epilepsy." Because there was no medical evidence of an organic basis to his attacks, I became curious as to how they could enter into his experience. After he came to see how pervasive the toxic effects of "self-erasing secrecy" were in his experience, the next step involved helping him recognize his own agency in escaping the secrecy. For instance, the act of discussing all of this with me was a crack in the armor of secrecy, as he reflected on how he felt better after discussing these secrets during therapy. Similarly, he noticed a decrease in the frequency and severity of his attacks.

Over a period of a few months, Jonathan judiciously came out, first to his parents (they were not surprised, and, although they admitted disappointment, they also expressed their love for him), and then to his only friends, one a woman, the other a man whom he had known for many years. In both instances, these friends surprised him by taking his gayness in stride and reaffirming their friendship with him. As he saw his own influence over secrecy, the effects of secrecy's tyranny to direct Jonathan's life receded rapidly. Rather than simply succumb to secrecy, he replaced secrecy with privacy—a privacy in which he was able to choose with whom he discussed his gayness.

Over the last months of our first work together, Jonathan made new friends at work, gained increased support and acceptance by his family of origin, and developed a "family of choice"—those friends and relatives who became his family through their acceptance of him.

Now, four years after our first meeting, I think to myself of the new Jonathan who has just left my office. At the age of 36, he has just reopened therapy in order to seek some supportive help in dealing with the loss of a significant eight-month relationship. Jonathan has received a number of promotions, has long been off his antiepileptic medication, and is now clear of mind. He had had another attack—the first in over two years—and was feeling exceptionally shaken. I asked him, "Can you think of any secrets that have gotten hold of you lately so intensely that you have inadvertently caved in to their expectations that you erase your own experience?" He said,

> I tried to pretend that our breakup would have no influence on my work, and yet it did. When my manager came and asked me if anything was wrong because my performance had slipped over the last few days, I denied it and said I was fine. By week's end, I was in bed asking friends to nurse me and to make the appointment with you.

This attack had less to do with gay issues than with simple human experiences of love and loss for a man who happens to be gay.

Although Jonathan's story may be dramatic because his symptoms were identified and diagnosed as a medical illness, the experience that he underwent "at the hands of secrecy" is by no means unique or uncommon. For 10–15% of the western world's population, Jonathan's story is all too experientially familiar. It is my opinion that there is no life experience more tyrannized by secrecy than that of being gay or lesbian.

PERSONAL REFLECTIONS

Once, when I was 11 years old, I was playing with my brother and sister in the backyard one sunny summer afternoon, when a tall, somewhat thin and effeminate young man came to the gate asking if we had seen his small poodle. I recognized him as the man from the end of the block who had recently moved in to look after his dying mother. My own mother called us in as she replied to the man in a cold and aloof voice, rather unlike her, that she had not seen his dog. Once he had left she turned to us and said, "Stay away from him, he's not of a good kind." This, of course, was a paradox to me as a child. Prior to this, I had thought to myself, "What a kind man he must be to come home from whatever life he had been leading in order to look after his dying mother." For him to spend those precious days of his youth with her during her last moments seemed to my young mind a rather generous thing to do. I could not see why he was "not of a good kind." It was only some years later that I came to understand that others thought he was gay.

Similarly, I remember a story of my great-uncle's son who had died at the age of 30 while with a male friend. The two were involved in a canoeing accident and both had drowned. Although I had never known this cousin, I grew up with stories of "it being for the best" that he had died. It wasn't until I was in my early 20's that I came to understand that this view of his death as being "for the best" was because he had been gay. Yet, he was my great-uncle's only son! Then, there was the older sister of one of my girlfriends from high school, who was asked to leave home at the age of 17 because she refused to wear party frocks and go to her school dances. Instead, she preferred to keep the company of a young woman. These two would laugh with joy when together, but the family would look on with disgust and revulsion.

I knew many such stories as I grew up. It wasn't until some time in my early 20's that I came to understand that these people were punished, not for any evil deeds they had done, but for an "affliction of the heart"—for truly loving someone of the same gender when others wished them to love only those of the opposite gender. It seemed so patently unfair, a crime without a victim, a sentence without a defense.

Although it was my awareness of the blatant and painful prejudice against same-sex love that first highlighted my understanding of discrimination, I quickly came to see that it came in other forms as well. Racism, ageism, religious discrimination, and cultural discrimination all seemed to be of the same ilk, but it was in the discriminatory practices against women, particularly those women of my own family, that I saw the greatest similarity with the oppressive discrimination of gay and lesbian people. However, there is one major difference. With gay and lesbian people, the oppression is of an invisible minority. They are not marked by any particular identifications, and they do not exhibit, in large part, the stereotypes of others who do not know them well.

OF LOVE AND LENSES

The word "homosexual" first appeared in 1891 in John Addington Symonds' treatise, *A Problem of Modern Ethics* (Persky, 1989). Its counterpart, "heterosexual," first appeared ten years later, in 1901. Persky writes,

> In Dorland's *Medical Dictionary* (1901), "heterosexual" was defined with unconscious poetic justice as "abnormal or perverted appetite toward the opposite sex." Some would say that under the tyrannical patriarchy, there is a sense in which all male heterosexuality is a "perverted appetite." . . . But not until the 1955 addenda to the third edition of the *Oxford English Dictionary* is *heterosexual* again required to officially define itself and, even then, does so in blatantly

ideological language as "pertaining to or characterized by the normal relations between the sexes." One only has to reflect glancingly on the monstrousness of the relations between the sexes, recorded in a torrent of studies, to absorb the impact of that usage of "normal."

For too many people the word homosexual brings forth a view of sexual *choice* embedded in a context of irresponsibility, immorality, and, occasionally, crime. However, most of us, both gay and straight, have been misled by the term homosexual. We orient towards the *genitalization* of human experience. As the title of this chapter suggests (based on the words of Oscar Wilde during his trial for being gay at the turn of the century in Ireland), homosexuality actually has more to do with one's love affiliation than simple genital lust:

> "The Love That Dares Not Speak Its Name" is such a great affection as there was between David and Jonathan, such as Plato made the very basis of his philosophy, and such as you find in the sonnets of Michelangelo and Shakespeare. It is that deep spiritual affection that is as pure as it is perfect. It dictates and pervades great works of art. It is in this century so much misunderstood that it may be described as the "love that dares not speak its name" and on account of it, I am placed where I am now. It is beautiful, it is fine, it is the noblest form of affection. There is nothing unnatural about it. That it is so, the world does not understand. The world mocks at it and sometimes puts one in the pilary for it. (Herrman, 1981)

I propose, like Oscar Wilde, that what we have come to call homosexuality has much less to do with sexuality than it does with the experience of human affiliation. Of course, by its very nature, there can be a sexual component to that affiliation, either in mind and/or in practice. However, it is my suggestion that we view homosexuality through the lens of human affiliation. This affiliation is based on a preferential love relationship along with, perhaps, a hope for congruence of sexual activity. I suggest this view instead of that which sees homosexuality through the lens of genital activity alone. That is, rather than simply privilege behaviors and subsequently confuse these behaviors with a person's inner experience, I propose to view the inner experience as more fundamental and the behavior as either being congruent with that experience or denying of it. Further, it is my belief that the existence of a compelling invitation to keep one's love affiliation secret, and the succumbing to that invitation, is the poison that robs gay and lesbian people of their joy in life and their hope for the future.

HISTORICAL OVERVIEW

It is believed that gay and lesbian people have existed since the beginning of time. Although the word homosexual was only recently coined in human history, descriptions of same-sex love exist in all human records from the earliest of writings to the thousands of human languages that are spoken today. Anthropologists (Tripp, 1975) suggest we look at the world's cultures as being divided into thirds when dealing with the issue of homosexuality. Approximately one third of human cultures have nothing to say about same-sex relationships. In these cultures, such as the pre-Christian Native Americans or the pre-Christian Polynesians, there were not even actual words to describe affiliative orientation. If words were used at all, they described lifestyle activities and were considered nonjudgmental and accepting. Another third of world cultures, say the anthropologists, view same-sex relationships from some degree of a positive perspective. The most obvious is the Golden Age of Greece. During this era, male homosexual love was valued above heterosexual love as being more pure and god-like. However, other than lesbianism being attributed to the island of Lesbos in classical Greek times, little was said of it; perhaps due to the patriarchal values of the times, which minimized the importance of women in Greek society. Recent examples of a positive valuing of same-sex love exist as well in the indigenous cultures of the Brazilian rain forests and equatorial Melanesia. The same anthropologists tell us that one third of the world's cultures have something negative to say about homosexuality. It is this latter third of the world's cultures that our North American, western, and Christian cultures are a part of. The anthropologists point out that the cultures that are most negative about homosexuality are also the most negative about affiliation and sexuality in general. In other words, these cultures have the greatest restrictions placed on the expression of *all* love and sexual liaisons, with the most prejudicial restrictions placed on same-sex expression. There are many examples of this prejudice, from Moslem to Latin American cultures and from Europe to North America. These cultures also tend to have rigid patriarchal hierarchies of social order.

It is in the neo-Christian tradition, as manifest mostly within North America, and particularly the southern parts of North America, where same-sex love has been viewed with the most vehement hate and the most vicious actions. Therefore, not only do people in such cultures experience an invitation to keep their orientations secret, but they are, in fact, invited to erase the secret from their own minds.

Since the time of St. Paul, various Christian traditions have emerged. Only relatively recently has the dominant Christian tradition reverted back

[2]Paul of Taursus, St. Paul, never met Jesus. He disapproved of sex in general, even between husband and wife and was desperately trying to establish some kind of regularity in the sex lives of converts who had come to Christianity from pagan religions that permitted all kinds of sex (Flood, 1989).

to Paul's[2] antisexual statements, in general, and antihomosexual comments, in particular. Boswell (1980) outlines how, for many centuries, love between men was condoned, accepted, and, at times, promoted within Christian tradition. Only since the beginning of the middle ages has there been an increasing preoccupation with same-sex love culminating in the coining of the term "homosexual" during the Victorian era of Europe to describe those who practice same-sex sexual behavior. Even though there are now some literalists who choose to believe the words of the apostles, as rewritten during those epochal times of tension between Church and belief, over the words of Christ who chose to say nothing of same-sex sexuality, there are others who choose to look to the inner intent of Christianity based on its message of acceptance and love. As a result of the diversity within the Christian faith, there is also diversity in the practical lives of those living within the Christian tradition. For instance, in Denmark, lesbians and gay men have access to legal and valued same-sex marriages, many in the western world have access to spiritual fellowship as lesbians or gay men; yet, in some parts of the United States, gay and lesbian people are legally persecuted, their love outlawed, and, if publicly known, they are shunned socially or their lives are put in danger.

PARTNERS IN OPPRESSION — PATRIARCHY, HETEROSEXISM, AND HOMOPHOBIA

It would be all too easy, however, to take the historical context of Christianity and some of its relatively recent overliteral interpretations to task for being the primary restraint that keeps same-gender love affiliations secret. I believe there are other factors that support such tyrannizing beliefs and further seduce the larger culture to blindly accept acting with violence toward lesbian and gay people.[3] For instance, the tradition of privileging one gender's view of the world over the other gender's experiences and beliefs can be tyrannizing. In many cultures, there is a *patriarchal* tradition where the values, beliefs, and experiences of men are valued more highly than

---

[3]Here, I use a definition of violence first proposed by Humberto Maturana (1986) in a personal communication. Maturana identifies violence as consisting of the following: the holding of a belief to be true such that another's is untrue *and* that this other view must change. Maturana states that all violence, including sectarian violence and warfare, emanates from such a belief. Note that it is not simply the difference of opinion that generates violence, but rather the belief that the other is not entitled to a different view. Therefore, it becomes the imposition of sameness that generates violence (see also Sanders 1988, 1989).

those of women, children, and other living beings. Similarly, western culture's habit of privileging an economic view of life[4] over an experiential knowing of life[5] depersonalizes everyone's love, but lesbian and gay love, in particular. Because western cultural tradition is one of patriarchy and *heterosexism* (the belief that the only true form of love occurs between males and females), it is also patriarchy and heterosexism that define any economic view of life. If, for example, one takes a position of patriarchy, believes, either blindly or knowingly, in heterosexism, and then privileges an economic view of the world (with accumulation of material wealth as success), a same-sex male union could be feared as an unfair advantage, and same-sex female relationships would traditionally be seen as nonthreatening (after all, women have for eons been the "property" of men). It becomes clear, then, how same-sex male unions would be disqualified, vilified, and punished.

However, in dealing with the issue of gay and lesbian love experiences, heterosexism is perhaps the greatest villain. Heterosexism is a culturally held belief, while individually internalized heterosexism can be described as *homophobia* (those negative feelings generated on becoming aware of gay or lesbian people or experiences). Heterosexism can be either conscious or unconscious. For instance, a person may not feel that they are disturbed by awareness of gay or lesbian love, yet act in ways that minimize the opportunities to be aware of it. On the other hand, someone may, in fact, consciously believe that heterosexual love is more natural or "normal" without being affectively negative toward gay or lesbian persons.

The belief systems of heterosexism and homophobia operate at any of three levels. One level is within a person's own inner experience. Most clinicians have seen someone who has experienced homophobia. These people can include gay and lesbian people who have come to believe the larger heterosexist discourse more than their own valued inner experiences. Another level of homophobic activity can be within an immediate community such as a family of origin, amongst friends, or in small social groupings such as church or place of work. Here, homophobia may be overt, such as gay and lesbian "jokes," which erase their subjects' humanity, disqualifier of valued relationships, or invites one to erase his or her positive sense of self for being different than the expected heterosexist stereotype. Or it can be covert, such as a refusal to acknowledge the importance of other persons of same gender in a gay person's life, a refusal to hear the beginning offerings of openness

---

[4]Such a view puts a commercial value on all aspects of life and the beings that live those lives.

[5]This view is based on an individual's experience being more fundamental than others' assumptions of those experiences, including others' assumptions of the value of those experiences.

on the part of a lesbian or gay person, or the persistent invitation to the lesbian or gay person to follow a more heterosexual life-style.

Finally, homophobia can be active within social institutions, where the internalized conversations that have been generated through heterosexist values come to form rules, regulations, and expectations. Here, a parallel can be drawn with the experience of women in our patriarchal culture. Women have often been socialized into disbelieving their own experience, reflecting negatively on those experiences in which they do believe, seeing themselves as inferior to men, and accepting the status quo as somehow the norm to which they must conform, even though it is defined in deference to men. Similar experiences occur for lesbian and gay people, except that, for them, the experiences often occur even more forcefully and less obviously.

Our culture has, over many centuries, come under the influence of an increasing tyranny of sameness. Such fundamental cultural beliefs — that we should be more similar than diverse, love through our genitals rather than through our souls, privilege property above experience, rules above relationships, and so on — when inculcated into most individuals within the society, are the true poisons that support the keeping of gay and lesbian love secret.

SECRECY AS A POISON

People who find that secrets control their lives rather than they control their secrets (e.g., through privacy rather than secrecy, or privileging openness rather than silence), often find many unwanted symptoms in their lived experience. Blindly accepting social and familial expectations and demands to keep one's love secret can certainly be life-restricting and even life-erasing. Such tyrannizing experiences can generate oppressive personal isolation, putting gay and lesbian people at risk of physical assault and potentially being murdered.

The invitations to erase oneself are offered to lesbian and gay people from many sources. Families of origin usually operate from a belief that all children will be heterosexual and, therefore, will grow up to follow heterosexual life-styles and experiences. Friends of the family, of the parents, and of the child (even if the child is actually gay or lesbian) are mostly chosen on the basis of fit with a heterosexual stereotype. Work and social interactions are based preferentially on a heterosexual life plan. All of these expectations, originally perceived externally, ultimately become an internalized dialogue for gay and lesbian people as well as their heterosexual peers. Eventually, the secret of being different from these expectations and values has poisonous effects, even on the reflective life of inner conversations that gay men and lesbians hold for themselves.

Perhaps the most poisonous effect of keeping a gay or lesbian inner life secret is death through murder or suicide. According to a recent U.S. study, the Report of the Secretary's Task Force on Youth Suicide, gay and lesbian youths are three times more likely to attempt suicide than other young people, and as many as 30% of all teen suicides may have to do with sexual identity issues (Hersch, 1991b). No matter whether these suicides result from *anomie* (the failure of an individual to experience life-embracing social interactions, usually because they are disqualified as not "fitting") or from beliefs such as stated earlier that "it's for the best" if a young gay or lesbian person were to die, suicide remains a life-erasing event. However, it is not only suicide that can erase a lesbian or gay person's life. Murder, sometimes called "fag-bashing" or "queer-beating" is an all too common result of one social group imposing its values about love relationships on another group.

Secrecy has many methods at its disposal for imposing restrictions on those who try to defy it. Fortunately, most lesbian and gay people do not face death or suicide in trying to escape the tyranny of secrecy. However, the fact that some people do must be borne in mind by therapists counselling strength in standing up to shame and secrecy.

TOXIC EFFECTS

Many lesbian and gay people suffer from what I have come to call the "if only you knew" syndrome. Here, a person begins to experience *anomie*, where the "demands" to live by simple social interaction fail to touch or have meaning to the gay or lesbian person, due to the internal disqualification of "if only you knew (about my secret gayness) you wouldn't say such things." Brent, who had severe suicidal ideation was suffering from such self-erasure. At age 40, he had come to see his life as an architect, father of three, and husband as meaningless. Growing up in Romania he had become aware, at an early age, of feeling an intense need for affiliation with other boys and men. Growing up in a communist country, he knew of no one with whom he could identify. When he went to a doctor at age 14 about fighting the behavior, he confided his fantasies of needing to be with a male. The physician sent him to a psychiatrist who, over a period of time, "helped" Brent see the need for secrecy and "helped" him follow the more usual path of development of dating women. After 26 years, he was now very much in the habit of disqualifying others' positive noticing with "if only you knew . . . ," which further emphasized his "difference" and, therefore, made him feel he was not entitled to the experiences of happiness, self-pride, and future positive thinking. The result was an exceptional state of experienced isolation and disconnection, which could have led to his giving up on life.

SUGGESTIONS FOR AIDING AND ABETTING AN ESCAPE FROM SECRECY

As many writers have said since the time of Don Clark's classic book, *Loving Someone Gay* (1977), the key word in dealing with gay and lesbian people is acceptance. It is important, however, for therapists to focus on what the acceptance is directed towards. Although one may not accept different life-styles, certain behaviors, job occupations, or choice of mates, acceptance, as it is being used here, means accepting the right of a person to love,[6] no matter if it be towards the same or opposite genders. It does not refer to acceptance of all activities, beliefs, etc. It is an invitation not to generate a "tyranny of sameness," but rather to introduce an acceptance of difference while respecting the fundamental similarities based on affiliative need.

Self-Reflection and Therapeutic Responsibility

Therapists also need to reflect on their own inner beliefs and how these beliefs may inadvertently act in ways that further solidify the effects of the secret in their clients' lives. Being aware of one's own homophobia, hetero-sexist assumptions, and blind subservience to patriarchy is a therapeutic requirement for therapists. A colleague, Dr. Marie Ellis, tells the story of meeting her first lesbian client, Heather N. Marie had gone into practice only months before and had been expanding her caseload. When Heather, a 32-year-old woman sat down, Marie asked her how she could be helpful. Heather stated that she had recently gone through a separation from her partner of eight years and was feeling sad and lethargic. Marie asked if the couple had been married (a heterosexist assumption—that all relationships can result in legal marriage); Heather said her partner was a woman. Heather noticed that her therapist's expression changed ever so slightly. In fact, Marie was trying to keep her surprise from registering so that she would not

---

[6]Here, I use Maturana's definition of love (personal communication, 1986) as the creation of space for the existence of another (i.e., context of acceptance) even at some cost to oneself. This is not necessarily a definition of romantic love, although it can include both limerance and being "in love," but rather it focuses on the experience of love as internally felt yet interpersonally oriented. I choose to see *privileged* love, that is, heterosexual or homosexual affiliative love, as that love which is most congruent between a person's inner experience and his or her interpersonal behaviors, given that the net experience and personal effect is positive and self-affirming. I choose not to see self-erasing "love" as love because the cost to self is greater than reward. Rather, I would call this self-sacrifice.

inadvertently offend Heather, for she knew enough to try to be accepting. Heather looked straight at Marie and said, "Don't worry, Dr. Ellis, I don't find you attractive." Marie was unsure whether to feel relieved or insulted!

This is a rather benign story that worked out well in the long run. However, there are too many stories, which lesbian and gay people can tell of how therapists have treated them poorly and with disrespect, even while they were trying to be helpful. For instance, not long ago, a common practice was to use aversive conditioning to "reassign" a gay person. Similarly, therapists would assume that lesbians or gay men should try heterosexual contact and relationships before coming to accept themselves as gay. Imagine if therapists suggested that their apparently heterosexual clients should try same-sex activity before deciding to marry, raise a traditional family, and so on.

There are many examples of how therapy and therapists can fall under the influence of gay-erasing ideas and assumptions. For instance, the belief that a person's exploration of same-sex love is simply a "phase" they are going through and that, in fact, they will "grow out of it" is a subtle yet obvious heterosexist statement. Similarly, the assumption that a gay or lesbian person may have no interest, whether sexual or emotional, in the opposite sex is evidence of heterosexist beliefs. To assume that gay men are together only out of sexual lust rather than the need for love, that lesbians are not really sexually interested in one another, that lesbian and gay men do not form families, or even that the therapist (whether gay, lesbian, or not) is truly free from homophobic and heterosexist ideology (i.e., has no need for self-examination regarding these issues), are further examples of how our culture's anti-gay beliefs can act subtly and pathologically, despite the therapist's intent to be healing. By not being aware of, and taking active steps to escape from such beliefs, we give our clients covert or even overt messages that allow the *secret* of same-gender affiliation to continue as a *nonchosen* influence in their lives. The lack of experienced choice brings forth the tyranny.

Therapists must help individuals reflect positively on their love experiences. They must be helped to see that these are based on human affiliation, on a privileging of life over property, on togetherness over isolation, on connectedness over separateness. As therapists, we must, through whatever skills and methods we use, invite our clients to side with positive life-sustaining sentiments over beliefs that are unfriendly and self-erasing. To do this, we must help our clients see themselves as being victims of inculcated ideas of heterosexism, homophobia, and patriarchy.

One way I do this is to invite the client to *externalize* (White, 1986) these ideas. This allows the person to have more influence over what ideas they choose to value and act on in their lives. When the context is one that positively connotes affiliation and negatively connotes self- or other-erasure, an invitation to escape the tyranny of heterosexist and homophobic beliefs is more easily joined by gay and lesbian people as well as their families and loved ones. In helping clients escape the negative beliefs of the past, therapists need to be aware of the different pace that individuals may use to escape such tyrannizing beliefs. Many gay and lesbian people are far ahead in their escape from tyranny compared to their loved ones, because they have been on their journey much longer than the family members have. This issue of timing cannot be overemphasized. What may appear to the therapist or an individual client as an opportune time to confront these erasing beliefs and actions may in fact not be the right time for the partner in life, the family of choice, or the family of origin. The experiences of others and how these experiences may in turn affect the experience of the client(s) must also be considered, although not necessarily as an excuse to avoid confrontation.

Another important therapeutic resource is *language use*. By reflecting on and becoming increasingly aware of how language maintains the status quo, therapists can choose alternate language constructions that orient clients to more respectful and accepting frames. For instance, by choosing to use the phrase "lesbian and gay people" rather than the word "homosexual", one brings forth the total experience of the people being discussed (primarily an affiliative event), rather than the narrow perception of those doing the discussing (primarily a sexual event). The use of the word "invitation" to describe the social and interpersonal expectations of conformity with the heterosexist values highlights the experience of choice that is implicit in such expectations. A therapist can help a client see that these are choices, where that client may not yet have experienced them as such.

There is no place for therapist neutrality when working with gay and lesbian people and inviting them to stand up to the secret with its poisonous effects on their experience. For, as feminist critiques of "neutral" therapies have stated (MacKinnon & Miller, 1987), to take a neutral perspective, either purposely or inadvertently, reinforces the status quo. The status quo has been far from kind to gay and lesbian people. One only need witness the intimidation, abuse, and death of gay and lesbian people during the Nazi years, leading up to and including the Second World War, to see the ultimate effects of the status quo. It was on hundreds of thousands of gay men and lesbians that the Nazis perfected their "final solution" techniques before including Jews, Gypsies, and others (Plant, 1986). The pink triangle that gays and lesbians were forced to wear in those death camps has now become a symbol of pride and self-determination. The status quo in our culture is, in fact, heterosexist, patriarchal, and homophobic. Therapists must, there-fore, side with the "victims" of these tyrannizing beliefs and actions—both the individual gay or lesbian person *and* those who love them—in their individual and combined efforts to escape from the tyranny of secrecy. A case example illustrates this:

Case Example: Melissa's Dilemma

A number of years ago, I was asked to consult to a therapist in her work with the family of a 13-year-old girl, Melissa. She had been brought to the Family Therapy Program after running away from home and trying to make her way back across Canada to the city from which the family had moved only months before. Her family was attending therapy reluctantly because it was their belief that their daughter was the one who was "broken."

The story unfolded that, after being apprehended by the police and returned home, Melissa disclosed with great distress that she had not wanted to leave her home city because she was in love with her best friend. When her parents realized the best friend she was speaking about was another girl, they became incensed and angry with Melissa, stating that this could not be so. Once the secret was out, Melissa stuck by her experience and maintained the truth of her disclosure. This further infuriated the parents, with the mother, at one point, actually stating to her daughter that if she were to remain a "lesbian" she would not be welcome in the home.

The next day Melissa tried running away, yet again. She was returned to the family by the police, and the family entered her in therapy. It was only at the insistence of the therapist that the parents attended therapy as well. They did, however, forbid Melissa's younger brother from attending, stating that he was to know nothing of her disclosure or the therapy. Ever since Melissa had been returned by the police, she had been placed with her maternal aunt, who was somewhat more sympathetic to Melissa's story of great grief on leaving her loved best friend, with whom she had begun an exploratory sexual relationship.

The therapist had come to the point in her work with this young woman and her family where she felt she was unable to move any further because of the intransigence of the family's belief that Melissa must forego her lesbian inclination in order to rejoin the family. Melissa, on the other hand, appeared just as firm in her belief that she had a right to her own experience and that the parents, therefore, must change their position. Such a story is common, although not as common as at least some form of acceptance by the family when they hear of their child's homosexuality. In this case, unlike many, the parents could not accept their daughter as different than they had envisioned her. In the end, the therapist recommended, with the aunt's support, a "parentectomy," allowing Melissa to live with her aunt and pursue a developmentally appropriate life-style based on the fact of her lesbianism. The parents, although unhappy at the prospect of not having their will done, were able to accept that their daughter might be different than they wished her to be, and that they would be unable to attend to her needs effectively. They chose to give over custody to the aunt.

It was in the light of siding with the "victim" rather than remaining with the status quo that the therapist suggested the "parentectomy."

Coming Out

One of the most damning effects of the invitations to secrecy on lesbian and gay people is to restrain them from claiming their own lives and experiences. The liberation from this restraint is called "coming out" (from the phrase, "coming out of the closet"—an obvious reference to the secrecy and invisibility that have permeated these people's lives). There are many heartfelt stories about the experience of coming out from both the lesbian or gay point of view and that of their loved ones (Borch, 1983; Penelope & Wolfe, 1989; Rafkin, 1987; Umans, 1988). These books and others like them are useful resources that enable clients who are struggling with the coming-out process to, in a sense, enlarge their community by reading the stories of others like themselves. They are also useful for helping therapists enlarge their own experience of the uniqueness of different peoples' coming out. Dahlheimer and Feigal (1991b), among many others (for example, Clark, 1977, 1987; Ikeberg, 1990; Herrman, 1990), have looked at the coming-out process in great detail and made specific suggestions to therapists working with lesbian and gay people and their loved ones.

In their "The Family That Came in from The Cold—A Five Point Plan," Dahlheimer and Feigal (1991b) underscore a number of important experiences that therapists can aid their clients in managing. They begin by addressing the need for gay and lesbian people to overcome personal emotional isolation—that isolation which invites craziness and suicide. They suggest reweaving the interpersonal relationships that gay and lesbian people are entitled to, but with a new theme of personal sufficiency and power. These clinicians then move on to aid their clients in understanding the cultural bias of messages being offered to people in regard to gayness and gender. By naming the "enemy," and it not being themselves or necessarily another person, but rather a system of beliefs and actions, clients can begin to experience feelings and needs to which they did not previously see themselves as entitled. Dahlheimer and Feigal suggest replacing negatives with esteem-building messages and experiences of celebration, what Imber-Black (1986) has called the "celebration of difference." Clients can be invited to validate their survivor history, validate their attractions and feelings as evidence of their humanity and of being alive, and use celebrations as "messages of hope" to counter the invitations to despair. By not taking a neutral position, but rather lending a professional alliance to gay and lesbian clients in the face of the attack by secrecy and hatred, these authors promote client self-advocacy. This, they say, helps clients to act not just as consumers, but also as activists. The right to have those needs fulfilled responsibly becomes uppermost in the client's mind. Finally, the therapist fosters client pride in diversity and the role of transformation. Here, gay and lesbian people are invited to be role models and enactors of opening up choice for all, promoting diversity, respect, and peacemaking. This is seen as the final step in the lesbian or gay person's taking control of her or his own life, living it fully in the context of positively valued experiences, and continuing his or her escape from the tyranny of secrecy and self-erasure.

Case Example: Eric's Oppression

Eric was referred to the clinic because of persistent depression, crying at work, and personal isolation. He looked much younger than his age, 28, and dressed in a contemporary "GQ" style. When I first met him, he looked sad, shy, and frightened. He told me of his secret — that he thought he was gay but wished he were not. He had been dating a woman who had left him three months before — ostensibly because the relationship was "going nowhere," but Eric said it was more because their sexual life was quite dull. Eric told me how, at age 14, he had been taken to a doctor because his voice was exceptionally high. Many tests were conducted, all showing no physical reason for his shrill speech. He was sent to speech therapy where, over a five-year period, he was eventually able to claim a voice that was more "masculine." By this time, however, he had also come to realize his preference for the love of men. But he did not value it, especially in light of his family's reaction to his high voice. Instead of dealing directly with these issues, he buried them deep within himself and tried, vainly, to live a life acceptable to others. He was outwardly successful, but inwardly, he was slowly being erased.

I began my work with Eric by accepting and listening to his story and then introduced uncertainties about his assertation that none of his family or friends could accept him as gay. I discussed his depressive symptoms in light of his intimate isolation. I externalized heterosexism, the habit of self-erasing self-criticism, and the habit of caving in to others' expectations. I guided him through a cultural journey of seeing the origins of these "enemies" of happiness and self-affirmation.

As he began slowly to question some of the "blind" assumptions that he had been under the influence of, I invited him to celebrate the first steps on the path different from the path he had been following. For instance, at one point in therapy, after Eric was able to go into a bookstore and purchase a gay-affirmative book (*The New Loving Someone Gay* by Clark, 1987), I suggested he invite a friend out for a meal, tell him or her that it was a celebration for the personal work he was doing in claiming his own experience, but left Eric free to tell no more if he so chose. He ended up speaking openly with his favorite cousin, a woman four years older than himself. Eric was doubly surprised — not only at her acceptance, but also at his own courage in countering secrecy. From here, Eric chose to be judiciously open with other friends and family while at the same time, coming to validate his own anger at heterosexist beliefs that had denied him the experience of self-sufficiency during childhood. Eventually, Eric began to see hope for the future and to start thinking of relationships with men as valuable and possible.

The effects of such secrecy, however, touch not only the individual who may be gay or lesbian, but also those who care about them. The most obvious are the families of origin, where often the secret appears to take on greater life than the individual who bears it. For Eric, the greatest difficulty in countering secrecy was in being open with his parents. He feared that they would not be able to accept him as a gay man, especially his father, who had appeared so concerned that his son might have a high voice all those years ago. Such a story can bring forth feelings of exclusion on the part of both the parents and the children. Experiences of imposition, misunderstanding, isolation, loneliness, and self-recrimination may continue and even become worse without grieving what actually was and is hoped for. It becomes the therapist's task to minimize the continuation of such experiences and to help the individuals involved in these situations heal as fully and as quickly as possible. I have found it helpful to first highlight the *affiliative nature* of gayness — to help the families see that their child is capable of and needs love, the only difference is *who* their child will find greatest happiness in loving. Then, I use Kübler-Ross' (1969) model of grief to help both the families grieve their lost expectations of the child and the child to grieve his or her expectations of the parents. Most importantly, however, I also suggest that this grief is emotional preparation for the birth of a new type of relationship, one that is a result of the conscious choice of both the lesbian or gay person and his or her family. The timing of being open with significant others is an important area for both therapists and clients to reflect on — different people require different paces for dealing with the same type of experience. It is my opinion that therapists should respect the pace of the client, even when it seems slow. However, a therapist can help the client explore what factors (such as fear of rejection, personal lack of information, lack of an alternative support system, etc.) may restrain her or his pace and what factors (such as relief from the burden of secrecy, privileging privacy, etc.) may invite a quicker pace.

Lesbian and Gay Families

Another area of great difficulty for lesbians and gay men is having children and raising them within their chosen families. Many gay and lesbian people try to keep the nature of their love orientation secret not only from their families of origin and the larger community, but also from their children. Here, secrecy becomes demeaning and toxic for the gay and lesbian person, the families of origin, the children, and even, potentially, for society. By not being involved in the community, lesbian- and gay-headed families are less likely to risk unwanted discovery with its attendant loss of control. The secrecy, therefore, keeps the family from being a social and community resource through volunteer work, community, home and school associations, and so on. The special experience of succumbing to secrecy as a family with gay parents is beyond the scope of this chapter, but has been addressed in other writings (Barret & Robinson, 1990; Dahlheimer & Feigel, 1991a; Herrman, 1981, 1990). However, the central theme for these families, as with gay and lesbian people themselves, is how to balance the need to escape the poisonous effects of secrecy with the necessity of some degree of personal privacy.

Secrecy or Privacy

In aiding gay and lesbian people and their loved ones to escape the toxic effects of secrets, therapists need to know the difference between secrecy and privacy. Secrecy, in my opinion, is the *necessity* of keeping something to oneself. Here, there is no choice experienced — secrecy is a requirement. Privacy, on the other hand, is the *choice* of keeping something to oneself. In this case, personal agency is privileged — privacy is a prerogative. The issue of secrecy versus privacy is relevant for clients and therapists alike.

Case Example: Denise's Privacy

Denise had been married for 20 years. When she was 18, she met a man at university who was different than many of the others. He appeared considerate, gentle, and interested in her experiences. He didn't seem to be "looking only for a place to park his penis." Her parents were thrilled that their only daughter had finally met a man, and the pressure to wed mounted. Her mother had always been concerned that Denise would never marry, since, as a girl she had said she would not, but rather would like to live with her best girlfriend for the rest of her life. Denise's mother took this in stride, only becoming concerned when this belief persisted into adolescence. Her mother never knew that Denise had had a failed affair with one of her girlfriends from university. It was in the throes of her despair following that breakup that Denise met her future husband, John. She wed, had children, practiced as a full-time homemaker, and lived, except for her children, what she would later call a "proper but empty life."

However, when she was 34, she went back to university to earn a master's degree in counselling and fell in love with a woman she met in class. The affair was intense, passionate, and unsettling. She feared that her husband would be publicly embarrassed by her actions, she worried that she would lose the respect of her children and her family. It was with these concerns that Denise came to therapy.

Work with Denise was not difficult. She was a bright and articulate woman, who was quickly able to see the double oppression of patriarchy and heterosexism for a lesbian woman. However, it was in her consideration of being "out" that she had the greatest difficulty. To her, this not only increased the risk of her husband (for whom she genuinely cared) being shamed, but also, she believed, put her academic and professional career at risk. However, to simply cave in to her fears was not in line with the "new" Denise emerging from under the tyranny of oppressive beliefs and invitations.

Denise eventually settled her dilemma by making a number of personal moves. The most difficult was telling John and asking him for a separation. Despite his pain, he did come to accept his wife as a lesbian and even remained friendly with her as he moved on in his own life. The most rewarding action that Denise engaged in was the generation of a family of choice with whom she could be fully open, and then coming out to her minister. His acceptance (she belongs to the United Church of Canada, a church that now accepts openly gay and lesbian parishioners and ministers as long as they lead Christian lives) helped her to find a gay-oriented congregation where she could be fully "out" but trust that people in the congregation would respect her wish for privacy. With the support of the congregation and her friends, Denise was then able to tell her children. Despite her oldest being angry at not being told sooner, both children eventually came to accept their mother and her partner in life. Through recognizing her right to privacy, while not falling prey to the scourge of secrecy, Denise was able to privilege choice — the antidote to oppression — in her experience.

When helping gay or lesbian people escape secrecy in their lives, different degrees of openness can be observed based on various levels of privacy. A person, for instance, may want to be open only in close, personal relationships (perhaps including family and close friends), while retaining privacy in the larger context of work, school, or social organizations. Alternatively, there may be judicious openness even within such larger contexts. Finally, there may be complete openness about one's love orientation. To be open, however, does not invalidate continued privacy about other aspects of one's life — intimate emotional and sexual details, for instance.

Openness and Personal Risk

Complete openness about being lesbian or gay does carry a potentially serious cost. Being fully open in a social setting that values homophobia and violence can put clients at excessive risk. Not long ago, two women and their 15-year-old daughter were part of a televised documentary series on alternative families. The women and the girl spoke of their experience of loving and playing as a family. In one poignant scene, the daughter spoke with obvious anger at being socially denied the full rights of being a family. She said, "We are as much, maybe even more, loving than most of what society calls 'normal' families, yet we aren't even allowed to be a family. It's not right!" A few weeks after this episode aired across North America, a man shot both women. One was killed and the other critically and permanently wounded. These women, their daughter, their friends and family have paid an unacceptable price in overcoming the socially imposed restraints and shame on being open about one's love affiliation. It highlights the ultimate dilemma facing all gay and lesbian people as they consider being more open about themselves in a homophobic and heterosexist culture — fear of reprisals, if not death itself. The murderer, in his own defense, said of his victims, "They were flaunting it" (Dahlheimer & Feigal, 1991b). Such a tragedy leaves one with the question, "Flaunting what?" The answer is: their love.

Tales like that of Oscar Wilde and his persecution before the legal courts of England continue even today in the United States (and other western hemisphere countries). As recently as 1986, a gay couple was found guilty of sodomy and sentenced before the courts despite the fact that this mutual "sodomy" occurred in the privacy of their own home and was only discovered once the police had broken down the door (Dahlheimer & Feigal, 1991b).

Yet, openness also carries with it other rewards if the danger is duly respected and defended against. Svend Robinson, a New Democrat member of Canada's Parliament, was the first person to publicly declare in Parliament his same-sex love orientation and make it a matter of public parliamentary record. In so doing, he says he has stilled the negative and disqualifying comments from other members of Parliament whenever he would get up to speak, such as "Here comes Mary." "What has the little fag to say today?" and "Aren't you dying of AIDS, yet?" Now, such comments are a matter of parliamentary record and attributable in the public domain to their speakers. Despite his coming-out in public and a right-wing, "neo-Christian" tirade against his reelection, Svend Robinson was reelected with the largest majority of his three terms in parliament and the largest majority of any member within the province from which he was elected. He also says that he has received tens of thousands of letters from gay and lesbian people, their loved ones, and others from across the country attesting to the significance of his public statement. Some value his public stand against the tyranny of secrecy, which permits them the hope of an escape from secrecy's toxic and poisonous effects. Others simply are glad to see a respected and valued public official who happens to be gay. Yet, the most telling are those letters he receives from young lesbian and gay people struggling with the poisonous effects of secrecy that invite them to kill themselves. These people attest to their newfound strength to stand up to homophobia and begin a personal journey towards happiness.

The decision to be open, whether to a family member, to a husband or wife, or to work associates, carries with it the ever-present danger of risk to self and loved ones. This danger is increased even more when it is women being open, for not only must women be on guard for unprovoked attacks from men who assume them to be genitally available to them, lesbian women must be doubly on guard against those who would further devalue them as homosexual in addition to being vulnerable as women. Many self-help organizations in the large North American cities teach gay men and lesbian women how to protect themselves from such attacks, yet, therapists must also help clients realistically evaluate the danger they may be in simply for being gay or lesbian.

Whatever therapists determine the risk of being open to be, the final decision is always the lesbian's or gay man's. Therapists need to set before clients their concerns, yet they must also balance worries with the advantages to standing up to fear and intimidation—those ever-ready tools of heterosexism, patriarchy, and oppression.

Cultural Openness

Openness, as with privacy, is very much a personal decision, but collectively, these personal decisions and the actions that follow from them create a subculture. Subcultures can create a venue of safety and acceptance that helps counter the dominant culture's imposition and violence. Gay and lesbian subcultures have existed for eons, however, it has mostly been since the advent of gay liberation that this subculture can be easily accessed and seen. Gay liberation began, in an obvious way, in 1969 with the Stonewall riots in New York City.[7] It is a movement that has organized and set examples for gay and lesbian people, as well as general society, ever since. It continues as a resource for individual and collective experiences today. Despite the personal empowerment many lesbians and gay men develop, in part from the gay liberation movement, it is of interest how small a place gay and lesbian cultural events have had in the experience of the larger, heterosexist community. For instance, in 1988, the largest civil rights demonstration in U.S. history took place. Over 600,000 people descended on Washington in support of gay and lesbian rights. This crowd dwarfed even Martin Luther King's "I Have a Dream" assembly on the Mall in front of the U.S. Capitol, and yet little was reported in the press, nor did it make a long lasting impression in the minds of most people. This, despite the percentage of gay and lesbian people in U.S. society being about the same as the number of African-Americans (12%). Similarly, during 1990 in Vancouver, Canada, the largest sporting event in the world for that year was the Gay Games and Cultural Celebration III. Here, 15,000 athletes and cultural celebrants participated before audiences in excess of 50,000 in internationally accredited athletics based on the motto of participation rather than simple competi-

---

[7]These riots in New York City began when a bar frequented by effeminate homosexuals was raided by the police simply because it was known to be frequented by gay men. The patrons, however, decided to not cave in to the invitation to self-erase and personally disqualify themselves but, instead, stood up to the police and fought back, creating a riot. It was here that the modern gay political protest was born in North America.

tion. Despite its dwarfing the 1990 Good Will Games in Seattle, very little was heard about this outside Vancouver. It is against such a backdrop of societal secrecy that individual gay and lesbian people are struggling in their attempts to escape their experience of victimization by secrecy.

Therapists can help counter the invisibility and secrecy cloaking gay and lesbian history and culture by inviting clients to become more aware of its richness. This history includes the place of lesbians and gay men in the Christian church (Boswell, 1980; Gordon, 1979; Scanzoni & Mollenkott, 1980), the arts, politics, philosophy (Katz, 1984), and the professions, (Vach, 1985). It is often of great surprise to someone who has been subjugated by secrecy to realize not only that there are these others like him or herself, but that these others have contributed greatly to human history.

"Outing" and Ethics

It is for these reasons that I cannot support the concept of indiscriminate "outing." In the last decade, an expanding number of gay and lesbian people have become increasingly frustrated with the continued dominance of oppression and intolerance toward lesbians and gays. In response to the criticisms that there are insufficient public figures identified as gay, "outing" them against their own choice began. In fact, a magazine, *Outweek*, was founded, which devotes itself to this practice. Many supporters of "outing" credit the process with helping to decrease the hypocrisy of a gay or lesbian person siding with the forces of heterosexism, homophobia, and oppression. While exposure of hypocrisy is certainly valid, indiscriminate "outing" does not pay respect to those gay and lesbian people who so far choose to be out only in contexts of personal acceptance and love. Of course, if every gay and lesbian person were to come out to their friends and family, every person in our larger culture would be affected to some extent. The likelihood of this occurring in the present atmosphere of violence and even death, remains remote. Rather, there will increasingly be those who take the forefront, those who congregate in large cities, those who express their opinions through direct actions, those who do so through indirect actions such as boycotts. Therapists, therefore, need to be respectful of individuals' right to choice. As far as therapeutic ethics, for a therapist to "out" a client (either publicly or simply within a family) violates confidentiality and is, therefore, unacceptable.

AIDS as Plague

One issue that has been highly publicized and dramatized in the public consciousness is the connection between gay men and AIDS (Odets, 1990).

In the minds of many, AIDS is seen as a gay disease. Even many gay and lesbian people succumb to this view and have taken on AIDS as the gay *cause célèbre*. AIDS is certainly devastating among the gay male communities in North America and, as such, deserves even more resources than it is currently allocated. But, because of the very fact that AIDS is seen in North America (particularly in the U.S.) as a "gay" illness, heterosexism, homophobia, and patriarchy conspire to keep resources from people living with AIDS in our societies. However, worldwide AIDS is primarily and predominantly a heterosexual illness, which affects tens of millions of people today.

The larger view of AIDS as a terrible worldwide epidemic is too often lost due to our culture's being blinded by homophobia and heterosexism. Those gay and lesbian people who are struggling with AIDS, therefore, must carry an even greater burden—the fact of being or seen as gay in a nonaccepting society, plus the devastation of a fatal and debilitating illness. Secrecy has a more omnipresent and pathologizing effect in such situations than it would for those not touched by AIDS. It is no wonder, then, that such groups as Act-Up, a radical gay rights group promoting the liberation of the people living with AIDS from the oppression of homophobia and heterosexism, have sprung up and received wide support in gay communities worldwide.

Therapists can help people see that AIDS affects those who practice unsafe behaviors, not those of a particular minority. Therapists can go even further by inviting lesbians, gay men, their loved ones, families, and friends to celebrate their being gay—that is, being able to love, commit, be intimate, respectful, and caring.

CONCLUSION

Being gay or lesbian in a homophobic and heterosexist culture can foster a particularly potent and poisonous secrecy. It is not simply a secret about a fact, an event, the hiding of a period of time, or a past relationship, but rather it is the hiding of the *essence* of a person, of that which invites this person to join the human race—the need to affiliate, albeit with persons of the same sex. It is the search for the congruence between an inner necessity and a valued opportunity that gay and lesbian people experience. This congruence is taken for granted by heterosexually oriented people but is often denied to gay and lesbian people if they succumb to the invitations of secrecy to erase their individual uniqueness—the ability to love and learn from that love.

Luckily, lesbian and gay people, and those who love them, are not silent anymore. They have loud, clear, reasoned, yet passionate voices that are claiming their lives and loves. Increasingly, their struggle is supported by others in society. This can be seen in how western culture is moving toward an acceptance of universal, nonconditional, and fundamental human values. Sympathetic and touching movies, documentaries, television programs, books, and articles are appearing with increasing regularity. The fact of chapters such as this, which would not have been even considered 20 years ago, is further testament to the changing times. A young premedical student wrote a treatise for his philosophy course entitled "Homosexual Acts: Are They Natural, Moral, or Either?" (Sanders, 1989). His answer was that, when they are based on love, they are both. The tides are turning in the battle against secrecy to love and the celebration of difference. One author recently wrote a dialogue between two middle-aged gay men:

'Is love an illusion?' 'No.' George immediately replies. A moment later, he adds, 'I have a new definition of love.' I wait. 'Love is the compassionate understanding of the discord between the heart and the world.' (Persky, 1989)

Not long ago, a lesbian mother told me of her response when confronted by a neighbor's statement that she loved to flaunt her lesbianism. She looked at the woman with a demure smile and replied, "Doesn't everyone love to flaunt their love?"

Therapists now have the opportunity to flaunt our therapeutic love by helping lesbian and gay clients escape the tyranny of secrecy and reclaim their right to joyful and intimate lives.

REFERENCES

Barret, R. L., & Robinson, B. E. (1990). *Gay fathers*. Toronto: Lexington Books.

Bell, A. P., & Weinberg, M. S. (1978). *Homosexualities: A study of diversity among men and women*. New York: Simon & Schuster.

Borch, M. V. (1983). *Coming out to parents: A two-way survival guide for lesbians and gay men and their parents*. New York: Pilgrim's Press.

Boswell, J. (1980). *Christianity, social tolerance and homosexuality*. Chicago, IL: University of Chicago Press.

Clark, D. (1977). *Loving someone gay*. Milbrae, CA: Celestial Arts.

Clark, D. (1987). *The new loving someone gay*. Berkeley, CA: Celestial Arts.

Dahlheimer, D. L., & Feigal, J. (1991a). Bridging the gap. *Family Therapy Networker*, Jan/Feb, 44–53.

Dahlheimer, D. L., & Feigal, J. (1991b, March). *The family that came in from the cold: Treating gays, lesbians, and their families*. Paper presented at the Family Therapy Networker Annual Conference. Washington, DC.

Flood, G. (1989). *I'm looking for Mr. Right*. Atlanta, GA: Brob House.

Gordon, M. (1979). *The unmentionable vice*. Santa Barbara, CA: Ros Erikson Publishers.

Herrman, B. (1981). *Gay fathers*. Toronto, Canada: Gay Fathers of Toronto Publications.

Herrman, B. (1990). *Being, being happy, being gay*. San Francisco, CA: Almo Square Press.

Hersch, P. (1991a). What is gay, what is straight? *Family Therapy Networker*, Jan/Feb, 40–43.

Hersch, P. (1991b). Secret lives. *Family Therapy Networker*, Jan/Feb, 36–39.

Imber-Black, E. (1986). Towards a resource model in systemic family therapy. In M. Karpel (Ed.), *Family resources: The hidden partner in family therapy*. New York: Guilford.

Ikeberg. B. (1990). *Coming out, an act of love*. New York: Penguin.

Isensee, R. (1990). *Of between men*. New York: Prentice Hall.

Katz, J. (1984). *Gay American history*. New York: Avon.

Kübler-Ross, E. (1969). *On death and dying*. New York: Macmillan.

MacKinnon, L., & Miller, D. (1987). The new epistemology and the Milan approach: Feminist and sociopolitical considerations. *Journal of Marital and Family Therapy, 13*(2), 139–155.

Markowitz, L. M. (1991). Homosexuality: Are we still in the dark? *Family Therapy Networker*, Jan/Feb, 27–35.

Odets, W. (1990). The homosexualization of AIDS. *Focus, 5*(11), 1–2.

Penelope, J., & Wolfe, S. (1989). *The original coming out stories*. Freedom, CA: The Crossing Press.

Persky, S. (1989). *Buddy's: Meditations on desire*. Vancouver, Canada: New Star Books.

Plant, R. (1986). *The pink triangle: The Nazi war against homosexuals*. New York: Henry Holt & Company.

Rafkin, L. (1987). *Different daughters: A book by mothers of lesbians*. Pittsburgh, PA: Cleis Press.

Sanders, G. L. (1988). An invitation to escape sexual tyranny. *Journal of Strategic and Systemic Therapies, 7*(3), 23–35.

Sanders, M. (1989). Homosexual acts — Are they natural, moral or either? Unpublished paper.

Sanders, G. L., & Tomm, K. T. (1989). A cybernetic–systems approach to problems in sexual functioning. In D. Kantor & B. Okun (Eds.), *Intimate environments*. London: Guilford.

Scanzoni, L., & Mollenkott, V. (1980). *Is the homosexual my neighbor, another Christian view*. San Francisco, CA: Harper & Row.

Selvini, M. Palazzoli, Boscolo, L., Cecchin, G., & Prata, G. (1980). Hypothesizing-circularity-neutrality: Three guidelines for the conductor of the session. *Family Process, 19*, 3–12.

Tripp, C. A. (1975). *The homosexual matrix*. New York: McGraw-Hill.

Umans, M. (1988). *Like coming home: Coming out letters*. Austin, TX: Banned Books.

Vach, K. (1985). *Quiet fire: Memoirs of older gay men*. New York: The Crossing Press.

White, M. (1986). Negative explanation, restraint, and double description: A template for family therapy. *Family Process, 25*(2), 169–184.

13

Women's Secrets — Women's Silences

JOAN LAIRD

[To be a woman] . . . is not yet a name for a way of being human.

— Rorty

Silence is the best ornament of a woman.

— English proverb

Many women, many words; many geese, many turds.

— English proverb

WOMEN AND WOMEN's lives have been one of the world's longest and best kept secrets. Their stories have oft gone untold, their voices unheard. Not only have women's lives not been given adequate voice or expression, but women's language and women's ways of storying have been discounted and ridiculed. Women's ways of knowing and speaking have been subjugated to the point where women have had and continue to have little power to shape or influence the larger social discourses in which the rules for speaking and acting are embedded. Why are women's experiences, even after two decades of a massive women's movement dedicated to breaking the silence, so hidden, their voices still so unheard? How are these larger social forces replicated and enacted in families and in family therapy? In this chapter, I explore the concepts of silence and secrecy as they relate to women's lives, moving from larger levels of social discourse to the family and to family therapy.

TOWARD DEFINITIONS OF SILENCE
AND SECRECY

Silence and secrecy are both socially constructed linguistic concepts that have different meanings in different cultures and contexts. But there are some common themes. Silence and secrecy are about, among other things, the relationship between knowledge[1] and power (Foucault, 1980). But there are also remarkably intimate relationships between knowledge and gender and between power and gender (Goodrich, 1991; Laird, 1991). Indeed, one of the most powerful lessons of feminist research over the last two decades has been that ways of knowing and speaking are gendered and are socially reproduced through mothering (Chodorow, 1978), through education (Belenky, Clinchy, Goldberger, & Tarule, 1986), through story and folklore (Laird, 1989) and ritual (Imber-Black, 1989; Laird, 1988), through the popular media and in the arts, in all of the contexts in which our lives are defined. It is white, middle- and upper-class males who largely control the making of social discourse and social meanings, that is, the making of "knowledge" and the defining of proper ways of knowing. The meanings of silence and secrecy in women's lives, then, cannot be explored without attending to knowledge/prevailing social discourse, to gender, to power, and to how these forces operate in the constituting of women's lives.

"Secrets" in Family Therapy: An Historical View

Family therapists, from the beginning of the movement, have been intrigued with the notion of the family secret. However, notions of the family secret, like conceptions of ritual and myth, have been rather narrow and decontextualized; the emphasis has been on the "pathological." Family theorists, with the exception of Grolnick (1983), have tended to view family secrets, at best, as homeostasis-maintaining or defensive maneuvers and, at worst, as negative and destructive phenomena. Secrets were seen as conspiratorial, usually growing out of and reinforced by experiences that fostered responses such as shame, guilt, humiliation, and fear. They were seen to bind the family and particularly family symptom-bearers in rigid and dysfunctional ways, maintaining paradoxes and particular power interests, restricting information, and cutting off access to needed knowledge or change.

It is understandable that secrecy has been negatively valenced in the family therapy field. Therapy, after all, was and is a "talking cure" and

---

[1]For the purposes of this paper, I define "knowledge" as "prevailing social discourse," that is, as the prevailing sets of meanings and constructs invested with the status of "truth" or "normativeness" in any particular sociocultural context.

secrecy, like silence, implies non-talk. Through talk or "the said" comes catharsis, understanding, liberation from past and present constraining narratives, and alternative stories. It is only through speaking the secret that its power to harm can be unravelled. Therapy, in general, is a ritual of breaking the silence, speaking the unspoken. The family secret, like the rigid family ritual or powerful myth, has been seen as maladaptive, as an agent of destruction that must be exposed or whose power must be dissipated. The family secret, then, posed a challenge to the family therapist. Solutions ranged from exposing the "secret" to tracking the intricate relational patterns in the dance of family secrecy.

Certainly some secrets *do* maintain harmful patterns and oppressive power imbalances in families, as well as in other social groups. In fact, the destructive use of secrecy as a weapon in family life mirrors its use in larger social groups. For example, in satanic cults, terrorist organizations, or in racist groups such as the Ku Klux Klan, the group's power hinges on the maintenance of secrecy, on denying outsiders access to the special knowledge and strategies that, in a sense, define the culture of the group and maintain its aura of mystery and fear. The same processes of secrecy — processes that keep its members bound, awed, and often blinded to latent goals for power and personal gain on the part of leaders and to the inhumanity and destruction wreaked on others — operate in some families.

Secrecy, Privacy, and Silence

However, secrets are not simply markers of dysfunctional family organization or defensive, self-protective maneuvers. Secrecy is a universal process and an important aspect of all social relationships at all sociopolitical levels in all societies (Tefft, 1980). Secrecy is not simply a tool of the male or of the powerful; it is used by children to demarcate themselves from elders and to enhance the autonomy-building process, by writers and artists to foster creativity, by the poor and otherwise disempowered as a strategy for validation and for resistance. Secrecy is, in fact, central to work of resistance fighters everywhere. Women, from all over the world, have learned how to use secrecy and silence for strategy and survival, to bide their time for another time or place, to preserve their stories and experiences, to protect themselves and their children, to enrich their lives, to define themselves (Arbab, Avakian, Clason-Hook, Gardner, Kwon, Ntloedibe-Disle, Nowa-Phiri, & Tsugawa, 1991).

Secrecy can help people to achieve certain important and necessary objectives, to demarcate appropriate and useful boundaries that foster a sense of specialness, or to protect the feelings or the reputation of a friend. Secrecy can be used by well-functioning individuals and groups to preserve cultural traditions, to better define identity, or to protect against possible sanctions or punishments from a stigmatizing context. For example, under *perestroika*, older women in Russia are now openly performing the folk music and dance of earlier times, secretly nurtured and preserved for a time of liberation. In the last decade, American women have been joining secret groups, which some liken to covens, groups that have their own sense of specialness and in which adult rites of passage are designed and enacted as part of an ongoing effort to better define adult women's identity in a supportive context (Shorin, 1988; Walker, 1990).

Whether we think secrecy is "bad" or "good," "healthy" or "pathological," adaptive or maladaptive, is at least, in part, a matter of values and context. The multiple meanings of secrecy cannot be interpreted without close attention to the context in which they are expressed, and to the values and agendas of those involved in the meaning-making process. For example, whether or not particular actions, interactions, or communications are considered "secrecy" or "privacy" depends, for one thing, on who is doing the defining and what is being defined. For Tefft (1980), secrecy generally is more "formal, conscious, and deliberate concealment of information" (p. 14), while privacy involves voluntary rather than obligatory concealment. When actions are socially sanctioned, such as most sexual practices between husbands and wives, they are seen as deserving of "privacy." These actions are defined as morally neutral or are valued by society (Warren & Laslett, 1980). There is no need to maintain secrecy; non-talk, except in certain contexts, as in a men's locker-room atmosphere or in women's confidence-sharing friendships, is considered socially appropriate. In their view, secrecy evolves as a defensive maneuver in the context of prevailing ideologies that define particular sets of practices or beliefs as deviant.

Certainly, there are contexts in which it makes considerable sense to hide one's identity behind a mask of secrecy. For example, some African-Americans or others whose ethnicity has been disparaged, like many lesbians and gay men, have chosen to try to fade into the dominant group by "passing," by concealing ethnic origins or sexual orientation in order to avoid social disapproval or even violence. Thus, many immigrants to these shores have Anglicized their names, bobbed their noses, or otherwise shed their ethnic customs or characteristics, variations on the theme of secrecy. These efforts to ward off economic and other kinds of social discrimination or punishment, while in one sense adaptive and self-protective, can also cut people off from potential sources of support and identity. Ethnic pride movements, the gay liberation movement, and many other self-help movements are efforts to break silence, to give voice to various kinds of oppression, to bring enforced secrets out of the closet. In an ironic twist, while most lesbians and gays agree that it is essential to educate the public about homosexuality and to affirm lesbian and gay pride, many would argue that the current "outing" movement strips necessary protections from homosexual men and women who have chosen to "pass," violating the right to self-determination. There are times when silence is golden.

Clearly, family secrets, like secrets in other social groups, cannot be understood without reference to the larger social contexts and the social discourses or culturally agreed upon sets of meanings that direct interpretations by lay person and professional alike. The story of the sexually abused daughter, for example, historically was suppressed by her father and perhaps her mother, as well, but also could not be heard by her caseworker or her therapist (Gordon, 1989; Masson, 1984). The story of the battered woman was not only silenced by her husband, but could not be heard by her neighbors or the police or the judge, while the rape victim often found that *she* had become the target of social blame and approbation. As Anita Hill showed us, recently, even a successful, well-educated, African-American attorney did not believe, as recently as ten years ago, that she could speak of the repeated experiences of sexual harassment by her supervisor without endangering her career. While these kinds of stories are being told today, the Hill-Thomas encounter provides dramatic example both of the personal costs of breaking silence and of the ways in which one narrative generates multiple meanings, some far from the narrator's own interpretations and intentions, and all reflecting, among other things, personal and political agendas and ideologies as well as community expectations for moral behavior. Each new "reading" of the text generates new possibilities for meaning. Even so, to break the silence is not necessarily to be "heard." As Senator Kennedy remarked to Anita Hill's corroborating witnesses, "These gentlemen cannot hear you, because they do not wish to hear you."

For better or worse, the processes of secrecy, then, are universal, common to all levels of social organization, seemingly adaptive in some times and places or maladaptive in others, sometimes oppressive and at other times representing a form of resistance to oppression. However, the concept of secrecy is far more complex than I have described thus far. Secrecy must be viewed in the larger context of "the said" and "the unsaid," of the spoken and the unspoken, in the context of the more comprehensive notion of *silence*.

Family therapists have been strangely silent on the subject of silence. Contemporary terms for family therapy such as "conversation" or "reflexive discourse" (e.g., Anderson & Goolishian, 1988; Hoffman, 1990; White & Epston, 1990) focus on the dialogic quality of the said. The emphasis is on the spoken word. Recently, however, linguists, anthropologists, and others have directed attention to the unspoken, the unsaid, to silence in its many forms. For linguist Steven Tyler,

> Every act of saying is a momentary intersection of the "said" and the "unsaid." Because it is surrounded by an aureola of the unsaid, an utterance speaks of more than it says, mediates between past and future, transcends the speaker's conscious thought, passes beyond his manipulative control, and creates in the mind of the hearer worlds unanticipated. From within the infinity of the "unsaid," the speaker and the hearer, by a joint act of will, bring into being what was "said." (1978, p. 459)

Linguists Tannen and Saville-Troike (1985) describe silence as "most often an out-of-awareness phenomenon — the ground against which the figure of talk is perceived" (1985, p. xi). In their book, *Perspectives on Silence*, in which the many meanings, forms, and functions of silence are explored, the complexity of this concept becomes manifest. Meanings and forms vary cross-culturally, in the ways that silence is used linguistically to foster talk, display anger, suppress or hide difference, maintain control, achieve certain ends, manage emotions, or as part of culturally institutionalized rituals. Silence can spring from fear, from loneliness, from resistance, from the will to survive, from the effort to escape stigmatization, from choice, from strength, from the desire to manipulate others. Silence is as powerful if not more powerful in intersubjective discourse as talk.

THE MANY FORMS OF SILENCE

There are as many kinds of silence as there are of talk. While it is important to recognize here that both men and women use silence in strategic ways and both are themselves silenced in ways that constrain their lives and their potentialities, in the pages that follow I explore silence as it is particularly relevant to the experiences of women.

The Unspeakable

There is no vocabulary for some human experiences. Golub (1989), an art therapist who worked with survivors of the Cambodian genocide, points out that not only are our words representative of our own cultures and often insufficient or irrelevant for cross-cultural work, but "words are by their very nature delimiting" (p. 7). In some cases, words can only desecrate the pain. "Only silence is infinite enough to contain the horror" (p. 7). Severely traumatic experiences, such as those of war or physical torture defy language, and when such experiences are finally put into words they are often misdescribed. Scarry (1985), in probing the ways in which the language of pain in war is obscured and distorted so as to allow and make tolerable and even acceptable the infliction of pain on others, argues that "physical pain does not simply resist language but actively destroys it, bringing about an immediate reversion to a state anterior to language, to the sounds and cries a human being makes before language is learned" (p. 4). When pain cannot be expressed or when it is attached to referents other than the human body, the failure "will always work to allow its appropriation and conflation with debased forms of power . . . " (p. 14).

Men's violence against women, not only during the rape and pillage of war but in everyday family and community life, also has been unspeakable. Like the 20-year silence following the Nazi holocaust, the extent and horror of male violence against women in this society still seems largely unspeakable and unheard. Not only do victimizer and victim alike maintain silence, but so does the world around them, protecting patriarchal definitions and power arrangements in the society and in the family (Herman, 1981). For the victimizer, the offender, the perpetrator or whatever gender-neutral words we develop to describe the (usually male) violent person, secrecy is often enforced through his threats of further violence. In cases of extreme wife battering or early and prolonged child sexual abuse, the pain may be so unspeakable that it can only be expressed through extreme dissociation or self-desecration. Women who have been battered or whose children have been molested by their fathers, stepfathers, brothers, or by more transient men passing through their families also help to maintain the silence and to protect the family from outside encroachment, for reasons of fear, shame, guilt; because they are afraid their families will disintegrate; because they have learned to be reliant on men; because they do not wish to give up their homes. Many such women are poor already or are dependent on men's income and are ill-prepared for the poverty and despair that can accompany single parenthood. Sexually harassed women do not wish to lose their jobs. (Why should *they* be the ones to have to leave?) Others blame themselves. They must have asked for it. They deserved it. They didn't protect their daughters enough.

The abusers not only enforce a code of secrecy and silence but, in Scarry's (1985) sense, they "shatter" the language of pain, that is, like other torturers or killers or soldiers, they detach the pain from its referent. For example, many fathers or stepfathers who abuse their children fail to recognize not only the moral failure of their role as parent or the destruction of the parent-child relationship, but the severe emotional and even physical pain they are inflicting on their own children. In what may be one of the more perverse efforts in modern times to shape a social discourse in order to protect such power injustices, some writers and researchers have greatly minimized the effects of child sexual molestation (e.g., Kinsey, Pomeroy,

Martin, & Gebhard, 1953), while others have attempted to redefine it as a natural phenomenon pleasurable to the child and positive for her development (Nobile, 1977; Ramey, 1979).

The spoken and the unspoken constitute each other. As Linda Gordon (1989) has shown us in her fascinating historical study documenting the shaping of social discourse around child sexual abuse, a number of special social categories of language and social institutions to support these social definitions were created to reconstitute the abuse of female children as female sexual delinquency. In a blaming-the-victim solution, father and the privacy and sanctity of home and family were protected from encroachments by the state through the creation of a huge complex for the institutionalizing of young girls. Also, by constructing the concept of the "town pervert" or the "dirty old man," the occasional deviant, the practice of fathers sexually exploiting their own daughters remained an unspoken part of the social discourse. And for those who were victims, the lack of language became a lack of consciousness, to the point where young females, in extreme cases, learned to deny their own experiences and to transform them into self-protective and self-destructive mechanisms. For others, the more well-meaning and benign among us, it is simply too troubling or too painful to think upon such acts, for they shatter our images of our culture and the institution of family; they imply profound and difficult commitments to change.

Professional Language and
the Maintenance of Silence

What is most troubling about the silence surrounding male violence in families is the role of professionals in supporting one of the most hostile of silences in human experience, for, here, the power of the expert is used to reinforce the subjugation of the least powerful, women and children. The long conspiracy of silence in Freudian thought about incest and other sexual abuse and its transformation into female fantasy has come under aggressive attack (Herman, 1981; Masson, 1984). Family therapists, when they wrote about it at all, with their language of systems, form, pattern, structure, and game also continued the silence, ignoring power differentials in the family, and even shifting major responsibility for the sexual abuse of their children and their own battering by their husbands to the wife-mother or to the marital interaction (see, e.g., Gutheil & Avery, 1977; Machotka, Pittman, & Flomenhaft, 1967). This stance has rightly earned the wrath and distrust of feminist thinkers from within and without, as family therapy emerged as a conservative force in protecting the patriarchal status quo in family life. Professional language plays a powerful role in maintaining silence. In a recent study of linguistic avoidance in professional writing and research on battering, Lamb (1991) points out that family therapists have not only followed the longstanding pattern of mother-blaming in the professional literature, but are leaders in the art of obfuscation of language. Lamb argues that, linguistically, responsibility for actions is assigned through the naming of the agents of acts. In the professional literature on men who batter women, male more than female authors and family therapists more than other mental health professionals use gender-neutral language such as "spouse abuse" or "domestic violence" to describe male acts of violence against women.

Women's Sexuality and the Maintenance of Silence

A final example will illustrate the notion of silence as the unspeakable. Women's sexuality and women's bodies constitute one of the central paradoxes, or series of paradoxes, in women's lives. Until the recent sexual revolution, the dominant social mythology for women's lives, at least for white, middle-class women, dictated that women were supposed to keep themselves sexually pure, virginity being the ideal for all unmarried women.

In fact, women who had transgressed against prevailing sexual mores, who had perhaps been forced to seek illegal abortions, to hide out in homes for unmarried pregnant women, and to relinquish their "secret" children (see Hartman, this book), hid these experiences in a shroud of shame. It is the sensuous, seductive, sexual woman who is seen as man's downfall, her raw, sexual nature seducing him from the finer pursuits of culture and learning (Ortner, 1974). Women's sexuality is seen, in many cultures, as potentially polluting, the source of male-to-male conflict and, indeed, the undoing of manhood (Douglas, 1966).

Not only is women's sexuality to be suppressed, defined as a source of shame, and ferociously guarded from encroachment by other males, but women's sexuality is so silenced that women have not even been able to speak about their own bodies, their sexual parts unsaid and misnamed. Lerner (1988), for example, describes the incomplete labelling of female genitals that served to keep women's bodies a secret even from themselves, leading to disturbances in reality testing. One of Lerner's clients describes the male organ, the penis, as "neat and simple," "without confusing or hidden parts," "validated" by others, while her own external genitals are "unspeakable." "Everyone knows that men have a penis and everyone can say the word — even at parties. But the only word that people will say to describe what women have is 'vagina'" (p. 30).

In the early part of this century, words for female body parts such as clitoris, vulva, or labia were not included in standard dictionaries. Until the work of Masters and Johnson (1966) first broke the silence, neither doctors, parents, nor females themselves gave language to those parts of the woman's anatomy, such as the clitoris, that might be sources of sexual pleasure. Menstruation has been defined not only as pollution but also as illness or syndrome, while infertility and hysterectomy represented the destruction of "womanhood." Thus, woman's biology, her sexuality, also became part of the silenced, the unspeakable, because women's identities in the past have been so directly linked with their reproductive capacities.

Paradoxically, in the public media, women's sexuality and female bodies, even those of female children, are sources of endless exploitation and display. Women and girl models are repeatedly pictured in sexually inviting ways, their breasts exposed, their legs spread, their secret parts inviting penetration. This public violation of women, endless grist for the violence mill, operates as a powerful means not only of reflecting but also of recreating a gender hierarchy in which women's bodies are the property of men. Women occupy far fewer of the top places of importance in acting, directing, producing, or writing and, thus, have far less opportunity to shape prevailing social discourse, to author alternative narratives.

When women do try to fight back, as in the case of Anita Hill, who apparently came forward most reluctantly, the backlash can be overwhelming. In a public double-binding process, Professor Hill was excoriated on the one hand for her years of silence, for not leaving the scene of the crime, for failing to repeat to her friends the graphic language allegedly used by Judge Thomas and, on the other, for speaking out, for viciously smearing a respected man, for destroying his life and his family, for seeking personal fame and money. Interestingly, both men and women overwhelmingly chose to align with Thomas, with his story, reflecting the power of prevailing social discourses around gender, sexuality, and violence. The meta-message was displayed in the context itself, the all-white male Senate Judiciary Committee vividly reinforcing our understandings about who controls the said, who makes the rules for social discourse, thus demonstrating the precarious future for any woman who does not know when to hold her tongue.

The Silence of Oppression

Maxine Hong Kingston's mythical warrior never discloses she is a woman at all for "Chinese executed women who disguised themselves as soldiers or students, no matter how bravely they fought or how high they scored on examinations" (1975, p. 46).

Clearly, all stories are not equal (Laird, 1989). We do not usually have equal opportunities to tell our stories and our differing ways of speaking are not equally validated. Some narratives are dominant, preferred, privileged, while others are subordinated, marginalized, or suppressed. For example, Belenky and her colleagues (1986) describe what they call "silent" women, women who see themselves as voiceless, powerless, unknowing, and subject to the whims of those in authority. Words are seen as weapons to be used against them. Perhaps it would be more accurate to describe such women as silenced, at least in certain contexts.

Tillie Olson (1978) revealed that women have been silent as literary voices. In the 20th century, only one out of 12 published and acclaimed writers is female. Heilbrun (1988) points out that women, in general, have been deprived of the narratives by which they might take control of their own lives. For her, to gain the right to tell one's own story is contingent upon the ability to act in the public domain. Women's storying, in contrast to men's, has been limited largely to the family. Heilbrun, revisiting the auto-biographies of a number of famous women, concluded that "male power has made certain stories unthinkable" for women (p. 44). Women whose lives do not revolve solely around their husbands and children, who seek adventures or quests independently of men, have few stories to emulate, for "lives do not serve as models; only stories do that" (p. 37). Conway (1983) notes the narrative flatness in which women of the Progressive Era, such as Jane Addams or Ida Tarbell, wrote about their lives. In their public stories, they portray themselves as feminine, that is, intuitive, passive, and nurturing. Their causes, their successes, occur almost fortuitously, accidently, not as the result of a conscious vision or purposeful quest. Other notable women, if they are grandiose enough to follow a vision and to describe it without modesty or qualification, risk public ridicule (Laird, 1986). Efforts are made to silence their influence through faulting their work as sentimental (feminine) or, paradoxically, by suggesting that such successful women are not womanly. They are manly and, it is implied, perhaps even lesbian (man-hating).

Not only are women's words suppressed through norms for storying and the largely male control over the media and other public forums for the making of social discourse, but certain storying genres have also excluded women. Written language, until the invention of the novel, was largely the province of men. In Eastern European Jewish culture, for example, women spoke Yiddish, the language of the commoner, but were forbidden to speak Hebrew, the language of the scholar and of writing (Zborowski & Herzog, 1952). (One colleague told me the story of her grandmother, who confessed on her deathbed that, as a child, she had secretly learned Hebrew by peeking in through the window of the boy's shul. Never in her life had she dared to tell of her hidden power!)

Women, in their historical assignment to the domestic sphere, have clear-ly had a far less powerful role than men in the development of the public collective stories we call knowledge or social discourse. Not only have women, bound by family and home, had less opportunity to shape social definitions of gender, for example, but "women's talk" itself is negatively defined in discourse about language (Andersen, 1988; Coates, 1986; Graddol & Swann, 1989; Lakoff, 1975). Those genres of language identified as female have frequently been demeaned and less valued. Women, as speakers, have been variously labelled gossips, chatterboxes, or naggers. Their speech, in various studies of and commentaries on language, has been seen as vacuous and restricted, more emotional than logical, full of useless adverbs and hyperbole. Women, it is said, are expert in the use of euphemism (Lakoff, 1975). Yet, said Rousseau, their writing lacks eloquence and passion. "They may show great wit but never any soul" (quoted in Coates, 1986, p. 28).

Women have been said to have vocabularies more restricted than those of men, yet to talk too much. Yet women talk less than men in heterosexual groups and are interrupted more (Coates, 1986). For women, silence is linked with obedience, while eloquence should be left to men. Coates (1986), in a study of historic folk-linguistic beliefs about sex differences in language, articulates the "androcentric rule": "Men will be seen to behave linguistically in a way that fits the writer's view of what is desirable or admirable; women on the other hand will be blamed for any linguistic state or development which is regarded by the writer as negative or reprehensible" (p. 15). At this stage of research on the relationship between language and gender, it is not clear whether women's words are fundamentally very different from those of men or whether their language is only stereotyped as different. However, because language is socially constructed, the more women's language is defined as different from and more negative than that of men, the more it is likely to be constituted differently.

Women's words are also subjugated through their exclusion from other forms of public storying. For example, until recently, the female comedienne was a rare occurrence, limited to the situation comedy and domestic humor. The public storyteller, the community humorists, have been men, and their humor is frequently about women. The Jewish mother, mothers-in-law of all ethnicities, and wives are particular targets. In an age where success is measured by Neilson ratings and sound bytes, it is largely men who control the images, the stories, and the icons of women. Through what is, but also through what is not talked about, particular roles for women and possible stories for their lives are reinforced.

Women are often pictured in the media as either mindless and voiceless or as rather scattered, talkative, and silly creatures. While the media is "still killing us softly" (and violently), there are exceptions. Television series such as "Cagney and Lacey" or "The Trials of Rosie O'Neill" and even "Murphy Brown" feature successful professional women who can be tough and gentle, courageous and afraid, competent and uncertain, women who are more androgynous, who learn how to speak in deeper and louder voices, who dare to swear and to use the more assertive language usually reserved for men, who are allowed to have their own adventures. Such portrayals provoke enormous controversy. The recent film, "Thelma and Louise," in which two women counter male violence with violence of their own and, in the process, find new voices and changed identities, has been highly criticized by both men and women, including feminist women, for it breaks all of the rules. While women are now permitted to "defend" their country, to meet violence with violence as part of the American armed forces, to shoot at men and women governmentally defined as oppressors, it is not clear that they may use violence to counter rape, battering, sexual harassment, and other forms of violence against their own persons.

Two points regarding women's language and its silencing should be stressed. First, what is important is the fact that women's language and women's storying is perceived and marked as different or "other" to the unmarked languaging of men; it is viewed as "less than." Second, the social discourse regarding women's language and women's writing is oppressive. It serves to silence; to be silenced is to be oppressed. "There is a Chinese word for the female I", wrote Kingston (1975), "which is 'slave.' Break the women with their own tongues" (p. 56).

Silencing Women of Color

The words and stories of women of color have been even more silenced than those of women associated with the dominant white culture. Oppressed by the virtue of both skin color and gender, and frequently because of poverty as well, such women experience subjugation both within their own groups and at the hands of the larger society. Denied education and literacy in the days of slavery, denied the power to preserve their own history in a society that prized writing, black men and women had to find alternate ways to story their lives. Barkley-Brown (1989), using quilt-making as an example of women's creative rituals, demonstrates how African-American women have "created their own lives, shaped their own meanings, and are the voices of authority on their own experiences" (p. 927). Similarly, Carpenter (1990) describes how African-American women, in their quilt-making rituals, and particularly in the making of narrative quilts, record and transform their lives. The quilts serve as powerful social documents in the case of these women, communicating their experiences of oppression and marking their fights for freedom. In contemporary society, black girls are still silenced in our educational systems. For example, from early on they are taught that their ways of storying and their ways of using language, are deficient (Michaels, 1981). Later on, if they hope to publicly tell their stories, they must embrace the dominant white language of literature (Jordan, 1985a). Many become multilingual, one language for the family, another for the streets or other peer contexts, and still another for white-dominated contexts. Clearly, the said and the unsaid are highly context dependent.

Differences between, for example, white and black women have been highlighted in the literature, and women of color have described their oppression by white women as well as by white men (Rollins, 1985). Men and women of color have faced a common oppressor. However, more recently, very courageous women of color have begun to speak out, to break the silence regarding their differences from each other, for example, differences between heterosexual and lesbian African-American women (White, 1991), differences in social class (Jordan, 1985b), as well as their subjugation in their own patriarchal cultures because of both gender and sexual orientation (Anzaldua, 1987).

Voluntary or Selected Silence: When Is Silence a Secret?

The speakers in any conversation, whether the participants have prepared their thoughts and rehearsed their words ahead of time or not, are constantly making choices about what to voice and what to leave unsaid. Each speech act is a blend of the spoken and unspoken, a process of selection in which each constitutes the other. This process of selection is highly dependent on the conversational context, although some silences are so powerful they may span generations. We vow we will never tell another about some things: the illegal abortion 30 years ago, a mother's infidelity, a father's seduction. But, we also screen and edit our own phrases, sentences, and paragraphs in everyday conversation, trying to think through what we wish to convey, how we think the other will respond, trying to present ourselves and our story in a way that will sound coherent to the other and is appropriate to the context, so that we will be understood and perhaps even liked and respected (Gergen & Gergen, 1983).

The motivations for choosing to say or not say are multiple. Perhaps a speaker thinks an idea isn't important or credible enough to occupy conversational space. Perhaps the effort is to protect the self or the other from emotional pain, to respect the privacy of the other or, conversely, to inflict pain, to gain the upper hand through the silence of rejection. We use silence in conversation to extend empathy, to "hold pain," to stimulate guilt and doubt, to convey a sense of mystery—the possibilities are endless. It is difficult to know when the decision not to speak is a matter of keeping one's own counsel and when it becomes a secret.

Similarly, the participants in the therapeutic conversation are each, moment by moment, making choices about what to keep silent about and what to give voice to, trying to interpret the words and silences of others, which potentiate the ongoing conversation. As therapists, we often puzzle about what the family is *not* talking about. What is the meaning of his seeming evasion of his wife's questions? Why can't the daughter explain her sadness or the father verbalize his rage? We tend to believe that talk, after all, is good—talk with each other and talk with us—while silence, particularly in the form of secrecy, inhibits change or resolution of problems.

Males and females "select" the said and the unsaid differently, not because of any inherent, biological differences between men and women, but because of the powerful ways in which language is gendered. Men and women frequently speak different languages, each misunderstanding and blaming the other for what may be differences in language (Tannen, 1990). A wife, for example, can only see her husband as critical and unloving, not pained by his own emotional and linguistic constraints, while he can only see her as undisciplined and perhaps angry, rather than joyful or exuberant. Women repeatedly berate men for their lack of expressiveness, for their silent suffering, for their failure to talk about issues women consider important, while men often argue that they cannot understand how it will help to obsess over an issue. Men tend to express their grief differently from women (Lister, 1991), sometimes making it difficult for couples to help each other through a major loss. The same may be said of joy, love, anger, difference, and all of the many emotions to be expressed and negotiated in relationship. It is clear that men and women have different linguistic styles in the languages of intimacy, of domesticity, of childrearing.

Often in family therapy, the effort has been to bring men's voices more clearly into the family, opening up a space by moving the woman to the background so as to make conversational room for father's or husband's ideas. The same recognition must be given to the ways that women select for silence, hold back, and devalue their own voices and ideas.

The Silence of Unknowing

Other kinds of silence emerge from a lack of knowledge or of alternative narratives, from a constricted repertoire of words, from a lack of ideas, or from a voluntary or enforced allegiance to a particular set of prior texts or meanings. The "why we came to therapy" narrative often exemplifies such constraints. Men, for example, usually come to therapy to solve problems, to help others, or because they have been forced by some outside authority, such as the court (Meth & Paskick, 1990). Women are very likely to view themselves as the "problem" or to view family difficulties as their own relationship failures. Many women cannot or choose not to complain about situations in which they are constricted or oppressed, either because they blame themselves or because they cannot conceive of any other options for themselves.

The silence of unknowing, of impoverished sets of ideas and meanings, constrains the possibilities for both sexes. Whatever else they may accomplish or fail to accomplish, one of the central purposes to the series of social movements today — the women's movement, the emerging men's movement, the various self-help movements (largely initiated and populated by women), the lesbian "children-by-choice" movement — all offer forums for giving voice to lived experiences, for giving sound to the silent, for admitting new words and ideas into the realm of possibility.

Often, words are not said internally because parts of one's own experience, the self-story, are inaccessible to the self. Lewis (personal communication, February 1991) calls this phenomenon the *dissociative unsaid*, arguing that such stories may be inaccessible to memory or repressed in some way, perhaps because they are unthinkable and unspeakable. Lax (personal communication, February 1991) argues that perhaps it is not that stories are repressed, but that one narrative becomes exclusionary, is seen as causal or explanatory, crowding out alternative possibilities. As participants in families and in other social groupings, in conversations, our own words are contingent on the space granted to us by the silence of others, on the encouragement we get to explore and express our ideas, to stretch, to dig deeply, to create new stories, to allow multiple meanings to emerge for consideration. One of the central purposes of therapy is to create a space where new ideas can be generated, new meanings considered, and the silences of oppression and unknowing can be exposed and challenged.

CLINICAL IMPLICATIONS

Much of therapy consists of creating space for the articulation of the unsaid, searching the unexplored region of potential. Given the many faces of silence and secrecy in the lives of women, what are the implications for family therapy as a clinical practice and as a profession?

First, we must make a conscious effort, in the therapy room and in the profession, to identify the unspeakable and to provide a context in which such silences can gradually find voice. If therapists are to help women and their families, they must understand the many ways in which women's oppression has generated secrecy and silence. If therapists are not sensitive to the sources of women's silences and to the ways silence constitutes the spoken, it is unlikely they will create the conversational spaces or continue the conversations in ways that the unspeakable can be voiced and its multiple meanings explored. Bearing witness, the process of the public storying of atrocities and oppression, of claiming one's own history, is a necessary path to healing, the context in which a new story can evolve.

The Case of the "Illegitimate" Family

Madelaine and David came to therapy some months after one of their five-year-old twin daughters was killed in a car accident in which everyone in the family was injured. David, less seriously injured than his wife, had been able to plan and attend his daughter's funeral while Madelaine, hospitalized for three months, found it very difficult after her return home to incorporate the loss and move on.

The initial task was one of finding ways, through conversation and ritual, to help with mourning and family restructuring. It was a very slow process and seemed impeded by something difficult for the family to articulate. In exploring intergenerational issues, I learned that Madelaine's mother, Viola, who lived close by and frequently provided child care for the surviving twin, believed that it was only a matter of time before this little girl too would be claimed by God. The grandmother often spoke of Madelaine's and David's "sins," implying they must have deserved their fate. Both Madelaine and David, while stating they did not really believe the grandmother and saw her as superstitious, were very anxious in her presence and somewhat afraid of her. Since Madelaine had been driving, even though the accident was determined to be the fault of the other driver, she could not help but wonder if she could have avoided it, which added to her pain, guilt, and denial.

In working on the family's genogram, Madelaine reported that she grew up in a family of six siblings but that she also had three other half-siblings whom she did not know and who were "illegitimate." In tracking this further, it gradually became clear that Madelaine's father, Arthur, had been married in Europe and had immigrated to America leaving behind a wife and children, intending to save money and to send for them as soon as possible. For whatever reasons, they never followed and/or he never sent for them. In the meantime, Arthur and Viola joined to create a family, over the years producing six children, including Madelaine. It was this second set of children that was clearly "illegitimate" and, I hypothesized, the unsanctified marriage a source of deep and continuing shame for Viola. Madelaine also reported that, tragically, her mother had lost most of her family in the tuberculosis epidemic of the 1920's and had herself

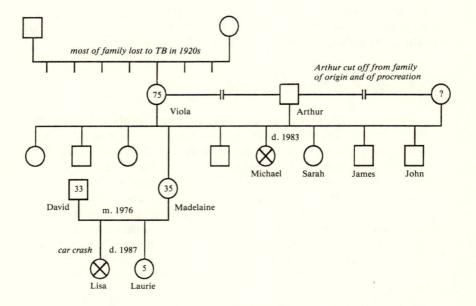

Figure 13.1: The Case of the Illegitimate Family

survived TB after extensive surgery. Viola had also lost one of her own children, Madelaine's younger brother, Michael, to cancer.

So powerful was the "secret" in this family that the father's earlier life was unstoried and Madelaine had never questioned the legality of her parents' marriage. Even with the family secret sketched out on the genogram and literally staring her in the face, Madelaine could not "see" it; it was an unspoken part of the family's historical narrative. It took a series of questions and comments from me, exploring what she knew of her father's first family, acknowledging the possibility that there may never have been a divorce, and a co-construction of the possible implications such a narrative might have for her mother's life, before Madelaine began to suspect that her mother was suffering from a long-standing and pervasive sense of shame and guilt. Madelaine then began to speculate that the effects of this "secret" and her mother's long silence was like a virus that was contaminating her mother's and her own ability to accept the loss of her child. With my encouragement, Madelaine soon talked with each of her siblings individually about what she suspected. One or two had figured out that their father probably either had never been married to the woman in England or had never divorced her, while the others, like Madelaine, had never thought about it. Each agreed it was important to help liberate their parents, and particularly their mother, from years of silence and shame. Each, in turn, told their parents of their love and respect, of how unimportant the fact of legal marriage was in shaping their own heritage or self-concept.

Madelaine and David soon reported that her mother had discontinued her warnings of impending doom, and their own progress in the resolution of the loss of their daughter proceeded in a less complicated way. Again with my encouragement, Madelaine learned more about her half siblings, her father's story, and her parents' early relationship. She learned that her father had kept in sporadic contact with the children from his first family. With her urging, he recontacted his children in Europe and learned that his first wife had divorced him several years earlier. As the case neared closing, Madelaine reported that her parents were planning a small family wedding and had invited the children from Arthur's first marriage to attend.

The case of the "illegitimate family" illustrates how a "secret" (which, in this case, was kept by each person for different reasons: in Viola's case, it was concealment born of shame and guilt, in the case of some of her children, it was a self-enforced silence intended to protect Viola, and in Madelaine's case, it was a story barred from consciousness) can fester and grow in power to the point where it can handicap the next generation. In this case, the simple act of breaking the silence, of saying the unsaid, released Viola (and thus her progeny) from the sense that she and all she begot would be punished through loss. A therapist not sensitive to a context in which women are shamed into silence and guilt around sexuality might not have created a therapeutic context in which the old story could be told and a new one shaped.

In a second example, a woman's "bad" sexuality again cannot be spoken of, neither in the marriage nor in relationships with medical professionals, as she and her husband try to understand their failure to have a child.

A Case of Hidden Infertility

Donna came to therapy because of her anxiety and confusion at finding herself attracted to another woman. As her story gradually unfolded, I learned that, some 20 years ago, while an honor student at a prestigious woman's college, Donna became pregnant. Because

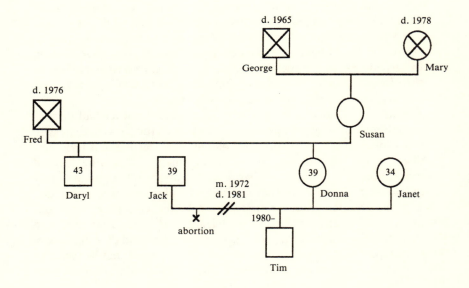

Figure 13.2: Hidden Infertility

her long-time boyfriend was reluctant to marry her, she, with pressure from her family and much talk about "disgrace," had an illegal abortion during spring break from college. She never told anyone, not her best friend or her brother or her beloved grandmother; she suffered tremendous shame, guilt, and pain in silence.

After graduation, anxious to be married and to have a child, the only options she could envision, she married a man she acknowledges she did not love or respect. After some five years of trying to conceive a child, she and her husband, Jack, finally sought the help of a fertility clinic. Donna wondered, from time to time, whether she was somehow being punished for her earlier "promiscuous" sexuality or whether the abortion had damaged her physically. But she knew that she had been pregnant once and that it probably was Jack who was sterile. She did not share her earlier experience with him or with the doctors. The fertility specialists soon learned that Jack was indeed sterile, but it was not so simple to determine if Donna could become pregnant. Over the next three years, Donna underwent numerous rather humiliating tests, never revealing her earlier pregnancy. The source of Jack's infertility was eventually discovered, corrected, and the couple went on to have a biological child. The marriage, however, ended in an acrimonious divorce.

Donna's current attraction to another woman seemed to have re-stimulated her latent sense of herself as a sexually "bad" woman, a feeling she had never been able to shed. Together, we began to examine the social and cultural constructions of "female" and "woman" that had shaped her family's and her own ideas about female sexuality, as well as the impact of her social and self-imposed silence on her self-concept. Gradually Donna began to differentiate her feelings about herself from sexist and homophobic biases in the external environment, freeing her to make a more self-determined choice about a future partner.

Only in the context of gender-sensitive therapy and in a world where premarital sexuality has become acceptable, where abortion was legally sanctioned, and where a lesbian life-style was an option, was Donna able to restory this part of her life, to create an alternative narrative. Only if the therapist is sensitive to the unspeakable in women's lives, and is willing to tolerate hearing it, will he or she provide the openings, the ideas, the reflections that will allow for certain women's stories to emerge. If we become more willing to listen to voices from the margin, we will learn more about ourselves.

REFLECTIONS

A central question in theory-building today is whether the neutral stance, respect, and de-powering of the therapist/expert implicit in new partnership models grounded in social constructionism (e.g., Andersen, 1987; Anderson & Goolishian, 1988, in press; Hoffman, 1990) and the therapeutic stance of the "interested stranger"/ethnographer whose only goal is to continue the conversation, will allow for the voices of the silenced to be heard. Or are these emerging theories and models, that at times seem sociopolitically neutral themselves, potentially conservative forces in the perpetuation of a patriarchal status quo (see MacKinnon & Miller, 1987). Why is it, asks, feminist theorist Nancy Hartsock (1990)

> that just at the moment when so many of us who have been silenced begin to demand the right to name ourselves, to act as subjects rather than objects of history, that just then the concept of subjecthood becomes problematic? Just when we are forming our own theories about the world, uncertainty emerges about whether the world can be theorized. Just when we are talking about the changes we want, ideas of process and the possibility of systematically and rationally organizing the world becomes dubious and suspect. (pp. 163–64)

In my view, it is not enough and, in fact, it is not possible to create a neutral conversational space from a "not knowing" position (Anderson & Goolishian, 1988). There is never anything "neutral" about the choices we, as therapists, make about when to speak or when to remain silent. Furthermore, there is probably very little neutrality in our own narratives, in those that we give voice to, in those we keep silent, or in those narrative possibilities that do not occur to us, because, as Goldner (1985) has argued, gender is a central organizing category for human experience. While this chapter explores some of the kinds of silences connected to women's lives, in particular, both men and women need special help in connecting their gendered personal silences with their public oppressions. While it may be true that the social context is always embedded in the individual narrative, the narratives of both therapist and client alike are shaped and constrained by their own gendered experiences. The therapist who is not particularly sensitive to gendered silences may not be able to create the conversational space in which the unsaid may be recognized or spoken.

In summary, therapists must be sensitive to the different ways that men and women story their experiences, as well as the ways that gendered conceptions for "male" and "female" tend to silence women's words and men's feelings. Therapists must be alert to the differential ways that men and women selectively use silence and secrecy. These uses of secrecy and silence may be connected to oppression, to differential exposure to "knowing," to gendered differences in the linguistic repertoire, to different intentions in trying to present a coherent self to others, to different ideas about how to use the said and unsaid in relationship with others. The therapist must be aware of his or her own gendered narratives and how they shape and constrain the ways we hear or don't hear the silences.

While the dysfunctional and deadly sides of secrecy have been more explored in family therapy theory, secrecy and silence are universal processes, which have their adaptive, protective, and necessary aspects as well as their maladaptive and subjugating aspects. They may be, but are not necessarily, dangerous or dysfunctional forces that "interfere with the person-to-person relationships essential in differentiated and reciprocally-balanced systems" (Karpel, 1980, p. 300). The conversational space we create between the said and the unsaid in the protected realm of therapy, however wide and open, is subject to the same sociopolitical rules for talk and silence that govern the larger contexts in which we are located.

Family therapists themselves constantly tack back and forth between the said and the unsaid, yet rarely examine the multiple meanings and the potential power of their own choices for silence in a larger conversational context, in which they reveal so little and expect others to reveal so much. Any analysis of secrecy and silence in therapeutic conversation must necessarily be sensitive to multiple interpretive frameworks, including those of context, the (gendered) forms of personal narrative with its aspects of the said and the unsaid, and narrator-interpreter, speaker-listener intentions and relations.

Finally, this chapter would not be complete without some comment on the very loud silence about gender in the field of family therapy itself. Many feminists, men and women, are observing that the effort to carry on the gender conversation in the profession repeatedly meets a wall of silence, a lack of response, and what seems an unwillingness to dialogue. Feminists are accused of not bringing up the issues in the right way, or for bringing them up too stridently or in ways that permit only certain, politically correct responses, while others are accused of failing to listen to women's voices, to read their works, or to engage in the conversation about gender at all. Whatever the sources of such silence, it is important we try to understand them and that we keep the conversation going.

REFERENCES

Andersen, R. (1988). *The power and the word*. London: Paladin Grafton Books.

Andersen, T. (1987). The reflecting team: Dialogue and meta-dialogue in clinical work. *Family Process, 26*, 415–428.

Anderson, H., & Goolishian, H. (1988). Human systems as linguistic systems: Preliminary and evolving ideas about the implications for clinical theory. *Family Process, 27*, 371–393.

Anderson, H., & Goolishian, H. (in press). The client is the expert: A not-knowing approach to therapy. In K. Gergen & S. McNamee (Eds.), *Inquires in social construction*. Newbury Park, CA: Sage.

Anzaldua, G. (1987). *Borderlands: La frontera: The new mestiza* (pp. 15–23). San Francisco: Spinsters/Aunt Lute.

Arbab, J., Avakian, A., Clason-Hook, C., Gardner, B., Kwon, M., Ntloedibe-Disle, M., Nowa-Phiri, M., & Tsugawa, T. (1991, January). *The vastness of silence: Expanding the definition of one of the ways of knowing*. Intercultural Panel, Conference on "Diversity in Ways of Knowing," Brattleboro, VT.

Barkley-Brown, E. (1989). African-American women's quilting: A framework for conceptualizing and teaching African-American women's history. *Signs: Journal of Women in Culture and Society, 14*, 921–29.

Belenky, M. F., Clinchy, B. M., Goldberger, N. R., & Tarule, J. M. (1986). *Women's ways of knowing: The development of self, voice, and mind*. New York: Basic.

Blumstein, P., & Schwartz, P. (1983). *American couples: Money, work, sex*. New York: William Morrow.

Carpenter, F. (1990). *Piecing life together: Therapeutic dimensions of African-American quilt-making*. Unpublished master's thesis, Smith College School for Social Work, Northampton, MA.

Coates, J. (1986). *Women, men and languages: A sociolinguistic account of sex differences in language*. London: Longman.

Chodorow, N. (1978). *The reproduction of mothering: Psychoanalysis and the sociology of gender*. Berkeley: University of California Press.

Conway, J. (1983). Convention versus self-revelation: Five types of autobiography by women of the Progressive Era. Unpublished paper for Project on Women and Social Change, Smith College, Northampton, MA. June 13, 1983.

Douglas, M. (1966). *Purity and danger: An analysis of the concepts of pollution and taboo.* London: Routledge, Kegan, & Paul.

Foucault, M. (1980). *Power/knowledge: Selected interviews and other writings.* New York: Pantheon.

Gergen, K., & Gergen, M. (1983). Narratives of the self. In T. R. Sarbin and K. E. Scheibe (Eds.), *Studies in social identity* (pp. 254–73). New York: Praeger.

Gilligan, C. (1982). *In a different voice: Psychological theory and women's development.* Cambridge, MA: Harvard University Press.

Goldner, V. (1985). Feminism and family therapy. *Family Process, 24,* 31–47.

Golub, D. (1989). Cross cultural dimensions of art psychotherapy: Cambodian survivors of war. In H. Waldeson, J. Durkin, & D. Perach (Eds.), *Advances in art therapy.* New York: Wiley.

Goodrich, T. J. (1991). *Women and power: Perspectives for family therapy.* New York: W.W. Norton.

Gordon, L. (1989). "Be careful about father": Incest, girls' resistance, and the construction of femininity. In L. Gordon, *Heroes of their own lives: The politics and history of family violence* (pp. 204–249). New York: Penguin.

Graddol, D., & Swann, J. (1989). *Gender voices.* Oxford: Basil Blackwell, Ltd.

Grolnick, L. (1983). Ibsen's truth, family secrets, and family therapy. *Family Process, 22,* 275–288.

Gutheil, T., & Avery, N. (1977). Multiple overt incest as family defense against loss. *Family Process, 16,* 106–116.

Hartsock, N. (1990). Foucault on power: A theory for women? In L. J. Nicholson (Ed.), *Feminism/post-modernism* (pp. 157–175). New York: Routledge.

Heilbrun, C. (1988). *Writing a woman's life.* New York: Ballantine.

Herman, J. L. (1982). *Father-daughter incest.* Cambridge, MA: Harvard University Press.

Hoffman, L. (1985). Beyond power and control: Toward a second-order family systems therapy. *Family Systems Medicine, 3,* 381–396.

Hoffman, L. (1990). Constructing realities: An art of lenses. *Family Process, 29,* 1–12.

Imber-Black, E. (1989). Rituals of stabilization and change in women's lives. In M. McGoldrick, C. Anderson, & F. Walsh (Eds.), *Women in families: A framework for family therapy* (pp. 451–469). New York: W.W. Norton.

Jordan, J. (1985a). Nobody mean more to me than you and the future life of Willie Jordan. In J. Jordan, *On call: Political essays* (pp. 123–139). Boston: South End Press.

Jordan, J. (1985b). Report from the Bahamas. In J. Jordan, *On call: Political essays* (pp. 39–49). Boston: South End Press.

Karpel, M. A. (1980). Family secrets: I. Conceptual and ethical issues in the relational context. II. Ethical and practical considerations in therapeutic management. *Family Process, 19,* 296–306.

Kingston, M. H. (1975). *The woman warrior: Memoirs of a girlhood among ghosts.* New York: Vintage.

Kinsey, A. C., Pomeroy, W. B., Martin, C. E., & Gebhard, P. H. (1953). *Sexual behavior in the human female.* Philadelphia, PA: Saunders.

Laird, J. (1986). Women, family therapists, and other mythical beasts. *American Family Therapy Association Newsletter.* No. 25, Fall, pp. 32, 35.

Laird, J. (1988). Women and ritual in family therapy. In E. Imber-Black, J. Roberts, & R. Whiting (Eds.), *Rituals in families and family therapy.* New York: W.W. Norton.

Laird, J. (1989). Women and stories: Restorying women's self-constructions. In M. McGoldrick, C. Anderson, & F. Walsh (Eds.), *Women in families* (pp. 428–49). New York: W.W. Norton.

Laird, J. (1991). Enactments of power through ritual. In T. J. Goodrich (Ed.), *Women and power: Perspectives for family therapy.* New York: W.W. Norton.

Lakoff, R. (1975). *Language and woman's place.* New York: Harper & Row.

Lamb, S. (1991). Acts without agents: An analysis of linguistic avoidance in journal articles on men who batter women. *American Journal of Orthopsychiatry, 61,* 250–57.

Lerner, H. (1988). *Women in therapy*. New York: Jason Aronson.

Lister, L. (1991). Men and grief: A review of research. *Smith College Studies in Social Work, 61*, 220–235.

Machotka, P., Pittman, F., & Flomenhaft, K. (1967). Incest as a family affair. *Family Process, 6*, 98–116.

MacKinnon, C. (1991). Doing something: The situation of women and the possibility of change. Smith College Medal acceptance speech, Rally Day, 1991. Northampton, MA.

MacKinnon, L. & Miller, D. (1987). The new epistemology and the Milan approach: Feminist and sociopolitical considerations. *Journal of Marital and Family Therapy, 13*, 139–55.

Masson, J. (1984). *The assault of truth: Freud's suppression of the seduction theory*. New York: Farrar, Straus, & Giroux.

Masters, W. H., & Johnson, V. E. (1966). *Human sexual response*. Boston: Little, Brown.

Meth, R. L., & Pasick, R. S. (1990). *Men in therapy: The challenge of change*. New York: Guilford.

Michaels, S. (1981). Sharing time: Children's narrative styles and differential access to literacy. *Language in Society, 10*, 423–42.

Nobile, P. (1977, Dec.). Incest: The last taboo. *Penthouse*, pp. 117–118, 126, 157–58.

Olson, T. (1978). *Silences*. New York: Delacorte Press.

Ortner, S. (1974). Is female to male as nature is to culture? In M. S. Rosaldo & L. Lamphere (Eds.), *Woman, culture, and society* (pp. 67–87). Stanford, CA: Stanford University Press.

Ramey, J. (1979, May). Dealing with the last taboo. *SIECUS Report 7*, 1–2, 6–7.

Rollins, J. (1985). *Between women: Domestics and their employers*. Philadelphia, PA: Temple University Press.

Scarry, E. (1985). *The body in pain: The making and unmaking of the world*. New York: Oxford University Press.

Shorin, J. (1988). *Creative ritual practice and adult identity consolidation in women*. Unpublished master's thesis, Smith College School for Social Work, Northampton, MA.

Tannen, D. (1990). *You just don't understand: Women and men in conversation*. New York: William Morrow.

Tannen, D., & Saville-Troike, M. (Eds.).(1985). *Perspectives on silence*. Norwood, NJ: Ablex Publishing Corporation.

Tefft, S. K. (1980). *Secrecy: A cross-cultural perspective*. New York: Human Sciences Press.

Tyler, S. A. (1978). *The said and the unsaid*. New York: Academic Press.

Walker, B. (1990). *Women's rituals: A sourcebook*. San Francisco: Harper & Row.

Warren, C., & Laslett, B. (1980). Privacy and secrecy: A conceptual comparison. In S. Tefft (Ed.), *Secrecy: A cross-cultural perspective*. New York: Human Sciences Press.

White, E. F. (1991, June 17). *Black feminist interventions*. Monday Night Lecture Series, Smith College School for Social Work, Northampton, MA.

White, M., & Epston, D. (1990). *Narrative means to therapeutic ends*. New York: W.W. Norton.

Zborowski, M., & Herzog, E. (1952). *Life is with people: The culture of the shtetl*. New York: Schocken Books.

14

Speaking the Unspoken:
A Work-Group Consultation
to Reopen Dialogue

SALLYANN ROTH

WHEN SOME MEMBERS of a group hold information not shared by other members, secrecy relationships are set up that can compromise the group's functioning. But secrecy relationships can arise even when there is no actual secret. They may develop when important, nonsecret information—whether fact, opinion, or feeling—is treated as irrelevant or nonexistent in interactions in which some people believe it to be relevant. Thus, secrecy relationships may also develop when groups avoid exploring information to which all have access but which some find uncomfortably sensitive.

Issues of difference—in gender, race, sexual preference, social class, and age, for example—are often highly sensitive. Within groups, some members may respond to such issues by minimizing their importance and emphasizing commonalities, treating difference as if it made no difference (Hare-Mustin,

I am grateful to the staff and administration at Health and Education Services, Inc., of Salem, Massachusetts, for the privilege of taking part in their work. They gave generously of their time, hearts, and minds in the consultation and follow-up and have carried their dialogue forward with courage, spirit, and determination. I thank Richard Chasin, M.D., and Caroline Marvin, Ph.D., for useful discussions about the preliminary consultation design, and my colleagues in the Family Institute of Cambridge's Public Conversations Project, Carol Becker, Ph.D., Laura Chasin, M.S.W., Richard Chasin, M.D., and Margaret Herzig, whose thinking nurtures my thinking and energy for this work. I also thank Claudia Bepko, M.S.W., Ann Fleck-Henderson, M.S.W., and Joan Laird, M.S.W., for their helpful comments on an earlier draft.

1987; Hare-Mustin & Maracek, 1988, 1990).[1] All know that difference exists, but some or all behave as if it were irrelevant. Commonality is viewed as central; issues of difference are relegated to the periphery or even rendered unspeakable. Unspoken rules may develop that restrict dialogue about difference in particular, inhibit communication and contact in general, and even stifle thoughts and feelings.

Other group members may respond to issues of difference by emphasizing their importance and minimizing commonalities, treating difference as if it made all the difference (Hare-Mustin, 1987; Hare-Mustin & Maracek, 1988, 1990). Everyone knows the commonalities exist, but some or all members behave as if they were irrelevant. Difference holds center stage; commonality is in the wings, or sometimes virtually unmentionable. People behave as if relevant commonalities were inconsequential or nonexistent.

Such emphasis or deemphasis on difference can foster the formation of subgroups and secrecy relationships. When subgroups hold opposite biases, tension may arise and impair the ability of all members to interact with an optimum degree of openness, whether from restraint of awareness or from restraint of expression. These biases are held at a sacrifice of richness and variety in the group's ongoing life and dialogue, and at a sacrifice of complexity in the understandings that members develop. Members of the group who are more fully aware of both commonalities and differences and the interplay between them may treat that awareness as an individual or shared secret. They may experience themselves as unable to speak or as unable to make themselves heard.

Secrecy relationships involving such biases can develop when people feel that avoided content is threatening to their sense of self or threatening to relationships about which they care. Secrecy relationships can also develop when group members disagree about whether or not a particular difference is important or relevant to their ongoing process. Members of a group who have greater access to power than other members (e.g., men, whites, heterosexuals) often minimize this key difference, while members with less access to power (e.g., women, people of color, gays and lesbians) often understand the difference in access to power (and the difference from which it arises) as defining of their experience. Once a secrecy relationship becomes estab-

---

[1]In a thorough discussion of gender bias, Hare-Mustin (1987) and Hare-Mustin and Maracek (1988, 1990) identified two prejudiced leanings: "alpha bias" (the exaggeration of differences between groups of people) and "beta bias" (the ignoring of differences between groups of people). Their work focuses particularly on the dimension of power as it relates to these biases, which I have purposely avoided here in the belief that any politicization would work against the goals of the consultation that is the focus of this chapter.

lished, from whatever source, trust is compromised and dialogue is interrupted.

This discussion of secrecy and openness, as they affect dialogue in a
group in which there are issues of difference, will be illustrated by a consultation I conducted for one unit of a mental health center,[2] in which secrecy
relationships had been fostered by emphasis on differences by one subgroup
and minimization of differences by another. In this work group, some members had come to feel that both speaking and not speaking were dangerous
to ongoing working relationships.

BACKGROUND

In the summer of 1990, I was asked to consult to a unit of a community
mental health center where issues of difference were said to be problematic.
In 1983, the agency had pioneered a program to serve the gay and lesbian
population of its catchment area. Known as the Gay and Lesbian Counseling Program, or GLCP, and staffed only by openly gay and lesbian workers,
it was the first program of its kind within a publicly funded community
mental health center in the United States.

In telephone calls from two workers at the agency — one from the adult
unit of the agency's outpatient services, under which the GLCP operated,
and the other from GLCP itself — requesting a day-long consultation, I
learned that an event had occurred two years earlier that many staff members still felt was unresolved. In a 1988 unit clinical meeting, two self-
described Christian staff members had revealed that they believed homosexuality to be morally wrong. Their comments were understood by the gay and
lesbian staff members as oppressive, homophobic, threatening, and attack-
ing. Since that event, a number of people within the unit, both straight and
gay, had not spoken to each other about the event and its meanings to them,
while others had spoken "secretly" in small subgroups.

The issues were indeed complex. Both staff members who contacted me
(one gay, one straight) believed that the incident represented more than itself
and that it had surfaced long-standing tension felt by some members of the
unit. Both callers reported that some staff members thought a consultation
was unnecessary, undesirable, or frightening, and that others felt they could
not go on without one. The former feared that a consultation would reopen

___
[2]This report on the consultation and its followup was, by agreement of all participants, reviewed by those participants remaining on the agency's staff at the time of
the chapter's completion. Our joint effort in this last phase of working together has
been to verify the reporting of participants' perceptions of the consultation and the
content of the follow-up interviews.

old wounds and make things worse. The latter experienced themselves as working in an unacceptable atmosphere of repression and dishonesty. Both callers strongly suggested that I meet separately and sequentially with members of GLCP, other members of the outpatient unit, and representatives of the agency's administration before bringing everyone together. I felt challenged to think of ways to respect reported staff concerns about coming together and having adequate separate hearings, and yet not limit the possibilities for what could happen by severely restricting the group's time together in the consultation.

I told the callers that I needed to invite all of the staff members to express their views of the unit's current dilemma and of what would constitute a positive outcome. Only then could I say what kind of format I would propose for work with the group, or even if doing work with the group to open the issues seemed to be a productive possibility. The callers expressed relief that I intended to invite input from their colleagues. They would not have to stand as the sole representatives for many disparate views, and could more fully voice their own views. They seemed to feel that offering all group members the opportunity to speak at the outset would help each person toward having a full voice.

PRELIMINARY PLANNING

In my preliminary thinking about the consultation, I wanted to build into its design many opportunities to explore whether opening up issues of difference could be safe enough for all group members. If members of the group could not experience it as a safe place to discuss difference, perhaps we could find a way to talk about that constraint, so that the reasons for not talking might themselves be out in the open. I wanted to facilitate opportunities for discussion of members' beliefs, feelings, and positions, with reference to the particular troubling "difference," and hoped to promote respectful curiosity and inquiry about those experienced as "other" and about each person's self. The option not to speak had to be respected and available to all.

In planning for contacts with the unit staff, I drew heavily on my experience as a member of the Family Institute of Cambridge's Public Conversations Project, a project undertaken to encourage productive dialogue on topics that usually engender fruitless, heated exchanges or avoidance of key issues (Chasin, Chasin, Herzig, Roth, & Becker, 1990, 1991; Ross, Chasin, Becker, & Herzig, in press). The project had developed guidelines for working with difference, which I adapted and expanded as guidelines for the consultation. They included:

1. pre-meeting contacts with participants (by telephone and/or letter) to orient them to the approach I planned to use and to make room for input from them
2. clarity and consistency of contracts, including those about
   a. time management
   b. the role of the facilitator
   c. an atmosphere of safety (proposing, getting agreement on, and adhering to clear ground rules, such as agreements about confidentiality and the voluntary nature of participation)
3. agreement about describing each participant's position using the language that person prefers, and avoiding the negative labels used in acrimonious confrontations
4. establishment of conditions for new listening (Andersen, 1988, 1991; Roth, 1988) as well as new speaking (e.g., no interruptions permitted; time for all to speak fully; clear agreement about taking turns to speak, and when and how each participant would be freed from the speaking role simply to listen; promotion of curiosity)
5. channeling of communication directly from participants to participants (not through the facilitator)
6. opportunity for expression of doubt as well as certainty in exploring the complexity of issues
7. opening of differences in personal beliefs, values, and experiences among participants on the same "side" of the issue
8. ongoing mutual assessment of the process through feedback from the participants (including the consultant)
9. focusing on the hypothetical future rather than the past or even the present (Chasin, Roth, & Bograd, 1989; Chasin & Roth, 1990; Penn, 1985; Tomm, 1987) to facilitate inquiry into the hopes and aspirations for a time beyond resolution

Following the initial telephone calls to request the consultation and a period of thinking about how to approach the work, my next contact was by letter to the entire staff:

It would help me to be grounded in as many perspectives as possible, so I am inviting signed or anonymous notes from any of you who wish to let me know your perspective on the clinic's present dilemma. I have been purposely vague in my description, "present dilemma," as I believe that there may be many different identifications of what the "present dilemma" actually is. I am also interested in your ideas about solutions. In other words, if things were happening as you would like, what, if anything, would be happening that is different from what is now happening?

Please do not talk with each other before responding to my questions. What will be most helpful here is not consensus, but individual understanding. Don't worry about formality or informality in your response. A reasonably legible scribble is as welcome as a typed note. Less helpful, but okay if you get in a time crunch, is a brief phone message.

In the letter I sought to incorporate many of the guidelines listed above. The letter offered equal access to the consultant. It positioned the consultant as equally interested in all views, which can be termed *equity of interest*. It suggested that the problem did not have to be "fixed" or defined by an "other." It suggested an emphasis on individual perspectives, not group-bound rhetoric, and assumed that multiple perspectives would be of value. It focused on the future, not on the past. Perhaps most importantly, by saying that responses could be anonymous and by expressing interest in difference and personal experience, I tried to engender a sense of privacy, as opposed to secrecy (Bok, 1989) and a sense of safety from which individuals could speak of the issues and state their concerns.

In this initial contact with group members, I also tried to reorient people who expected that they would hear a presentation from an expert. They learned that they would be asked to participate with colleagues and a consultant in a problem-solving effort. (One respondent wrote, "I don't understand. I thought you were coming to teach us about homophobia.")

Eight of the eighteen participants responded. Here is a sampling of the kinds of responses members made, which helped to guide my planning for the day.

- . . . Homophobia . . . and the incident have not been dealt with. Attempts . . . felt frustrating, in that beliefs held by several staff members . . . were dealt with in the secrecy of one-to-one supervision. It has felt very much like an alcoholic family — like there is a big pink elephant in the room which everyone sees to some degree, but we are not supposed to mention it. . . . It's difficult to talk about differences of any kind when we encompass so many.

- Individuals were obliterated, and replaced by dogma and ideology. [People] became representations of a cause, rather than themselves.

- For months after [the incident] . . . people appeared to be frightened, hurt, and/or angry. Instead of trying to resolve it together, people began to ignore one another and relationships changed significantly. The administration talked to a few people behind closed doors. . . . Since that time the atmosphere for discussion of any potentially controversial subject has been strained. It seems to be understood by all that there are serious consequences for expressing one's opinion. . . .

- Your visit frightens me. I do not believe a happy resolution is possible — and I very much would want a happy resolution. Damaging things have been said. . . . I fear it is all going to start up again by your visit here.

These and other comments suggested that the unit's dialogue had stopped or become exclusive, and revealed that many people felt frustrated about important talk occurring behind closed doors. I felt it important to work with the full group in a way that would not echo the perceived hiddenness that had been distressing to many people and that also would provide safety to those who feared the hurt that greater openness might bring. I believed, too, that it was important to be responsive to and respectful of the requests that separate meetings occur. To address both agendas, I proposed that all of the unit's workers clear the entire day and that we start out in the full group with options to move in and out of large and small group formats within the same room as the day unfolded.

I saw the unit as a place in which dialogue had been interrupted, foreclosing the possibility that new meanings and new understandings could be created or could evolve (Anderson & Goolishian, 1988, in press). The discussion of difference, once so creative, open, and vigorous in the agency that it had given rise to a pioneering counseling program, was experienced by some unit staff members as having broken down in their work group into subdialogues, one emphasizing commonalities, the other, differences. I hoped that the dialogue in the unit could be resumed, but recognized that we might get no further in the consultation itself than what Gurevitch (1989, p. 161) calls the experience of "not understanding," which is one of " . . . setting the other at a distance as an other who stands at her or his own separate center and cannot be reduced to common understanding." If openly "not understanding" others replaced secretly held beliefs of "understanding" others, it could become the starting point from which more productive dialogue would resume in the future.

INTRODUCTION OF THE DAY'S PLAN AND THE CONSULTANT

As our meeting began, I said that I saw my role as facilitating the process of their meeting their goal, which I understood to be that of speaking with each other about sensitive topics of difference, if such a discussion could take place without anyone feeling devalued or obliterated or without making matters worse. I presented myself as the servant of the group, not as an evaluator of actions or ideas, or even necessarily as a contributor of them. I said that the plan for the day had already been influenced by their answers to my letter as well as the two original phone calls and that it would continue to evolve as we shared experiences during the day.

I said that I had learned from their letters that there were varying wishes and expectations, that I had tried to design the day to take all of them into account to some extent, and that I understood there would be much still undone at the end of the day. In this way, I attempted to address expectations and to keep them moderate.

Next, I introduced myself professionally as a family therapist and then self-disclosed to an extent that I believed would encourage other participants' greater openness. I named my sexual preference. I spoke of my enjoyment of sports involving some physical risk. I described my professional focus in a way that would signal my hope for the consultation — as a long-standing interest in finding ways to engage in full and authentic dialogue in situations people usually experienced as polarized and limiting. In that work, I said that I had noticed that the success of a dialogue was connected to new listening as well as new speaking (Andersen, 1988, 1991, 1992; Roth, 1988). I hoped to dispel any secrecy about the approach I was using with the group by sharing my thinking about the process throughout the day.

CLARITY AND SAFETY OF THE CONTRACT

Finally, I discussed the kind of contract I hoped we could make together. For the maximum safety of all participants, I asked that our contract include agreements about time management, confidentiality, noncoercive participation, and the role of the consultant, as described below. Participants agreed to all of the suggested provisions.

1. *Structure of the day.* I laid out my general plan, specifying the time segments I had tentatively allocated for each part.

2. *Noncoercive atmosphere and the right to pass.* In the interests of safety and the creation of a noncoercive atmosphere, I asked everyone to agree that anyone could ask about anything seemingly relevant or important at any time, and that the rest of us would have the freedom to respond or not, with no explanation required. This provision was originated by James Sacks and is known as the "right

to pass" (Chasin & Roth, 1990; Chasin, Roth & Bograd, 1989; Lee, 1981, 1986). If one of us should choose not to respond, we would do so by saying "pass" or "pass for now," and passing would not preclude making a response later. I asked that the right to pass, whether temporarily or indefinitely, hold for any aspect of participation throughout the day.

3. *Confidentiality*. I suggested that, outside this group, people could speak freely about their own experience and discoveries only in ways that did not reveal who had made any particular statement, unless they specifically had asked for and received permission to do otherwise.

Because some members entered the consultation meeting tense and fearful, I asked group members to specify one word or phrase that expressed a feeling they brought to the meeting. They used such terms as "fearful," "hopeful," "cautious," "tentative," and "anxiously excited." It seemed to me, as I heard the words and phrases people brought forth and remembered the notes they had written, that some well-meaning, highly motivated, and caring individuals who wanted to be connected with each other had had their developing dialogue interrupted in a way that they had, thus far, been unable to surmount. As I understood the task we shared for the day, it was to work toward creating conditions more favorable to the resumption of the dialogue they had begun (Chasin et al., 1990) — conditions of openness, curiosity, and interest that would invite new listening as well as new speaking.

I saw the group as divided on two levels: on the content level by issues of difference, and on the process level by secrecy relationships around the complex meanings of these differences. I expected that a starting point that offered the opportunity to bring forth what was and was not "understood" could lead most directly to open dialogue and the releasing of constraints on conversation. Gurevitch (1989, p. 166) states that "the problem associated with dialogue is that of overcoming the tendency to not listen, which results from seeking to understand before listening and from imposing a complete set of meanings on the situation in an effort to define it as exclusive." Andersen (in press) calls this tendency "pre-understanding (prejudice and assumptions)."

An extended role reversal seemed to have the potential to make evident how each group was perceived by the other. These beliefs, then, would no longer be imagined, hidden, or secret, would no longer be the subject of covert speculation or assumption, and, once shared, could be explored. The extended role reversal, in which everyone agreed to participate, called for members of each group to enroll as members of the other group as a first step in moving from group identity and group perception to personal identity and personal perception. As the focus moved to personal statements and to full and open listening, I hoped that a multiplicity of viewpoints and beliefs would enrich the store of material available to the group and its members, from which they could make new meaning and more fully shared understanding.

AN EXTENDED ROLE REVERSAL

Asking those staff members who identified themselves within the agency as lesbian and gay to go to one side of the room and those who identified themselves within the agency as straight to go to the other side of the room, I enrolled each group as its counterpart in the following way:

> As soon as you are there, something strange is going to happen. You will remain you — that is, you will have your own personality and most of your family history — but, for a while you are going to have a different sexual preference than the one with which you usually walk through life.
>
> Take a moment, remembering that you now have a different sexual preference. Think about the family in which you grew up. How was that for you, around your becoming a sexual person? Imagine yourself — alone and with your family — at the important periods of your own development, given this alteration in your history. Take your time. [This is followed by five minutes of silence.]
>
> Given this new history, at this time, the present time, you are working in an agency like this one, one that has a predominantly straight outpatient unit staff and an entirely gay and lesbian GLCP staff working within the unit. Think silently for a few minutes. [I paused after each of the following questions, allowing people time to think.]
>
> • What questions and concerns come up for you about work?
> • About work with clients?
> • About your work environment?
> • About your family?
> • About colleagues and staff in this unit?
> • About colleagues and staff in other agencies?
> • About friends?
>
> Finally, a situation has occurred in the unit in which there is tension between the gay and lesbian and the straight staff. In role, with this new sexual preference, what issues might you want to raise?
>
> Be careful to avoid stereotyping and dogma in your role. Try to avoid generalities and try to use words that describe specific situations.
>
> Take a half an hour, in your separate groups, to discuss what issues and concerns have come up for you that you want to raise with the large group. We'll then put them on the blackboard.

After thirty minutes, I collected a long and full list of topics from the heterosexual workers who had been enrolled as gay and lesbian. Their list included such items as:

- I wonder if I'll be seen for who I am, or if they'll see me through their own prejudices?
- They are nice enough to my face, but I wonder what they really think of me?
- They talk nicely enough with me, but would they trust me with their kids?
- What would happen if I brought my partner to the Christmas party?
- I trust their clinical ability, but can they deal with differences?
- I'm tired of always having to justify my existence.

I suggested a particular form for listening and responding. The actual lesbians and gays (who had been enrolled as straight) would, without interruption, listen (as themselves) without comment until all of the issues and concerns had been written on the board. Then, taking turns in the order in which they were seated, the lesbian and gay staff members could, without interruption, share personal reflections on whatever had come up while listening to the concerns that the other group had raised (Andersen, 1987, 1991, 1992; LaChapelle, 1988). Each would ponder aloud to him or herself: What is stirred up in me by hearing these things? What have I heard here that I respond to? What questions does this raise for me? What does it make me wonder?

I suggested that people in the reflecting group take as many speaking turns, in seating order, as needed for all members to feel finished reflecting. Each person would mark the end of a turn by passing along a ceremonial object (LaChapelle, 1988). In this way, there would be no ambiguity about when someone was finished with a turn. As agreed, each person had the "right to pass" at any time—and, indeed, not to share reflections at all (Chasin & Roth, 1990; Chasin, Roth & Bograd, 1989; Lee, 1981, 1986). We would know that the gay and lesbian group members felt that they had spoken enough for the present when the ceremonial object was passed through that group one complete time in silence. Then turns would rotate in the same way around the straight group, whose members would be invited to share personal reflections on the contributions their gay and lesbian colleagues had just made.

The choice to avoid direct discussion and to solicit personal reflections from group members, a modification of the Reflecting Team model originated by Tom Andersen (1987), and the Talking Staff Council method originated by Elizabeth Cogburn (LaChapelle, 1988), might seem to interrupt dialogue rather than encourage it. Actually, however, the approach moves dialogue forward by forestalling any tendency people may have to cut off what they might hear before they have fully heard it and by providing an almost sacred listening space. Knowing that they will not be speaking immediately, people are able to listen more fully than in ordinary conversation. When they do speak, they know they have all the time they want to be fully expressive and are often exceptionally thoughtful and in touch with previously unrecognized feelings.

In this format, all comments are reflections on what has been heard. I suggested guidelines for speaking (after Andersen, 1987, 1991) that aimed to keep the process moving toward opening up, not closing down, and to increase the multiplicity of available ideas and feelings. I suggested that people reflect aloud on the associations that had been stirred up for them as they listened, and that they do so in a spirit of elaboration and addition, not in one of negation. I also asked that comments relate only to the day's experience, and that, when they concerned other people, they be framed as "wonderings" rather than statements.

When the lesbian and gay staff members, who had been the first listeners, finally spoke, it was with amazement at how well the straight staff members had understood their concerns. Perceiving some of their concerns as being accurately expressed by those whom they had seen earlier as discrediting these concerns established a context in which the lesbian and gay members could more powerfully voice those concerns and even venture into previously unarticulated territory. They found new freedom to abandon the unified front they had once felt necessary. One woman said, "I am torn. If I feel connectedness to the straight world, am I being disloyal to my own community?"

As they spoke to the content of what they had heard, they were self-exploratory, not reactive. One lesbian staff member spoke movingly of homophobia within herself, something she had not done before. Differences within the gay and lesbian staff group began to emerge. For example, tension arose over what it meant that some dressed and behaved in a way that could be seen as straight. Individual distinctions were drawn as members of the GLCP began to speak more as individuals and less as representatives of a group. Reflecting in turns for about an hour, they continued to share what had been stirred in them by the list of issues and concerns the others had placed on the board.

As the ceremonial object went around the circle of first listeners, who were now speakers, I became increasingly certain that they would achieve full expression. But, as timekeeper, I became concerned that the day-long format would not be long enough for full speaking by all. In keeping with my view of the consultant's role as facilitating the safe discussion of sensitive topics of difference, I asked the group's permission to participate more actively. I briefly described the psychodramatic technique of doubling (Moreno, 1975), in which the facilitator moves beside and a bit behind the person who has just spoken, places a hand on that person's shoulder and, speaking as the speaker, offers a statement supplementary to what the speaker has just said. The double's efforts are to bring forth the speaker's as-yet-unspoken thoughts and feelings, by providing a stimulus statement (Yablonsky, 1976). The speaker always has the last word, either restating the double's comment in his or her own language if it has been experienced as accurate, revising it if it has not been experienced as correct, or stating what comes up as more to the point. If the speaker does not wish to be doubled, he or she declines with a simple hand signal.

Doubling statements often serve to shift the tone of the conversation by shifting its focus — perhaps from cognition to feeling or vice versa. Although cast as statements, doubling comments do not direct or impose but, rather, increase the range of focus of the person being doubled, whose experience is consistently one of clarifying his or her own thoughts. Doubling statements are always recast, revised, or replaced. Doubling can enable very full expression, make possible a wide range of inquiry for the speaker in a very short time, and enhance self-observation. For example, when one staff member referred several times to "them," I doubled, "I am speaking of 'them' when I could be speaking about myself." He recast the doubled comment as "It's easier sometimes to talk about others than it is to talk about myself," and began to consistently use "I" language for the rest of the meeting.

I explained that I wished to use this technique to hasten movement to the heart of what people had to say within the limited time available. The group agreed to its use, and I employed it in the morning and afternoon feedback segments as both groups responded to the lists of concerns on the board. The doubling, I believe, did not introduce new content, but enabled participants to express themselves more fully.

When the time came for the straight staff members to reflect, most did so with softness and emotion. Their listening had clearly moved most of them to a greater sense of empathy and connection and had offered them a chance to reflect on themselves as well as on those to whom they had been listening.

One woman, for example, spoke with emotion and humility of how her Jewish immigrant grandmother had often warned her of grave perils in the world and had pushed her to be hypervigilant and suspicious. She recalled her irritation and easy dismissal of her grandmother and her belief that her grandmother was living in a bygone, no longer relevant world. In listening to the gay and lesbian staff, she had come to feel that, by not recognizing there might be some actual danger for them, she had been treating them as she had treated her grandmother, and that many of them, like her grandmother, had already experienced direct injury as a consequence of being seen as "other."

A Christian staff member who had participated in the precipitating incident spoke of how important it had been for her to be seen more fully, of how she had been afraid to let people know of her beliefs, and of how she had felt silenced by staff responses to her statements. In the aftermath of the event, she felt forced back into the closet as a Christian, as if her beliefs and others' responses to them were a dangerous secret.

The thrust in the morning meeting was consistently toward "understanding" between members of both groups. In the afternoon, we went to the next step in the process with a different outcome, one of "not understanding" and "not being understood."

The gay and lesbian staff filled the blackboard with the concerns they had listed when they were enrolled as straight workers in the unit. Their list included such items as:

- If we get a few of *them* here, will this turn into a gay agency?
- What will we look like in the community to be the only place with a gay/lesbian unit?
- If a client who is ambivalent about his or her sexual orientation goes to a gay or lesbian therapist, the therapist will push the client to that side and won't remain objective.

After the list had been put on the board, the actual straight staff took the ceremonial object to offer their reflections in response to the list of concerns. They spoke of feeling angry, hurt, and misunderstood. They felt they had been seen in stereotypes and had not been seen or responded to as themselves. They felt that their caring for their colleagues had gone unrecognized. They were shocked to have been seen as misusing their power, as insisting that others fit into their mold, and as fearing being identified as connected to gays and lesbians. They had treated the GLCP staff as they would treat anyone, as if there were no difference, some said. They were as astonished at the levels of misunderstanding as the gay and lesbian staff had been at the levels of understanding.

The warmth and accord that had been generated in the morning were supplanted in the afternoon by anger, hurt, and discord. The entire group had moved from "understanding" and "being understood" to "not understanding" and "not being understood," from "knowing" to "not knowing."[3] The morning's hopefulness and excitement were gone, and in their place were discouragement and sadness. In the course of the day, the movement in the group was from assumptions of sameness and ability to empathize with each other about basic human issues to assumptions of difference and a seemingly unyielding impasse.

Completion of the extended role reversal was followed by a full group discussion to conclude the day. In the group discussion, participants asked questions of each other and made statements that continued to bring forth perceptions of "not understanding" and of "not being understood."

To address the group's discouragement about issues of difference, I asked people's permission to briefly participate in a different way, to share some ideas I had been reading and thinking about, to see if they might be useful. I spoke to the group about Gurevitch's (1988, p. 1197) idea that people cannot reach understanding of one another unless they also arrive at the point of realizing that they do not understand each other:

> Conversing with the other necessitates both the construction of sameness and familiarity and the recognition of otherness and strangeness. The true understanding of dialogue may be reached only when disparate selves are acknowledged within the larger common framework of meaning.

Several participants expressed relief that both the issues of what they believed staff members had in common and did not have in common were finally out in the open. Some lesbian and gay staff members said that they wanted their difference to be recognized, that they did not want to be seen as if they were "just like everyone else." Their lives really were different, they said, and the attempt to see them as "just like straights" felt disqualifying. "I want you to ask me how it was for me, and for my children, when I marched in the Gay Pride parade," one woman said. "It doesn't feel like care if your response to my doing that is as if I told you I had gone to the movies this

---

[3]Anderson and Goolishian (1988, in press), Andersen (1992), and others have written persuasively of the importance of the therapist's taking a "not knowing" position to prevent impeding the client's story with the therapist's preconceived ideas.

The work reported here is grounded in the belief that it is central to the work of the therapist/facilitator to establish conditions that invite clients/participants to be in a not-knowing position in relation *to each other*, and even in relation to themselves. The challenge for the therapist/facilitator is to find ways to establish conditions safe enough to encourage people who are used to believing that they "know" and "understand" each other to open themselves to taking "not knowing" and "not understanding" positions within the very situations and relationships they have experienced as foreclosed.

weekend." Another said, "I'm different, not just like you. And when you don't get it, I feel invisible."

In this discussion, people asked questions out of curiosity and made statements that brought forth important differences. A white group member recalled having lived with a black person who, when the issue of racial difference came up, had quoted from a poem by Pat Parker (1990, p. 68):[4]

> For the white person who wants to know
> how to be my friend.
>
> The first thing you do is to forget that i'm Black.
> Second, you must never forget that i'm Black.

There were nods of assent and understanding in the group as she spoke these words. Many participants seemed to respond to the idea that in order to be able to continue being in contact and conversation, they would have to put themselves to the seemingly impossible task posed in Pat Parker's poem, that of holding two opposing realities simultaneously, and recognizing and acknowledging them both.

As we moved toward the end of the day, I invited comments on how free people felt to speak of other differences. I felt that the day's efforts could be most useful for the future if they were seen as opening conversations about differences across the board, and were not limited to gay/straight issues. People named issues of class, gender, and large discrepancies in pay as examples of differences they had found it difficult to discuss openly. As the meeting moved to a close, members of the staff expressed measured hopefulness that the breaking of silence through surfacing and honoring of differences would continue and that working relationships would grow and change.

FOLLOW-UP TO THE CONSULTATION

When I conducted follow-up interviews[5] with over two-thirds of the participants, approximately one year later, I found that the process had moved forward in ways I could not have predicted. Staff and administration members who spoke with me were abundantly generous with their time and

---

[4]Quoted by permission of Firebrand Books (Ithaca, New York). From "for the white person who wants to know how to be my friend" by Pat Parker in *Movement in Black*. Copyright © 1978.
[5]Comments quoted from these interviews have been excerpted from tape transcripts and have been slightly edited for clarity. Comments reported in each section have substantial overlap and can also be categorized in numerous other ways.

deeply thoughtful in their observations. Much of what they said will guide me in future work. Many reported transformative experiences on multiple levels and expressed the belief that the process had catalyzed the group's development of productive ways to address difference and complexity in unit relationships.

Several people reported having experienced great pain during the consultation, but attributed it to personal issues or unit relationships beyond the scope of this chapter. Nevertheless, their experiences need to be acknowledged here.

Many of the changes participants reported can be loosely categorized as

- Movement from silence toward openness around issues of difference
- Movement toward bringing more complex and less dichotomous views into every level of the conversation
- Movement from the political to the personal in dialogue with self and others

While these shifts followed the consultation, the consultation did not bring them about. Rather, it created a safe place in which shifts could occur and facilitated the group's reopening of their dialogue so that unit members could more fully share and develop their own ideas as they responded to numerous changes in their work world—disruptions such as relocation of their offices, massive budget cuts, staff changes, and externally, a deteriorating social and economic environment.

From Silence Toward Openness

Staff reported that movement from silence toward openness had emerged on many levels—in reflections on themselves, in personal relationships within the unit, in ways that a number of difficult work issues were handled, and in the relationship of the unit to the community. Reflecting on the time prior to the consultation, one worker said, "I was so unaware! A dynamic about difference was covert, not overt. It's not that there was a secret, something someone was hiding, but something about how things were going that was so little talked about openly that it felt distancing—as if something secret was going on." Speaking of that same period, another worker said, "There were such powerful forces toward silence." A third staff member said, "Some things that had felt unspeakable became able to be spoken, and whether or not they were spoken was less important than that there was a pathway carved out to speak." Another observed, "It's the sense of secrecy or taboo that cuts off pathways."

For some, personal pathways had opened, and their conversation with themselves, about themselves, was altered. A lesbian noticed her own "homophobia" for the first time; a straight woman reported, "I inherited subtle stereotypes and actually thought I didn't have any!" Another person said, "I remember feeling sad. How can I not have seen how painful this was for the gays and lesbians! I ended up looking at my own defensiveness, at how much I hadn't seen because I was so closed off."

In the follow-up interviews, some people noted that personal relationships had developed or deepened. One staff member observed, "Something happened that opened people to knowing each other more personally." Another said, "I had this idea before that I had to be constrained. Constraint built tremendous separations. Now I feel a real bond and connection with the staff—and I'm not sure how it happened. There's more openness. I'd been censoring myself, my spontaneity. Now I joke about who I am. I'm right out there, less hidden—and I've made some really nice relationships." Another explained the development of new friendships across sexual preference lines by saying, "I felt more comfortable [afterward] with those who took off a layer of mask. Then I felt I could take off mine. I didn't feel that openness before then; it was more like a wall. But I didn't appreciate that I had a wall, too."

Several staff members spoke of the situation in the unit as echoing their families of origin and of their responding accordingly. As one person commented, "When things got so bad in the unit, it was no surprise to me. That's what I expected to happen when differences were raised. That's why it was easy to get silent afterward. Since last summer, I've been much more ready to say, 'This is what I believe, I'm not trying to hurt you, and we do have conflict.' Living with this and seeing that another way can work has been great for me, an experience I never had in my family!" Another person spoke of being freed, in part, by the form of the consultation from an old sense of "having to make things better, to fix them" when there was conflict. That freedom, she reported, had carried forward.

Within the unit, ways of addressing difference seemed to have opened up. "It was around gay/lesbian issues that [the change] started, but it ended up across the year to allow other differences to be discussed, too." These other differences were being dealt with, on the whole, in more open ways. Two issues that had been named at the end of the consultation meeting as being historically difficult to discuss—pay differences and gender roles—were mentioned specifically in the follow-up interviews as having been openly discussed.

For example, a gay man reported that "a few months after the consultation, the women in GLCP confronted me on my maleness and male leadership style, on how I use power from that angle. We were then also able to speak about *their* ways of using power. It was very helpful in changing our ways of working with each other."

Additionally, a new set of issues of difference was currently on the table, as the agency had since added a unit for services to the deaf. Difficulties around what was assumed, known, and not known, had already come up. These issues had been more promptly and openly addressed than some people believed they would have been prior to the consultation. Staff members made such comments as, "Before the consultation, I would have felt it was too dangerous to bring up 'X' directly, but this time I was able to," and, "I was feeling before that differences shouldn't come into play, but it's a kind of paradox. To recognize difference out loud allows the differences to be less important in the interaction."

There were also signs of shifts in how some members of the GLCP perceived the agency's support of the Program. In the past, in dealing with certain funding sources in a changing human-services environment, financial concerns had led the agency to play up some programs and to play down others, including the GLCP. In 1980, the agency had published a brochure listing all of its programs then in existence. By the time the GLCP was established in 1983, the agency had changed to unit-specific and specialty brochures, including one for the GLCP. The GLCP has received additional publicity over the years since its inception through press releases, newspaper articles, and presentations at national conferences. In 1991, the agency returned to the use of an agency-wide brochure that included all units and specialty programs. Some members of the GLCP experienced what the agency considered careful attention to funding politics and advertising decisions emphasizing unit specialties as hushing GLCP up and failing in its commitment to the GLCP. Those members perceived the return to an agency-wide brochure as a strengthening of the agency's support for the gay and lesbian program.

One worker felt that "the agency really made more of a commitment to the GLCP unit. We now have a brochure listing all of the specialty units, including the GLCP. Since last August, I have felt the GLCP more validated, as though we really belong now to the larger agency. Before, it felt to me like we'd snuck in and could be snuffed out quickly. [Before] it felt like the agency was keeping the program a secret. There were concerns that [outsiders] would get upset, that it might affect our state or federal funding. 'Don't flaunt it' was the message."

From Polarizing Conversation Toward Conversation of Greater Complexity

In the summer of 1990, conversation in the unit had been rife with dichotomies, even as some staff members privately held more complex views. Issues had been discussed as if they were about gay/straight concerns or about similarities and differences. In the follow-up interviews about a year later, people's descriptions were filled with complexity. Many spoke of holding multiple, even opposing, views as valid and even useful and had brought these complex views into their conversation. Many spoke of valuing "freedom to ask questions, express concerns, and hold different ideas, freedom to not agree."

A lesbian staff member spoke of learning that she had the "capability to meet people in that kind of difference and be respectful of them"—and still feel that she was "okay": "I had always thought that I had to hate anyone who hated me or was prejudiced against me. And then I'd feel that I was abusive, so I'd feel bad about myself. It didn't fit, because I'd then be doing the same thing that I said I hated the other person for—so I was being like them! But I couldn't figure out how to move out of that place. Being vulnerable with those I felt were against me so they could really see me offered me a way out. It's such a relief to not have it as an 'us and them.'"

Others had broadened their frames of reference to embrace substantially richer descriptions than had previously been available to them for understanding unit relationships. The following comment represents a sentiment expressed by many: "There's a real sense in the unit now of not just accepting differences, but of valuing them. It makes a contribution to the whole, rather than being something to worry about."

Others were very specific about how this less dichotomous way of thinking had surfaced in the life of the unit: "After that day, I went to the Christian person with whom I had a conflict, and I said that what I had experienced that day was the recognition of how much alike we are in our difference, that she was speaking from the deepest place in her about what she really believes in and who she is, and I was speaking from the very same place in me. And so for me it became about being more alike than different."

Suspending the Political to Focus on the Personal in Conversation with Self and Others

Participants reported that moving from politicized to personal language had powerful effects on their own experience of themselves as well as on their relationships within the unit. This movement had helped them transcend the limitations of one set of ideas and eventually move toward larger, more encompassing frames of reference: "I'm a person who can use the political language. I love it and always prided myself on being political. I'd let you see that, but not the personal. I felt safe enough on that day to make a decision to go into my center and operate from that place," one person reported.

A gay man, who had been angrily political in his response to my initial letter, spoke eloquently of his experience: "The evening after the consultation I was tearful, grieving. I came to understand that day that there was no way I'd ever know what it was to be straight, no matter how hard I tried. It was painful and a relief. It was when we wrote all the things down about what we thought when we were pretending to be straight and the straight staff said, 'No, that's not how we think about someone being gay.' There was no way any attempts I made to fit in the straight world were going to work. I couldn't pass. I mourned that I would never know what it is like to be straight. And when I really got that, I wondered how I could have expected the straights to do what I couldn't do myself! That made it less important — we all just seemed to be more human. It didn't make sense anymore to be angry about that."

THE CONSULTATION AS CATALYST TO THE RESUMPTION OF DIALOGUE

When the agency administration and unit staff agreed to have a consultation, issues of difference had begun to impair the ability of some group members to interact and to work together. The once creative and productive group dialogue had broken down into a subdialogue of difference running counter to a subdialogue of commonality, and a subdialogue of one set of religious values vying with another subdialogue based on a different set of values.

Some members of the group experienced silence and a sense of constraint. For them, secrecy had replaced openness and the conviction of understanding had replaced awareness of not understanding. Meanings became frozen. Some felt inaccurately seen and inadequately understood. They wanted their views to be known and respected, but had become too guarded to risk showing curiosity, interest, and openness toward the views of others. Misapprehensions flourished where the ideas and beliefs of others were not understood but were believed to be understood. New meanings and new understandings were no longer being created.

The first task of the consultation was to establish conditions that all members found conducive to safe engagement in the dialogue. People had to perceive conditions as favorable to openness, curiosity, and interest in order for new listening and new speaking to take place. Safety required that all participants feel assured of not being attacked or disqualified for expressing their views, and that each person be guaranteed the opportunity to be fully enough heard to risk granting to others the same full listening.

Each of the guidelines was important in inspiring confidence in the group as a safe place — clarity, consistency, confidentiality, voluntary participation, word choice to describe others, time to speak without interruption and to listen fully, the order of speaking and listening, acceptance of doubt as well as certainty, openness about the process, encouragement to express differences, a focus on the future, the emergent nature of the process, and—the *sine qua non*—full agreement to each of these provisions. Another important contributor to the sense of safety was the use of a ceremonial object to designate who held the right to speak fully and without interruption at any given moment—and, for those not then holding the object, who held the right to listen fully without the burden of having to formulate a response to the speaker. For those who already felt safe in the group, perhaps the guidelines did no more than make safe conditions explicit. For those who had not felt safe, the guidelines seemed to delineate the terms under which they believed they could safely reenter.

With this arrangement in place, the speaking and listening began, increasing in emotional intensity, as participants experienced first understanding and being understood, and then not understanding and not being understood. Some group members had held their beliefs and feelings in secret, including their beliefs that they understood others. Speaking and listening in safety, they told their beliefs and feelings and heard those of others. Their experiences were mixed—some of understanding and being understood, some of not understanding and not being understood.

The creation of an environment inviting both experiences was the second task of the consultation. Awareness of not understanding and of not being understood were conditions as necessary to the resumption of dialogue as safety:

> The ability to not understand has two major implications for the process of understanding in relationships. The first is clearer, and relates to the recognition and conception of the other in the eyes of the self. The second is that of seeing oneself in the eyes of the other. This too, requires one to have the power of not understanding to activate the process of making strange. A shift must be made from the centered self to the perspective of the other, whereby one attains a separate and strange perceptive center of consciousness enabling one to view the self as other. . . . Shifting the center from the self toward the other and taking the other's role allows one to gain not only a new understanding of the other, but also a new understanding of the self. This consequently alters the terms of the dialogue and revises and re-activates the understanding of both the self and the other. (Gurevitch, 1989, p. 164)

The extended role reversal enabled participants to address questions of how they saw others and were seen by others and to make these perceptions evident.

The consultation did no more than establish conditions of safety and provide a process to facilitate participants' arrival at a place of curiosity and discovery. Only because the will to establish these conditions was already present in the group and the participants had the courage to open themselves to not understanding and not being understood, to understanding and being understood, could the consultation catalyze the resumption of their dialogue. The work of the group since then has been to keep the dialogue open, creating new meanings and new understandings that are shared, forged from the complexities of their differences and not understandings as well as their commonalities and understandings.

REFERENCES

Andersen, T. (1987). The reflecting team: Dialogue and meta-dialogue in clinical work. *Family Process, 26*, 415–428.

Andersen, T. (1988). Personal communication.

Andersen, T. (1991). The reflecting team. In T. Andersen (Ed.), *The reflecting team: Dialogues and dialogues about the dialogues.* New York: W. W. Norton.

Andersen, T. (1992). Relationship, language, and understanding. *The Australian and New Zealand Journal of Family Therapy,* June.

Anderson, H., & Goolishian, H. A. (1988). Human systems as linguistic systems: Some preliminary and evolving ideas about the implications for clinical theory. *Family Process, 26*, 371–393.

Anderson, H., & Goolishian, H. A. (in press). The client is the expert: A not-knowing approach to therapy. In S. McNamee & K. Gergen (Eds.), *Constructing therapy: Social construction and the therapeutic process.* London: Sage.

Bok, S. (1989). *Secrets: On the ethics of concealment and revelation.* New York: Vintage.

Chasin, L., Chasin, R., Herzig, M., Roth, S., & Becker, C. (1991). The citizen clinician: The family therapist in the public forum. *American Family Therapy Association Newsletter, 46*, 36–42.

Chasin, R., & Herzig, M. (in press). Creating systemic interventions for the socio-political arena. In B. Gould & D. DeMuth (Eds.), *Family therapy in the global context.* Boston: Allyn & Bacon.

Chasin, R., & Roth, S. (1990). Future perfect, past perfect: A positive approach to opening couple therapy. In R. Chasin, H. Grunebaum, & M. Herzig (Eds.), *One couple, four realities: Multiple perspectives on couple therapy.* New York: Guilford.

Chasin, R., Roth, S., & Bograd, M. (1989). Action methods in systemic therapy: Dramatizing ideal futures and reformed pasts with couples. *Family Process, 28*, 121–136.

Gurevitch, Z. D. (1988). The other side of dialogue: On making the other strange and the experience of otherness. *American Journal of Sociology, 93*, 1179–1199.

Gurevitch, Z. D. (1989). The power of not understanding. *Journal of Applied Behavioral Sciences, 25*, 161–173.

Hare-Mustin, R. T. (1987). The problem of gender in family therapy theory. *Family Process, 26*, 15–27.

Hare-Mustin, R. T., & Maracek, J. (1988). The meaning of difference: Gender theory, postmodernism, and psychology. *American Psychologist, 43*, 455–464.

Hare-Mustin, R. T., & Maracek, J. (1990). Gender and the meaning of difference. In R. T. Hare-Mustin & J. Maracek (Eds.), *Making a difference: Psychology and construction of gender.* New Haven, CT: Yale University Press.

LaChapelle, D. (1988). *Sacred land, sacred sex: Rapture of the deep.* Silverton, CO: Finn Hill Arts.

Lee, R. (1981). Video as adjunct to psychodrama and role-playing. In J. L. Fryrear & R. Fleshman (Eds.), *Videotherapy and mental health.* Springfield, IL: Charles C. Thomas.

Lee, R. (1986). The family therapy trainer as coaching double. *Journal of Group Psychotherapy, Psychodrama and Sociometry, 39*, 52–57.

Moreno, J. L. (1975). *Psychodrama: Action therapy and principles of practice* (vol. III). Beacon, NY: Beacon House.

Parker, P. (1990). "For the white person who wants to know how to be my friend." In *Movement in black: The collected poetry of Pat Parker 1961–1978* (p. 68). Ithaca, NY: Firebrand Books.

Penn, P. (1985). Feed-forward: Future questions, future maps. *Family Process, 24*, 299–310.

Roth, S. (1988, November). The opening meeting: Therapist position and action. Plenary paper presented at Harvard Medical School Conference, *Treating Couples*.

Roth, S., Chasin, L., Chasin, R., Becker, C., & Herzig, M. (in press). From debate to dialogue: A facilitating role for family therapists in the public forum, *Dulwich Centre Newsletter*.

Tomm, K. (1987). Interventive interviewing: Part II. Reflexive questioning as a means to enable self-healing. *Family Process, 26*, 167–183.

Yablonsky, L. (1976). *Resolving emotional difficulties through role-playing*. New York: Basic.

15

Taboos and Social Order: New Encounters for Family and Therapist

ALAN COOKLIN
GILL GORELL BARNES

THIS IS A CHAPTER about what is not allowed. The idea of what is not allowed has gone through a number of changes. Originally, it referred to what is not allowed to happen or what is not allowed to be talked about by the family within the family. Increasingly, it became apparent to us that this aspect of a family's behavior could not be considered without inclusion of the therapist's contribution. Therapists may, albeit unwittingly, disallow certain subjects and interactions as much as may the members of a family. Therapists are often — or at least should be — concerned lest their own prejudices amplify or intensify issues that are not of real concern to the family. Of equal interest to us are issues that may be of concern to the client or family, but that the therapist unknowingly supresses. This may be because he or she is either very uncomfortable with a topic, or it may just be related to the narrowness of thought or limits of the therapist's repertoire through lack of exposure. When based on discomfort, this, in turn, may be related to topics that are both personally painful and highly sensitive — such as incest, sexual abuse, and certain forms of violence, torture, and deliberate brutality. Other topics may be avoided when they accentuate difference between the therapist and family. These can include social issues such as poverty, homelessness, race, or other factors. Thus, this chapter is about what is disallowed by the family, the prohibitions being, to some extent, supported by the therapist and the culture in which they both operate.

FACTORS IN FAMILY AND SOCIAL PATTERN: RIGIDITY AND INCONGRUENT ADAPTATION

While the family therapy field is currently engaged in controversies about what is a system and to what extent "systems" descriptions can be generally applied to human relations, in practically all the frameworks of thinking it is implied that increasing flexibility of response is a central goal. "Unbalancing" (Minuchin & Fishman, 1981) and "creating perturbations" (Maturana & Varela, 1987) are two obvious examples from different perspectives. This flexibility is related to some implied "rigidity" (Bateson, 1972) in family patterns. How one perceives the basis of such rigidity can lead to different responses. We use the term "incongruent adaptation" on the assumption that the family that presents a problem is, in some way, adapting to new situations, but in a way that is incongruent to the mastery of that situation. Such situations, of course, include the culture, and may include the therapist or other professionals.

Our assumption is that a rigidifying of pattern is almost universal in situations of fear. Illness, cultural isolation following immigration, unemployment, poverty, racial harassment, and the various events in which one has to face great loss, in fact, any frightening problem will tend to be responded to by an increase in rigidity of pattern. "Freezing" is a common alarm response in animals (Milner, 1966). The metaphor of "freezing" (or in Spanish, "paralysis") is commonly used to describe individual responses to fear. We suggest that patterns of behavior and organization in families and other groups may become frozen in response to some perceived fear threatening the *group*.

What we will describe are rigidified systems, which are organized around incongruent, ineffective, or outdated responses to fear, the manifestations of which will often increase the likelihood of attack or of the feared event.

This has implications for the process of change. Physiological rigidity is most often associated with states of tension or in the body's reparative response to injury (scars, adhesions, etc.). The physiotherapist uses, among other techniques, gradual and alternate stretching and relaxation of the affected area. Together, they are effective, but neither work on their own. As a metaphor, this aptly describes much of the way we have used ourselves as therapists in these "rigidified" situations. We have taken the position that if one can "release the spasm" then, in large measure, development at whatever age will proceed.

DIMINISHING RIGIDITY OR INCONGRUENT ADAPTATION OR INCREASING FLEXIBILITY OF ADAPTATION

Rigidity in the relationships between the people and between the different sets of relationships within the family, is often organized in a way that maintains certain facets of family life as *hidden*. Previous interest in the hidden has focused particularly on family secrets (Pincus & Dare, 1978). Their definition of secrets, however, related much to what is "not known," particularly through what is kept out of consciousness. In the Oxford dictionary (*Shorter O.E.D.*, 1973), "secret" is defined as:

> That which is kept from public knowledge or from the knowledge of persons specified . . . not openly avowed or expressed . . . concealed, disguised . . . designed to escape observation or detection.

Thus, secrets are information that one or more people withhold from others. In relation to the family, it can exclude or protect certain family members from others or from the perceived noxious effects of the information to either party. Alternatively, it can exclude those outside the family from information that is restricted to family members. The people who don't have the information may or may not be aware that they do not have it.

The focus of this chapter differs in that we are concerned more with the apparently mutual acceptance by family members that a particular event or aspect of family life *should* remain hidden or prohibited. Of course, this acceptance may be relatively imposed on some members, depending on the way the relationships of power are organized within the family. Clearly, there is much overlap between secrets and taboos, and we will describe cases in which there are secrets, but we will view secrets through the lens of the taboo, rather than vice versa. In relation to taboos, the information is more likely to be generally available even if not explicitly shared. In addition, the maintenance of the taboo is more likely to be seen as in the service and/or preservation of some higher social order. There are also more likely to be specific representations (totems) of the taboo subject—i.e., things that may not be said or done.

But, if family taboos fulfill the function of maintaining an often necessary degree of family order, then why should a family therapist challenge them? If they do so, then how can it be done?

The most important reason for challenging a taboo is when it has become associated with seriously destructive behavior in the family. This behavior (violence, stealing, arson, or self-destructive acts, such as attempted suicide) may be an attempt, albeit in an incompetent and distorted form, to create greater flexibility or randomness in a rigid system without a head-on challenge to the social order. Thus, one may see a young person's behavior as attempting to create "room" for change, while preserving the stability of the family "order" (via a potentially destructive act) at a time of great potential change, such as late adolescence.

Gorell Barnes (1983a) has presented the case of a 16-year-old young man who attempted to shoot himself on the school stage with an air pistol. The question she posed was: Why did he need to choose such a dramatic and potentially dangerous protest to the social order of the family, in order to be able to engage in the issues of independence and sexuality that he now faced?

Case Example: Eric

With the onset of Eric's adolescence, his parents were faced with a painful dilemma about their value system. For them, sexuality was intertwined with loss of control and was associated with a tradition of severe violence in the father's family of origin. The event that precipitated the conflict occurred when Eric told them he wanted to have a party. Their response was to suggest he invite a couple of friends out to dinner and the theatre. They presented their imagery of the imagined party: "Bottoms heaving on beds, and fish ponds filled with gin." The therapist's interest was to help the family find a less destructive way to continue the struggle about change.

In the father's story about growing up, sexuality had been associated with beating, humiliation, and fear. By talking openly about "fucking" as a normal part of the range of a young man's required experience in the pathway to adulthood, Gorell Barnes introduced some more open conversations that the family, in the safety of the clinic setting, were keen to take up. Eric's attempt to draw attention to an area of life in the family—sexuality, pleasure, and fun—was explored along a number of dimensions, between mother and father, between each parent and their children, among the brother, sister, and their peer group, and finally between each parent and their own experience of growing up.

Widening the context of meaning in this way allowed the family to see Eric's attempt at self-harm as a failed solution among a set of more life-enhancing alternatives. Helping them to find a framework to negotiate about the risks and potential pleasures of the party became the central issue for negotiation, rather than the question about the dangers of Eric killing himself. However, the degree of taboo around this issue for this family was sufficiently prohibitive for Eric to have to invent a second scenario of self-destruction, this time a fantasy about his death in a violent automobile accident. His parents got the message that "once is not enough" for therapy to change a life script. This first successful attempt at contextualizing enjoyment as part of the family's story of themselves as a family who "could enjoy life," then allowed them to consider more permanent change in their own relationship patterns. Taking the slogan from their church, "The family who prays together, stays together," we adapted it to "The family who plays together, stays together." Subsequent meetings were spent with the family describing the many innovative ways that they had incorporated having fun into their own family script, including the "restorying" by mother of her own adolescence to include a raunchy account of parties in her youth, nights spent in the hay at barn dances, and some gentle and affectionate reminiscences of the courting days with Eric's shy, but apparently eager, father.

The taboo implies that some or all family members share an image — often ill defined, inexplicit, and by the very nature of its being taboo, unchallengable — of disastrous consequences that will ensue if the taboo subject is acknowledged and faced. Family therapists have tended to assume that this image of disaster hinged on the fear of the possible breakup of the family (Bentovim & Kinston, 1990). There are, in fact, many subtler and more specific fears that a family may share. The fear of breakup is, of course, real and is present in the minds of many victims of child sexual abuse in powerful ways that carry forward to their families of procreation or to subsequent relationship patterns. For others, it is more a metaphor for any disaster that cannot be thought about. The therapist must, therefore, believe that these things can be usefully thought about and that the capacity of the family to manage potential disasters will be enhanced if they are faced.

THE NATURE OF TABOO

In Heinemann's English dictionary (1979), "taboo" is defined as:

1) Being banned by social custom.
2) Excluded from use, approach or mention because of the sacred quality of an object (Polynesian).

The word originates from the Polynesian "tapu," meaning forbidden. It was originally used to combine that which is holy with that which is prohibited, and it may express either sacredness or uncleanness. Either way the thing tabooed is in some way dangerous (Douglas, 1984; Leach, 1982). The most common taboos are incest and food taboos. There are certain key characteristics of taboos relevant to our topic:

1. The origin of the prohibition is unmotivated and enigmatic.
2. The nucleus of the prohibition is often an act of touching.
3. The prohibition shows a capacity for displacement — there is a risk of "infection" from the prohibited object.
4. Violators of taboos become taboo themselves.
5. The situation is usually handled by inventing elaborate ceremonies to expiate the taboo. (Fox, 1983)

In addition, both the sacred and unclean aspects of taboo are inextricably bound up with manifestations or representations of the sacred in the form of totems. Cultures in which totem and taboo are explicitly embedded in the way people think and conceive of nature often clearly distinguish between customs and proscriptions that are related to propriety or public authority and taboos that hold the danger of mystical retribution.[1] It is the latter that most closely fit our theme, while the former are closer to political proscriptions, which may involve immediate retribution from earthly authorities and result in a more "conventional" secret (i.e., wife abuse, alcoholism).

As currently used, the concept of taboo implies a block on communication as well as action. It is, of course, culturally determined. In Bali, there is a taboo on engaging a third person in a dispute, a practice that is quite common in most Western cultures. Thus, what is treated as taboo is often a function of the particular culture, family, locality, religious, ethnic, or political group. Incest taboos varies greatly depending on whether a culture is matrilineal or patrilineal. For example, the matrilineal societies stress proscriptions on incest with the sister, while patrilineal societies are more concerned about adultery with wives or other members of the lineage and incest with the mother (Fox, 1983). In Western culture, the proscriptions against incest, while originally based on a patrilineal taboo regarding incest, have become increasingly influenced by "Western" perspectives about individual psychological development. The "ethic" that prescribes "leaving the nest" is naturally weakest in isolated rural areas, in which there is some

[1]These differences have been described in detail in relation to the Tallensi people by Fortes (1966).

evidence that incest is more common. However, Western concern is now focused on the abuse of power and the psychological impact of parent-child incest as defined by "child sexual abuse." If one assumes that all taboos at some time had one or more functions, the incest taboo provides an example at three levels:

societal — maintaining exogeny and protecting against consanguinity

family — maintaining the "order" between different generations

biological/psychological — protecting the developing organism from excessive interference with the self-regulated developmental process

What becomes taboo may, therefore, be a manifestation of the constraints that play, or have played, a part in maintaining the order of that culture. Blasphemy is an example of the use of a number of taboos in the maintenance of the order of a particular religion. One could argue that a religion — which can cut across and transcend native cultural rules and which may be less rooted in any one culture, and often not the local culture — is more vulnerable to social change. A religion may, therefore, become reliant on the stabilizing function of taboos. Although clearly related to other factors, the recent outcry by the international Islamic community over Salman Rushdie's book, *The Satanic Verses*, seems a good example of this process in action.

Our proposal is that taboos in the family fulfill a similar stabilizing function, although there is a difference: Societal taboos are often explicit, while "smaller" or idiosyncratic family taboos may be both implicit and may include a proscription against the naming of the taboo. The most commonly cited family taboos in Western culture used to be about sex. It is easy to see how uncontrolled sexuality could be perceived as a threat to the social order of the family. Sexuality implies the possibility of bringing newcomers into the family, or of the individual "moving out" literally or metaphorically, thus diminishing or disrupting the influence of family norms. It also implies a greater government of the behavior of the individuals by affect or passion, and less by the "rules" of the family.

While specific elements may need to remain "closed" within specific subsystemic units (for example, details of the parents' sexual relationship being excluded from the children), in the service of maintaining intergenerational boundaries, the tendency to hide can easily become not only redundant, but also can constrain against necessary change.

All families and all relationships have some taboos, some issues that the participants avoid. We are not, therefore, suggesting a sort of witch hunt against "all that is hidden." Rather, we are interested in these key issues as a source of inflexibility, which a family may need to overcome when negotiating certain changes. The taboo may be confined to the current generation, but will often have a pattern of two or three generational conflicts associated with it, as in the example of Eric's family.

Many of the issues are "universals" (i.e., sex, death, torture, incest, madness, cowardice, deformity), others are relatively universal within a particular culture (like intimacy and loss in the upper middle class in Britain) while some are more "family specific."

A "Family-Specific" Taboo

The Bond family presented a more universal taboo about suicide in the family, as well as a taboo against male displays of distress, vulnerability, or passion. This was considered a family-specific taboo, as they were not part of the British aristocratic class in which this attitude might have been more commonly expected.

The husband had developed a woodworking business and was happiest when he was in his shop away from the emotional demands of family life. The couple had two children, a boy, 10, and a girl, 7. The boy had been sent to boarding school at age 9, partly because he was having difficulties at his local school, partly because there was no choice of school in the countryside where they lived, and partly because it was expected in this family that boys, in particular, would go to boarding school. The school he went to, however, was not typical of English boarding schools, but was a liberal, co-ed school.

Jason had been away from home for longish periods before. However, six months after starting at this school, he began to seek out the school matron at night and to stay up for much of the night, holding onto his penis and complaining that there was something wrong with it and that it might fall off. He was also becoming increasingly unpopular with the other children.

When I (Cooklin) met the family, what I encountered was the rather bland disconnection of the father and an intense but rather curious relationship between Jason and his mother. It was curious because he seemed to miss her when he was at school, but avoided her, both in front of me and at home when he returned every weekend. For her part, she seemed genuinely to want to respond to him and nurture him but always pulled away from him whenever she felt at all emotional. In the course of asking how the family was constructed, I asked how Mrs. Bond's father had died (this was just over a year before). The response I received to this question was very hostile.

The parents agreed to discuss this without the children present, and the mother eventually told me, in a flat voice, how her father had shot himself the previous year. The mother then became extremely distressed and increasingly enraged with me for having made her face what she felt about this suicide. She suggested there must be a better way to help Jason other than this "family therapy stuff," but, by this time, her husband was beginning to find a place for himself in the emotional life of the family and had become more connected to Jason. He did not accept his wife's sudden attempt to change directions (by seeking a referral to an educational psychologist or a guidance counsellor). They returned a month later saying that the effects of the intervention had been devastating for the mother, but that Jason was much more settled. Jason also agreed with the school's suggestion that I should meet with the family and the school together. The "devastation" had been the breaking of a taboo on the sharing of powerful and depressing emotions between the couple, as the mother allowed herself to share with her husband, for the first time, her shock and despair about the suicide of her father.

This vignette illustrates another important point about the nature of taboo: namely, that a taboo is not present or absent, or true or untrue. It is an experiential description about a state, which can only be detected by the degree of discomfort it engenders in the participant observer. This, in turn, is a function of the interaction between the therapist and the family and between the therapist's and family's areas of discomfort and fear. What is it in the processes in the family and in the interaction between the family and the therapist that gives the therapist access to the taboo area? What are the implications of this being a co-constructed process for therapists who open themselves up to different sorts of "taboo" experiences? How does the therapist acquire the capacity to develop this awareness and to utilize it?

TABOOS IN THE THERAPIST

There are two particular areas — certainly in Britain — in which the therapist's taboos are manifested in the way he or she responds to information from the family. These are: sexual abuse — particularly including individuals who report, or begin to recall in adulthood, often brutal childhood sexual abuse — and race and ethnicity.

Incest as Taboo

Throughout the Western world during the past ten years, there has been a massive increase in awareness that very large numbers of children are victims of sexual abuse. We used to not hear about these cases and knew very little about the impact on children until recent years, but recently we have seen several adults—many of whom had first sought therapy with their families—who are beginning to describe and remember these abusive childhood experiences for the first time, with what appears to be considerable benefit. What was it that prevented us from receiving these reports in the past? There is growing evidence that many abused people sought therapy in the past; they must have harbored a hope that the therapist would help them confront these experiences. Unfortunately, this did not happen in the past, as often as it does now. Therefore, there must have been some shift in therapists' accessibility or responsiveness to hearing of such events: that is, a change in therapists' taboos.

A recent example, in which Cooklin referred one of his patients to Gorell Barnes, illustrates some of these questions. Eva, a woman in her 40's, had originally come to therapy with her family. The marriage had always been rather distant. The husband spent long periods of time away on business in the Far East. She had entered a passionate lesbian relationship, and the family was at the point of breakup. The couple separated and, with our intervention, managed to maintain a mutually supportive relationship as parents.

> Eva returned to see Cooklin because she was becoming increasingly uneasy about the way her relationship with her woman partner was developing. She felt it was becoming emotionally abusive in a way that was analogous to her relationship with her husband. She discussed her discomfort about being seen as "pretty" by her current lover, by her husband, by her parents, and by Cooklin. Two constructions of the process follow. First is Cooklin's account.

> Although reading this now, I might well think about sexual abuse, at that time it was not that content that organized me. While noticing that Eva was in fact "pretty" in a quite alluring way, I experienced a strangely disconcerting mixture of attraction and discomfort. Eventually, this became organized in my mind, and I said, rather simply, "Well, were you sexually abused as a child?" as though it were the most obvious thing to ask. Her first response was one of shock and amazement. She then burst into tears while telling me she could remember no such thing. She reported being unable to recall almost anything between the ages of six and 14, seemed genuinely puzzled by her response, and remained very distressed but curious. After a few

weeks, the patient organized an idea that perhaps her mother had sexually stimulated her (her father was now dead), as she hated the intrusive way her mother had continued to kiss her until quite recently. It took several weeks before she gradually began to recall what actually happened to her during those eight forgotten years. Her parents had been divorced, and she had both missed and felt sorry for her father. She had stayed with him quite frequently. The abuse by her father had been regular and included frequent and painful sodomy. She had actively taught herself to forget.

This again raises the question: What is the quality of the interaction between therapist (Cooklin, a male in this case) and client that allows the one to sense issues that the other has not yet articulated? In previous years, we are sure we have both missed the point in such cases, partly because it was not a familiar idea until fairly recently, but partly because of a therapist taboo on hearing the cues. Reviewing this case, we tried to determine what cues had led Cooklin to suspect that this issue pertained to this case. In his notes, Cooklin had simply written "I think she's been abused." Key factors that led to this suspicion were: (a) Eva's "loss" of memory for a large part of her childhood, (b) the distaste she described about being "seen as pretty," and (c) a quality in her responses to him as a male therapist:

- The process of interaction seemed very open, but she gave little information.
- She showed discomfort in Cooklin's presence as she tried to recall events.
- There was a mixture of "matter of factness" in her descriptions coupled with constant cues for Cooklin to validate her perceptions.

The important point here was that the relationship needed to be actively and, to some extent, mutually participant; close to what Winnicott has called the "overlap between two play areas" (Winnicott, 1971). We believe that it was this process rather than a reevocation of the therapist's taboo that eventually led Eva and therapist to mutually agree on a limit about how far they could go in exploring these events together. They eventually decided that facing the details of the abuse would be easier with a woman therapist.

Following is Eva's perspective on her work with Cooklin:

The first thing is that Dr. Cooklin gave me the message that I was acceptable, and that all things, as a human being, are okay. As I have always had difficulty believing I am part of the human race, that was pretty important to me. The next thing is something about being able to let the ideas hang out there . . . that felt better than the way I had packaged everything . . . looking inside some of those boxes was better than having everything boxed up and filed away, and all that containing I had done in order to live. The third thing is something about my father. Even though I didn't know about my father and myself there was something protective operating, so that I didn't want my father to be judged, either.

As men and women work with other men and women who have been abused, the mapping of territories will develop between clients and therapists in ways that will have gendered distinctions. Areas that were previously uncharted will be named. Language will evolve to describe processes that were previously undiscussed. In deconstructing the experience of sexual abuse, many texts will be written, and these will have importance in different domains. The discussion of sexual abuse between women, for example, moves from the private to the public domain and becomes part of a wider politicized process of women finding their own voices in relation to a wider context of gender and power. It is more difficult for women clients who are or were abuse victims to make this transition from private to public when their therapist is male.

Gorell Barnes, in reviewing this three-fold perspective on the process of "uncovering" the taboo, was intrigued by Cooklin's choice of metaphor, the "overlap of play areas." Sexually abused children often cannot safely perceive play as a desirable activity, because it is within the domain of play that abuse often takes place. The use of this metaphor, therefore, raises important questions about the boundaries of play in therapy, as well as the language we use in making constructions about the therapeutic process. As men and women develop shared constructs about abusive relationships, therapists will learn more from their clients' experiences about ways of using appropriate language. This language, as well as aspects of the attunement process may have gendered distinctions that we have not yet named, relating as they will to gender, power, coercion and intimacy at different developmental levels.

In subsequent work with Gorell Barnes, Eva described how she could not have talked further with Cooklin, because she believed he would laugh at her for her stupidity: not only for "making a fuss" about her abuse experience, but also because of her incompetent way of expressing herself. To develop a voice in which her own language was heard and valued would not have been possible without the safe and intimate context she had with him.

Race as Taboo

The second taboo—race—has been equally problematic in different ways. With both taboos, people do not believe they exist. Professionals like to believe that they are not racially prejudiced. However, we know that, in Britain, Blacks are much less likely to be appointed to senior jobs (Brown, 1984; Dept. of Employment, 1987). Blacks are more often involuntarily hospitalized for psychosis than are whites (Burke, 1986). Black offenders are less likely to be recommended for probation and are more likely to receive custodial sentences (Guest, 1984; Taylor, 1981). Poor urban centers in Britain tend to have a high percentage of Blacks (Brown, 1984; Blair, 1988; Champion, 1989; Diamond & Clarke, 1989). The professional may be unaware of the extent to which he or she participates in this institutionalised racism.

Working with the taboo of race in therapy was hampered by the fact that recognizing the existence of prejudice in Britain contradicts the predominent culture's self-image of fairness and reasonableness. Because of the power differential between therapist and client, Black and ethnic minority patients would be unlikely to question the therapist's racial stance. The failure to recognize the significance of race in the culture turned that reluctance into a taboo, which was perceived as humiliating to anyone who dared to break it. Therapeutic teams who were concerned about their failure in this respect tended to adopt one or more of three main approaches:

1. They developed an explicit antiracist policy, which was commonly advertised on notices to those attending a clinic.
2. They examined the practices and infrastructure of the clinic in terms of antiracist practice. This includes the kind of information provided by the clinic, the kind of letters written, greetings, furnishings, pictures, etc., and often requires some form of antiracist consultation for it to be effected.
3. They instituted antiracist training.

To varying degrees and at different paces these approaches were used in the Marlborough Family Service, the Tavistock Clinic, and the Institute of Family Therapy (the three settings where the two authors work).

In the Marlborough Family Service, the staff noticed that Blacks and other ethnic minorities made proportionately much less use of our service than whites, while often having as many problems for which they thought they could be potentially useful. The staff team decided to employ Black consultants to provide antiracist training for the whole group in an attempt to ensure that the service equally served all ethnic groups in the community.

In the follow-up to that training, the staff examined everything associated with the clinic (their building, literature, language) in terms of what would make them more friendly to ethnic minorities. One of the practices they began to adopt was to talk to the family about their feelings about having a white therapist when they must have experienced discriminatory relationships with other white professionals, who may have been in positions of relative power similar to the current relationship. They would further point out that the family could not, as yet, be sure that they (the therapists) would not behave similarly.

I (Cooklin) had been working with a young couple, in which the husband, Rajiv, was of Indian-Hindu background. His father had brought the family to Britain after the Tanzanian government introduced discriminatory legislation against the employment of Asians in academic jobs. He was married to a French woman, Odette, and they had a three-year-old child. They were both well-educated, and although Rajiv was unemployed when Cooklin first saw them, they could not have been described as obviously socially disadvantaged. Three months after the first meeting, Rajiv was asked to run an engineering firm, and a year later, the firm was expanding fast. Odette complained that after Rajiv had had an affair, he had become obsessed with work and never listened to her. He complained that she was depressed and depressing, as well as sexually restrictive. When Odette was pregnant with the couple's second child, these problems were exacerbated; she considered an abortion, but instead they consulted me again.

When I saw them, Rajiv told me that Odette was always complaining that his mind was never with her and that she would speak and he would not hear her. Because of our service's emphasis on race, I imagined the voices of my team asking, "Why are you not discussing the racial issue with this man?" despite the fact that this middle-class, successful man's problems seemed far removed from racism. After all, he seemed so "British." The voices continued to argue with me. Rajiv was telling me about the problems of relocating his factory, and there was something in his description that led me to wonder why he was moving from one part of the country to another. The "team" won, and I rather clumsily asked whether racism was involved in this move. He looked surprised, so I added that he had never acknowledged his racial difference, perhaps because he thought I "would be prejudiced against him in favour of Odette." He continued to look surprised but also seemed relieved by this statement. He replied that he had never talked to anybody about his race and ethnicity, *includ-*

ing Odette. When the family had migrated to England, his father had moved from an academic job to a lowly manual one, and he blamed this for his father later becoming depressed and alcoholic. He had bitterly despised his father's reaction and vowed never to allow himself to be in a situation in which he was vulnerable and could be humiliated. This explained the move, as he felt the community in which the factory was placed to be prejudiced against him because of his color, but had not been able to say this to Odette. He then linked this to the way he kept aloof from Odette.

The result of this initially uncomfortable conversation was that we broke a taboo; one that had been operating on me as well as on him. Having broken it, however, he was left, in some sense, vulnerable in relation to me, perhaps before he was ready. One practice the team had recently developed was to try to find some area of life that could be shared by therapist and family or patient and that could cut across culture and power differences. At one point, Rajiv was talking about the way he absolutely could not hear Odette when he was so obsessed by work; without really thinking, I told him that the only time that I ever had that experience was when I was working on my wind generators. I told him of the three wind-driven electric generators I had developed; I would often work with them or "play with them," which involved working up a ten-meter pole. At these times, I was "exactly like" him, and could hear nobody, but added that it was more limited and pleasurable for me than it seemed to be for him. The next time he came with Odette, he brought a design for a new wind generator with a cordless motor that he was considering developing.

Thus, through the process of my eventually challenging what had become a shared taboo subject, and through accidentally discovering an area of mutual interest, we both were freed of some unhelpful constraints. The result was that Rajiv then used the consultation to question his own "aloof" stance to both his wife and his employees, which had become a form of incongruent adaptation to his discomfort with the host culture. This, in turn, led to a more mutually respectful debate by the couple about the management of their family life. The result was that the taboo of discussing race dissolved allowing for more flexibility around other issues.

This vignette illustrates how therapists' and family members' feelings about race can lead to realistic mistrust of the therapist, which consequently interferes with his or her usefulness to the family. In this case, however, Rajiv had much in common with the therapist in terms of social class and interests. An even greater sensitivity and a greater effort to connect is called for when the family is also socioeconomically disadvantaged.

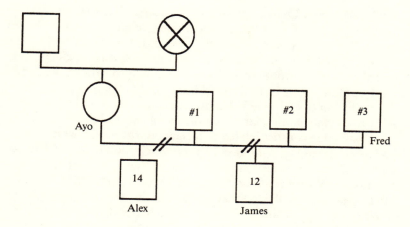

Figure 15.1: Case of Ayo

Case Example: Race and Poverty as Taboo

Ayo, was a 34-year-old Black woman whose parents had emigrated from Jamaica; she was the mother of two boys, Alex, 14, and James, 12. The boys had different fathers and both had been made wards of the court in infancy on the basis of abuse by their fathers. Ayo said her own father had, at times, beaten her severely during her child-hood. The two boys had been placed in long-term foster care with different foster parents. Ayo, however, had never accepted this and had fought hard to get her children back. She had kept in as much contact with them as the social services would allow and, several years previously, had used the Marlborough Family Service Intensive Treatment Programme as a way of being united with Alex; as a result, he was eventually returned to her care.

The situation with James had been more difficult. James' foster home was in a community and culture that was totally different from that of his original family and quite different from that in which he would live in London with his mother. Ayo, however, was determined to get him back and complied with every possible ruling made by the social service department. She had a stable boyfriend, Fred, also a second-generation immigrant from Jamaica, who had formed a good relationship with Alex.

In a family meeting in which all members of the family (including

Ayo's father and Fred) were present, I (Cooklin) sensed great reluctance to discuss any of the problems they might face when James returned home. At the same time, the obvious discomfort in the room, coupled with anxious looks among the family members, suggested that there probably was some kind of problem about James returning. James was a lively, intelligent, and outspoken young man. I sensed from their nonverbal communication that Fred was not sure if he had Ayo's permission to say what was on his mind. I asked if there was some conflict related to race about the way in which James had been brought up in foster care, which would be difficult to discuss if Fred assumed he would be on the "side" of the foster parents, who were white and hated by Ayo. Eventually, after much uneasiness, Fred explained that he was worried that James would get into trouble with the police in the area where they lived, as he was too "trustful." This area of London was one in which there had been much racial tension between the Black community and the police, with many claims of arbitrary and groundless arrests by police. If James was to survive "in our area," he would have to learn to mistrust the police and all "white" authorities and to avoid contact with them. It turned out that each member of the family had tried to say this to James in different ways, but had been so worried "that it might go against us" with the "authorities," (i.e., that Ayo would lose custody) that they had not discussed this with each other. I pointed out that they could not be certain about my trustworthiness, either, and we would need to discuss how they were going to deal with that.

After many reassurances to me that I was "okay" Ayo eventually admitted she felt she must hide from me any potential problems about James returning or she might lose her fight to get him back. She then acknowledged that she had believed that the two children had been made wards of the court without any other options being considered, and that she believed this was because of her race. Once all of this had been acknowledged, and the therapist had acknowledged the bad relationship between the police and the Black community in their neighborhood, the family was able to plan much more realistically for James' return home. They faced the housing authority with the need for new housing (which they had been afraid to do before) so that the two boys could have separate rooms and, in doing so, were able to acknowledge possible problems with Alex's adjustment to James' return as well as the need for James to have some space to effect the considerable cultural transition that the return to his mother entailed. Thus, dissolving the taboo on race allowed them the freedom to solve the problems of their impending transition.

People in such circumstances need to be appropriately suspicious and mistrustful. It is important that therapists do not interpret this as "pathology," but find a way to acknowledge the disadvantage faced by the family, encourage them to see the aspects of this disadvantage that they can realistically fight, and show respect for the successful ways they have managed despite these extra burdens.

TABOO AND THE PROCESS OF CHANGE

The last two examples illustrated incongruent adaptation to change, in which the taboo plays a part in the maintenance of a certain rigidity. Sluzki (1989) has suggested this rigidity may be a normal, appropriate, or in some situations even useful response in a process of great change, but it quickly may cease to be useful and then is incongruent to the current issues facing the members of the family.

Earlier it was suggested that the constraints represented by the taboo "play or have played a part in maintaining the order of that culture." By the time the constraints are challenged, they are often unnecessary or have lost any effective power. If one applies this thinking to a family, it would suggest that, by the time the family comes to a therapist, this "maintenance" function may well be redundant; The order that the members perceive as requiring preservation may have been permanently lost — at least in the form in which it exists in their minds. The members of a family may share some image of a social order that they are trying to preserve, but that already has been replaced by a new set of values, which they could perhaps even enjoy, if they would acknowledge and face the loss of the "old order."[2]

Redundant Taboos

An unusual example of "redundant" taboos comes from a family that I (Cooklin) visited some years ago. A number of taboos were included in the unspoken rules about what could or couldn't be discussed at the dinner table, one of which included the way men were given unfair precedence in the inheritance of money. The mother's brother inherited all the money, but the fact of the money was never discussed, although it was known to be a source of great bitterness. Instead, there was an almost slavish concern with maintaining the trappings of a social order, which had existed before the various divisions had developed. The family lived in the heart of the coun-

[2]Cooklin explored a similar concept from a more psychoanalytic perspective some years ago; then labeled The Family Group Preoccupation (Cooklin, 1979).

try. Those at home were the 70-year-old mother, a withdrawn, 40-year-old son, and a 35-year-old daughter crippled with severe rheumatoid arthritis.

It was the first time I had met the family and, after some rather formal drinks, we all sat down to lunch. What was surprising to me was the very restricted range of topics that were discussed during lunch and the looks that were passed between members if other topics were raised. I was also surprised at the way these adult children would ask their mother's permission before leaving the table, taking a further helping of food, collecting the next course, etc. Thus, a set of constraints, which may have had some relevance when the children were very young and required some check on their behavior and table manners, were carried over into adult life and had thus become a manifestation of the difficulties in facing what has already changed: in this case, two of the children had left home, an older son was still living at home, with a severely restricted mental life, and the only daughter was also at home and bitterly angry about her fate. Their dogged adherence to the old family traditions may have provided some protection from feeling helpless or humiliated by their sense of abandonment at not being provided for financially and at having dependent and incapacitated children. Thus, the taboo was redundant, in that it maintained a set of "required" relationships, which were neither relevant to nor functional for the current context.

There are many lesser examples of redundant taboos, which may have been functional for very young children, but which have ceased to have relevance as the children approach adulthood and the family faces quite different life-cycle issues. While the taboo remains, members of the family will, to varying degrees and with different levels of specificity, entertain an image of a set of potential relationships that are to be avoided. If one talks to the family about such relationships — e.g., by inviting them to "imagine" how things will be five or 10 years on, who will be "at home," and who will have left, or who will agree to stay to "look after the parents" — references to possible disasters or calamities will often ensue.

ENCOUNTERING, DISCOVERING, OR CATCHING TABOOS, AND WHAT TO DO WITH THEM

The foregoing has some implications for therapy. Therapy assumes that the function of the taboo is anachronistic and either no longer offers protection or protects something whose value is of questionable priority in comparison with other needs/requirements. Therapy, therefore, takes a position of promoting change that may be in conflict with the social order.

However, the therapist first needs to have some way of sensing what is taboo. One route, that I believe is close to the approach used by Carl

Whitaker, although only written about by Minuchin (Minuchin & Fishman, 1981), is to assume a number of universal taboos and talk about these. Another way is to be "bloody minded" and insist on talking about all the issues in the family about which you sense there is discomfort. By definition, these are invasive or "deconstructivist" techniques. They require that the therapist hold onto his or her belief system of what is important, of what may be meaningful to this family, in this context, with this presenting problem, at this time. This requires a number of qualities on the part of the therapist:

1. a level of tenacity in listening
2. sensitivity to the "sore" areas in the family and following these through with questions
3. a capacity to engage in conversations that are potentially conflictual and sometimes to take a partisan position in these

This defines a particular kind of therapist. This therapist is not only seeking to validate and relate to the "conversations" offered by the family, but is prepared to "inject" a different version of reality if she or he believes the latter reality is more adaptable to change. This resembles the practice of reframing as defined by Watzlawick et al. (1974) and is very similar to the way Minuchin (1974; Minuchin & Fishman, 1981) defines "different realities" with a family. However, it is important to recognize that this represents a different image of the therapist from that commonly expected by those taking a "co-constructivist" stance. In practice, the definition of realities is no less mutually constructed by the family and therapist together, but in this situation, the therapist makes no pretense of only "following." Our reason for taking this position is based on the belief that the therapist has to take a leadership role in finding "safe routes" for the family to begin a discourse on subjects that have been taboo. Without this guidance, family members may not be able to judge that these are "safe routes" until they are actually following them. When encountering taboo areas we may display a level of tenaciousness more fitting to a dog "worrying" a bone. This is because we believe that the taboo area of thinking has an intensely pervasive impact on all the interactions of family life. To counterbalance this requires an equivalent intensity of interaction on the part of the therapist. What follows are a number of areas of family life in which we frequently encounter taboos:

- sex in all or various forms and with different degrees of explicitness
- violence, violent death, and suicide
- money and property
- religion

- "shameful" events, such as criminal acts or imprisonment
- race and ethnicity

The existence of societal taboos can lead to a common misconception that if they are broken then one will be free. This is both a nonsequitur and a "logical typing error" (in that "freedom" and "constraints" are members of different classes of experience). Consider the compound taboos on sex and religion in this next example.

Case Example: Taboos on Sex and Religion

Angela, aged 38, and her husband, Bob, aged 46, had three children. The family was Roman Catholic and was active in practicing their religion. Bob was a highly successful executive in a multinational firm. He would often return home from work tired and preoccupied with the worries and excitement of the workday. The couple had met when Angela was 18 and had married when she was 20. Soon after, she had qualified as a school teacher.

The couple's sexual relationship had been good, and they had enormously enjoyed freedom from what they had previously perceived as constraints of family life and religious morality. Thus, as Angela began to feel that Bob was being drawn away from her by work, she made great efforts to intensity their sexual relationship. She would dress up in sexy clothes to await his homecoming, and they would then frequently engage in highly erotic and active lovemaking. The role of the "sexpot" that Angela adopted had been an attempt to counter Bob's investment in his work. However, what began as an attempt to maintain their freedom as a couple, soon began to feel like a prison from Angela's point of view, but she continued to play the role.

About 12 years into the marriage, Angela began to drink heavily and, after several crises in which the children found her drunk, she joined Alcoholics Anonymous. Her husband saw this joining of another organization as a betrayal, and, in essence, this developed into a more potent pull away from his work than their sexual life had been. There was an increase in the distance between the couple, and Angela experienced increased loneliness. She became involved emotionally, and later sexually, with a parish priest. The priest fulfilled her image of the man who would "free her" from the constraints of her restrictive upbringing as Bob had begun to represent just those constraints.

In a curious way, sexuality had become a taboo for this couple. They enacted a set of erotic routines, but these were never discussed between them and the different meaning for each partner was, therefore, never explored or shared. The sexual relationship with the priest broke some obvious religious taboos, but it was as though this taboo were easier to break than the barrier against discussion of the couple's own sexual relationship. However, by breaking the church's taboo, Angela did not achieve any greater sense of emotional freedom and, in fact, at the outset of therapy she was feeling more trapped than ever.

During the first part of the couple's therapy, Bob began to face the degree to which he had abandoned Angela and made overtures to find out how he could rediscover her. Angela oscillated between Bob and the priest, until the priest was finally removed from the parish, after which she became depressed. Bob took this as a confirmation that she had no further interest in him and decided to leave her. At this point, the couple came to see me (Cooklin) for a crisis session to discuss the arrangements for separation. Angela insisted that she would once again like to develop a sexual relationship with Bob, but was terrified of the constraints it would involve. I began to describe a ritual, insisting that it was nonerotic, but did not let the couple know exactly what it would involve. Angela was terrified, and Bob was fascinated, and I found myself with a "secret weapon."

I decided not to tell the couple what the task was, but to let them know that there was such a task, that it was nonsexual, very difficult, and highly physical and intimate, but that I did not believe they were "ready for it." Thus, I turned the task into a symbol, but one that was not yet disclosed and, therefore, almost analogous to a taboo. This not only put the couple on the same level in relation to me, by removing the idea that the task was something which would be "done" to Angela, but also unwittingly placed myself in a role similar to that of a priest (having an available ritual for which the couple was "not yet ready"). The unexpected result was that the couple eventually came together to dissociate themselves from the power they had previously allocated first to the priest, and then to the therapist. When they returned home they had a great row about the task, and eventually shared their fantasies (which were quite disparate) about what the task would be. Three weeks later they returned having reestablished a sexual relationship, one in which Angela no longer felt that she was used (either at her own or Bob's volition). When they heard what the task would have been, they were both amused, and left saying that they "just might do it anyway."

I could have challenged the taboo that sex with priests is not allowed. However, it was the *couple's* sexual relationship that was the significant taboo. What the therapy, and in particular the crisis session, appeared to do was to provide a different framework for the couple's relationship. This was a framework within which they could begin to negotiate issues of freedom. It also created a crisis that virtually compelled them to break the taboos about their sexual relationship and allowed them to discuss their experiences of it.

MAKING THE TABOO EXPLICIT AND CHANGING ITS FUNCTION

There are, of course, no clinical rules for this any more than there are for any other therapeutic goal. We have found, however, that we commonly use a number of approaches, some borrowed and some our own. Following are some techniques we have used:

1. Talk about universals, which can include all the issues on the previous list of common taboo subjects. We owe this technique to the fascinating work of Carl Whitaker. He has a way of talking to the family, in what at first appears to be an indiscriminate manner, about all that is commonly most taboo: sex, incest, murder, suicide, etc.. He speaks in a bland and charming way so that the participants don't immediately tune out the "shocking" words at first.

2. Be explicit with detail. For example, with a discussion about money: If one person owes another money, then insist that they specify whether this includes interest, at what rate, whether simple or compound, whether the debt is corrected for inflation, what are the possible tax consequences, etc. Thus, whenever people are talking in a general way about a "manifestation" of some unthinkable or unworkable aspect of a belief system, which is in charge of them in ways they do not like, help them to be specific and to look at the *details* of its operation in their everyday lives.

3. Track and search areas of discomfort. This requires the therapist to "hear" allusions and innuendos and to make logical leaps. It also requires that the therapist be willing to interrupt the standard family pattern and "inject" questions, comments, or jokes that "break the rules." This also usually requires one to be "bloody mindedly" persistent.

Steven was 19 when seen for a consultation on behalf of a physician who was considering him for hospitalization. He lived with his mother and two older sisters. His father had left his mother when Steven was 6, and Steven had not seen him since. It was believed that the father had since been remarried twice, and the family's views of men in general was not positive.

His maternal grandfather had died from cancer, his mother's new partner was ill with cancer, his attractive older sister had always had disastrous relationships with men, and the other sister had isolated herself from all emotional relationships. This sister had begun to stoop to try to hide her breasts as they developed at age 16. She had eventually given up this habit, although her posture remained awkward. At age 15, Steven also began to stoop, to such a degree that he stood less than two-thirds of his normal height. During the four years before I saw him, many treatments had been attempted, including 16 months in an adolescent psychiatric unit, manipulation under anesthesia, treatment with a plaster cast (which had to be removed as a result of pressure sores), and family therapy for himself and his mother and sisters. His stoop had continued to worsen, to the point where he required a Zimmer frame to walk into the first consultation, and he had developed a strange, high-pitched voice.

The physician and I agreed that we would insist on a number of family sessions aimed at testing the flexibility of adaptation of both Steven and the family and finding an agreed framework for change, before we would hospitalize Steven to "straighten him out." We faced the dilemma that "everything" had been tried, and the focus remained on Steven's back. Something else of at least equal affective consequence was required if we were to achieve any lasting change. The only other such topic was the father, who was alluded to rather than directly spoken about, and whose definition as "evil" was well-established. I took the risk and insisted that our attempts to help would be useless unless the father participated. The older sister, Sheila, who knew the address of her paternal grandmother, agreed to try to contact him. He did not arrive at the agreed hour, but since we now had the telephone number of his office, Steven agreed to telephone the father himself.

STEVEN: I think I know what to say now.

SR: (the other therapist) I will get the table (all of us found ourselves unwittingly responding to Steven as though he could not walk). (Steven dialing number.)

THERAPIST: (Alan Cooklin) While Steven is doing that, can you remind me how old he was when your husband left?

MOTHER: He was 6 in August, and he left in December, he was 6½. (Telephone now answers.)

S: Hello, please may I speak to Mr. Brian Marks. I am . . . this is

Steven Marks—Hello is Mr. Brian Marks . . . I am . . . could
you please . . . could you please tell him he was expected for a
meeting this morning, and could you please tell him that . . . er
. . . if I could possibly speak to him, please. Hello, is Mr. Brian
Marks there? Oh, hello, I am Steven, this is a very difficult
phone call to make because . . . I am . . . what I wanted to tell
you about was to ask . . . the doctor has asked me because it
was quite important, um, because there was a meeting here at
half past nine and unfortunately you have not arrived, and the
doctor wanted me to ask you if you could possibly attend another meeting, so if you cannot attend another meeting—he
said it was very important that all the family is involved with
the meeting as there is a chance that the situation could be put
right or much better . . . (There is a long pause as the others in
the room realize the confusion: The father has not realized to
whom he is talking.) . . . This is Steven, I am Steven Marks,
yes, yes. Hello, I am all right thank you . . . oh yes, oh yes, and
please could I just speak to the doctor as he is here.
(Turns to me.)
He said that he would look forward to seeing me anytime,
which would be convenient?

Following the phone call, the father did attend sessions. With his
help, it was possible to shift the focus to the question of Steven's
identity as a man and away from his back. The taboo regarding the
role of men in the family was broken, and an absent father was
reinvolved in his son's life.

4. Talk silly/serious to children in a way "grown-ups won't understand"
about taboo areas, but in a way that respects the different levels of development in the family.

Shona was 10. Her mother had committed suicide three years
before. Her father had remarried, and the stepmother was warm and
very concerned about Shona, but complained with frustration that
she could not "reach her." The problem presented was that Shona was
failing at school and complaining of many and recurrent pains, particularly pains in the vagina. Shona had perceived her mother as a
very powerful and, at times, dominating person, while her father was
seen as somewhat passive and distant until after the mother's death.
Apart from the pains, the father's and stepmother's main complaint
was that Shona would never "talk about it" (the death).

THERAPIST: But what happened? Who told you about it? (the suicide)

SHONA: My daddy.

TH: What did he say?

S: That she's committed suicide.

TH: Did you know what that meant?

S: Yes.

TH: Did you ask him any questions about it?

S: No.

TH: So you don't know really what happened, do you?

S: I don't like talking about it.

TH: Well . . . no . . . I can understand that, who would? (Shona begins to cry) Well I don't mind if you cry a bit, because I cry, and I'm used to people crying, but I'd still like to know about it because it would help me to understand the family, you see, because I take it your mummy's still here with us in some way, in people's minds.

S: I don't know. She took aspirins, I think.

TH: She took aspirins. Did she have pain or was it just the kind of pain everybody has when they get upset?

S: I don't know.

TH: How old were you?

S: Six, I think, six.

TH: Do you remember worrying about her before she died?

S: No.

TH: Because kids always do worry about their mummys, you know. I mean she (the father's and stepmother's new baby) worries about this mummy, you can see the way she always makes sure that she gives her mummy plenty to do. So, who let her do it?

S: I don't know, I was not at home, I think.

TH: Who was at home?

S: Nobody, I think. So she just killed herself, and I was left at school.

TH: Nobody collected you from school?

S: Yes. She didn't come and. . . .

TH: You must have been furious.

S: Yes, I was.

TH: So she, not only did she kill herself, but she left you at school?

S: Yes.

TH: Is that the first time she's dumped you in school? (So the idea of her being angry with the dead mother is tolerable and not taboo.)

S: Yes.

TH: And how have you got your daddy to make sense of what she
     did? Because it's crazy to kill yourself, isn't it, because you can't
     even talk about it afterwards.

S: Daddy didn't tell me she killed herself, he would only tell me she
     died. I just found out that she killed herself.

TH: Can you remember how it was that you got him to tell you the
     truth?

S: No, I don't know. I just knew that my father and Olga (her
     stepmother) said she killed herself, and I hate talking about it.

TH: Did you go to the funeral?

S: NO.

TH: Do you know what happened to her? Where she is now?

S: Yes.

TH: Where?

S: Well, I know where they put her after she died.

TH: Where?

S: In the cemetery.

TH: In the cemetery? Did you see her after she was dead?

S: No.

TH: What was her name?

S: Katherine. . . .

TH: But you couldn't punish mummy for killing herself, could you,
     because she wasn't there?

S : No.

TH: Who have you been able to punish?

S: Nobody.

TH: Really? Haven't you tried punishing daddy?

S: No.

TH: Maybe he's a bit difficult to punish?

S: No, 'cause I don't think he did it.

TH: Who do you think did it then?

S: Don't know. Maybe she didn't like herself. (crying freely while
     she talks now)

TH: Do you think that's crazy?

S: Yes.

TH: Somebody must have helped her to not like herself, mustn't
     they?

S: Maybe.

TH: Where were her mummy and daddy?

S: in . . .

TH: In Israel?

s: Yes.

TH: Did she have brothers and sisters?

s: Yes. Two sisters and one brother.

TH: Did they ever talk with you about what happened?

s: My aunt Sophie did, she's . . . like you.

TH: You mean crazy?

s: (She laughs while still crying) No! She was—I don't know what to call it—psychologist, I think. And I talked to her, but I told her "I don't want to talk about it." So, we don't talk about it anymore.

TH: Oh, she is crazy. She gave in. . . . So that's a problem you have. Do you mean that whenever you don't want to do something which is upsetting, nobody pushes you to do it?

s: Sometimes, yes.

TH: What kinds of things?

s: Well, I play the piano, and I don't want to go.

TH: Do you cry like this when you have to play the piano?

s: No, no.

TH: So, wouldn't it be good if you could cry about playing the piano and talk about mummy?

s: I play the piano, but I say I don't want to play anymore, and my mummy (meaning her stepmother) cause she also plays the piano, and the first time she didn't like to go out, so she understands that I don't want to go on right away with the piano.

TH: Oh, that's bad.

s: So she let me stop, and my teachers, they say "No!" so I go on.

TH: Would it be better if your mummy said you'd had to go on and the teacher said you could stop?

s: Yes, yes. (laughing)

TH: Yes, it would be much better that way.

s: Yes.

TH: I tell you how it happened in my family. My little girl, she's much bigger than you, she's 17 now, and she plays the oboe and the recorder, but she used to forget to practice, and she had an oboe teacher, who was just like your teacher, they had a tremendous row, they nearly had a fight, you know. She and the recorder teacher were about to know each other . . . and her solution to that, maybe you should try this with your piano teacher . . . her solution was that she started teaching other kids.

s: Who? (looking very interested but bemused)

TH: My little girl, then she enjoyed it.

s: Oh . . . (thoughtfully)
TH: Have you ever thought if you could teach the piano?
s: Yeah. (laughs again)
TH: If you could teach, if you could teach Olga the piano, or is she good at it?
s: She is a lot better than me.
TH: What about daddy, is he any good at the piano?
s: No.
TH: Would you like to teach daddy the piano?
s: It sounds funny . . . (giggles)
TH: Maybe you could teach your daddy and that would really, really punish him.
s: Yes. (laughing)
TH: That would be a good punishment, you could really . . .
s: Yeah. . . .

You will see that I sensed there was a taboo against the idea of Shona blaming anybody other than her mother for the death. What I used was a mixture of "bloody mindedness" and humor, as well as a search for a safe metaphor in which some blame or "punishment" of the father could become part of the family's currency.

5. Use metaphors and tell stories that relate to the taboo, but that include different frames for thinking about its meaning, and, therefore, how it might be used in different, more flexible ways. This both allows the idea of the taboo having value, but also allows this value to be reconsidered. The Jungian idea of befriending the shadow side of the self plays a part in this way of thinking about owning, and therefore taking charge of dissociated aspects of family patterns and former or current views about these patterns. An example of such a metaphor was the use of "punishment" in the case of Shona above, and the slightly exaggerated story of my daughter's row with her teacher introduced an idea of passionately violent feelings between child and adult, but in a frame that allowed the possibility of reconciliation.

6. Bring in other generations (usually the prior generation) either to challenge maintenance of the "executive" authority in the family or "to get their permission for these things to be talked about."

Joanna, her husband, James, and baby, Jemima, had been referred to us during Jemima's first year. When Jemima was five months old, Joanna's grandmother, who had been the "good grandmother" in her family, died. She had acted as a support when Joanna's mother had been severely incapacitated, after suffering brain

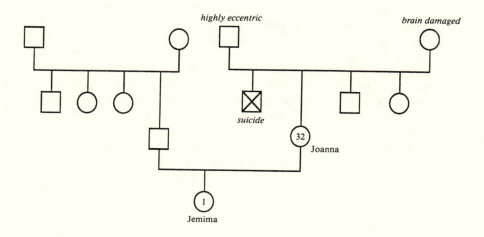

Figure 15.2: Case of Joanna

damage in a car accident. This had left Joanna as the eldest responsible female in her family of origin. The grandmother's death recreated
for Joanna a pattern in which she felt left alone to take care of others
and also posed a new challenge about how she was to do this. Was
she to do it in the style of her family of origin, which had made many
unusual adaptations to give the handicapped mother the "illusion"
that she was still in charge, or was she to adapt to a carefully cultivat-
ed norm of health and well-being that her husband's family consciously paraded? She became acutely depressed, started drinking
heavily, and was hospitalized three times, each time discharging herself and refusing to take medication.

Joanna and her husband both came to see us with the baby, Jemima, throughout most of the first two years of Jemima's life. Joanna
retained a hostile view of the whole process of these "conversations,"
which often consisted of long monologues about her precarious attempts to maintain a daily structure by driving around London with
her dog and her baby and dropping in unexpectedly on friends, who
were becoming less sympathetic as time went by. She described her
home as a "trap," talked obsessively of "being inside a concrete box"
and of "a tiny dirty window" through which she would peer at a
hostile world from which she felt excluded. She would often respond
to any attempt at contact by the therapists or by her husband by
repeating ad nauseam, "I only see four walls." Nonetheless, Jemima

continued to thrive, Joanna's housekeeping was adequate, and she remained out of the hospital. Joanna clearly enjoyed aspects of the therapeutic conversation, in which much teasing and humor would go on, as the therapist introduced a number of other frames through which her dilemmas might be considered. However, her continued obsessive preoccupation with "the four walls" suggested to us that the choices she saw herself as having needed to be contextualized in a wider family arena for her to believe that her position could ever change.

We called together both sets of Jemima's grandparents and all the living siblings. One of Joanna's brothers had hanged himself the previous year; the reasons for his suicide remained obscure. However, it was clear that, in Joanna's mind, his death was associated with remaining in their home, a farm in a remote part of England. Joanna herself used to visit this farm nearly every weekend. She expressed a longing to be free of the compulsion to visit. The rationale we gave to the family for this "clan" gathering was that we would explore together the ways in which people carry the traditions and influences of their families of origin into marriage, and the way in which these influences may form part of the difficulties any couple might have. As the whole family was very concerned about the well-being of the joint grandchild, Jemima, as well as that of the couple, all four grandparents and the adult siblings on both sides of the family attended.

The definition of the couple as part of the wider family system was well-received by Joanna's father, who had been described to us previously as highly eccentric. Throughout the meeting he remained highly self-referential and continued an uninterrupted stream of talk, which seemed at first unrelated to the concurrent family discussion. However, he also interjected messages that suggested he had a better understanding of his daughter's dilemma than anyone else. Observing that he and his wife also had problems and that, while the focus today might be on the young couple, it might more appropriately center on the senior generation tomorrow. He commented on how "Joanna has had to evolve by herself over the last 25 years since her mother's accident." He described how he saw himself and his wife as actors, playing the part of normality. He constructed it for the two of them, with himself acting as his wife's memory (the young adults confirmed that her memory was lost). He contrasted the positive qualities of the grandmother Joanna had lost (his own mother) with the more eccentric and clinically disturbed qualities of his wife's family: "Everyone used to go to psychiatrists in Jane's family." He portrayed a world in which all "parental" figures were perceived as being psychiatrically disturbed and in need of treatment. This presented a marked contrast to James' parents. They busied themselves with trying to pin down the many ways in which Joanna's "mad" behavior was an annoyance to the rest of the family and the ways in which this might be changed; they also made many practical suggestions about what would constitute good child care for Jemima.

During the course of the conversation, Joanna revealed that she thought she would never make the transition from being a Brown, her family of origin, to being a Drewitt (the family name of her husband). This became a metaphor for the two different worlds of experience she was contending with, the world of her brain-damaged mother and illogical, eccentric father—a domain within which her elder brother had recently killed himself—and a world of healthy child development, which she saw herself as having lost because of the absence of an active participant "mother" in her own childhood. This world was now represented by the Drewitt family, as her husband's sisters had many healthy, bright children, and Joanna did not always feel that her own child was welcome there. She viewed joining the "normal" world as an active betrayal of the world of her childhood and of her family of origin. To be "normal" was taboo.

Confronted by the power of Joanna's father's rambling and random stream of interruptions, her husband challenged her more directly with the dilemma: "Your father's world is more real to you than my world." She denied it, but went on to show how compelling the reality of the world of her family of origin was for her: "Every weekend when I visit, I feel I am going back into a Brown world. I have this hammering in my head to become a Brown again." Her husband engaged her in an intense conversation about his family's readiness to have her "enter" their family, although he was unaware of all the issues of perceived disloyalty outlined above. In the middle of this, her father began to talk to her in a compelling, low-key voice. Gradually, her head turned as her attention was drawn back to her father, who was saying without any logical sequence, "I don't worship any family . . . Jo and James have got to find their own way somehow . . . they got married in the Western Isles . . . where do you want to be on Friday, Saturday, and Sunday?" At the point where she turned her head, both therapists, her husband, and her father engaged in a lively and direct critique of the very brief and highly packed sequence that had just taken place. The taboo against discussing the interconnection of Joanna's behavior with that of her father, the Brown world, and the pain of transition from her father's domain of logic (in which as the keeper of his wife's memory he held the power for two parents) to that of a more everyday reality, was vigorously debated. Her father, accepting both his power and the necessity of its overthrow, cheerfully said, "I'm older you see . . . some weeks I accomplish nothing, other weeks I write to Washington, I write to Moscow." His inability to achieve much in the "everyday" world and Joanna's competence in surviving in it were highlighted.

Many constructions could be made from this densely packed text, but those that overtly showed themselves as freeing Joanna began with the open highlighting of the power of her father's voice in a context where other voices, her husband's and her own could be heard in a new way by the whole family. This allowed the beginning of new constructions of how she herself could be a parent. These could develop because her husband, far from "holding" her memory during her "mad" episodes, as her father had done for her mother, had always held out for her memories having their own validity, although their meaning was not yet revealed. Joanna and James needed much further support as their family grew in size, but the intervals between our meetings became longer and longer as they gained in confidence.

7. Use a co-therapy relationship to discuss, in front of the family, things that they may think it unwise to discuss. This technique, which we originally learned many years ago from observing Papp and Silverstein's rigorous way of working as a team in front of the family (Papp & Silverstein, 1984), has developed between us in a number of idiosyncratic ways. We always try to move away from one fixed meaning that a family is currently ascribing to part of its own process, and to develop other meanings, which offer different possibilities of viewing, construing, or changing patterns of behavior. As we have worked together for many years, these conversations may be minimal and tangential. They develop in relation to the use the family makes of them. The tendency in Western thought to pose values in terms of interrelated opposites is found in families, as well as in other systems, but our tendency, as co-therapists of different genders, is to deconstruct such attempts to create "order" and to introduce a number of ways that meaning can be assigned to the interactions, words, and silences in the room.

Sarah was originally referred to us because she had become very underweight, her menstrual periods had stopped, and she had given up a promising career as a musician and returned home to live with her parents. Both parents seemed to derive much comfort from Sarah's presence at home, and she continued to lose weight. Following several meetings with Sarah and her parents, we decided that a wider context was needed for this living arrangement to be discussed, one that included Sarah's three siblings.

The meeting of Sarah's four adult siblings took some weeks to arrange and involved complex international travel. As a group, the young adults showed complex patterns of emotional connection built up around illness. The eldest daughter in the family had a rare progressive disease, which had led to her being accorded a "special" status in the eyes of her brothers and sisters. Not only was this seen to have led to her receiving more love than the other children, but the illness itself was seen to have a stabilizing effect on the parents' violent and emotional relationship. As each of the children had reached their late teens, they had developed symptoms of anorexia and had spent time being of concern to their parents. The power of this arrangement as a shared but unacknowledged secret in the younger generation had not become apparent to us, or to them, until we called this meeting.

Throughout the family meeting, the way in which the development of all four children had been shadowed by the developing handicap of the eldest daughter, and the competitiveness this had aroused, was increasingly revealed. After their sister had left home, it appeared that each, in turn, had done their best to fill the place she had vacated in their parents' hearts and lives. Each, in turn, had "given up" this position as the next child reached his or her late teens. Sarah, as the youngest, who currently held this position, believed that, if she left home, the "family as it was" would fragment.

Sarah, throughout the meeting, had continuously addressed the family in the third person, as "they," demanding that she be allowed to harangue them without interruption. Her siblings challenged the necessity of her sacrifice for the well-being of the "guts of the family." At the same time, they were empathic, having experienced a similar illusion. Sarah was unable to listen to these differing voices and continued to attack the whole family, particularly her eldest sister, for "ruining her life" by not taking enough responsibility for their parents. The taboo area, the power of the handicap, had been discussed, but the pattern of competing for parental love and non-communication, which maintained the power, remained. The mother continued to be used as the channel of communication between the siblings, so that little direct discussion took place.

At one key point, when Sarah was "filibustering," Gorell Barnes challenged her right to control others in this way; she persistently interrupted Sarah until she began to address her eldest sister directly.

Her thinking immediately became less dualistic as she engaged in a dialogue: "You are only showing me now, Katie, how it is that I let you have power over me. Either you must remove yourself from my life and I will remove myself from yours, or we must start again and try and have a few good talks as grown-up sisters." Katie responded positively to this direct appeal for change.

As the sisters then began to sort things out between themselves, the mother, who was normally the family switchboard, became highly agitated and tried to interrupt by making a long speech about how she would "like to see change taking place." She was kindly but firmly shut up by different family members, who pointed out to her that change was at that moment taking place and that the effect of her intervention was to stop it. One of the other siblings commented about how hard it was for a new interaction to develop in the family without somebody else trying to put it down. The following commentary then began between the two therapists.

"Do you think that these two young women of 27 and 22 need their parents' permission to talk to each other direct?"

"Yes, I do."

"Who do you think they might have feared would be hurt most if they talked to each other direct?"

"Perhaps it's the idea of the family as it was that they don't want to lose."

"To talk to each other in the presence of their parents and the rest of the family seems very important."

The father joined in the "discussion about the discussion," "I think it's the most important thing that's happened in the family for a long time."

GORELL BARNES: Well, they needed your blessing to have the conversation direct.

FATHER: I think it needed the two of you to be here.

COOKLIN: (reflective) I have always thought I should be a vicar.

FATHER: (referring obliquely to the fact that it was Good Friday) You've got the most difficult thing of all to handle today.

This curious mixture of indirect allusion to sacrifice and blessing, within the powerful mesh of the loving patterns of the family, created a shift, which allowed Sarah to develop new perceptions of the role she was playing in the family. Following the beginning of this new conversation, the family went away and talked for three hours, later returning for a further session with fresh ideas about their relationships. As adult siblings and adult children to two parents who had stayed together for over 30 years, they were prepared to offer Sarah a range of different perspectives on what growing up in this family might mean to the youngest child.

Gossiping or reflecting in front of the family has been used as a technique by many family therapists of widely differing "schools" of therapy. It holds the family in an observer and "reflecting" position, while allowing comments to be made that address the taboo area at different levels. Members of the family, in turn, can move to these other levels through the channels created by the breaking up of former rigid constructions.

CONCLUSION

In this chapter, we have outlined a way of conceptualizing entrenched and rigidified patterns in the family. We have suggested that when these patterns are incongruently adaptive, they may need to be released by discussing taboo areas of family life to which they relate. We have not offered any prepackaged tools for achieving this, although we have suggested some different ways in which taboos may be addressed and detoxified. These ideas have a number of implications for training and the development of the therapist's self-knowledge about their own forbidden areas. How can the therapist introduce discrepant information if she or he does not know to what it is discrepant? How can the therapist be trained to sense and use discomfort rather than just respond to it? If the therapist is to be free to take whatever is useful out of his or her repertoire of life experience, then he or she has to be ready for examining such material, and feel comfortable enough with the result; that is, with what the family, in turn, makes of this mutual experience. This requires an ability to be comfortable with "unknowing" and a capacity for therapeutic containment in the therapist that makes the risk area safe enough to explore within the session. It also involves commitment to the venture, continuity of the family-therapist conversation, and a grasp of when the family is ready to "go it alone."

ACKNOWLEDGMENTS

Thank you from Gill Gorell Barnes to Virginia Goldner for conversations at the Womens' Colloquium, Denmark, 1991, and to Elsa Jones for many conversations.

Thank you from Alan Cooklin and Gill Gorell Barnes to the staff and teams we have shared and developed ideas with in our separate and shared institutions: The Marlborough Family Service, The Tavistock Clinic, and The Institute of Family Therapy, London.

REFERENCES

Bateson, G. (1972). *Steps to an ecology of mind*. New York: Ballantine.

Bentovim, A., & Kinston, W. (1990). Focal family therapy: Joining systems with psychodynamic understanding. In A. S. Gurman & D. P. Kniskern (Eds.), *Handbook of family therapy*. New York: Basic.

Blair, T. C. (1988). Building an urban future: Race and planning in London. *Cities, 5*:1, pp. 41–56.

Brown, C. (1984). *Black and white Britain — The third PSI survey*. London: Heineman Books.

Burke, A. (1986). Social work and intervention in West Indian psychiatric disorder. In V. Coombe & A. Little (Eds.), *Race and social work*. London: Tavistock.

Champion, T. (1989). Internal migration and spatial population distribution. In H. Joshi (Ed.), *The changing population of Britain*. Oxford: Blackwell.

Cooklin, A. (1979). A psychoanalytic framework for a systemic approach to family therapy. *Journal Family Therapy, 1*, 153–165.

Department of Employment (1987). Ethnic origin and economic status. *Employment Gazette*, 18–26.

Diamond, I., & Clarke, S. (1989). Demographic patterns among Britain's ethnic groups. In H. Joshi (Ed.), *The changing population of Britain*. Oxford: Blackwell.

Douglas, M. (1984). *Purity and danger: An analysis of the concepts of pollution and taboo*. London: Ark Paperbacks.

Ezriel, H. (1950). A psychoanalytic approach to group treatment. *British Journal of Modern Psychiatry, 11*, 59–74.

Fortes, M. (1966). Totem and taboo. London: Proceedings of the Royal Anthropological Institute, 5–22.

Fox, R. (1983). *The red lamp of incest: An enquiry into the origins of mind and society*. Indiana: University of Notre Dame Press.

Gorell, Barnes, G. (1983a, June). Time and intergenerational pattern. Presentation at joint Ackerman Institute, New York, and Institute of Family Therapy, London, conference, New York.

Gorell, Barnes, G. (1983b). A difference that makes a difference. *Journal of Family Therapy, 5*, 37–52.

Guest, C. L. (1984). A comparative analysis of the career patterns of Black and White young offenders. Unpublished dissertation.

Leach, E. (1982). *Social anthropology*. Glasgow, Scotland: Fontana.

Maturana, H. R., & Varela, F. J. (1987). *The tree of knowledge: The biological roots of understanding*. Boston: New Science Library.

Milner, P. M. (1966). The role of the brain in motivation. In B. M. Foss (Ed.), *New horizons in psychology*. Harmondsworth: Penguin.

Minuchin, S. (1974). *Families and family therapy*. London: Tavistock.

Minuchin, S., & Fishman, H. C. (1981). *Family therapy techniques*. Cambridge, MA: Harvard University Press.

Pincus, L., & Dare, C. (1978). *Secrets in the family*. New York: Pantheon.

Papp, P., & Silverstein, O. (1984, June). The debate in front of the family. Presentation at Institute of Family Therapy conference, London.

Ramseyer, U. (1977). *The art and culture of Bali*. Oxford, England: University Press of Oxford.

Sluzki, C. E. (1989). Network disruption and network reconstruction in the process of migration/relocation. *The Bulletin — A Journal of the Berkshire Medical Center, 2*(3): 2–5.

Taylor, W. (1981). *Probation and aftercare of a multi-racial society*. London: London Commission for Racial Equality.

Watzlawick, P., Weakland, J., & Fisch, R. (1974). *Change*. New York: W. W. Norton.

Winnicott, D. W. (1971). *Playing and reality*. London: Tavistock.

VI

FAMILIES, SECRETS, AND THE WIDER SOCIAL CONTEXT

16

Racism, Secret-Keeping, and African-American Families

NANCY BOYD-FRANKLIN

EVERY CULTURE AND each individual family has its own secrets. However, the history of slavery and the subsequent realities of racism, oppression, and discrimination have created a special meaning to the secrets of African-American families in this country. This chapter will explore the complex issues and many levels of secrets within African-American families from both the historical and the current cultural context. It will also explore the implications of these secrets for therapists who are treating these families.

CAUTION AGAINST STEREOTYPING

Before the historical context is explored, it is very important to clarify that there is no entity which can be identified as "*the* Black family" or "*the* African-American family" (Boyd-Franklin, 1989). Black families come from many parts of the world and share a common history of their African heritage. However, the cultures of Black people in Africa, the West Indies or the Caribbean, and South America are quite different from African-American families whose ancestors were brought here from Africa as slaves. Even within African-American families, there are differences among families living in the rural South, the urban South, the Northeast, the Midwest, or the West. There are many similarities and also subtle differences. This paper will focus primarily on African-American families and the unique ways in which secrets manifest within these families.

AFRICAN HERITAGE

African societies were primarily tribal societies. They were closely-knit extended families in which there was often some level of kinship between all members. Nobles (1974) and Mbiti (1969) have stressed the collective identity of an Afrocentric as opposed to a Eurocentric or individual focus. This collective identity meant that the good of the tribe was always considered above that of the individual. This was a more open society, in which people knew about each other's lives and business, and relationships were based on trust. Within this context, "secrets" related more to the ancient stories, which were entrusted to a few of the elders and were passed on, through the oral tradition, to future generations. "Secrets" were special knowledge related to rituals, healing, protection, and life events, such as birth, puberty rites of passage, illness, and death. With the impact of slavery, however, African people were torn from their homeland and brought to a very different and oppressive world.

THE IMPACT OF SLAVERY

Slavery disrupted traditional African tribal life. Families were torn apart (Giddings, 1984; Pinkney, 1975; Rose, 1982). Members of the same tribe were separated and put with members of other tribes, which prevented communication. Many of the secrets within African-American families, as well as those which are kept from "outsiders," have their roots in the oppression of slavery. Slave masters attempted to control all aspects of the slaves' lives. It is a tribute to the survival skills and strength of these men and women that they were able to persevere. The ability to keep secrets became linked to these survival skills.

During slavery, African-American children learned at a very young age that words were dangerous and that anyone who disobeyed the orders of the master or his overseer could be killed or punished severely. Escape and freedom became a driving force for many African-Americans. Messages were given "in secret" through spirituals such as "Wade in the Water," for instance, which signaled a meeting down at the river to escape. Themes such as "Let my people go" were common. The innate spirituality, which had been such an integral part of African tribal life, was incorporated into the lives of African slaves and into their freedom plans. Many spiritual messages of "freedom in the next life" or through death had a double meaning and gave a secret message of imminent escape from slavery.

Many slaves secretly practiced African rituals and spoke the language of their ancestors. Children were given "slave" names by their masters and

African names by their parents. Because tribal languages were forbidden, these were only spoken in secret.

Many authors have documented the ways in which the "dehumanizing process of slavery attempted to deprive African people of their families ties, customs, language, food and spiritual rituals" (Boyd-Franklin, 1989; Kinney, 1971). Many spiritual rituals survived in secret. Often within the slave communities, there were healers or root doctors who used special herbs to treat illnesses. These were often kept secret. Medical doctors and therapists who practice in African-American communities today often find a "secret" level of medicine and health care within these communities.

Some of the practices of slavery were designed to destroy families and to keep slaves from developing relationships and kinship ties. Boyd-Franklin (1989) states that "traditional tribal marriages were not allowed; but nor were slaves allowed to marry according to European practices. Since men and women could not legalize their marriage, every child born to a slave was thus not a legally recognized family member. Mothers, fathers and children could be sold away from each other, disrupting any semblance of family security or stability" (p. 9).

In response to these practices, African-Americans developed a number of secret rituals through which they created their own families and marriages. Practices such as "jumping the broom" were common and subsequently became marriage rituals. If a man and woman who were slaves wanted to "marry" and start a family, they called together members of the slave community and "jumped" a broom together. This became a symbol of their commitment. In some plantations where marriage was forbidden, this was done in secret. Because mothers and fathers were often sold to other plantations, children were often informally adopted by non-blood relatives. Because of the fear associated with the separation from loved ones, children were often not told the secret of their parentage. This practice of informal adoption is very common today. The implications of this for the development of family secrets will be discussed below.

Both African-American men and women were "abused sexually (during slavery) — men as breeders to increase the labor supply and women as sexual objects for white slave masters" (Boyd-Franklin, 1989, p. 9; Giddings, 1984; Pinkney, 1975; Rose, 1982). The rape and sexual exploitation of African women by slave masters produced a large number of light-skinned babies. These children were valued more highly by their white fathers and were often given certain privileges. Because American society valued these lighter-skinned offspring, this was the beginning of the skin color distinctions and biases within African-American families. Slavery thus created a number of different kinds of "toxic secrets," some of which were kept from outsiders and some of which were kept from other family members.

SECRETS ABOUT SKIN COLOR

Given the history of slavery discussed above, the issue of skin color has always been a very loaded and complex issue in African-American communities. As stated above, in the days of slavery, lighter skin color was often the result of the rape or clandestine sexual relationship between the white slave master and a female slave. The children of these unions were given certain privileges based on their lighter skin color and were often allowed to be house servants rather than work in the fields. This created a double bind, in which skin color often brought privilege, freedom, and even educational opportunities, but it was often also a "badge of shame" because of its relation to the earlier sexual exploitation of Black women.

Today, skin color is a complex issue within African-American families. In some families, light-skinned members are favored and dark-skinned members are scapegoated, rejected, or treated as inferior. In others, the reverse is true. Often, skin color issues are idiosyncratic to a particular family. In these situations, often it is the person who is most "different" who is scapegoated. In some circumstances, a family may reject a child who is far lighter than all of the other children, particularly if that child has a different father.

At other times, skin color is an overt representation of what may be a toxic family secret. In some families, light-skinned members would "pass for white" in order to gain entry into work and educational opportunities particularly in the pre-1960's segregated South. This often created either an extreme emotional cut off from the family of origin or a very complicated "double life." In these circumstances, light-skinned individuals would often live as white in their work life, and possibly "marry white," but then see their families of origin in secret. The following case is an example of how secrets dating back to the legacy of slavery and issues of skin color can contaminate a mother-daughter relationship in the present.

Case Example: The Bailor Family Secrets

The Bailor family entered treatment when their daughter, Ann, began to act out in high school. She began wearing her hair in "dreadlocks," wore African dress, and was dating a boy of whom her parents did not approve. He was seen by her parents, a suburban New Jersey couple, as "too militant." He had started an organization for African-American students at their high school, of which Ann was a member. When her parents forbade her to see this young man, Ann stayed out late, broke curfew, and blatantly disobeyed them. Her grades began to suffer, and her parents were concerned that she would

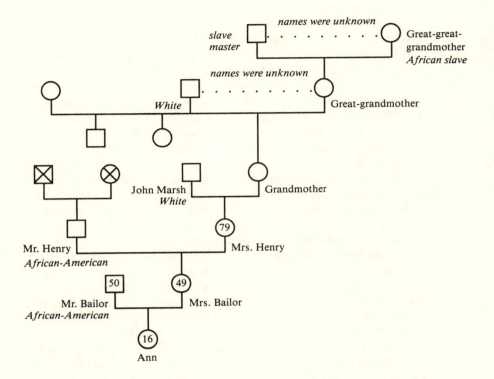

Figure 16.1

fail courses during her junior year in high school and would not get into college.

In the first session, Mrs. Bailor (age 49), a light-skinned, African-American woman, bitterly complained that in the last year her daughter, Ann (age 16), who was also light-skinned, had become "too Black." Mr. Bailor (age 50), a dark-skinned man, passively agreed. The level of emotionality was very charged between the mother and daughter. Therefore, I first put Mr. Bailor in charge of Ann's behavior. He was responsible for negotiating a clear curfew with her and sticking to it.

Change began to occur, but I still had the sense that there were "toxic" issues for this family, particularly for the mother, which were not being discussed. I suspected that there might be a family secret in the mother's own history. Therefore, I arranged to see the mother alone and told her that I was concerned that the conflict with Ann was stirring up many painful memories for her. I shared this with her as a hunch and asked if this was true. She was very quiet for a while and then began to cry softly. She told me that Ann reminded her a great deal of herself at the same age. Mrs. Bailor then began to share her own complicated family history with me. It was difficult for her to decide what part of this history was, in fact, true and what part was "family myth," which had been embellished over the years.

She explained that ever since the days of slavery skin color had always been a loaded issue in her family. Her great-great-grandmother had been a slave in New Orleans, Louisiana. The family "secret," passed down through generations, was that she had been raped by her slave master and had produced a very fair-skinned daughter, who had blonde hair and blue eyes. This was Mrs. Bailor's great-grandmother. After the Civil War, she became the mistress of a white man and had a daughter with him (Mrs. Bailor's grandmother). They were never married. He was married to a white woman and kept his mistress and her daughter a secret from his "real" family.

Mrs. Bailor's great-grandmother encouraged her daughter to pass for white as she was also blonde-haired and blue-eyed. The great-grandmother later had a number of children by Black men who had more obvious African-American features. Mrs. Bailor's grandmother, Martha, separated herself from the rest of the family and "passed" for white. She moved to New Jersey and lived a very separate life. No one at her job nor any of the men she dated knew about her African ancestry. Finally, she married a white man, John Marsh. Mrs. Bailor's mother was her first-born daughter.

Although Mrs. Bailor's mother is very light-skinned, her features are definitely indicative of her African heritage. Mrs. Bailor has an uncle who looks white and an aunt with light-brown skin. Shortly after that child's birth, her father, John Marsh, left. This raised questions in the family. Mrs. Bailor's mother was the family rebel who acted out and raised the questions that her parents were afraid to address. She confronted her mother and father, and her mother told her the secrets, going back to slavery, of skin color and of the African heritage in her family. In rebellion, Mrs. Bailor's mother married a very dark-skinned, African-American man, Mr. Henry, whom her grandmother refused to acknowledge. Thus, Mrs. Bailor was born into a very charged family atmosphere in which these secrets were still being acted out in the multigenerational cut off between her mother and her grandmother.

Mrs. Bailor's mother and father had a very stormy marriage, with her father frequently accusing her mother of infidelity with other men. Although this was never proven, it had a profound effect on Mrs. Bailor. As a teenager, she began to rebel. She chose a man who reminded her of her father, both in his dark skin color and in his temperament. She tearfully shared that she had done many of the same things as Ann was doing at the same age.

This type of complicated and confused family history is often overwhelming to both the family and the therapist. As the therapist, I certainly felt this. There was a sense that Mrs. Bailor had taken a tremendous risk in revealing her background to me, and I first complimented her for taking that risk and told her that it must have been very painful for her to do so. She cried, and I supported her in letting the feelings out. This was very new and very frightening for her.

I joined with her as a parent and told her that, as parents, we often don't realize how these painful parts of our past can affect us and our children. We discussed how this pain had affected her relationship with Ann. I helped her to see how this legacy of toxic secrets had set the stage for her relationship with her daughter. With my help, many sessions later, she was able to share her family history and secrets with her husband and her daughter in a family session. This session was the first time either Mr. Bailor or Ann had ever seen Mrs. Bailor cry. Mrs. Bailor was able to be honest with Ann about how much she had feared being a parent and how when she was growing up, she had often heard how she had to "look out for her children's appearance" by choosing a light-skinned mate. Although Mrs. Bailor had rebelled against this as a teenager and in her choice of husband, she was repeating this multigenerational legacy with her daughter.

Although this was a very difficult and long course of family therapy, this session proved to be a turning point and the beginning of a reconciliation between mother and daughter. Nor surprisingly, a stormy but important intervention involved encouraging Mrs. Bailor to go back and open up a dialogue with her own mother and with her grandmother, who had had no contact with her for most of her adult life. Mrs. Bailor reported that she shared her own pain with both of these women. They discussed the never before spoken skin color secrets in their family and the question of racial identity, which had never been addressed. Mr. Bailor and Ann were able to support Mrs. Bailor in this very difficult work. As Mrs. Bailor worked through her own multigenerational secrets, she was able to acknowledge to Ann that it had been very threatening to her to cope with Ann's emerging sense of her own racial identity, when Mrs. Bailor was in such conflict about her own. At the end of treatment, both Mr. and Mrs.

Bailor were able to discuss these issues more openly with Ann and to understand for the first time Ann's own struggles to define herself. By the end of treatment, Ann was able to successfully complete high school and was preparing to leave for college with the support and encouragement of both of her parents.

SECRETS RELATED TO EXTENDED FAMILY, INFORMAL ADOPTION, AND PARENTAGE

Billingsley (1968), Hill (1972, 1977), and Boyd-Franklin (1989) have described the complex extended family networks of African-American families. It is very common for extended family members to raise a child whose parents are unable to do so. In many African-American families this form of informal adoption or taking in of children occurs very frequently. At times, this informal adoption is a permanent, long-term relationship, at other times, it is a short-term, intermittent experience. Informal adoptions can occur when a parent dies, is hospitalized, is incarcerated, or in times of extreme economic stress. Older relatives will often remove children if the parents are involved with drugs, alcohol, or if there is evidence of physical or sexual abuse. Thus, this informal adoption process serves as an informal social service system. This originated in the days of slavery, when families were arbitrarily separated or sold apart from each other. It also has its roots in the pre-1960's segregated South, in which African-American children were not served by the segregated adoption and social service systems.

Secrets About Informal Adoption

The informal adoption process, while clearly beneficial to many generations of African-American children, is a system that is quite vulnerable to the development of secrets. For example, if a girl became pregnant as a teenager, families often sent this child to be raised by a distant family member. This person was often a grandmother figure who now had an "empty nest" or an aunt who could not have children of her own. In some families, the natural mother is known to the child. This is quite common in three-generational families, in which a fairly young grandmother (34–50) will raise her grandchild in the home while the child's teenage mother is raised simultaneously as a sibling. In these cases, grandmother often becomes "Mama," and the biological mother is referred to by her first name.

When there are problematic circumstances surrounding the informal adoption process, secrets often result. The following case example illustrates both the ways in which secrets can develop and the complicated and sensitive therapeutic process which is necessary to explore them.

The following is a complex case example that illustrates the ways in which family secrets about informal adoption, together with differences in skin color, can create feelings of intense inferiority and depression. These painful secrets take many forms. Often in the treatment of African-American young adults, these complex secrets and the burden of holding or colluding to deny them becomes too great. In these situations, because these adults may no longer live in their families of origin, the use of family therapy with one person (McGoldrick & Gerson, 1985), the completion of a genogram, and the coaching of an individual to first seek out adult family members who may know the complete story, are often helpful steps. This case is also a good example of how, by careful coaching of family members, extended family members can be involved in the treatment, even though they may live too far away to attend sessions.

Case Example: Multiple Secrets

Miriam was a beautiful, dark-skinned, African-American woman who entered therapy at age 29 with very low self-esteem. She was profoundly depressed and reported that she had been "sad" for most of her life. Things had become worse for her two years previously, when her "mother" had died, and Miriam had learned at her funeral that the person she knew as her mother was in fact her aunt.

Her history emerged as follows: Miriam had been raised as the only child of Mr. and Mrs. Williams in Memphis, Tennessee. She always felt "strange" in her family because both her "mother" and "father" had very light complexions, and she was very dark skinned. As a child, she had been called names like "darkie" and "ink spot" by children in the schoolyard and in her neighborhood. When she tried to discuss this with her parents, they became uncomfortable and quickly changed the topic. For years, Miriam had felt unwanted and "not good enough." Although she had been given every material advantage, she did not feel loved. When she was 12, her parents divorced. After this, she saw little of her father, and her mother became very bitter and resentful. She turned her anger on Miriam, whom she often abused, emotionally as well as physically. Miriam had never been able to leave home until her mother's death of a heart attack two years previously. At this point, she abruptly lost her home and came to live with an aunt in New York.

The secret regarding her parentage had begun to emerge at her mother's funeral. A stunning woman (who in fact looked a great deal like Miriam) introduced herself at the funeral and referred to her tearfully as "my baby." Miriam was drawn to this woman. After she left, an aunt told her that this woman, Janet Law, was, in fact, her

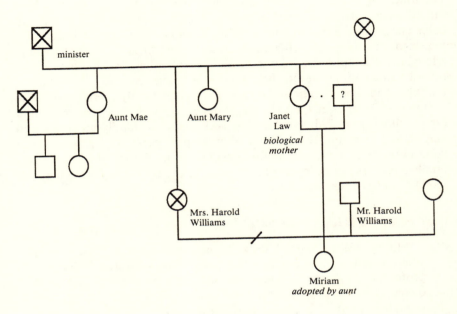

Figure 16.2

mother. She had become pregnant at 15 and could not raise her child. That child (Miriam) was sent to live with an aunt in Memphis (Mrs. Williams) who raised Miriam as her own.

Miriam had been shaken by this knowledge, but she had been afraid to pursue it with anyone. This hesitation is indicative of the power of keeping secrets in this family system. After her mother's death, she moved in with an aunt in New York, found a job at a department store, and became profoundly depressed.

When I first saw Miriam for therapy, she felt very defeated and cried through the first session. As trust was gained, she shared her complex history. Together, we constructed her genogram and realized that there were many gaps. She made a list of the family members who might help her to understand and come to terms with the secrets in her past. She listed her father, whom she had not seen for many years; her Aunt Mary, with whom she was living; her Aunt Mae, who had first shared the secret; and finally, her biological mother.

Miriam was terrified of contacting any of these people. Therefore, I asked her to pick the person who was least threatening to her. She chose her Aunt Mary, with whom she was living. She made a list of questions about her past that troubled her. After this discussion, she was able to disclose to her Aunt Mary what she had learned about her biological mother. Although her Aunt Mary confirmed this fact and was supportive, Miriam did not feel comfortable asking the many questions that still remained. With my coaching, Miriam was able to invite her Aunt Mary for a family therapy session, explaining that she needed her help to understand her past. We rehearsed and role-played the questions Miriam would ask prior to the session.

Aunt Mary was a warm, caring woman who obviously cared a great deal about Miriam. She was honest and open with Miriam in the session. Miriam asked many questions, particularly related to why she had been "given up" by her mother. Finally, tearfully, she admitted her worst fear to her aunt, which was that she had been rejected because she was dark skinned. She explained to her aunt how other kids, as well as her adopted mother, had often been cruel to her about her skin color.

Aunt Mary was visibly upset by this disclosure and assured her that this was not the case. She promised to show Miriam more pictures of her mother, whom she described as a "beautiful, brown-skinned woman." She had sent her to the Williams family, not as a rejection but because she was only 15 and too young to raise a child herself. As the session proceeded, Aunt Mary explained to Miriam that skin color had always been a "loaded" issue in the family. She also spoke honestly with Miriam about her own guilt at never having known how badly Miriam had been treated while she was growing up. She explained that the Williamses had been into "keeping up appearances" and that they had seen very little of the rest of the family because they lived so far away.

A number of other sessions were held with Aunt Mary. As that bond was solidified, she offered to accompany Miriam to see her other aunt, her adopted father, and finally her biological mother and to talk at length with each. With my encouragement, they each composed letters to each person and made arrangements for a visit.

We talked openly in our sessions about Miriam's fantasies of what might occur, and Aunt Mary was helpful in terms of reality testing and helping her to guard against disappointment.

Although Miriam's adopted father, Mr. Williams, was somewhat rejecting of her, he did answer her questions and helped her to understand what a tension-filled household she had grown up in. He acknowledged that he and Mrs. Williams had been very pleased to informally adopt Miriam at first, as they had no children of their own. However, as the couple's relationship began to deteriorate, they both began to resent each other and Miriam. Her adopted father told her that when she was a child, they felt that she didn't need to know about her "real mother." After her adopted parents divorced when she was 12, they never "got around" to telling her. Miriam found this explanation very unsatisfying. Unfortunately, Miriam's fantasy of an ongoing relationship with her adopted father was never realized. He was in a new relationship and had no desire to see Miriam on an ongoing basis. This demonstrates the reality that opening secrets *doesn't always* make for "new, happy relationships," but does resolve mysteries, provide clarity about oneself, and often allows a person to bring closure to this chapter of his or her life.

Miriam's contact with her Aunt Mae and Janet Law, her biological mother, were more positive experiences for her. Aunt Mary also accompanied her on both of these trips. Aunt Mae was able to share much more of the family background and to explain how mortified the family had been when Janet (her biological mother) had become pregnant. She explained that their father was a minister and was frankly embarrassed by her pregnancy. She was sent to live with Mr. and Mrs. Williams until Miriam was born and then they informally "adopted" the baby.

Her meeting with her biological mother was very moving. Janet Law lived in Mississippi near the Tennessee border. She had never married or had other children, but had lived with her guilt about "giving Miriam up" for many years. After seeing her at Mrs. Williams' funeral, she had wanted to contact her but had been afraid. They left their brief meeting with a tentative bond between them.

After these dramatic events, Miriam was seen in therapy for approximately another year. She was seen both in individual sessions and in family sessions with her aunt and occasionally other key family members. With this opening up of the family secrets, she was able to work through her anger at her adopted mother and father as well as her biological mother. She was able to rebuild her self-esteem and her sense of "family." She continued to strengthen her relationships with Aunt Mary, Aunt Mae, and Janet Law, her biological mother.

SECRETS RELATED TO ALCOHOL, DRUG ABUSE, AND AIDS

Another area that can be very loaded for African-American families involves secrets concerning family members who are alcoholic, drug abusers, or who have AIDS. As in many other cultures, these issues are often secrets in African-American communities. This type of secret can be manifested in many ways. Often it is "known" but not discussed throughout the community.

Parents or grandparents who are church-involved or who have middle-class aspirations may be embarrassed by these behaviors and may see them as an indication of their failure at parenting. These issues are then kept secret from the church family, as well as the extended family. In the grandparents' generation, often these issues are kept as secrets from the grandchildren, who may not be told that their parent is drug-involved or incarcerated or has AIDS. There are many ways in which these secrets can manifest as symptoms in children. Sometimes the effort at denial or maintaining the "toxic secret" also emerges as symptoms in a child.

Case Example: AIDS as a Family Secret

Mrs. Patterson, a 51-year-old African-American grandmother, brought her grandson, Dwayne (age 10), to our community mental health center for treatment. Dwayne had been living with his grandmother intermittently for most of his life. She had been given custody by the courts two years previously when he and his two brothers, Paul (9) and Darryl (6), had been abandoned by their mother at a shelter. Dwayne had been acting out ever since. He was disobedient toward his grandmother and was disruptive in school. He had been suspended in the week prior to treatment because of a fight with another child at school.

In the first session, the therapist* had asked the grandmother to bring the entire family. She brought all three boys. In the course of the session, it became clear that Dwayne had begun acting out after his abandonment by his mother. During the course of the session, Mrs. Patterson reluctantly shared that all of the boys' behavior had become worse since their mother's death six months prior to treatment.

The therapist sensed that the grandmother was uncomfortable answering questions about the boys' mother and, therefore, he asked the boys to sit in the waiting area so that he could speak to her alone. Mrs. Patterson was very reluctant to discuss the issue with the therapist. He acknowledged that she was just meeting him and that it must be very hard to trust someone enough to share personal information this early in a relationship. The therapist told the grandmother that he felt that there were some other important issues in the family,

*The therapist in this case was a white male. I was the supervisor.

which he needed to understand in order to help her with the boys. He still sensed her discomfort so he told her that they should go slow. He would begin working to help her with the boys, and when she had greater trust in him perhaps she would tell him more about her family.

The therapist worked hard in the next two sessions to help put the grandmother back in charge of the boys' behavior. They worked out a system of rewards and clear consequences for negative behavior. The boys began to change. They had a week when there were no incidents in school. The therapist praised the grandmother for the excellent job she had done. The therapist continued to work with Mrs. Patterson and the boys in family therapy. Their school behavior as well as their behavior at home improved as the therapist reinforced Mrs. Patterson's role as the (grand)parent in charge. The therapist's credibility with the family grew, and trust increased.

Finally, about four months after the initial session, the grandmother called the therapist and asked if he had any free time on that day. She came in and said that she had prayed over what he had said to her in the beginning of treatment about her needing to trust him before she could really talk about her daughter. She told him that her daughter, Maxine, had been drug-involved since her teen years. She had used many substances including marijuana, cocaine, and I.V. heroin. Approximately two years before she had been diagnosed HIV-positive, and six months ago, she had died of AIDS.

Mrs. Patterson was very upset by this disclosure. She stated that she had prayed over whether to even tell the therapist. It was a secret in her extended family, her church and, although she suspected that the boys might have "heard something," she had attempted to keep the secret from them. She had never discussed with them how their mother had died nor the reason why she had abandoned them. Mrs. Patterson was very embarrassed by all of this. She was concerned that she and her grandsons would be stigmatized in their community if people knew their mother had died of AIDS.

Her feelings were very complex; she was afraid that the boys could never keep a secret like this and would blurt it out. She was feeling very guilty about her daughter's substance abuse and felt that she had failed as a mother. She was determined to "make it up to" her grandsons and to "raise them better." Ironically, she therefore found it very difficult to set limits for them and to discipline them appropriately. The therapist assured her that he knew how difficult it was for her to share all of this with him. He also stressed how impressed he was that she could trust him with this special information in order to help her grandchildren.

While continuing the family sessions and working on Mrs. Patterson's limit-setting with the boys, the therapist conducted a number of individual sessions with her to explore her own guilt regarding her daughter and help her to resolve it. He also began to introduce the concept of how a "toxic secret" can cause problems in a family and how children can begin to act out in response. Initially, Mrs. Patterson was not ready to tell the boys. The therapist accepted this and asked her what she thought the boys knew about their mother's death. She wasn't sure. With the therapist's help and role-playing she was able to prepare for a session in which she would ask the boys what they knew. The therapist also prepared her for the fact that children often "know" much more than their parents think they do, even if they are conscious of a "taboo" against discussing the secret.

With the therapist's support, Mrs. Patterson met with all of her grandsons in a family session. She asked them what they knew about their mother's death. The youngest boy, Darryl (6), sheepishly replied that the other kids often teased him about his mother's death. Dwayne (10) replied that the fight he had had at school had occurred because a kid had said something "bad" about his mother. He was reluctant to answer when pressed by the therapist about what the "something bad" had been. He mumbled that she was on drugs. Paul (9) became very agitated while his brothers talked and surprised everyone by blurting out that a kid on the block had told him his mother had AIDS. The grandmother was startled. She asked if the other boys had heard such things, also. They all nodded. She cried openly and, with the therapist's help, was able to pull them all close to her and tell them yes, that their mother had died of AIDS, which she had gotten by shooting heroin from contaminated needles. All of the boys cried with her.

This session marked the beginning of the next phase of therapy, attending to the grief and the mourning and the sadness and anger that the boys felt about their mother's death. The opening up of the secret allowed this second phase to begin.

Here again, the therapist was able to pace the family and build trust with the grandmother. He respected her hesitancy. Although therapy continued for many months after this disclosure, this session was very significant in that it released the toxicity of the secret, which all were investing a great deal of energy in maintaining. It is not unusual that when parents actually ask their children, they "know the secret" on some level, even if they do not know all of the details. All family members then collude to deny it, and the effects are increased, including acting out in children and lack of open communication.

THE IMPACT OF RACISM AND DISCRIMINATION

Racism has its roots in a society that allowed slavery to exist. "Slavery set the tone for Black people to be treated as inferior. Skin color is a badge of difference" (Boyd-Franklin, 1989). Pinderhughes (1982) has described the ways in which this led to a "victim system," in which overt and covert barriers exist for African-Americans in achievement and employment, as well as access to the benefits of prosperity. In 1991, African-Americans are still disproportionately represented among the poor.

In response to racism and this "victim system," African-Americans have developed what Grier and Cobbs (1968) have called "healthy cultural paranoia." In response to the oppression of slavery and the years of segregation and discrimination that followed, African-American families have developed a healthy suspicion of the motives and intentions of white people and institutions. As a result, there are many secrets that these families keep from the outside world. This is a stance intended to protect the family from intrusion by outside agencies. Much of this has roots more recent than the experience of slavery. For example, the welfare system often penalized African-American families by threatening to cut off the family's financial support if a man was living in the household.

SECRETS RELATED TO THE WELFARE SYSTEM AND THE INVISIBILITY OF BLACK MEN

Because of the history of slavery and the legacy of the welfare system described above, African-American families have learned the often painful lesson of keeping their "family business" secret from outsiders. This has been particularly true of male-female relationships. Because slave masters did not allow formal marriages, slaves often had these relationships in secret. This created the beginning of the experience of the invisibility of Black men. Often, they were helpless to stop the disruption of their families or the sexual abuse of women.

This legacy of the "invisibility" of African-American men has been further exacerbated by the experience of the welfare system. Aid to Families with Dependent Children could only be given if it was proven that a man was not living in the home. This created another "secret" around the issue of male-female relationships. All signs of a man's presence had to be hidden from the prying eyes of caseworkers, who paid surprise visits to the home and often searched closets for a man's clothes. It is no wonder that African-American "single mothers" often keep secret from a therapist that they are living with a boyfriend, for fear that this information will be given to the welfare department. This is only one example of the intrusion that many African-American families have experienced within this society. As a result, these families are often cautious, guarded, and suspicious when they are approached by outsiders. Children are taught from an early age that family issues are "nobody's business but our own."

Secrets Related to the Fear of Child Protective Agencies

For many poor African-American families, there is also a fear of the power of child protective agencies. These agencies can remove a child from his or her home for abuse or neglect. The process leading to the return of the child is often very complicated. Also, because of the involvement of extended family, particularly the older generation of grandmothers, grandfathers, aunts, and uncles who may be raising a child, complex custody issues can result. This is often complicated by internal family secrets about informal adoption and fears about loss of legal custody. The following case illustrates this dilemma.

Case Example: The Holmes Family

Carl was a nine-year-old, African-American boy who was brought for treatment by his grandfather, Mr. Holmes. They had been referred by the pediatric clinic at a local hospital. Carl was very obese and the nurses and doctors at his clinic felt that his weight was a health risk. He was also profoundly depressed.

Both Carl and his grandfather presented as very sad and withdrawn. The therapist, a white male, began treating the family and joined with Carl and Mr. Holmes. As their therapeutic relationship became stronger, Mr. Holmes asked for an individual session with the therapist and told him the story of his informal adoption of Carl. The grandfather assured the therapist that Carl "did not know" this history.

The following story emerged: Carl had been born to Mr. Holmes' daughter, Tanya, when she was 20 years old. Both Carl's mother and

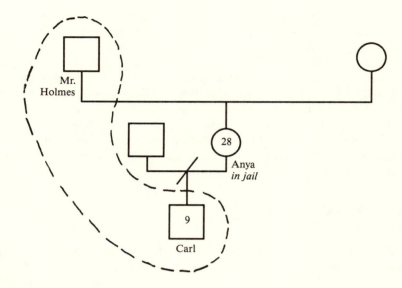

Figure 16.3

father were substance abusers who shoplifted to support their habits.
Carl's mother was frequently evicted by her landlords because she
would spend her rent money (from Welfare and AFDC) on drugs.
The strain between Mr. Holmes and his daughter was so great that
she did not come to the family when she was evicted; she lived in an
abandoned building with her infant. A neighbor called the Child
Protective Agency when Carl was left alone by his mother in an
abandoned building. His cries brought help and he was taken into the
care of the Child Protective Agency. Mr. Holmes heard about this
occurrence from neighbors. He then contacted the Child Protective
Agency and asked for custody of Carl. The process of obtaining
custody took a year, during which time Carl was in a foster home and
Mr. Holmes was not allowed to see him. Mr. Holmes and his home
were thoroughly investigated by the Child Protective Agency.

As Mr. Holmes talked about this experience, his rage and bitterness were evident. He was finally awarded legal custody when Carl
was one and a half years old, but he resented the Child Protective
Agency and its power over his family. He was always fearful that Carl
would be taken away from him. Mr. Holmes became very attached to
Carl. He saw this child as his "second chance." Feeling that he had
failed as a parent with his daughter, he intended to "make up for it"
with Carl.

When Carl was two and a half, his mother attempted to regain custody of him. Mr. Holmes went to court to fight this request. Once again, the custody was awarded to Mr. Holmes. All of this was kept secret from Carl. Shortly thereafter, Carl's mother was involved in an armed robbery in which a bystander was killed. Although she did not commit the murder, she was involved in the crime and was sentenced to five years in prison. Mr. Holmes, fearful that his daughter would "want Carl back" when she was released from prison, chose to keep Carl's mother's whereabouts and her incarceration a secret from Carl. He was very ashamed that his daughter had become a drug addict and in his words a "convicted criminal." Carl was told only that his mother had left him with his grandfather and that he had no idea where she had gone.

As the therapist listened to this secret, it was clear that the grandfather loved his grandson deeply and was also involved in a very enmeshed relationship with him. He kept a "tight rein" on Carl and did everything for him. Carl had no chores or responsibilities at home, and his grandfather still bathed him and chose his clothes for him. He also worked in Carl's school as a volunteer so that he could "keep an eye on him."

The therapist decided to say to the grandfather that it was clear he loved his grandson so much that he was trying desperately to keep him from all harm. The grandfather understood this and saw that in some ways he loved his grandchild "too much" and was trying to make up for whatever he may have "done wrong" in raising the child's mother.

The therapist chose not to intervene in the secret immediately, but to address it by saying to the grandfather that children often "know" a family secret even if they don't know all the details. The therapist told the grandfather that often when kids become as depressed as Carl, it is because they sense that something is very wrong in the family, but they can't talk about it. The therapist introduced the thought to the grandfather that he sensed that Mr. Holmes knew that for Carl to improve, eventually the secret would have to be explored, but that he also knew Mr. Holmes was not ready at that time. This was done in order to acknowledge the secret and not collude to ignore it. but also to let the grandfather know that his fears were understood.

The therapist built credibility with the family by working on Carl's depression and obesity and by helping the grandfather to treat him in a more age-appropriate manner. The grandfather talked openly with Carl about his need to begin to grow up and do more things on his own. A reward system was devised whereby the grandfather could reward Carl for monitoring his own diet. Gradually, changes began to occur. Carl became more verbal with his grandfather, and Mr. Holmes could allow him to do more on his own. Although Carl did not lose weight, his depression began to lift.

As trust emerged, the therapist had a session with the grandfather in which he pointed out the improvements that Carl had made. He told Mr. Holmes that this progress could only continue if Carl and his grandfather had a relationship built on trust. The grandfather shared with the therapist that Carl had been asking a number of questions about his mother recently. The therapist responded that he sensed that the grandfather was ready to share information about Carl's mother, but was scared. The grandfather agreed and talked about his fear of losing Carl. The therapist helped the grandfather to approach the Child Protective Agency and discuss his fears about losing custody of Carl if his mother was released from prison. Although they could give him no guarantees, in the process of discussing the issue, he received reassurance that others saw and recognized his care of his grandchild and that it was likely he would remain the legal guardian.

With this fear at least addressed, the grandfather was able to begin to raise issues with Carl about his mother. In a family session, he was able to ask Carl if he ever thought about his mother. Carl replied "Yes," and was eager to ask questions. With the therapist's help, the grandfather told Carl the story of how he had come to live with him. It was only in subsequent sessions that he was able to tell his grandson about his mother's incarceration. He cried as he shared with Carl his shame and guilt about raising his daughter. This was the first time Carl had ever understood his grandfather's pain and the reasons why he was "on him all the time."

Gradually, the therapist was able to support the grandfather in discussing his fears of losing custody. Carl made it very clear, in a very age-appropriate way, that although he wanted to know his mother, he had no desire to go and live with her. The grandfather was then able to give Carl permission to write to his mother. This led to a telephone call. Eventually, he allowed Carl one visit with his mother, but he was very concerned about Carl seeing her in prison. As this secret was opened up, Carl's depression began to lift. Although he did not develop a real relationship with his mother, he and his grandfather had the beginnings of a more open communication. The secret that had existed between them was finally lifted, and they could begin to build a new relationship.

RESPONSE OF AFRICAN-AMERICAN FAMILIES TO THERAPY

African-American families often respond to therapy initially with mistrust and hesitancy. This has many implications for therapists who are working with these families. Often, this mistrust is interpreted as resistance, and families are dismissed as not suitable for therapy. This is unfortunate and is complicated by the fact that therapy itself is often a secret in African-American communities. Therapy is often viewed negatively and is seen as being "for crazy people," for "sick people," for "white folks"; you are seen as "weak" if you are in therapy. Because of this, many African-Americans are very hesitant to enter therapy. Therapists, who had been trained to ask many questions and to take a detailed history during intake, often fuel the suspicion of these families and cause them to drop out of therapy. These questions are perceived as prying into the family business, and families will often keep secrets from therapists initially.

The Issue of Timing in the Exploration of Secrets

Because of the multiple issues related to secrets in African-American families and the many levels that may exist, a word of caution is necessary. Many therapists are trained to explore and open up family secrets as soon as possible and often become intrigued with this process. With African-American families, however, the legacy of mistrust is ever-present, particularly in the early phase of treatment. It began with slavery and was enhanced by the "healthy cultural paranoia" (Grier & Cobbs, 1968) that grew from living in an oppressive, obtrusive society. With this in mind, therapists must proceed slowly and build trust before exploring these intimate family secrets. If this exploration takes place before sufficient trust has been established with the therapist, the family will flee treatment. Therefore, therapists must be attuned to the issue of timing in the course of treatment. It is very important to invest the time in joining and establishing credibility with a family before "exposing" its secrets. This is particularly important in cross-racial therapy.

Another issue of timing is related to generational boundaries in African-American families. In some families there are very rigid boundaries between adults and children. Within African-American culture, therefore, there are many "family secrets" that one does not tell to children. This tradition can persist even after these "children" have grown up and have children or grandchildren of their own.

When the therapist senses that adults are reluctant to discuss an issue in front of the children, it is important initially to show respect by tracking this family preference and meeting alone with the adults in the family. The therapist can state quite openly in such a meeting: "I sensed that there was something important that you wanted to tell me but that you couldn't discuss in front of the children." Therapists in this situation often must have the patience to work this through with the parents or other extended family members until they are ready to address this issue with the children.

The therapist, whether Black or white, must struggle with the question of which secrets are important to open up in African-American families. Therapists often find that they must walk a fine line between not colluding with the family to deny the secrets and strategically deciding the timing of the exploration.

Recommendations for Therapists in Working with Secrets in African-American Families

Hesitancy to enter and embrace therapy is so common among African-American families that I have recommended a different approach to the treatment process based on a multisystems model (Boyd-Franklin, 1989). Although most therapists have been trained to provide treatment for patients and families who want it, this model teaches therapists to work with families who are very suspicious of the process. I recommend that therapists use the first few sessions to build trust with African-American families. Therapists are discouraged from collecting genograms and extensive history in the first few sessions, but to be more solution focused. This allows African-American families the time to begin to know and trust the therapist and to begin to believe in the process. It is only then that these families will begin to share their personal family business and secrets.

Throughout this chapter, I have focused on the process of opening up secrets. However, it is also important for therapists to understand that it may not be necessary for *all* of the family secrets to be opened up in order for effective treatment to occur. Therapists often must make choices as to whether these secrets are relevant to the problem that they are trying to solve.

Haley (1976) describes such a case (known as "Modern Little Hans") in which a middle-aged, African-American couple bring in their son who has a fear of dogs. The therapist cures the child's dog phobia and then turns his attention to the couple. In the course of his work with the couple, the therapist discovers that there is a secret within the relationship. He encourages them to act as if they have told him the secret and go on from there. This is, in fact, a very elegant intervention. It becomes obvious that the husband had an affair early in the marriage when the wife was preoccupied with caring for their newly-adopted infant son. This had been a painful but unspoken issue between them ever since.

While Haley never mentions this, it is fascinating to note that the child's symptom, i.e., his fear of dogs, takes on a new significance when we recognize that a "dog" in the African-American community can be used to refer to a man who "messes around on his wife" or who has affairs. This intervention takes into account the cultural values and allows this couple to move forward and discuss healing their relationship so that their son does not have to again become the family's symptom-bearer. The therapist does not collude with the family to deny the "secret" of the affair. He does, however, wait until he has the trust and credibility with the family to open up this difficult area. By telling them to proceed as if they have told him what occurred, he allows both parties to deal with the resentment generated by this time in their lives and talk about this issue. They can then move forward in their relationship.

CONCLUSION

The treatment of African-American families is a challenge for therapists of any ethnicity. In working with the rich fabric of this culture, the therapist must often unravel the complexities of family secrets in order to produce therapeutic change. However, in order to be effective with African-American families, each clinician must struggle to fully understand the history of slavery, oppression, and racism, which has contributed to the process of creating these family secrets. From this perspective, each therapist must build trust with each African-American family. It is this joining and trusting that will allow us to find the appropriate therapeutic balance necessary to avoid being too intrusive and, at the same time, to avoid colluding and covering up "toxic" secrets. The key ingredient in this process is the issue of timing. This chapter has offered suggestions to therapists regarding this process. It is hoped that it will serve as a beginning for future exploration of the issue of secrets in African-American families.

REFERENCES

Billingsley, A. (1968). *Black families in white America*. Englewood Cliffs, NJ: Prentice-Hall.
Boyd-Franklin, N. (1989). *Black families in therapy: A multisystems approach*. New York: Guilford.
Giddings, P. (1984). *When and where I enter*. New York: William Morrow.
Grier, W., & Cobbs, P. (1968). *Black rage*. New York: Basic.
Haley, J. (1976). *Problem-solving therapy*. San Francisco: Jossey-Bass.
Hill, R. (1972). *The strengths of Black families*. New York: Emerson-Hall.
Hill, R. (1977). *Informal adoption among Black families*. Washington, DC: National Urban League Research Department.
Kinney, E. (1971). Africanism in the music and dance of the Americas. In R. Goldstein (Ed.), *Black life and culture in the United States*. New York: Crowell.

17

AIDS and Secrets

LASCELLES W. BLACK

IN AN ORDINARY WEEK in my work with patients at risk for infection with the Human Immunodeficiency Virus (HIV), I listen to people speaking of their secrets relating to Acquired Immune Deficiency Syndrome (AIDS) and their families. These secrets illustrate the complexities for patients, their families, and the therapist when HIV and/or AIDS pertains.

A young mother, Betty, is crying because she has been diagnosed HIV-positive, and she is terrified that if her husband, Tim, tests HIV-negative, he will take their child and leave her. During a difficult period in their marriage they separated, and she had a brief affair with a man whom she later learned has AIDS, which is why she chose to be tested. Betty did not tell her husband about this affair when they reconciled, and she can't bring herself to reveal the secret to Tim in this time of crisis. In her desperation, she prays that Tim will also test positive for HIV so that he will not discover the affair and desert her because of his own fear and anger.

Joseph has been told he has AIDS. He is a teacher with graduate degrees in mathematics and education and close to ten years experience teaching in inner city schools. He is afraid that if his diagnosis is revealed, he will lose his job or be given an administrative position when all he has ever wanted to do is teach children with special needs. He feels compelled to keep his illness a secret from his closest friend and colleague at his school.

An 11-year-old boy, Adolfo, has returned home from a weekend visit with his father, and he tells his mother, Elena, that his dad instructed him not to

This chapter is dedicated to the memory of William Ramos. Willie was a personal friend and colleague. He was a devoted family man, an educator, and an advocate for people with AIDS. He will be remembered in the Bronx as a leader in the struggle against ignorance, prejudice, and AIDS. Willie died of AIDS December 7th, 1991.

touch his stepfather or use any utensils or household items that his step-father might have used because his stepfather has AIDS. Elena is frightened and agonized because she has not yet told her son that she is also HIV-positive.

Edward and Clive, a gay couple, have had frequent arguments because Clive refuses to tell his ex-wife, whom he left less than a year ago, that he is HIV-positive and that she should be tested because she may have been infected while he was still living with her. Edward does not know what is keeping Clive from revealing this vital piece of information, and he is seri-ously reconsidering whether he should continue a relationship with a man who shows such little concern for the health and life of someone he once loved.

Cynthia, a law student, has been told that she has AIDS, but she still will not tell her boyfriend that she has HIV. She says that he refuses to use condoms, so she uses a diaphragm and a spermicide with nonoxynol-9 for birth control, but she will not inform him of the risk he is taking for fear of facing his anger and being rejected.

A mother, Shirley, whose T-cell count has fallen precipitously, worries over how she will tell her teenage children about her health problems when she has allowed them to believe that their father died of pneumonia instead of AIDS. A low T-cell count (also called CD-4 cells, these cells are special-ized for defense against infections) is an indication that the person's immune system is compromised and that the person is more vulnerable to opportu-nistic infections.

Jake is a gay man who is afraid to tell his family that he is homosexual. When asked, he denies all risk factors for HIV, but shows symptoms of the early onset of AIDS. He refuses to permit the physician to test him for HIV infection. Jake wishes to keep the secret from everyone, including himself.

Clara is a young woman who is a prostitute. She knows she is at high risk for HIV. When she develops several opportunistic infections that would indicate that she is likely HIV-positive, she refuses to be tested for HIV. She will only permit the physician to treat her for the opportunistic infections. Clara understands that she is at risk for reinfection if she has sex without a condom, so she practices safer sex. She keeps her HIV status a secret even from herself, but behaves in ways that suggest she knows she carries the virus.

As the above examples indicate, issues of HIV/AIDS are fraught with secrets. Marcia Abramson's (1990) study of the practices of hospital social workers who work with people with AIDS identified secrecy as the most relevant and salient ethical problem faced by these clinicians. She describes three areas of secret-keeping, including keeping secrets from the person with

AIDS, due to the clinician's own discomfort; keeping secrets from those who may be at risk, due to the requirements of confidentiality; and keeping secrets from the rest of the world, due to the overwhelming sense of stigma. Her research supports the idea that the therapist, in fact, becomes the designated keeper of many secrets.

However, not all secrets operate on the same level or have the same potential for danger. Some secrets pertain to personal privacy and choice, while others bear significance for public safety. In the case of Cynthia, the law student, clearly her boyfriend is at risk for HIV infection and he should be informed. But she refuses to tell him and will not divulge his name to health-care providers. Instead, she changed her story and denied that she had a boyfriend. So this man, if he does exist, may be infected and, if he is unfaithful to Cynthia, could also spread the virus to others.

Walker (1991) and the Ackerman Institute team dealt with this issue by giving a client a specific time frame in which to notify a partner at risk or they would cease to work with the person. This approach to dealing with a dangerous secret — i.e., a patient's need to disclose to a sexual partner and the clinician's ethical duty to warn if this is not carried out by an agreed upon time — has worked when people have chosen to remain in treatment.

Jake, the young gay man who does not want his family to know his sexual orientation, has every right to his privacy, and his health care should be maintained until he is ready to reveal those matters to his family. As long as he practices safer sex, his secrets are his own concern. Brill (1990) writes of this right of a person to keep a secret from himself. If in exercising that right he also denies himself needed medical attention are moral principles being breached? The therapist would have to work carefully with the patient to help him realize what keeping this secret from himself is costing him.

Epidemiological research suggests that keeping the secret of HIV from oneself can put others at risk. Winiarski (1991) reports that denial of risk factors (meaning the person states that he has no idea how he got the infection) seems to be more prevalent in middle-class and upper-class men. He states that 27% of HIV infected men in the New York City borough of Queens denied all risk factors. This compares with 6% for New York City as a whole. A higher percentage of women were infected through heterosexual contact in the Queens sample when compared to a New York City sample. It would appear that the men's denial of risk factors is linked to the higher rate of heterosexual transmission. It is apparent that the secrets that these men are keeping have had dire consequences for the women in their lives. The dilemma of dealing with such secret-keeping in a culture that so highly stigmatizes the person with AIDS confronts any therapist working in this area daily.

STIGMA AND SECRECY

The secret of AIDS is of a nature that is different from all others because of the multiple levels at which the secrecy occurs. Walker (1991) stresses that the secrecy that is attached to AIDS in families is a direct reflection of societal views that stigmatize the AIDS patient.[1] In the mind of much of the public, the disease is often associated with sin and shame and generally disapproved behaviors. These attitudes have led to the stigmatization of people with AIDS and their families, and, in at least one country (Cuba), there have been incarcerations under the guise of quarantine. The fear of being stigmatized leads individuals and families to keep the disease a secret.

Individuals may deny the real cause of their illness and only acknowledge the opportunistic diseases from which they suffer so that these may be treated. Thus, people may speak of having cancer or pneumonia, but not AIDS. This denial may serve to protect some secret behavior such as drug use or sexual orientation, which, if exposed, may lead to stigmatization, loss of employment and status, and erosion of support from the family. Revelation of the illness may also cause a person to lose housing, insurance, and friendships (Walker, 1991). Although discrimination based on a person's HIV-positive status is illegal, it still continues to happen. Employers, landlords, and others who choose to discriminate against HIV-positive people simply use other excuses, which hide the real nature of their intentions.

At the level of couples' relationships, a husband, for instance, may keep the information from his wife (or vice versa), out of fear of recrimination and abandonment. Because drug use or extramarital sexual activity has often been kept secret from the partner, opening the secret of being HIV-positive becomes doubly difficult. Because the partner may also become infected, this secret-keeping is especially dangerous. The secret may pertain in both heterosexual and homosexual couples. However, the gay community is generally more aware and educated about HIV, and so such secret-keeping is less likely within the boundaries of gay couples.

At the family level, parents may keep information of their positive HIV status from their children, from their in-laws, and from other members of the extended family. Sometimes the reason given is they think the children or the grandparents can't "handle" such devastating news, or they can't be relied on to keep the secret within family boundaries. An aging parent or very sick relative may be singled out for protection from the secret informa-

---

[1]The reader is referred to Gillian Walker's book, *In the Midst of Winter*, which offers the only family therapy text solely devoted to working with persons with AIDS and their families from a systemic perspective. Her chapter on secrecy orients the reader to many of the legal issues involving confidentiality and duty to warn.

tion and so is excluded from all communication relating to the health of the HIV-positive relative.

Elements of classism, racism, and heterosexism have combined to contribute to denial and secrecy. In the early days of the epidemic, many cultural and ethnic groups thought they were safe from the virus because the image of the "AIDS patient" projected in the media was a white, middle-class, homosexual man. This denial continued when the new "at risk person," a Black or Hispanic, male, intravenous drug user did not fit their group. Each group imagined safety being guaranteed by their appearances and identities and so did not examine the specific behaviors that placed them at risk. Preventive measures such as condom use, safer sex education, information on the cleaning of I.V. drug apparatus conflicted with religious teachings, and cultural and moral norms. Such beliefs have put people at risk through a kind of secret-keeping at the widest cultural level. Until the late 1980's, some nations denied the existence of the virus within their borders, claiming they had no PWA's (People With AIDS).

THE AIDS SECRET AS DIVISIVE

When a part of a family or a group insists on keeping AIDS a secret from other members of the family, the results can be quite divisive, and the effects can have an impact on others outside of the group who are also connected to the person with AIDS. In denying that the family member has AIDS, it then becomes necessary to exclude those members not party to the secret from any discussions pertaining to the true nature of the illness. Sometimes elaborate stories have to be created to maintain the subterfuge. Close relatives and friends are sometimes not informed when the person with AIDS is hospitalized. They may be told he is not allowed visitors so that the secret is not revealed to them by seeing the patient in the context of a ward with other persons with AIDS. Energy and resources that could more profitably be spent on coping with the illness and its effects are instead spent on guarding the secret. Those who are excluded eventually realize that they are being treated differently from other family members. Resentment corrodes relationships, replacing needed compassion and support.

The results of this exclusion may be that family members start to distance themselves from each other. Those who are outside the secret circle feel shut out by those on the inside. They may begin to exclude those family members from their own gatherings and celebrations just at the time when such support and involvement is most needed. The patient and his or her family may soon be isolated from the rest of the family.

Sometimes a person with AIDS may keep his diagnosis a secret from his immediate family, while relying on close friends for support. Such friends become the person's most loving and comforting network, but they are vulnerable to being excluded when family members discover the diagnosis during a final illness or at death.

Case Example: Mourning Charley's Death

A patient, Cecil, tells me that his friend Charley died recently. Charley's family came to the hospital and claimed his body even though they had shunned him for years because they could not accept his homosexuality. Charley's illness had been a secret from his family, and their grief was colored by anger. Charley's lover, Michael, and his gay friends were told they were not welcome at the funeral. Cecil and Michael went to the church anyway, but they did not go to the cemetery. Charley's obituary stated that he died of cancer, and he was buried in the family plot.

Cecil and his friends felt ignored, frustrated, and robbed of the opportunity to mourn openly. They were the ones who lived with, shared with, and cared for Charley all his short adult life. They were the ones who stood by him and helped him during his suffering from the ravages of the opportunistic infections to which people with AIDS are subject, including Kaposi's sarcoma. But they were excluded from the rituals of burial and mourning because the family rejected Charley's homosexuality and denied that he died of AIDS.

I helped Cecil to affirm that he and his friends are also Charley's family and that the memory of Charley will always be with them. The good times they shared cannot be lost. Michael needed the support of his group of friends at this time and, while they were deprived of participation in the burial ceremony, the mourning process could still take place. I talked with Cecil about designing a ritual to express their grief in their own particular way. They designed a ritual where the group went together to the cemetery on a Saturday afternoon and said goodbye to Charley and left flowers and a lavender colored candle burning on his gravestone. Then, they went back to the apartment that Charley had shared with Michael and performed an upbeat memorial service singing songs and talking about the good times they had enjoyed with Charley and assuring Michael and each other that they would be there for one another in good times as well as in times of need and sadness. Reconciliation with Charley's family remained impossible.

AIDS AS A FAMILY SECRET

Claude and his wife Mary are both HIV-positive. In fact, Claude's diagnosis is AIDS, and he has had several hospitalizations for pneumocystis carinii pneumonia (PCP), tuberculosis (TB), and other opportunistic infections and his CD-4 cell count is less than 50. Mary has had fewer opportunistic infections and her CD-4 cell count is just below 300. (Normal CD-4 cell count is 700.) They have four children: a 21-year-old son, a 17-year-old daughter, a 15-year-old son, and a 9-year-old daughter. They have not told their children or their extended family about the true nature of their illness.

The only family member they have taken into their confidence is Claude's older sister, Clarisa, who lives in another state. Clarisa has no children of her own, so they have agreed that when they die or become unable to care for the younger children she will take them into her home.

Claude and Mary are afraid to tell the family about their HIV status because of Claude's history as an intravenous drug user, which is also a family secret. Claude was able to keep his secret because he continued to work and support his family for more than 20 years. It was only when his health started to fail that his problems became known at work; he has been kept on the payroll as a part-time worker and given lighter duties. The family is reasonably secure financially, and their main concern is what will become of their children.

The children see their parents taking a lot of medication daily, they are aware of Claude's hospitalizations, so they know Claude and Mary are not well. With the amount of publicity that HIV/AIDS gets in the media now, it would be unlikely that the children have not guessed the true nature of their parents' health problems. What they are more likely to be speculating about is the mode of transmission that caused the infection. This is probably also true for other members of the extended family who are aware of Claude's hospitalizations and weight loss.

To assist the family with the opening up of this secret, I asked Claude to tell me how old his eldest son needs to be in order to handle his parents' secret responsibly. The way that this question was framed implied that there was an age at which the secret should be opened. He thought about it and then said that 21 is old enough. I then asked Mary to name the person on her side of the extended family whom she would be most likely to trust with the information. Without hesitation she named her mother, and we made plans for how she could tell her mother.

Then, I asked them to say who would supervise the two teenagers
in the event that Mary and Claude should be hospitalized at the same
time. This was a hard question to answer because they had assumed
Mary would be able to take care of the children the way she always
did. They had not considered the possibility of her hospitalization.

Claude and Mary discussed this problem together and decided
that her mother would be the best person to take temporary charge of
the teenagers, but she would need the help of their eldest son. They
also decided to tell these two people the full nature of the problem as
soon as possible so that they could deal with emergencies when they
are called on. Mary then admitted that it had been very hard to talk
with her mother while preserving the secret and fending off questions
about why Claude got ill so often. Claude acknowledged that he had
experienced the same feeling with his eldest son and had been avoiding one-to-one meetings with him for a long time. They still dreaded
the reactions of the selected two when they disclosed their history of
drug use. I helped them to see that it is also important to state that
they have maintained more than six years of sobriety, they attend
Narcotics Anonymous meetings, and they are determined to spend
the rest of their lives drug free.

Following this session, they both spoke to their son, and Mary
talked with her mother. Once the secret was opened in this part of the
system, we were able to make plans for telling their other three children. It is common in this work that the secret will be opened gradually to various family members, either on a basis of their immediate
need to know or because the patient has been helped to draw distinctions among family members to determine who might be most accepting of the information.

WHEN AIDS IS A SECRET IN A MARRIAGE

The opening of secrets when AIDS pertains can have deleterious effects with
which the therapist must be willing to work. Often a person becomes infected with HIV due to other behaviors that have been kept secret from a
spouse. Thus, many secrets may emerge at the point of diagnosis.

When Betty found out that a man she had an affair with had
AIDS, she took the HIV test and learned that she was infected by the
virus. Her husband, Tim, a man with a long history of intravenous
drug use but now two years into recovery, immediately assumed he
had given her the infection. Secretly, Betty prayed that Tim would

also test positive, for she feared that he would take their two-year-old son and leave her if he were negative.

When his result proved him HIV-negative, Tim refused to believe that a man with his background did not have the virus. He insisted on being retested, and he continued to feel guilty because he was convinced that he had given the disease to his wife. Betty also demanded a retest, stating that if Tim was negative then she was, too. When the second set of tests confirmed the first, Betty wept bitterly but still denied any knowledge of how she contracted the virus.

Tim accepted the results of the second test but then he dropped out of couples' therapy and his behavior at home changed. I tried repeatedly to get him to return to therapy, but he refused. He forbade Betty to talk about HIV in the home and tried to stop her attending support groups. Betty reported that Tim often became angry when he saw her taking her medications, saying she should not be taking pills when there is nothing wrong with her. Betty continued to attend family therapy sessions when she could, and I worked with her on the issue of the secret she was keeping, which was clearly a secret that Tim knew but could not discuss.

After a month, she decided to tell Tim about the affair. But Tim did not want to hear about it. He said he did not care how she got it, they would just have to live with it. He became more controlling and stopped her from attending church because he was concerned that she might tell the pastor that she had HIV. He also spent less time with her and the baby and mostly watched TV by himself. As Tim distanced from Betty, she reached out to her mother and younger sister, and they started to visit her more often. One afternoon, Betty phoned me to say that Tim had not come home the night before, and his clothes were gone from the closet. She called his job and was told he had not shown up for work that whole week. Betty said, "He might have moved out yesterday, but he left me a long time ago." Betty's younger sister moved in with her to help her care for the baby.

WHEN AIDS IS A SECRET BETWEEN A PARENT AND A CHILD

One of the major issues when AIDS is kept a secret from children is that someone else will reveal the secret. Such revelation takes the information and appropriate ways to handle the child's response out of the parents' hands. The secret may also be revealed by the parent during a moment of stress or anger. Effective work with AIDS patients requires using a genogram to talk through who knows and who does not know the diagnosis.

Such a conversation enables the therapist to begin to assess beliefs about opening the secret and to coach people to do so where appropriate. When this has not happened, reparative strategies are needed as in the following example.

> Elena and her husband, Hector, were too frightened tell Elena's 11-year-old son from her first marriage that Hector had AIDS and that Elena was HIV-positive. Keeping the secret was stressful, but they wanted to protect him from such upsetting information.
>
> When Elena's son, Adolfo, informed her that his father instructed him not to touch his stepfather or use any household items that his stepfather used because he had AIDS, she became frightened and shouted at her son that he would have to treat her the same way because she also had the virus. The child was shocked because this was the first time he had heard that his mother was HIV-positive. Subsequently, the boy started acting out at home and school, talking back to his stepfather and making trouble in class, especially classes run by male teachers.
>
> By the time the family came for therapy, the secret was out, and the work needed was to address Adolfo's response. I began by making it possible for Elena and Hector to explain that they had wanted to protect him. At first, Adolfo would not speak to me or to his parents. He seemed willing, however, to speak to me through a hand puppet, a bear that he had chosen. Using the puppet, Adolfo spoke about all of the things that the little bear was afraid of, including his parents' illness, his biological father's anger towards his mother and stepfather, their possible deaths, and what would become of him. All of these fears had been kept secret from his mother and stepfather, who were able to begin to respond. Over several meetings, Adolfo began to speak without the puppet, and his behavior at home and school settled down.

WHEN AIDS IS A SECRET
FROM ONESELF

Denial is an important strategy in the preservation of a secret, and the more frightening the secret the stronger the denial is likely to be. Drug users, while feeding their habit, have denied their addiction to family members, friends, and themselves. "I can stop anytime I want" is a statement that indicates that the user is already out of control. It should not be surprising, then, that this frequent use of denial is also applied when the drug user is required to deal with HIV. If the person is not yet ready to face being HIV-positive he may try to keep the secret from himself.

Evelyn is a drug user who has been in recovery less than two years. I knew that her test results were HIV-positive, so when she dropped by to see me after a session with her physician and told me that her doctor had given her good news, I was surprised. I asked Evelyn what the good news was, and she told me that her CD-4 cell count was high. When I inquired about her HIV test, she told me that the results were negative. I reframed the question and received the same reply. I told Evelyn that I was getting contradictory information from her. She seemed confused. I asked her to think about why the doctor would mention her CD-4 cell count if she were HIV-negative. She thought about this a while then said she had been using the wrong words. She said she suspected she would be HIV-positive because of her drug use in the past, but she said, "I prayed and prayed that I would be HIV-negative, and I just kept on saying the same thing."

I helped Evelyn to understand that being HIV-positive does not mean she is dying. Sometimes people think HIV-positive means AIDS, and AIDS equals death. I also helped her to understand that because her CD-4 cell count is still in the normal range, her body is able to fight off opportunistic infections. All of this is information I had discussed with her in pretest counseling two weeks earlier, but the shock of hearing that she is HIV-positive made her forget, and she fell back on old coping skills, like denial.

I acknowledge that it is not always the best therapeutic strategy to confront a person's denial in a time of stress but, in this case, I was guided to make that intervention for several reasons. Because she agreed to be tested for HIV and returned for the results, Evelyn clearly wanted to know the truth. If she had been allowed to leave the clinic without clarification of her diagnosis, Evelyn might have become even more confused when she realized what the doctor had really told her. It was important that she have an accurate knowledge of what being HIV-positive means. I also knew that she was recently reunited with her husband and misinformation about her HIV status could be dangerous.

But denial can sometimes serve a protective function. It can be a way of buying time or postponing dealing with the problem until one feels strong enough to face and accept it. A person has a right to this temporary security blanket as long as it does not lead to engaging in unsafe behavior that may place others at risk.

When Joseph was released from the hospital, he was very angry that the physician told him he had had pneumocystis carinii pneumonia (PCP). While he agreed that he had symptoms of PCP, and the illness had responded favorably to standard PCP treatments, he said the doctor had not explored the possibility of other infections but made his diagnosis "out of the blue." I asked him what having PCP signified to him. He replied, "That would mean I have AIDS. I can't have people going around saying I have AIDS without real proof."

Joseph was afraid that if he had AIDS he could no longer be a teacher. He had known for some time that he was HIV-positive. The task was not to get him to accept that he had PCP and, therefore, AIDS; it was more important that he understood that he can continue to teach as long as he felt strong enough to do so. His illness is no threat to the children. We worked together over several months. During this time, Joseph taught school and his confidence grew about dealing with his illness. As he began to be able to talk about having AIDS, we were able to make plans for telling his family members.

ASSESSING DANGER WHEN AIDS IS A SECRET

When AIDS and HIV are kept a secret, danger may exist on many levels. Such danger requires the therapist to establish an ethical position regarding secrecy and openness. Clearly, when AIDS is a secret within an intimate sexual relationship, a partner may be put at risk. It is important, however, to establish what other dangers may exist in opening the secret, as illustrated in the following case.

Edward came from a very religious family who rejected him when he told them he was gay. His lover, Clive, is also religious and, though they live together, they have kept their relationship a secret from everyone except Hilda, Clive's ex-wife. When both men tested positive for HIV, Edward insisted that Hilda should be informed because she might have been infected. Clive agreed that she should be told, but he kept putting it off. Edward began to doubt Clive's integrity.

The keeping of the secret caused many arguments between the two men. Edward was angered by Clive's continued procrastination. I asked Clive what he feared the most about telling Hilda, and he began to cry and said, "Edward's safety." I asked him to explain. Clive told Edward that Hilda had a cousin who got HIV from her boyfriend, and two of Hilda's brothers have threatened to kill him. That man fled the state in fear for his life. Clive is afraid that if Hilda also tests HIV-positive, her brothers will come after him and Edward.

Edward had not known that there were dangerous men in Hilda's family and that the virus had already infected someone close to her.

He had known nothing of the threat that these men posed. He now had a better understanding of the levels of secrets and fears with which Clive was struggling. I reminded Clive that he had a moral responsibility to inform his ex-wife that she might have been infected with HIV. Clive agreed and decided that he would feel safer doing this in the context of therapy, so Hilda was invited to their next session. Hilda was informed of the men's diagnosis and why Clive had been afraid to tell her. I gave basic HIV information to Hilda so that she understood that she might have been exposed to the virus. Hilda was frightened of her brothers' response. As the therapist, it seemed to me that this was a situation that called for urging secrecy, at least temporarily, until the true danger could be adequately assessed. She decided she would not discuss the issue with her family until after she got her results. She chose to go to an anonymous test site for HIV testing. This way she knew her HIV status but there would be no record kept. Hilda proved to be HIV-negative. This took a lot of stress off everyone concerned. She made a decision to keep the entire matter private, telling me that she had decided it was none of her brothers' concern. Clive and Edward's relationship improved following the resolution of this secret.

SECRECY, PRIVACY, AND CONFIDENTIALITY

The issues of secrecy, openness, privacy, and confidentiality that all AIDS patients, their families, and their caregivers struggle with have recently played out in the arena of professional sports and the media.

When basketball player Earvin "Magic" Johnson chose to disclose his HIV status to the public, it was probably the most courageous act of his life. The effect of his self-chosen openness was immediate. His candid acknowledgment of his infection with HIV caused many black politicians and civic and religious leaders to pay open attention to the epidemic that is devastating inner-city neighborhoods. In the summer of 1991, a workshop organized by advocates for programs to fight the spread of AIDS was able to attract only two of the 26 members of the Congressional Black Caucus. Since Magic Johnson's announcement, that caucus has pledged to make AIDS one of its legislative priorities (Gruson, 1992). Denial is a vital component in secret-keeping and, for over a decade, minority populations sheltered themselves behind the media projected image of the HIV-infected person as being primarily a gay man or an intravenous drug user while they secretly took care of their infected heterosexuals.

Bobby "Doc Case" Bostic, a performer who does an AIDS education rap called "Stop the Madness," has stated that he used to be booed when he did his act. Now the word is that "If Magic can get it then anyone can" (Flynn, 1991). Clearly, the disclosure of HIV infection by a prominent and well-respected African-American athlete does a lot to increase national awareness of the epidemic and decrease the stigma associated with being HIV-positive. Decreasing the stigma will likely decrease the need for secrecy.

But does this then mean that all prominent people must disclose their HIV status? If they do not, should they then be forced to do so? The rules pertaining to privacy and the protection of the confidentiality of a person's medical records, especially those that deal with HIV/AIDS, must be separated from the issue of secrecy. The confusion of privacy with secrecy can be seen in the situation of tennis star Arthur Ashe, who was forced to reveal his HIV status by the media. If a celebrity cannot choose to protect his own privacy regarding HIV, what implications does this have for an average person with much less power and status? As therapists work to enable AIDS patients to lift the veil of secrecy, it is critical that this work be done in a context that draws adequate distinctions between the privacy that is essential in a free society and secrecy that is a result of stigma and shame.

UNANSWERED QUESTIONS AND DILEMMAS

While there are many effective strategies for dealing with the secrets that arise with AIDS and HIV, there are many questions left unanswered as we enter the second decade of this disease. What does it mean to intimate relationships that secrets and the lies that are necessary to support secrets are embedded in their fabric? What are the long-term psychological and mental health effects, especially on children, of living in families where some secrets must be kept in order to provide safety and protection? What are the effects on individual well-being and the health of relationships of needing to deny one's obvious perceptions in order to survive?

CONCLUSION

As I close this chapter, new people with new secrets have come to me for help. Peggy has tested HIV-positive. She is a single, middle-age woman with a teenaged daughter and an elderly, ailing mother. She has been the breadwinner and the strength of the family for many years. She can't bring herself to tell her family. She also just started a new job, and she is afraid that the company may deny her health and life insurance when they find out her HIV status. What can she do?

Eric is a gay man living with his father who is a retired Baptist minister. He relies on his father for assistance in defraying the costs of his college education. How can he tell his father he is gay and HIV-positive at the same time?

Graham describes himself as a recreational drug user who only shoots up occasionally with his buddies. He has tested HIV-positive. When I tell him he needs to inform his friends with whom he shoots up, he says, "No way. Why bother—one of them gave it to me!"

Tomorrow, no doubt, I will hear other painful secrets and face continuing ethical dilemmas. The secrets people feel compelled to keep in the face of AIDS and HIV will continue as long as those struggling with this illness are stigmatized and made to feel ashamed.

REFERENCES

Abramson, M. (1990). Keeping secrets: Social workers and AIDS. *Social Work, 35*(2), 169–172.

Brill, A. (1990). *Nobody's business: The paradoxes of privacy.* New York: Addison-Wesley.

Flynn, S. (1991, November 22). Not by Magic: African-Americans face an uphill struggle in the fight against AIDS. *The Boston Phoenix,* 18–20.

Gruson, L. (1992, March 9). Black politicians discover AIDS issue. *The New York Times* (National edition), Section A, p. 7.

Walker, G. (1991). *In the midst of winter: Systemic therapy with families, couples, and individuals with AIDS infection.* New York: W. W. Norton.

Winiarski, M. G. (1991). *AIDS-related psychotherapy.* New York: Pergamon Press.

VII

TEACHING TRAINEES

ABOUT SECRETS

18

On Lies, Secrets, and Not Telling the Truth: A Training Curriculum

KATHY WEINGARTEN

THE TEMPTATION IN a paper on this topic is to go too far. Thinking about secrets, planning what I will write, I have found myself drawn to the artifice of embedding a secret in its midst so that I can evoke in you, the reader, a response that will viscerally remind you of what secrets can do in even the most neutral and harmless contexts. I notice, however, that the prospect fills me with an unnerving glee. My energy for this task is diverted from the literature review I intended, from the theoretical framework I wanted to devise, from the refinement of the case illustrations to the subtle traceries of clues I am thinking of placing and then erasing. So, I have stopped. My fantasy—this plan—lasted about one minute. But I am already in a different relation to my reader. I feel guilty. I feel that I need to make amends—for instance, by making this chapter easy to read. In any event, I am sobered up and penitent.

Yesterday, during a supervision group, talk serendipitously turned to secrets, as one had been revealed by an individual client to a seasoned therapist. Now, does the reader need to know the sex of the client and therapist, I ask myself right off? Have I concealed it on purpose? Have I followed a conventional literary tactic of setting up the scene and then filling in the detail? Are my intentions relevant or only their effects on the reader? What if I had never called notice to the genderless constructions I located in the sentence? Would it make a difference if nobody thought there was information I was withholding? Can I even know if, outside the context of this chapter, I would have considered the possibility that I was intentionally not telling the truth or holding a secret? Will I be lying if I don't share with the reader that, a second ago, I had the thought, "This is why you always tell the truth. It's too anxiety-producing to lie and keep a secret. You can't even keep it up for didactic purposes. Stop."

Perhaps this extra space will help us establish a needed break from the interaction we have been having. I hope that the reader has experienced some of the pulls, the tensions, the feelings that get stirred up when one is in the presence — even such a diluted presence as a page of print — of lies, secrets, and truth distortions. I hope I have engaged the reader on a personal level with my principal training premise: though there are resources available that suggest strategies for family members and therapists who need to deal with secrets, the most important resource of all is the therapist's awareness of her own feelings and ideas, biases and reactions, to the actual or potential presence of lies, secrets, and truth distortions. Without this fully explored resource, therapists are critically constrained from doing work with others in as effective a way as possible.

I have a training perspective on secrets that comes directly from my own experience and history. I have worked as a family therapist for 20 years and trained others for nearly as many years. In those 20 years, I can see that both my personal and professional positions on secrets have changed over time. Some of these changes reflect shifts in theoretical allegiance; some reflect an abundance of life experience with my own and others' secrets; some reflect the accumulation of clinical opportunities to try out and see the effects of different strategies. All these changes have reinforced my idea that a professional in training needs help in figuring out not just his position on secrets, lies, and truth distortions among family members or close associates but his position about his position.

There are many positions on a position that a therapist might take: for example, a position on a position might be that once a therapist has articulated a position with his clients, he must maintain it under any circumstances; or the position on a position might be to shift position according to what emerges in the work. Another is that a therapist needs to be neutral; or that a therapist needs to offer a way of thinking about the situation rather than a plan of action; or, conversely, that a therapist needs to offer concrete suggestions for action rather than just a way of thinking about the situation. Regardless of which position on a position a therapist takes, it has been my experience that a therapist does better with a position on a position that is flexible enough that he can change his thinking midstream about how to work clinically with a secret, whether that "midstream" comes in the middle of a case or over the years of his practice.

Let me turn now to the elements of a training curriculum that I hope can promote both the acquisition of a position and a position on a position. The curricular suggestions I make in this chapter come from a number of courses taught over many years. I am not suggesting that this module on secrets, lies, and truth distortions be plunked down into a training program as *the* way to train about secrets. Rather, I am suggesting ways of thinking about the issue in training and some exercises that apply the ideas. I would hope that each trainer would select what is useful and incorporate the ideas into his or her way of working.

A TRAINING MODULE ON LIES, SECRETS, AND TRUTH DISTORTION

My training module consists of several parts, each of which is guided by a single operative framework. I believe that people develop meaning with others, including meanings about secrets, lies, and truth distortions. Definitions of secrets, lies, and truth distortions do not tell us, for example, what a secret is but reveal the meanings that make sense to the community of people with whom we are in dialogue (Anderson & Goolishian, 1988, 1990; Gergen, 1985).

A training course develops its own local culture of stories about secrets, lies, and truth distortions, which reflects and expresses the wider cultures that members represent from other conversations and experiences. Though there are experts on this subject (Bok, 1989a & b), I bring to the course the perspective that, as therapists, we do not need to search for "correct approaches," but rather to learn which ones we prefer or choose to live with or need to invent. I have a strong preference for learning that combines the personal with the academic, the abstract with the applied. If the course has worked well, people will leave with a range of ideas about how others work with secrets, lies, and truth distortions. They will have a sense of how they work best with these processes at this moment in their lives, and they will know to "check in" with themselves about whether their current practice fits their present values and beliefs.

Over time, I have identified two basic orientations towards secrets, lies, and truth distortions that therapists and clients bring into therapy. In one, there is a belief that secrets maintain and protect relationships. Lies and truth distortions are the necessary and inevitable burden that must be borne to avoid hurting others, which can be the result of telling the truth. Truth-telling is seen as self-indulgence. It damages relationships and creates "monsters" that wreak catastrophe.

The other orientation is one that views secrets, lies, and truth distortions as impediments to intimacy. Telling the truth is seen as the start of a process of restoration and repair in which the capacity for shared meanings can eventually be rebuilt. This process moves along more smoothly in a non-blaming atmosphere of support, in which people listen attentively to and speak thoughtfully with each other.

My orientation falls into this latter view, and the curriculum reflects this. I hope that it provides an atmosphere in which trainees feel that it is safe to reveal their fumblings and their foibles. In creating an environment in which they feel safe, I hope they experience, in the context of the course, what I think people, in general, need in order to work their way from secrets, lies, and truth distortions: the feeling that relationships will hold as they reveal themselves to others.

Introduction

The introduction include an exercise and readings that bring the therapist into the ambience of secrets. The intention of this section is to stir up feelings that secrets often evoke: curiosity, "paranoia," excitement, fear, illicitness, anxiety, panic, anger, giddiness, guilt, and sadness. A second intention is to generate distinctions amongst and notice connections across ideas like privacy, deception, concealment, silence, protection, hiding, and confidentiality.

Exercise: My first inclination in any training situation is to design a process in which the participants can have a shared experience of what they will be studying. With secrets, lies, and truth distortions, I think it is particularly crucial to collaborate with the group on what would constitute acceptable parameters for such a process, i.e., what is an acceptable "level" of deception to introduce into this particular newly forming group?

I warm up to such a group task by asking the group to associate to the word "secret," perhaps with several go-arounds of talking, and then repeating the exercise for the words "lies" and "truth distortions." For some groups, doing this and discussing the associations could easily be a first class. This provides a rich foundation for posing the question to the group of how they might like to experiment with introducing a secret into their midst. If a group is not enthusiastic about this plan, I will not proceed with it.

If the group is interested, I then ask them to anticipate how a secret—the content and pathway of which is still unspecified at this point—might shape the group process, be maintained by group members during (and, inadvertently, beyond) the "experimental" time period, affect individual members, subgroups, and the entire group, intersect with extra-group issues, and be handled by the group members or the leader. This, too, can prove a valuable conversation for generating ideas on the subject.

Once the group has identified some of the issues that arise with the introduction of a secret into a cooperative group sharing a task, they are more able to give "informed consent" as to whether or not they want to proceed. I do this to underscore my experience that secrets introduce powerful processes into a group and that, a little like playing with fire, one must handle them carefully and with one's eyes open. Should the group wish to continue, I then solicit ideas about how to introduce the secret. Some ideas might include:

1. A member is designated by the group to share a secret with another member. Whether the identity of the secret-holder is known or not known to the other members generates interesting differences in the group process. If the two members who share a secret are known, the focus tends to be on behaviors that may distinguish these two from the other group members. When the identity of the secret-sharer is unknown, group members tend to become more vigilant about the behavior of all group members. A variation might be to choose the secret initiator by selecting names from a hat so that the identities of the secret initiator and the secret-sharer are not known to the group as a whole.

2. The group leader could call a few members of the group in advance of the next class and share a secret, either the same one or different ones. In this procedure, the group would not know how many classmates know a secret or whether those who know a secret share the same one. This clearly would introduce a different dynamic into the group, one that explicitly involves the group leader.

For any experiment such as this, a time frame must be established. I would suggest one to two meetings at the most, including the time needed to discuss the exercise. The shorter the period in which the secret is "kept," the cooler the effects; the longer, the hotter. The potential for people feeling isolated or buffeted by processes that are uncomfortable, even when they understand them, is high, and the leader must be willing to call the experiment off at any time. I think it is also important to foresee that long-term, unpredictable effects could be generated. Any group that selected to do this opening experiment would need to contract with each other to be in a continuing conversation with each other about feelings, responses, thoughts, and fantasies that are stirred up throughout — and perhaps, beyond — the course.

Readings: Fiction provides another source of learning about the topic of secrets, lies, and truth distortions. I believe that clinicians greatly enlarge their experience by immersing themselves in the lives of people they meet in the pages of books. There are wonderfully powerful and evocative stories of secrets in books, and the beauty is that, as a reader, we have no responsibility for what evolves. Though I have my own favorites, I like to generate a reading list from the group, pooling our resources during one class and then asking people to add to the list for the duration of the course.

Though I recommend *Nicholas Nickelby, Jane Eyre, The Mother's Recompense, The Scarlet Letter, Oedipus Rex, Ordinary Love, Les Miserables, The Little Drummer Girl, Possession*, and *Beloved*, I often read from the opening passages of *In Every Woman's Life . . .* :

> Sometimes the secrets bursting from the Streeter hearts are too large to be contained within their rooms, too explosive to be safely stored beneath the high ceilings of the comfortable East Side apartment. Then, like certain toxic wastes condemned to be endlessly transported from place to place at ever increasing danger to the populace because there is no acceptable repository for them, the secrets must be taken out into the world in search of an adequate hiding place. The danger of witnesses increases. Lies must be compounded. Acts that seem perfectly acceptable under ordinary circumstances — like standing in line at the post office — may suddenly leave one feeling vulnerable as a rabbit on the highway if one happens to be picking up mail under an assumed name. (Shulman, 1987, p. 5)

The passage suggests the layers, the complexities, the tangles, the webs, the depth and extent of effects secrets can have. With the metaphor of toxic waste, the author reveals her position about secrets. Every person takes a position, even if the position is to take no position. In the next section of the course, we work on identifying one's own and others' positions.

From Theory to Practice

Identifying theory: In this segment, we work on developing the ability to locate the underlying theoretical and value assumptions embedded in any approach to working with secrets, lies, and truth distortions. I believe that trainees need to understand the relation between their own theory, practice, and values as well as be able to identify the theory and values that inform the practice of their clients and colleagues.

Positions are built up out of many variables, chief among them one's clinical theory, one's familiarity with the literature on secrets, lies, and truth distortions, one's professional and personal experience, and one's values and ethical/moral posture in the world. In this section of the course we try to look at the implications of the therapist's own clinical theory for practice regarding secrets and learn to identify the clinical theory embedded in writing on and practice with secrets, lies, and truth distortions.

Most family therapists work with a clinical theory whether they can name it or not. It is a bias of mine that people operate more effectively in their professional work if they know which clinical theories underlie their work. In the brief introduction to this section, I ask people to describe the theories they draw on (or are drawn to) in their work,[1] and then ask them to discuss the position on secrets either that this theory espouses, if they know, or that would be consistent with this theory, if they do not know.

Many people are unable to extrapolate a position on secrets from their understanding of the clinical theory. This, then, becomes a homework assignment: to figure out the clinical theory's position on secrets. If there is no literature on this topic, I suggest that trainees contact family therapists who are associated with or who have, perhaps, contributed to the formalization of the clinical theory, and ask them.

In addition to the practical applications that the primary schools of family therapy suggest — for instance, psychoanalytic and object relations, intergenerational, behavioral, systems-oriented (structural, strategic, and systemic), and narrative approaches — there is also a literature on secrets outside our field (Bok, 1989a & b). This book is a primary resource for researching the topic. I think it is useful for trainees to do some directed library research and report back.

The task is to identify not only the practical suggestions offered about handling secrets in families and between families and therapists, but the value premises that underlie the suggestions. For instance, one author's premise may be that "any secret in a family is harmful" and another's may be that "therapists need to protect the value of privacy in families, but families need to protect the value of openness of therapists." If the value premises are hard to identify, this can become a group task.

Case Example

To conclude this module, I present a family case that I worked with in 1982[2] that illustrates the kinds of challenges regarding secrets that clinicians face. I show the link to the clinical theory that I was using then, describe the value premises that supported the work, and discuss the shifts in my own thinking about this case that have occurred over the years as I have used this case as a teaching illustration.

The different theoretical perspective I have now, a decade later, influences my thinking about how to work with the family's secret. I use this case to

---

[1] I might ask a trainee who was uncertain about which theories provided the foundation for his or her work to videotape a session or let me observe a session. We could then look at it together and develop a description of the underlying theory. This, in and of itself, is always a fascinating training experience for me and for the trainee.

[2] Phoebe Schnitzer, Ph.D., supervised this case with me. The two co-therapists were Jenny Hull, M.S.W., and Paul Guillory, Ph.D.

illustrate how important it has been for me, and why I think this may be generally useful for others, to develop a position about one's position on secrets that can accommodate change in one's thinking about how to work with secrets in clinical practice.

The case was one that I supervised with co-therapists who worked with the family as part of a team learning, Milan-style systemic therapy. The mother called requesting help for her 12-year-old son, who was physically abusing himself. Initial individual evaluations of the mother and the son were done at the clinic, and a referral to our family therapy program was made. We saw the family for a total of seven sessions, during which time the child's self-abuse stopped.

> This family had a secret that the mother requested that the treatment team keep. The team immediately got "entangled" in how to proceed — whether or not to honor the request — because the team could not do its routine genogram without either colluding in the parents' secret or exposing the secret. (Nor can I write about the situation without taking a position regarding the secret, i.e., that I am electing to share the family's secret with you, the reader.)
>
> The mother, Marge, told the individual therapist that the 12-year-old John, whose last name was different from that of the rest of the family, was the product of an earlier relationship that the mother had been in before her marriage to her husband, Brad, with whom she had three children. Brad, who had been married and divorced before, had two children from the previous marriage who were 10 and 12 years older than John. At the time the father and mother married, John was 3, and one of Brad's children lived with them. Marge claimed (notice the non-neutral word choice) that no one in the family knew that John was not Brad's child. Marge insisted that the therapists had to keep the family secret because it would be very dangerous if John knew that Brad was not his father.
>
> The team members, pre-masters and pre-doctoral level trainees in family therapy, were all convinced that John had to be told the secret and that his self-abusive behavior was linked to the secret. They believed he was forcing the secret out into the open by frightening his mother into asking for help for him.
>
> My colleague and I led many discussions with the trainees asking them to distinguish amongst secrets, privacy, and confidentiality (Bok, 1989b), to consider multiple hypotheses, and to design questions to check their own and elicit the family's hypotheses. Though we had been primarily interviewing whole families, we did separate this family during some interviews so that we could talk with Brad

and Marge about their ideas about what would happen if John and others "learned" that Brad was not John's father.

Reacting to the material that came up in the interviews with Marge and Brad, the team developed an increasingly complex position on the family secret. Marge and Brad believed that if John knew that Brad was not his father, he would say, "I don't have to listen to you," which would cause so much fighting between Marge and Brad that the parents would divorce. Further, John's father had been incarcerated for rape. The parents believed that if John knew his father was a rapist, he would begin a life of crime himself.

As this material emerged, the team conversations became more nuanced. My colleague and I asked them to examine their positions to see how the premises that supported these positions did or did not fit the parents' position. The trainees saw that they were considering the situation primarily from the child's perspective. They believed that secrets are *always* problematic for children, especially during adolescence, when a child is beginning to deal with adolescent identity issues. By hearing the parents' perspective, they were able to add these concerns to the ones they had initially considered.

At the conclusion of the seven meetings, the co-therapists delivered a message to the parents that used positive connotation and restraint from change, connected behaviors of all family members to the presenting problem, used the family's language, and avoided blame. The message revealed the team's position that we were not going to tell the parents what they should do about the secret. Rather, issues were indirectly raised in the message about what might happen if they did or did not tell the secret.

In a telephone follow-up interview done 18 months later, Brad indicated that John continued to be symptom-free and that he still had not been told about his father. When asked how he explained John's improvement, Brad said, "His problems were with me. I changed my routine. I do more things with him. Now, there's no more fighting. I'm there for him. Now, I take an interest in him. He doesn't do as much, but what he does, I help him with it."

Brad's remarks moved me; at the time, I heard them as confirmation of the work that had been done in general, and the intervention, in particular. His remarks can be used to demonstrate how our interpretations are influenced by many factors, including our clinical theory. I can just as easily, it turns out, interpret Brad's remarks from the clinical theory I am using now, and fit them with my current position on secrets. It is the elucidation of these changes that is the heart of the matter of this training curriculum.

In my experience, the theory that I use, the position that I take changes over time. I accept that and am comfortable with the fact that my intellectual style favors newness over familiarity. I am also open to the influence of my peers. I value being open to change even though it may make those who must accommodate to shifts in my thinking uneasy.

As I think about this case ten years later, I am aware that I think quite differently about this family and the work that we did. For me, this is positive. I am aware of how hard it was to write up this case using an idiom that belongs to a theory and clinical approach on which I no longer rely. I had to restrain myself from switching words or calling attention to words that I would never let go unremarked now. For instance, the first sentence that sets up the secret is the one in which Marge tells the therapist that "It would be very dangerous if John knew that Brad was not his father."

From my current clinical perspective, which draws on feminist social constructionist (or postmodern) theory and a narrative approach to therapy, I would immediately be alerted to the use of the word "father" (Weingarten, 1991). What is a father? Is a father the person who contributes the genetic material, the person who assumes the legal and social role of fatherhood, or the person who takes on the task of making a child feel cared about and "at home?" I would be very interested in bringing into the therapy questions such as these, questions that allow us to make distinctions about the experience of being a father and having a father.

I inte pret Brad's remarks at the time of the follow-up as meaning he moved from occupying a social role with John to becoming a "hands on" father (Daniels & Weingarten, 1982). In that context, the secret of John's paternity became less salient for the family. Perhaps, even, a space had been created for people to know what they already knew. At the very least, the therapy had not made John and Brad more distant from each other. At best, the therapy did not interfere with the two of them moving closer to each other.

Now, I prefer working more directly with families. I prefer a stance in which neither I nor my teammates, if I have them, work from an expert position, constructing messages and sending them in for the family to react to on its own. Rather, I prefer to work from a radically collaborative stance, one in which I make my expertise available so that together family members and I can figure out how to participate in conversations that allow new meanings to emerge, meanings that create new options for thinking, feeling, and behaving with others (Anderson & Goolishian, 1988, 1990; Weingarten, 1992).

Though we did create a context for new options, both for the family and the trainees, I am not sure that the process was sufficiently collaborative to change the supervisors' thinking. Speaking just for myself, I do not think I thought very differently about the case after hearing the trainees' arguments than I did before. With my current approach to therapy, this would signal me that the process was not fully collaborative.

Approaching the case now, if I were the therapist, I would call the mother and ask with whom she thought it made sense to meet first. I would then talk with her about her ideas and my reactions to them. Together, I imagine we would come to some agreement about the membership of the first meeting.

If the first meeting were with Marge and Brad, I would cover the issues surrounding the presenting problem and, if they talked about the family secret, I might ask if they saw any connection between John's behaviors and the secret. From the work that was done, I know that they did. I would then explore these. I would also ask them what their thoughts were about secrets in general, secrets in their families, and the effects of this secret on family members if they thought there were any. I would attempt to develop a collaborative approach both to thinking through ways of understanding and helping John with his self-abusive behaviors, as well as ways of thinking about the implications for the family at this particular moment in time of this particular secret.

I can imagine asking them if they are content with the decision they've made or whether they would be interested in hearing alternative views, mine or professional experts'? I can imagine giving them selected chapters from this book as examples of how some people think about secrets. If I had a position myself about what I thought they should do, I would tell them. I would not do this in the spirit that my opinion is right, but that it is one more opinion to consider. Also, it is an opinion of which they should be aware because it can't help but influence my work with them.

At the moment, I don't think I have a position on an action they should take, though I do have ideas about possible meanings of telling or not telling the secret now or later for various family members, possible meanings to somebody of knowing something he doesn't feel he is supposed to acknowledge knowing, and the possible constraints on other relationships in which people believe that they know something that someone else is not supposed to know.

In describing my current views on how I would approach this case, trainees can see that many pieces of the work are different from Milan-style practice. It is my hope that in sharing my changes, trainees will become more comfortable with the possibility of change in themselves. The further elaboration of these differences leads to the next component of the course.

Interviewing Practice through Role-plays

The third section of the course consists of a sequence of role-plays that introduce a variety of clinical situations that allow trainees to learn more about their own and others' positions. Though one can rarely simulate the emotional force-field that is often a part of clinical work, role-play allows practice with a variety of situations in which it is possible to stop the clock, stop the tape, and discuss actions, feelings, and thinking.

In this section, I use simulated role-play work in two different ways. First, we role-play a range of difficult clinical situations in which lies, truth distortions, and secrets are present, and trainees imagine they are the therapist in session. By rotating trainee-therapists, the group generates many issues to consider.

The second purpose for which I use role-play is to identify which position(s) fit comfortably for the therapist and work well for the client(s), and what is a workable position on a position. By role-playing a single family session, therapists can try out a number of positions regarding secrets, lies, and truth distortions within the same meeting to see what fits, what kinds of flexibility each position offers, what options remain open and which narrow with different therapeutic positions.

Though the first set of role-plays needs to be challenging, they can't overwhelm. I like to warm up to the most difficult clinical role-plays, using a gradient of challenge that is idiosyncratic to me. For instance, secrets, lies, and truth distortions regarding sexual affairs are commonplace in my practice and not as challenging as secrets involving organized crime, which frighten me quite a bit.

Role-play #1: This role-play helps therapists consider how they would respond to a client who asks for help regarding a secret in her life.

> You are the individual therapist to a married client who has confided in you that she is having an affair. You have "explored" this with her. You have not offered an opinion on, but you have suggested she consider the consequences of, telling or not telling her husband. One day she tells you that she is distressed because she has told a friend that she is having an affair and asked that friend not to tell either her own or her friend's husband about it. The friend has told her own husband, and now your client is furious and is asking you what she should do.

In this role-play, the therapist could try a number of responses. I would suggest that those watching, who will later offer their reflections on the role-play, listen "as if" in a role: for instance, listen as the client, the friend, the client's husband, and the friend's husband (Anderson & Goolishian, 1991).

Role-play #2: This role-play helps therapists consider what aspects of their own lives they wish to keep private (or secret) from clients and what situational factors influence their attitude.

A therapist is meeting with a client after the therapist's absence of two months due to an illness that has been left purposefully vague. In this session, the client asks the therapist what was wrong. I imagine multiple twists: the therapist has had a ruptured appendix and peritinitis, a heart attack, cancer, breast cancer and the client's mother died of breast cancer, breast cancer and the client, who is 10, is in treatment because her mother died of breast cancer the previous year. Or, to further complicate the situation, we role-play that the trainee is the client's couple therapist who has heard through the grapevine about the individual therapist's illness. The client asks the couple therapist what happened to the therapist or asks whether or not she knows what happened.

In all these variations, the therapist's ideas about what is and is not the truth, a lie, or a secret may shift. One point of this exercise is to identify the degree to which one's own position fluctuates according to contextual factors.

Role-play #3: In another situation, the difficulties of assessing the presence or absence of secrets, lies, and truth distortions can be role-played.

A wife accuses her husband of having an affair with his law partner, which he vehemently denies. From her perspective, she has caught him in a string of deceits and lies that he claims represents her paranoia. He says that she is so sensitive about the issue of fidelity that he has stopped telling her everything he does with his partner in the interests of stilling the waters.

The therapist must first confront within herself whether or not she thinks she knows if the husband is having an affair or the wife is paranoid. From this assessment, she must identify a position that she can take with the couple that will allow her the flexibility she needs to help them sort out what they want to do without becoming entangled herself in her own assessments — paralleling the wife's — of whether or not the husband has a secret, is lying, or is "merely" distorting the truth for "protective" reasons.

Role-play #4: The next role-play deals with multiple systems involved with a family.

The Department of Social Services is investigating parents for neglect because their child sexually molested another child in the school bathroom. The parents say that the child briefly attended a day-care center in which a friend's child is now reporting that she was ritually abused by the care provider's husband. The parents hire a lawyer to prevent DSS from interrogating their child, which they fear may cause harm. The case has been brought to court.

In the role-play, the trainee can adopt multiple roles to notice shifts in perspective from the roles of therapist or consultant to the child, the parents, the molested child's parents, the school principal, the DSS worker, the lawyer, and the judge.

Role-play #5: This role-play exposes the way in which values and biases influence therapists' positions on secrets as much as or even more than empirical or experiential "evidence." Therapists can describe their positions as "correct," or they can describe their positions as merely theirs, stemming from a host of complex and personal historical factors. Either way, treatment involves reckoning with not only their position but their position on their position.

> A couple enter therapy deeply divided about a secret that they and only a few others know. The mother was artificially inseminated to conceive the couple's now-grown children. Both parents have had extensive individual therapy, and the two therapists disagree about whether the children should be told. The parents are considering divorce. If they do, they know that the secret will be told.

Role-play #6: The final group of role-plays enables the trainee to adopt a range of positions in relation to the same case. This helps identify a position.

> A couple seeks treatment for conflicts over combining work and family life. As the work progresses, the wife requests an individual session during which she tells the therapist that she had an affair five years ago.

Additionally, the trainee can experiment with a number of positions on his position. During this role-play, the question isn't what would he do, but rather what kind of position does he want to take? For example, does the therapist want to behave as if he knows the "correct" action to take but that he will work with the client toward finding her own path? Does he want to tell her what he thinks she should do? Does he want to put forward that they will learn together what makes sense for her at this point in her life? Any of these positions on a position (of which these three are just a few) are workable; the trainee needs to identify which works for him in clinical work.

The beauty of role-playing in a group context is that the variations that emerge are usually abundant and are themselves the best lessons about the complexities of the issues involved and the positions that can be taken. The role-plays break up the idea of "Truth" in favor of truths.

At the same time, it is inevitable that some positions will seem to the leader and to the group members more desirable than others. When this happens, I encourage more discussion about why this might be so. For instance, I may interview a trainee, or others may do this, asking what the trainee thinks would be stirred up if he took position X instead of Y? I might ask what she understands about why one position with regard to one situation is harder to work with than another? There are myriad possibilities for working with the trainees at their growing edge.

CONCLUSION

I have saved my own thoughts about my position with regard to secrets, lies, and truth distortions for the end. I am happy to share my thinking with readers, as with trainees, but I am clear that my thinking cannot be adopted wholesale by anyone else. I have lived my way into my position. It fits me. It fits with my thinking, my experience, my reading, and my conversations with colleagues, friends, and family members. My position and my position on my position is the achievement of many conversations with many individuals and many dialogues — internal and spoken — with the many groups I belong to.

I see myself as part of the process that happens in my office, not apart from it, and this sets up certain parameters of flexibility. I have not kept secrets from clients or supported them in doing so; I have given some clients a lot of information about myself when I felt that not to do so would seem like "secret-keeping" to me; I have also been clear that with some clients withholding a fact that I had told others did not feel like secret-keeping, lying, or a truth distortion.

With this said, I do not have invariant policies. I respond to the situation and to the individuals involved, including myself. I have to feel comfortable myself to do my best work. When I don't feel comfortable, this negatively affects my work, and I tell clients that I am not comfortable. This becomes part of the dilemma. If they want my best effort, and I feel constrained by what I cannot say to X because they have not spoken to Y, I discuss this as one consequence of holding a secret.

I will not lie for clients, under any circumstance, no matter how trivial the item. I am usually clear about what I would do if I were in a particular situation, but I usually don't think I know from the outset what my clients should do or, for example, what "really" is going on, or whether someone is or is not lying, distorting the truth, or telling secrets. I see therapy as an opportunity to explore each person's perspective or, in some cases, to figure out what that perspective is.

Though a training curriculum on secrets, lies, and truth distortions might seem to have a narrow focus, in my experience, the issues that one gets to address are as wide-ranging as families themselves. There is passion and pain, persuasion and perversion, past, present, and future. Above all, a course on this topic provides a stunning exposure to the complexity and diversity of human response. Perhaps more than anything else, this promotes the respect for difference that is so essential in working with families who live with secrets, lies, and truth distortions.

REFERENCES

Anderson, H., & Goolishian, H. A. (1988). Human systems as linguistic systems: Preliminary and evolving ideas about the implications for clinical theory. *Family Process, 27*:371–393.

Anderson, H., & Goolishian, H. A. (1990). Beyond cybernetics: Comments on Atkinson and Heath's "Further thoughts on second-order family therapy." *Family Process, 29*:157–163.

Anderson, H., & Goolishian, H. A. (1991). Thinking about multi-agency work with substance abusers and their families: A language systems approach. *Journal of Strategic and Systemic Therapies, 10*:20–35.

Bok, S. (1989a). *Lying: Moral choice in public and private life.* New York: Vintage.

Bok, S. (1989b). *Secrets: On the ethics of concealment and revelation.* New York: Vintage.

Bronte, C. (1960). *Jane Eyre.* New York: Signet Classics.

Byatt, A. S. (1990). *Possession: A romance.* New York: Random House.

Daniels, P., & Weingarten, K. (1982). *Sooner or later: The timing of parenthood in adult lives.* New York: W. W. Norton.

Dickens, C. (1990). *Nicholas Nickelby.* Oxford, England: Oxford University Press.

Gergen, K. J. (1985). The social constructionist movement in modern psychology. *American Psychologist, 40*:266–275.

Hugo, V. (1987). *Les miserables.* New York: NAL.

Le Carre, J. (1983). *The little drummer girl.* New York: Knopf.

Morrison, T. (1987). *Beloved.* New York: NAL.

Shulman, A. K. (1987). *In every woman's life. . . .* New York: Knopf.

Smiley, J. (1989). *Ordinary love & good will.* New York: Ivy Books.

Weingarten, K. (1991). *A mother's voice.* Unpublished manuscript.

Weingarten, K. (1992). A consideration of intimate and non-intimate interactions in therapy. *Family Process,* 31:45–59.

Wharton, E. (1986). *The mother's recompense.* New York: Charles Scribner's Sons.

19

On Trainees and Training:
Safety, Secrets, and Revelation

JANINE ROBERTS

Bob, an early childhood specialist, was in his first family therapy course. As he did a genogram and exercises about his family of origin, he became increasingly convinced that his older brother had to have had a different father than he and his other siblings. As he pieced together the information, he talked to two younger sisters and his mother, in order to corroborate what he had figured out. His mother did not want to discuss it. One sister talked openly with him about it, the other thought it best not to bring it up after so many years. In class, Bob was confused on how to map the relationship lines of his family. He was unsure of how much of the story to tell, as he was in the middle of putting it together himself. He wanted to tell his older brother.

Shawna, in working on a paper analyzing and comparing her family to a family in literature,[1] came up against both spoken and unspoken taboos by her parents and siblings about sharing certain information

With many thanks to Evan Imber-Black for editing assistance, to Georgi Locker-man for helping to try out many of the ideas, to Joan Friebley for her careful reading of an earlier draft, and to Pietro Barbetta, Carey Dimmitt, Didi Firman, Bill Griffin, Irina Pond, and Paolo Sacchetti.

[1]Shawna used the novel *A Wrestling Season* by Sharon Sheehe Stark. For a list of primarily contemporary novels and plays that intricately describe family life and that can be used for training, please write the author: School, Consulting and Counseling Psychology Program, University of Massachusetts, Amherst, MA 01003.

outside of the family. For years, there had been a protective boundary around the secret of her mother's alcoholism. If Shawna wrote about it now and others read it, she would be breaking family rules of 30 years duration. The paper remained unwritten. She talked with her instructor about what it meant to change this family pattern. Finally, she called several family members and asked for permission to discuss some things. She began to write.

Working with secrets in family therapy training raises different issues than most other content areas because of the nature of the subject. In teaching, using families that are already well known to trainees (e.g., their family of origin, friends and neighbors, or families of others in the group) offers a rich pool of "normal" families to use as a base for examining various theories. This usually balances the skew of the focus on dysfunction in the family therapy literature, while it provides more detailed information about family interactions than is available in case write-ups. However, when working with secrets, accessibility to content cannot be assumed in the same way as when working, for instance, with family stories, rituals, or photos. Concerns are raised about members of the group having access to confidential data. Participants can feel that they are being disloyal to their families. And, as was the case with Bob in the opening vignette, the person himself may be just uncovering family information that was unknown before.

Care needs to be taken to handle these issues sensitively, providing protection from unwanted disclosure and support when there is unclarity or a new awareness of family patterns. In addition, careful distinctions need to be made among privacy, secrets, and confidentiality. The concerns that can arise for trainees about secrets in their lives are similar to issues that arise in treatment for both clients and helping professionals. If they are worked with thoughtfully in training, trainees can both experience first-hand some of the relational complexities of secrets and also make connections regarding how secrets can be worked with in therapy. Also, people can be helped to articulate how their own ideas about secrets evolved. This may help them to see how ways they think secrets should be worked with in treatment are connected to their own values and experiences.

Along with this more personal understanding of secrets, trainees need to look at the schemas for working with secrets that various clinicians have proposed, and to develop their own skills and techniques to work with secrecy in therapy. Unfortunately, few of the major textbooks have any reference to secrets and how to work with them.[2] Sourcebooks for family

[2]Carter & McGoldrick's *Changing Family Life Cycle* (1989), Gurman & Kniskern's *Handbook of Family Therapy* (1980), Hoffman's *Foundations of Family Therapy* (1981), Nichols' *Family Therapy Concepts and Methods* (1984).

therapy teaching (Piercy, Sprenkle, & assoc., 1986; Sherman & Fredman, 1986) also do not include any exercises or ideas on working with trainees and secrets. Yet, secrets in some form or other, pervade many of the case presentations made in the family therapy literature. As people read these case histories, implicit information is given on how to work with secrets. But working with secrets needs to be dealt with more explicitly because (1) of the many ethical issues involved, (2) secrets are often a part of difficult problem cycles such as abuse, violence, and addictions, and (3) secrets frequently involve personal values. Also, as secrets can be made out of any content, a wide range of aspects of family life can involve secrets. That means that secrets of client families may hook into some part of the trainee's own experience that has not been examined in relationship to secrets.

In the following sections, issues are raised and discussed in much the same sequence as they might be worked with in training. Exercises and/or charts that can be used as handouts are given to help think through and organize the ideas presented in each part. The emphasis is on both engaging the trainee in a meaningful dialogue about his or her experience with secret-keeping and secret-revealing, as well as looking at current therapeutic methodologies that are available to help clinicians make sense of how families construct secrets and where they are located.

First, I discuss issues of definition. Then, values and secrets are examined, including the values the trainees bring with them. Both a values continuum experience and a family-of-origin exercise are described. Next, secrets are explored from the perspective of how interpersonal relationships can be marked by who knows what and when they know it. The content of secrets is also looked at, with a particular emphasis on what messages the larger culture gives about what does and does not need to be kept secret in families. Policies that have been proposed by various clinicians to work with secrets in treatment are then explored. The use of simulated therapy interviews where secrets are introduced is presented as a training tool for this section. Finally, issues about secrecy, training teams, videotaping, and one-way mirrors are discussed. Throughout, there is an emphasis on creating a safe context to learn about secrets, as well as respect for the complexities of making decisions on how to do work with secrets in therapy. Opportunities are built in to engage with the material on different levels depending on the comfort and experience of participants.

WHAT IS SECRECY?:
THE PROBLEM OF DEFINITION

Awareness of the allure and the dangers of secrecy . . . is central to human experience of what is hidden and set apart. Rooted in encounters with the powerful, the sacred, and the forbidden, this experience goes far deeper than the partaking

of any one secret. . . . If we do not take this into account in considering particular forms of concealment . . . then we shall but skim the surface; and the secrets,
once revealed, will seem paltry and out of proportion to all that went into guarding them. Similar care is needed in approaching and defining the concept of
secrecy itself. (Bok, 1984, p. 5)

The definition of secrets that is held by a therapist needs to be one that
takes a stance that secret-keeping is neither inherently positive or negative. If
this is not done, the clinician can miss distinct meanings of secrets as they
relate to cultural, gender, and generational differences. Also, if the therapist
has predetermined values about secrets that are then reflected in how secrets
are viewed, this will very much influence how they work with secrets. Secrets
are contextual. They take on different meanings at different times, and they
define personal relationships in unique ways depending on how the family,
ethnic group, and community views both the process of secret-keeping and
the content of secrets. Information that should or should not be kept secret
shifts according to cultural and societal mores. A family in the 1990's who
introduces their adopted child to her biological parents at an early age
would probably receive support for this from some adoption agencies and
social workers. Thirty years ago, the helpers would more than likely have
reinforced the necessity of keeping the adoption secret when the child was
young, and certainly no support would have been given for open adoption.
A person with AIDS may openly disclose his illness in one community and
receive much needed support — in another part of his life, it may be impossible to let people know. Secrets function differently in different contexts.

Yet, a number of family therapists have taken a negative position on
secrets without examining the impact of this stance. Ed Friedman has probably taken the strongest one. He states that the five major effects of secrecy
on a family are:

1. **Distortion** of perception and information, at the fact gathering
   level.
2. Creation of **pseudo-bonds** and unnecessary **estrangements**.
3. Stabilizing of triangles and support for **pathological** family processes.
4. **Dilution** of family strengths.
5. Maintenance of **anxiety** at higher energy levels." [emphasis added]
   (Friedman, 1973–74, p. 64)

As might be expected, in the four case examples that Friedman then presents
in the same article, the emphasis is on revealing the secrets. A person's view
of secrets strongly influences how she or he works with them.

Bok (1984)[3] makes the case for a neutral *definition of secrets* that focuses primarily on *"concealment, or hiding, to be the defining trait of secrecy"* (p. 6, italics added). She also notes how this concealment presupposes the different positions of insider and outsider, with those knowing the secret on the inside, and those unaware of the secret excluded to the outside.

Pittman (1989), focusing more on how the content affects interpersonal relationships, defines *secrets* as information that is relevant to a person that is kept from him or her. For example, an affair that is hidden from a spouse may be relevant to him because it has key implications for how he understands his relationship to his partner. On the other hand, in a family with young children, information about the parents' sexual relationship may not be relevant to the younger generation. The sexual bonding between the parents can be seen as *private* information. Of course, this raises the issue of who decides what is relevant information and when and to whom it is relevant.

Bok (1984) also speaks to the importance of distinguishing privacy from secrecy. *Privacy* is the *"condition of being protected from unwanted access by others—either physical access, personal information, or attention. . . .* Privacy and secrecy overlap whenever the efforts at such control rely on hiding. But privacy need not hide; and secrecy hides far more than what is private"* (p. 10, italics added). This is a key distinction in therapy that is often not made.

The interplay of secrecy and privacy leads to the question of confidentiality in therapeutic relationships. In order to implement a policy of confidentiality, therapists need to be clear with their clients about what is kept confidential and why, and how it is to be kept confidential. This marks the boundaries of the therapeutic relationship. "Confidentiality *refers to the boundaries surrounding shared secrets and to the process of guarding these boundaries. While confidentiality protects much that is not in fact secret, personal secrets lie at its core"* (Bok, 1984, p. 119, italics added). In family therapy, because there are often different generations, different agendas, and different needs of family members, the lines separating secrets, privacy, and/or confidential information often are not immediately clear.

One way to introduce distinctions among secrecy, privacy and confidentiality is to ask trainees to take a piece of paper and write down these three phrases on it: "Secrecy is . . . ," "Privacy is . . . ," "Confidentiality is. . . ." Then, ask them to complete the phrases with whatever thoughts first come to mind. After they have finished the sentences, have them exchange their

---

[3]The first chapter of this book, entitled "Approaches to Secrecy," makes an excellent handout for initial reading about secrets.

sheet with one other person and discuss what they have written. For instance, Michelle, a 39-year-old graduate student wrote, "Secrecy is two layers away from exposure. It's about things dug in—about facts bricked over by values one is uncertain about." "Privacy is my business. Personal." "Confidentiality is an agreement between at least two people to exclude others from information the two share." In exchanging her sheet with a partner, her partner then asked her, "Okay, you link secrecy to uncertain values. But what about values one holds as fundamental and then one creates secrets because of it such as during the cold war with, 'The Russians are bad so we need spies and the CIA'?" Giving words to one's thoughts and then dialoguing about them can help people to become clearer about their own ideas and to think about the complexities of making distinctions among the three concepts.[4]

A variation of this exercise that can be done if there is more time is to have one person start a sheet with "Secrecy is . . . " and pass it to someone else in the group to add onto. The same can be done with a sheet for "Privacy is . . . " and "Confidentiality is. . . . " After four or five people have written down something, the sheet can be read aloud to everyone, allowing more of a group comment on the distinctions among secrecy, privacy, and confidentiality. For instance, in one group of nine in which this was done, one person wrote, "Secrecy is not telling anyone what they cannot understand." Another person added, "The idea of a contract. The idea that telling them the secret would cause them potential distress." Yet another person wrote, "Secrecy is more common than you think." This led to a discussion about how one decides what someone else can understand and how this varies with the values of different eras.

These are good opening exercises to do before talking about any of the issues. People immediately become personally involved with the material. At the *end* of any work with secrets, participants can come back to this exercise to see how they might rewrite their statements.

Once some of the definitional problems have been clarified, secrets and the value systems of families and trainees can be addressed.

---

[4]Another way to think about the distinctions among secrecy, privacy, and confidentiality is to ask people to write down on a piece of paper, which they do not necessarily share, something that is secret in their lives, something that is private, and something that is confidential. This exercise needs to be done with careful attention to issues of disclosure and safety, so that people do not reveal more than is comfortable for them. However, it has the power of vividly illustrating distinctions among the three concepts because they are defined in the personal realm. Thanks to Georgi Lockerman for this idea.

SECRETS AND VALUES

Few would question the scruples of people planning a surprise birthday party for a family member and keeping it secret. The secrecy is time limited, it is done in a spirit of fun, and ultimately it provides some support in the form of the celebration for the person who does not know the secret. The goal of keeping the secret is revealing it. This kind of secret can provide important bonding for subsystems of the family and can introduce humor and a sense of playfulness to daily life.

On the other hand, there would be many different opinions on whether a woman having an abortion has the right to keep it secret from her husband or boyfriend. People have stronger opinions about if, when, where, and how information should be disclosed when it involves more intricate life decisions.

It is also important to note that we do not know what is "normal" secret-keeping or secret-revealing in a particular family. As Linda Berg-Cross states, "The number of secrets kept by varying types of families has not been systematically studied and is therefore unknown. It is unknown how often family secrets get revealed; also unknown is whether the consequences of revealing a secret vary with either its content or its function" (1988, p. 144).

Two different exercises can help trainees learn about their own value system as well as think about what is "normal" secret keeping in families. The first is a values continuum about secrets, families, and therapy. The group leader presents two different positions about secrets (see below) with two different corners of the room representing each of those positions. People then place themselves along an imaginary line depending on what they think about the issues raised. If they agree with the position, they move closer to that corner. In dyads or triads people then share why they have put themselves in a particular spot. Many discussions are generated with this exercise because of the issues that are raised with the statements at each of the "poles," and because people can quickly turn to someone and speak their ideas immediately, rather than waiting for a few moments to speak in a large group discussion.

DIRECTIONS FOR DOING
THE *VALUES CONTINUUM*

Push the chairs aside in a room, and make an imaginary diagonal line down the center of the space. This is your continuum. One corner represents one side of an issue (one pole), the other corner represents the other. Read out the first of the two points of view, indicating physically which end of the continuum represents this stance. Then, read the second point of view, indicating the other corner. Ask people to place themselves along the line with their placement representing where they see themselves in relation to these two statements. After they have placed themselves, ask people to turn to a neighbor and take a minute or two to explain why they placed themselves there. Or, you can have people go to the other side of the room and hear the rationale given by someone who put themselves in quite a different position from their's (people often prefer doing this).

Statements for the group facilitator to read out:

1. (One "pole"): Secret information within families is generally destructive to the long-term growth of family members.

   (Other "pole") Secrets can provide necessary protection and/or support for family members.

2. Generally, therapists should disclose their policy on secrets early in treatment whether or not this is brought up by the family as an issue. This helps prevent inadvertent disclosure of secrets.

   If the therapist highlights secrets early on as an issue, this may force things underground and ultimately not allow the therapist and/or family access to important information.

3. Therapists should never hold secrets from the family, including those told to them by other family members or by other helpers (including diagnoses, reports written about the family or individual members, etc.).

   Therapists should keep those confidences that family members as well as helpers feel are essential.

4. In order to keep generational boundaries clear, some secrets are necessary (e.g., in terms of money, sexuality, certain problems, etc.).

   Intergenerational relationships work best if there is open information exchanged about most major issues.

5. In order that therapists and teams do not inadvertently keep secrets, formats such as the reflecting team should be used.

   Therapists and teams need boundaries too, and times when they can talk and consult in private are essential to their work.

After finishing the five poles, the group is asked to come back together to reflect on the issues that are raised as well as to process the exercise. This activity usually stimulates participants to refer to actual situations that they have read about or observed, or been involved with in the treatment arena. For instance, Roger, who does a lot of work with teenagers and substance abuse, was much more concerned about being upfront on a policy about secrets with clients than was Beatrice who worked primarily with young children as a consultant to schools and day-care centers. Secrecy and denial are of central concerns in addictions work, and the age of Roger's clients leads to a different set of issues about what the teenagers wanted family members and others to know or not know. Many questions come up about distinctions in *practice* among privacy, confidentiality, and secrets. For some people this means that they have to "keep walking" along the poles because different variables would put them in a different position. After the two poles were read for number 3 (see above), Desiree found herself going back and forth between the two ends. She first articulated her strong belief that when helpers keep secret from clients about their mental status and other reports and diagnostic labels, that automatically puts clients in a one-down position. On the other hand, she felt strongly that *within* the family there might be some appropriate secret-keeping, such as if an older daughter was raped, younger siblings might not need to know.

People also wanted to know more about how each individual's position had evolved. To look further at their own values, trainees can be asked, in dyads, to look at what they have learned about secrets, privacy, and confidentiality in their families of origin and communities (see Table 19.1). This exercise is designed so that it can be done with no disclosure of secrets and should be presented as an activity where people feel safe about what they do or do not share. Connections can be made to treatment concerns for helping families feel safe about what they disclose.

How, when, where, why, and to whom information is disclosed can be as important as the content of information. A 50-year-old man standing on a street corner trying to talk to an unknown passerby about his abusive father is viewed in one way; the same man saying the same things to a therapist in a private therapy room is seen in another manner. Each of these two contexts provide two very different frames. In the first, there is no clear relationship within which information is being disclosed. The second context provides a potentially safer context regarding issues of safety, trust, relationship connections, and how information will be used. These are all key in working with secrets.

Again, the large group can be brought back together to share what they learned about families and secrecy, privacy, and confidentiality. In one group, Malika wanted to adapt and use these same questions with couples in treatment. She felt like they could really help couples learn about important differences and similarities as to how information was shared within their family and without. Brian commented that how the questions were framed let him have a sense of control over what he did and did not tell. He felt like he had more empathy for the need for clients to have a similar sense of control. Another trainee, Maria, said these kinds of questions, which pro-

TABLE 19.1

Secrecy, Privacy, and Confidentiality in Your Family of Origin

1. What was the role of privacy in relation to your living space? In relation to the rest of the community? (Think about private spaces, private time, open or closed doors, people from the community coming in or out of your apartment or home, etc.)

2. What was the role of secrets in your family? Were some secrets playful or protective? Were they manipulative, supportive, or perhaps avoidant? Did they work differently for different people? Would other people agree with your description of how they worked in the family for either the group or individual family members?

3. In your family, what did each of the three generations (grandparents, parents, and children) think was information that was important to keep private? How was this the same or different for other families in the same neighborhood or from the same ethnic and/or religious or class background?

4. Over the family life cycle, how did things shift in terms of how secrecy, privacy, and confidentiality were dealt with?

5. If secrets were disclosed, what was their impact? How did family roles and/or alliances shift (for instance, did the role of the revealer change in any way)? What was the duration of the secret, the number of people involved, and in what kinds of ways were they involved?

6. If there is a family secret that is not disclosed, what do you think the effect would be if it were disclosed? How would it happen? How would family relationships shift? Relationships outside the family?

7. If you could change one way that your family handled secrets, what would it be?

8. How do you think what you learned about secrets influences how you think/work (or would work) with them now in family treatment?

9. How do you (or would you like to) differentiate with clients among secrets, privacy, and confidentiality?

10. What do you think should happen with clinical information between clients and larger systems that is often kept secret (eg. reports, diagnoses, clinical summaries, etc.)?

moted *open* talk about the processes of secrecy, privacy, and confidentiality, shifted possibilities of thinking about secrets to a new level. The relational aspects of secrets were no longer masked.

Depending on the size of the overall group, how well people know each other, and how long they will continue to work together, different amounts of information will be disclosed with this exercise. For instance, a group of 30 trainees were working together every week for nine months. Six months into the year, people worked on these questions together in four-person Bowenian support groups (created for family-of-origin coaching).[5] An

---

[5]In these support groups that meet over a semester or longer, trainees decide what their policies will be about confidentiality of material that is discussed. In general, the same kinds of guidelines that define confidentiality in a therapist-client relationship hold within these groups.

amazing amount of energy and a high level of disclosure occurred. In contrast, in a workshop with 75 people who were only meeting for one day, there was less disclosure and more emphasis on implications of these questions for how they might work clinically.

LOCATING SECRETS

To look more closely at how relationships are affected when there are secrets, it can be useful to think about where secrets are located. Alliances, boundaries, and hidden coalitions can all be marked by who does and does not know about the existence of a secret as well as its content.

Karpel (1980) describes three levels of secrets. The first one he calls *individual*, where one person in the family knows a secret and keeps it to herself (e.g., having AIDS). Another level is *internal*, where some people within the family share a secret and keep it from others (e.g., daughter had an abortion, mother knows about it). The third level is *shared* family secrets, where the whole family knows something but does not share it with the outside world (e.g., family violence where all are aware of it). Using some of my own and Imber-Black's ideas (personal communication), I have expanded Karpel's original typology to include the location of secrets when therapists and other larger systems are involved. This chart (Table 19.2) can be used in training to visually demonstrate the range of levels where secrets can be located.

This chart can be used in conjunction with a case example so that people do not think about location as a static concept. Secrets "move" and change locations. This "movement" is central to understanding interpersonal aspects of secrecy. Case examples can demonstrate to trainees what can happen in therapy as "locations" shift.

> Anna, a woman in her 30's, had been sexually abused just before her 12th birthday by a man she trusted and knew well who worked at her school. Her parents found out about it and, in their confusion about who was responsible for what, took away her 12th birthday party. The secret of the abuse was kept within the family to protect Anna, but nothing was done to punish the man or hold him accountable. (To the best of Anna's knowledge, he was simply transferred to another location.) Anna did not disclose this secret to anyone for years. She was not sure what her siblings did or did not know about what had happened and why the birthday party was cancelled. Anna never discussed it further with her parents.
>
> In therapy, Anna first shared what had happened with her therapist. With coaching from her therapist, she then approached her

TABLE 19.2

Location of Secrets in the System*

- located inside individual family member (e.g., member is contemplating an abortion)
- located in dyad of individual in family and person outside the family (e.g., helper, friend, person having an affair with parent, etc.)
- located in subsystem of family (e.g., incest that only father and daughter know about)
- located within and between subsystem of family and larger system (e.g., failing grades on a report card that are known only to mother, son, and school)
- located within whole family (e.g., someone has lost job, alcoholism, family violence)
- located between family and larger system (e.g., probation, IRS fine)
- located within larger system (e.g., labels/diagnoses unknown to family members)
- located within whole community (e.g., songs that African-American slaves sang that communicated messages about slaves escaping, etc.)

---

*adapted from Karpel & Imber-Black by Roberts

parents to talk through with them why they had punished her by taking her party away, and why they had not confronted the abuser. She then opened up the secret with two of her siblings. As she was able to rework her relationships with her family, Anna decided she wanted to tell some of her close friends. This seemed to balance some of the deep shame she had felt when her party was cancelled and her childhood friends all knew something had happened and were whispering about it, yet nothing was said openly. With her friends, Anna planned the birthday party her parents had cancelled when she was 12 — complete with presents, games, and food that might have all been there when she was a child. Pictures of the party were shared with the therapist and other family members.

As the location of the secret changed and broadened, Anna was able to rebuild connections as well as recreate a community of people that gave her different messages about what had happened to her. The birthday party became a chance to celebrate herself with pride (not shame) with witnesses who knew her story. When treatment ended, Anna (who was in a helping profession) saw herself as a person who was developing a particular competence in working with children and families where there was sexual abuse. Three years later, she called her therapist to let her know that she was developing, along with a team of other people, programs that offered help to younger girls who had been sexually abused. Thus, she ultimately relocated her own secret to a broad sociocultural level.

SECRETS: A CONTENT APPROACH

Grolnick (1983) offers a different way to think about secrets by focusing on their content (see Table 19.3). Any content can become a secret. However, secrets also exist in a societal context, shaping how various behaviors are viewed and what the consequences are if secret information is disclosed. This societal context keeps shifting depending on current values. This is reflected in Table 19.3 by regular and boldface type. The regular type presents the content areas of secrets Grolnick thought were important in 1983. In bold type, other areas have been added. In some instances, these are areas (such as violence and addictive behaviors) that we have become more willing to acknowledge as secrets in our culture since the early 1980's.

TABLE 19.3

Classification of Secrets by Content

---

1. Events
   A. Birth-related: "illegitimacy" (quotes added), abortion, **adoption, miscarriage, parentage, foster care**
   B. Sex-related: affair, **sexual orientation/preference (this was listed on the original chart as homosexuality)**
   C. Money-related: concealed income, inheritance, family business dealings, blackmail, wills, **loss of money***
   D. **Legal system related***: past [prison] sentence, ongoing illegalities, **jobs that "break" the law such as midwifery done in home of family***
   E. Job-related: job firings, demotions, conflicts, **jobs that require secrecy from others***
   F. **Death-related: suicide, cause of death (e.g., AIDS, cancer), violence and death (e.g., the "disappeared" in South America)**
   G. **Violence-related: to oneself, to another (e.g., rape, incest) (note: Grolnick originally placed rape and incest under the category of "sex-related.")**
   H. **Mental illness-realted**
   I. **Seeking assistance from professional helpers***
2. Personal Facts
   A. Biologic
      1. Physiologic (reversible): sexual dysfunction, infertility, and **new birth technologies**
      2. Organic (irreversible): chronic illness (diabetes, epilepsy), **terminal illness***
      3. Genetic: inherited disorder
   B. Functional
      1. Behavior: phobic, sexual, ritualistic, **addicitve**
      2. Thought and attitudes: pretense of an interest or belief whose absence is the secret; fantasies
      3. Emotions: real likes, dislikes
   C. **Background: class differences, immigrant experiences, wartime experiences, etc.**

Original chart, Grolnick, L. (1983). Ibsen's truth, family secrets, and family therapy. *Family Process, 22*(3): 275–288.
Sections of the chart in **bold** have been added by Janine Roberts.

*Thanks to Georgi Lockerman and Carey Dimmit for these additions.

Like Karpel, Grolnick focuses on the fact that secrets tend to be not about thought and emotions, but rather about actual events that happen. What neither author brings into play is that the feelings and thoughts that people have about these events are based on their own experiences within the larger culture and on messages they have received about what can and cannot be talked about. These contextual messages are central to whether people decide to keep events secret or not. Years ago, when people had cancer, they often did not tell others. Now, it is more routinely shared. In the 1970's and 80's a list of prominent American women who had had abortions appeared in newspaper ads supporting reproductive rights. This would have been unheard of 30 or 40 years ago.

The meaning of the different events in this chart may vary greatly depending on cultural background, gender, class, or different neighborhoods. An out-of-wedlock birth may be kept secret in one community, while in another community it is seen as a common life-cycle transition. Boyd-Franklin (1989) also highlights the importance of a given cultural group's position vis-à-vis sharing information with helping professionals. She notes that because of the "legacy of mistrust" that has occurred between African-American families and the predominant culture, there may be many personal issues that Black families are unwilling to share until a trusting relationship has been carefully built. Other ethnic groups will have different positions regarding helpers and secrets, and it is important for trainees to learn about these.

This chart can be used to stimulate discussion on how secrecy is embedded within a shifting cultural and societal context. Any one of the content areas can be taken and discussed from the perspective of where, when, and how it has been emphasized or not as something that should be kept secret. For instance, women's addictive behaviors were hidden for many years. Infertility was often not discussed openly. That is not the case as much today.

Areas of the chart can also be taken singly and examined across different cultural backgrounds represented in the training group. For instance, sexual orientation or preference might be much more openly shared in some ethnic or religious groups than in others. This may lead to a discussion of meaning and values within different ethnic groups.

In working with the chart in training situations, several trainees commented that it does not cover a whole area of secrets in human relationships that occur commonly, such as gift-giving, creative work in progress, scientific discoveries, and secret clubs that children have. These would generally be seen as more "benign" secrets. They felt that this negatively skewed thinking about secrets. Other trainees commented that it was striking to see visually how, in the space of less than ten years, there were considerable differences in how to think about the content of secrets. This spurred them to question what aspects of secrets are morality related and/or status related and how these change as morals and status measures change in the larger culture.

PROCEDURES, POLICY, AND SECRETS

Once trainees have examined some of the distinctions among secrecy, privacy, and confidentiality and have looked at the relational and content aspects of secrets in families, it is important to think more specifically about how to handle secrets in treatment. In therapy, information revealed or unrevealed and *how* it is revealed has deep implications for the relationship the therapist has with the family, its individual members, and their relationships with each other.

In thinking about how secrets affect relationships, Karpel looks at three roles: (a) the subject(s) of the secret, (b) the holder(s) of the secret (may be one and the same person as the subject), and (c) those who are unaware of the secret.[6] Karpel goes on to look at what can happen when someone in the family privately discloses a secret to the therapist (therapist moves positions from one who was unaware of the secret to a holder of the secret). It becomes almost impossible for the therapist to stay out of hidden alliances, the therapist has to handle his or her own emotional reaction, and therapeutic planning can become contorted as the therapist tries to weave a plan that takes into account that different people know different things.

In three case examples,[7] Karpel explicates two strategies that can be used in working with secrets: *reparative* and *preventive*. *Reparative* strategies focus on working with the person(s) that discloses the secret as to how he or she might disclose it to others that need to know. The therapist functions as a supportive facilitator of this process. When the therapist is told that some sort of secret exists (but the content of it is not yet disclosed), a *preventive* approach can be taken. Karpel advises therapists to then ask the client(s) how he or she would like the therapist to handle any secret information that emerges. However, little is presented by Karpel on a policy about secrets at the beginning of therapy that would clarify to family members the therapist's own stance on secrets and treatment.

Wendorf and Wendorf (1985) discuss this issue at length. They take the position that therapists should openly state that they have a policy regarding

[6]Besides these three roles, it seems that there is an important role at times of therapist and others as listener/witness to a secret. If a secret is disclosed, an essential part of the process can be an acknowledgment of the boundary shifts as to who knows the secret and when, where, and how it can be talked about.

[7]Each of the situations arose when helpers met privately with individuals.

whether things are confidential or not that considers what is best for all the members of the family and for the treatment. Family members can then choose what they want to disclose, and the therapist can work with them as to how and when this information should be shared with other people. In this way, family members know that information they present will be considered in the context of the best interests of everyone, including any protection that any individuals might need. This begins a dialogue that centers on such issues as who owns the secret and who has the right to disclose it. However, Wendorf and Wendorf provide no guidelines to think about "what is best for all members of the family."

Other authors feel that it is not always necessary for the therapist to know the content of secrets to be able to work with them effectively. Imber-Black (1985) describes a couple that had something that had happened in the past between them that they kept referring to and that seemed to be keeping them stuck. In this case, both the husband and wife knew what the secret was, and it did not appear to involve current behavior or to be abusive or dangerous. Without discussing what these secret events were, the therapist was able to help the couple design a ritual that put these events in their rightful place, rather than at the center of their current life.

Cecchin and Boscolo (Boscolo, Cecchin, Hoffman, & Penn, 1987) encourage therapists to ask circular questions about the process of the secret-keeping and the effect it has on people, rather than the content of the secret. Thus, they ask people when the secret started, how long it has been going on, what would happen if other people knew about it, who else knows about it, etc. Secrecy can also be a central part of an intervention that they prescribe when they ask some people (often the parents) to go out together with no one else knowing when and where they are going. (This is a variation of the invariant prescription as used by Selvini Palazzoli and her group in Milan [Selvini Palazzoli et al., 1989].)

Distinctions need to be made, though, between content of a secret that puts a family member at risk or involves violence or abuse, and secrets that do not involve dangerous behavior. Cecchin states that, "The fact that something is a secret is more important than the content of the secret" (1987, p. 140). But the content of the secret can also hold deep meaning and have key implications for action. This overemphasis on the relational aspects of secrecy becomes problematic in an extensive case example that Boscolo and Cecchin recently published (see "The Family with a Secret," Boscolo, Cecchin, Hoffman, & Penn, 1987). In this case, the therapists know that the stepfather has made several attempts to have sexual intercourse with his 21-year-old stepdaughter, Lisa, who is now suicidal and has run away from home. The parents disclose this information to the therapists, but do not want it discussed with either Lisa or two younger daughters. The therapists never work directly with this secret with the family. A year and a half later, when Boscolo and Cecchin see the family again, Diane (age 15) wants to leave the home and live alone or with Lisa (who had since moved out of the house). Diane is also refusing to go to school and had checked herself into a psychiatric hospital rather than be at home near her father. Lisa, pointing to Diane, said to the therapists, " . . . you left your work unfinished!" (1987, p. 176). Diane obviously felt that she was in a very unsafe position and was exhibiting similar symptoms to those Lisa had when her father was making overtures to her. By not working with the family more openly regarding the content of the secret, the therapists failed to protect the daughters in the family, or hold the father accountable for his actions. The importance of acknowledging the differences in content of secrets when danger and safety are involved is vividly highlighted. This is a good case example to use with trainees to look at how therapists need to work with both the relational and content aspects of secrets.

ROLE-PLAYS

Simulated interviews can help with the careful exploration of secrets in the therapeutic process. Two distinct types of role-plays can be used. One is an interview with a family in which no secrets are intentionally introduced into the situation, at first. After about ten minutes, a secret is introduced to some or all of the participants, and observers can watch the shift in dynamics after this happens. This is an excellent demonstration of the impact secrets can have on systems. It also provides an opportunity for trainees to begin to think about how they might actually work with secrets.

DIRECTIONS FOR
ROLE-PLAY EXERCISE

1. Ask trainees to split up in groups of from five to seven people. Each group should then pick a therapist, two observers, and the rest of the group will role-play family members. Ask the family members to include a depressed mother among them.
2. Have them begin a basic family interview. It is usually most effective for family members to spontaneously create their family history as well as a problem that brings them to treatment, rather than planning this out ahead of time.
3. Observers should be asked to watch for communication patterns and nonverbal interaction and to think about the relationship between the therapist and various family members.

4. About 10–12 minutes into the role-play, give a slip of paper to each person in the role-play with instructions as to whether they know the secret or not. This is so that observers and people in the simulation do not know where the secret has been introduced. Give to the therapist a slip that says, "You are unaware of the secret at this time." Give to each family member a slip that says, "The mother in this family is physically abused by her partner. It is episodic and each time you believe it will be the last. All family members know, but have not told the therapist." These slips should not be shared with anyone else.

5. Let the role-play continue for another 10–15 minutes with the observers continuing to note changes in affect, interactional patterns, and content discussed.

6. Finish off the role-play and then process it. Observers can comment first on how they saw relationship patterns before the secret was introduced, and how they shifted once the system knew there was a secret. If there was disclosure, observers can also speak to any changes around the revelation. Clients and therapists can be asked to talk about relationship patterns before and after the secret was given, and how it felt the same and different for them. If there was no disclosure, a good question to ask is, "Do you think disclosure should happen, and if so, when, where, and how should it happen?"

   It is important to allow time for people to share the secret with everyone at the end of the role-play and to "de-role." A good way to do the latter is have people name who they are in the "here and now" to a partner in the group.

7. If you have a large group, different scenarios can be enacted at the same time to locate the secret-keeping in a different part of the system. For instance, if you wanted to have the *therapist involved in a secret with a family member*, you could ask a group to make sure they include a husband in the role-play. Then, once the role-play is underway, you could give a slip of paper to the husband saying, "You have told the therapist that you are having an affair. No one else in the family knows about it." The therapist would receive a similar slip. The family members would all receive slips saying, "You are unaware of the secret at this time." Other simulations can be designed where the *therapist has a secret* (say a diagnosis that has been given to an adolescent in the family during a hospitalization) or *someone in the family has a secret with helpers outside of the therapeutic system* (e.g., a teenager shares her pregnancy with her probation officer).

In one group that enacted the first role-play described, the observers were struck by how communication patterns shifted once the secret was introduced. Body language of family members changed a lot. Children moved away from parents and the therapist. People carefully eyed each other and checked out what they could and could not say. Verbal communication became more and more indirect and confusing. The observers were also amazed at how they distorted information they heard in order to support their imaginative ideas about what the secret might be.

The therapist in the role-play described herself as becoming more and more suspicious as the role-play went on and less clear what her relationship was with the family. Family members described their roles as more uncomfortable and unclear once the secret was introduced. Some of them wanted out of their roles! The focus of the interview became convoluted. In this role-play, the secret was not disclosed.

Trainees felt that the role-play gave them the opportunity to experience the power of secrets in systems, as well as a chance to begin to think about how to work with them. They were surprised at how influential the notion of a "secret" seemed to be in changing their behavior. A second kind of role-play can work more with policy issues in therapy. These are scenarios where secrets are part of the role-play from the beginning. The focus is not just on observing the dynamics around the secret, but also on creating a therapeutic context where they can be worked with effectively. The therapist is encouraged to go into the role-play with some possible strategies (as described above) for how to deal with secrets. The family role-play members make sure they have some element of secrecy in the problems they are bringing to therapy. These role-plays can be processed in a similar manner as the first ones, with particular emphasis on giving feedback about whether the therapeutic strategies worked in addressing issues of secrecy.

Role-plays provide the opportunity to work with issues around secrecy in a protected atmosphere, where participants can communicate about what they intended as strategies, get feedback about how they worked, and retry different approaches. Therapy simulations are the closest step trainees can take before actual practice. As trainees enter practicums and internships, there are further opportunities to more directly examine secrets and therapy.

TRAINING TEAMS AND SECRETS

The way family therapy training is often conducted adds another set of unique issues that need to be considered when thinking about secrets. The use of teams, phone hook-ups, and the one-way mirror can create situations where secrets are inherent to the process. People watch other people anonymously, talk about them privately, and then share some of their ideas through a spokesperson (usually the therapist who is in the room). Videotaping of sessions can lead to questions about what needs to be kept private and what will and will not be shared while the videotape is on. Families may request to have the taping stopped while they talk about certain subjects. Sometimes families are taped without their awareness. A well-known presenter recently showed a video clip of a family talking alone without their therapist. They had asked to talk without the therapist present. At the presentation, someone in the audience asked, "Did the family know they were being taped?" The presenter brushed the question off by responding, "Well, they knew they were in the room that had the cameras and microphones."

With the public showing of training tapes all over the United States and the world, what might ordinarily be kept secret or private is, in fact, disclosed to strangers with whom the family will never have any contact. Trainees watching videos can also have access to information that might not necessarily be in their best interest to have. For instance, a student in a class began to watch a demonstration videotape from a well-known institute, when he realized that he had known the family on the tape some ten years previously. He discussed this with the instructor and, given that he had no continuing ongoing contact with the family, he and the instructor decided that he could continue to watch the tape. However, this left the student with information about this family that they did not know he had. He ultimately felt uncomfortable with this situation.[8]

Some of the formats currently being used, like the reflecting team (Andersen, 1991), offer different possibilities about secrecy and privacy in training. The team does not meet privately, but discusses their ideas in front of the family. There is a more reciprocal relationship in regard to how information is shared and what is shared. Given the variety of team structures available for training (Roberts, 1983; Roberts et al., 1989), training teams can choose what will work for them and families organizationally, depending on what issues are salient in their work with secrets. Attention needs to be paid to ways structures in training may inadvertently lead to secret keeping, too much disclosure, and/or worries about hidden information.

Here are some guidelines to use in team situations and to give clarity for both team and family members about how, when, where, and with whom information is shared. These guidelines are intended both to help clients have a strong sense of control about what is disclosed and how it is taken in

---

[8]Professional organizations such as the American Association for Marriage and Family Therapy (1100 17th St. NW, 10th floor, Washington, DC 20036-4601) and the American Family Therapy Association (2020 Pennsylvania Ave. NW, Suite 273, Washington, DC 20006) have available ethical guidelines about confidentiality and videotaping.

by others, and to build in possibilities for people to openly discuss with each other about whether the process is working for them or not. They are intended for use after the standard kinds of permission are obtained from the family to be observed by a team and to have sessions videotaped.

1. Ways to ensure that family members feel safe and in control of boundaries around information:
   a. Ask family members if they would like to meet members of the team and know their names and credentials.
   b. Make clear that they have a choice about times when they do not want to be observed.
   c. Offer the possibility for family members to ask at any time what their therapist and/or team members think about particular things that have been said.
2. Ways the technology of team supervision can support clients being in control of information:
   a. Make it clear that videotaping can be stopped at any point if clients do not want something taped.
   b. Let families know exactly when they are being videotaped and observed.
   c. Invite families back behind the one-way mirror to see the set-up.
   d. Let them know that the phone is a tool for them, as well. For instance, they can call the team to ask them what they are thinking.
   e. Make videotapes of sessions available for family members to watch if they think it would be helpful.
3. Have regular check-ins with both family and team members to reflect on whether or not the process is working for them and to answer further questions they may have.

SUMMARY

Trainees need to understand their own values and biases about secrets and what implications these have for how they view therapeutic work with secrets, and to get involved with some of the complexities of working with secrets in therapy. The intent of the exercises and charts presented here is to help trainees participate in meaningful dialogues about secrets so that they have some conceptual tools to understand secrets, they are attentive to the impact secrets have had on their own lives, and they have some clinical expertise to begin to work with them. Throughout, trainers need to model sensitivity to the different ways secrets can work for families, to make thoughtful distinctions among secrets, privacy, and confidentiality, and to provide support and protection around issues of disclosure. In doing this, they can then help trainees to begin to do the same for and with clients.

REFERENCES

Andersen, T. (1991). *The reflecting team: Dialogues and dialogues about the dialogues*. New York: W. W. Norton.

Berg-Cross, L. (1988). *Basic concepts in family therapy: An introductory text*. New York: Haworth Press.

Bok, S. (1984). *Secrets: On the ethics of concealment and revelation*. New York: Vintage.

Boscolo, L., Cecchin, G., Hoffman, L., & Penn, P. (1987). *Milan systemic family therapy: Conversations in theory and practice*. New York: Basic.

Boyd-Franklin, N. (1989). *Black families in therapy: A multisystems approach*. New York: Guilford.

Carter, E., & McGoldrick, M. (1989). *The changing family life cycle*. Boston: Allyn & Bacon.

Friedman, E. H. (1973–74). Secrets and systems. In J. P. Lorio & L. McClenathen (Eds.), *The Georgetown family symposia* (vol. 2). Washington, DC: Georgetown University Family Center Publishers.

Grolnick, L. (1983). Ibsen's truth, family secrets, and family therapy. *Family Process, 22*, 275–288.

Gurman, A., & Kniskern, D. F. (Eds.). (1980). *Handbook of family therapy*. New York: Brunner/Mazel.

Hoffman, L. (1981). *Foundations of family therapy*. New York: Basic.

Imber-Black, E. (1985). "We've got a secret!" A nonmarital marital therapy. In A. S. Gurman (Ed.), *Casebook of marital therapy*. New York: Guilford.

Karpel, M. A. (1980). Family secrets: I. Conceptual and ethical issues in the relational context. II. Ethical and practical considerations in therapeutic management. *Family Process, 19*, 295–306.

Nichols, M. (1984). *Family therapy: Concepts and methods*. New York: Gardner.

Piercy, F., Sprenkle, D., & assoc. (1986). *Family therapy sourcebook*. New York: Guilford.

Pittman, F. (1989). *Private lies*. New York: W. W. Norton.

Roberts, J. (1983). Two models of live supervision: Collaborative team and supervisor guided. *Journal of Strategic and Systemic Therapies, II*(2), 68–84.

Roberts, J., Matthews, W., Bodin, A., Cohen, D., et al. (1989). Training with O (observing) and T (treatment) teams in live supervision: Reflections in the looking glass. *Journal of Marital and Family Therapy, 15*, 197–214.

Selvini Palazzoli, M., Cirillo, S., Selvini, M., & Sorrentino, A. M. (1989). *Family games: General models of psychotic processes in the family*. New York: W. W. Norton.

Sherman, R., & Fredman, N. (1986). *Handbook of structured techniques in marriage and family therapy*. New York: Brunner/Mazel.

Wendorf, D. J., & Wendorf, R. J. (1985). A systemic view of family therapy ethics. *Family Process, 24*, 443–453.

Index